LABYRINTH

An International Journal for Philosophy,
Value Theory and Sociocultural Hermeneutics

Printed ISSN 2410-4817
Online ISSN 1561-8927

Vol. 18, No. 2, Winter 2016

**PRAXIS, VIRTUES, AND VALUES:
THE LEGACIES OF ARISTOTLE**

Editor-in-Chief:
Prof. Dr. Yvanka B. Raynova

Managing Editor:
Dr. Susanne Moser

Advisory Board:

Prof. Dr. Seyla Benhabib (Boston), Prof. Dr. Debra Bergoffen (Fairfax), Prof. Dr. Peter Caws (Washington), Prof. Dr. Lester Embree (Florida), Prof. Dr. Reinhold Esterbauer (Graz), Prof. Dr. Nancy Fraser (New York), Prof. Dr. Alison M. Jaggar (Boulder), Prof. Dr. Domenico Jervolino (Roma/Napoli), Prof. Dr. Andrzej M. Kaniowski (Łódź), Prof. Dr. Alexis Klimov † (Trois-Rivières), Prof. Dr. François Laruelle (Paris), Prof. Dr. Hedwig Meyer Wilmes (Nijmegen), Prof. Dr. Herta Nagl-Docekal (Wien), Prof. Dr. Elit Nikolov (Sofia), Prof. Dr. Sonja Rinofner-Kreidl (Graz), Prof. Dr. Hans-Walter Ruckenbauer (Graz), Prof. Dr. Ronald E. Santoni (Granville), Prof. Dr. Anne-Françoise Schmid (Paris), Prof. Dr. Hans-Reiner Sepp (Prague), Prof. Dr. Helmuth Vetter (Wien), Dr. Brigitte Weisshaupt (Zürich), Prof. Dr. Kurt Weisshaupt † (Zürich), Prof. Dr. Andrzej Wiercinski, Prof. Dr. Richard Wisser (Mainz)

Axia Academic Publishers

Bibliographische Information der Deutschen Nationalbibliothek:
Die Deutsche Nationalbibliothek verzeichnet diese Publikation in der Deutschen
Nationalbibliographie, detaillierte bibliographische Daten sind im Internet unter
http://dnb.dnb.de aufrufbar.

Die wissenschaftliche und redaktionelle Arbeit wurde von der Kulturabteilung
der Stadt Wien – Wissenschafts- und Forschungsförderung unterstützt.

Labyrinth: An International Journal for Philosophy, Value Theory and Sociocultural Hermeneutics is a serial publication of the Institut für Axiologische Forschungen / Institute for Axiological Research, Vienna – www.iaf.ac.at
For more information, please visit the Journal's homepage:
www.labyrinth.axiapublishers.com

© 2016 Axia Academic Publishers
Vienna
All Rights Reserved
Journal & Cover © 1999 Institut für Axiologische Forschungen
Printed in Germany

ISSN 2410-4817 / ISBN 978-3-903068-22-3

www.axiapublishers.com

PRAXIS, VIRTUES, AND VALUES:
THE LEGACIES OF ARISTOTLE

Table of Contents

EDITORIAL

Yvanka B. Raynova (Sofia/Vienna)
Back to the Sources of Value Theory and Practical Philosophy — 5

ARISTOTLE: SOURCES, INTERPRETATIONS, AND DISCUSSIONS

Markus Riedenauer (Vienna)
Basic Evaluation and the Virtuous Realisation of Values:
The Integrative Model of Aristotle — 7

Olav Eikeland (Oslo)
If phrónêsis does not develop and define virtue as its own deliberative goal –
what does? — 27

Wei Liu (Beijing)
Aristotle on Prohairesis — 50

Audrey L. Anton (Bowling Green, KY)
Sculpting Character: Aristotle's Voluntary as Affectability — 75

Dimka Gicheva-Gocheva (Sofia)
The Influence of Herodotus on the Practical Philosophy of Aristotle — 104

RECEPTIONS OF ARISTOTLE'S ETHICS AND PRACTICAL PHILOSOPHY

Martin Huth (Vienna)
Humans, Animals, and Aristotle. Aristotelian Traces in the Current Critique
of Moral Individualism — 117

Kathi Beier (Leuven)
The Soul, the Virtues, and the Human Good:
Comments on Aristotle's Moral Psychology — 137

Susanne Moser (Vienna)
Tugend als Wert: Christoph Halbig und Max Scheler im Vergleich　　　158

Yvanka B. Raynova (Sofia/Vienna)
Paul Ricœurs Suche nach einer Neubegründung der Menschenrechte
und der Würde durch die Fähigkeiten und die Anwendung der phronèsis　　　193

Sabeen Ahmed (Nashville, TN)
The Genesis of Secular Politics in Medieval Philosophy:
The King of Averroes and the Emperor of Dante　　　209

EDITORIAL

Back to the Sources of Value Theory and Practical Philosophy

The international philosophical community will certainly remember 2016 as the Year of Aristotle. The reason for this is the impressive number of conferences, colloquia and lectures organized worldwide on the occasion of the 2400th anniversary of the birth of the ancient philosopher, and in particular the International Multiple Congress "Aristotle Today", which took place in Athens, Heidelberg, Padua, Paris, Helsinki, Lisbon, Notre Dame (Indiana), Moscow, Córdoba, Leuven, and Sofia. However, if we have chosen to dedicate the second issue of *Labyrinth* 2016 to Aristotle, it is not simply in order to take part in this splendid anniversary celebration, but also to recall that "in the history of value theory (…) Aristotle should always be mentioned in the first place not only chronologically, but also in view of his importance", as once stated Oskar Kraus. In this context, the main objective of this issue is to offer some new readings of Aristotle's axiological ideas and practical philosophy in view of their historical impact and persisting importance. Thus, it is divided in two parts.

The articles included in the first part discuss the origins and the foundations of Aristotelian value theory and practical philosophy. Reinterpreting the meaning of certain fundamental anthropological, ethical and political concepts of Aristotelian philosophy, such as *orexis, pathe, phronèsis, prohairesis, boulēsis, bouleusis,* a/o, the authors show their importance for the understanding of human being and human action. As a subject of reason, emotions, aspirations, will, and desires, and having a specific character and individuality, the human being is moved in his/her actions by different motives and instances. Markus Riedenauer shows how emotions function as primary evaluators of situations, and form the basis for virtue ethics by calling human beings to realize the call to morally good and fulfilling action. In this sense, as stated by Audrey L. Anton, "since the vicious person fails to know the good, she neither acts in accordance with it voluntarily nor does she feel appropriately towards the good." Thus, it is important to elucidate the connection between the voluntary and the character as a person's set of fixed dispositions to feel and act in certain ways. Anton's analysis reveals in particular the role of interplay between the internal (character) and external (praise and blame) aspects for steering moral improvement, i.e., a good voluntary behavior. For his part, Wei Liu argues, that "decision" (*prohairesis*), which includes desiderative and deliberative components, provides the moving cause of rational action, and that it better reveals the person's character than does the action itself. With reference to previous publications and debates, Olav Eikeland offers a detailed reexamination of the relation between "reason", "knowledge", and virtue, in setting the goal for ethical deliberation.

The articles in the second part of the issue aim to show the historical impact of Aristotelian ethics and theory of action, and especially the diversity of their receptions. In particular, the authors show how problems in modern and contemporary ethical theories (modern virtue ethics, moral individualism, utilitarianism, recursive ethics etc.) can be resolved by using Aristotle's conceptual framework. Thus, Martin Huth investigates the Aristotelian sources of the current critique of moral individualism presented by Cora Diamond, Alice Crary, Paul Ricoeur, Klaus Held, Bernhard Waldenfels, a/o, and analyzes the way they use certain key Aristotelian concepts: (a) "ethos" as the lived moral sense, ground and horizon of moral decision-making and ethical reflection; (b) "hexis" as the morally relevant habituation of perceiving and acting; (c) "phronèsis" as practical wisdom, which is considered to be a specific practical know-how as opposed to the scientific knowledge of the episteme; and (d) the definition of the human being as "zoon politikon", who is "by nature" dependent on social relations, including the development of moral skills. Following Elisabeth Anscombe, Kathi Beier tries to overcome the baselessness of modern virtue ethics by exploring the conceptual connections between virtue and soul in Aristotle's moral philosophy. She claims that the human soul is the principle of virtue since reflections on the soul help us to define the nature of virtue, to understand the different kinds of virtues, and to answer the question as to why human beings need virtues at all. By comparing the virtue conceptions of Christoph Halbig and Max Scheler, Susanne Moser shows that Scheler, similar to Aristotle, understands virtues as a kind of transformers from the negative to the positive, because they fix the right way of dealing with negative emotions and switch over the negative basic mood into a positive, joyful one. In the context of Paul Ricoeur's understandings of human rights and human dignity, Yvanka B. Raynova demonstrates the fruitfulness of the Ricoeurian application of Aristotle's phronèsis in (bio)ethical discussions and cases, where decisions are difficult to take.

We are perfectly aware that no publication can cover even a single subject of Aristotle's gigantic philosophical heritage. Nevertheless, with the present volume we hope to disclose some new aspects of his conceptual framework, which could be helpful for further axiological debates.

Yvanka B. Raynova

ARISTOTLE:
SOURCES, INTERPRETATIONS AND DISCUSSIONS

MARKUS RIEDENAUER (Wien)

Basic Evaluation and the Virtuous Realisation of Values: The Integrative Model of Aristotle[1]

Abstract

Human affectivity is a research topic situated at the intersection of psychology, philosophical anthropology, theory of action and ethics. This article reconstructs the Aristotelian theory of emotions in the context of his theory of aspiration (ὄρεξις) and in terms of their function as primary evaluators of situations, which forms the basis for virtue ethics. The Aristotelian model integrates desire, motivation and morality for a rational being in community. Affects (πάϑη) reveal the profile of relevance of the world to a person as an indispensable basis for the work of practical reason. They are analysed in the dimensions of their cognitive core, their social, bodily, and motivational aspects. Affectivity constitutes a primary evaluative response to situations and thereby disposes human beings to realise their call to morally good, virtuous and fulfilling action.

Keywords: emotions, evaluation, virtues, desire, motivation.

The ethics of Aristotle is readily designated as "eudaimonian" or "eudaimonistic". This is reasonable, as the argumentation of the first chapters of the *NE* establishes the formal notion of the highest goal of human conduct, which is called by the generally recognised name of *eudaimonia* at 1095a 19, and in the following chapters, Aristotle enquires as to the content of this concept.

> But presumably the remark that the best good is happiness is apparently something agreed, and we still need a clearer statement of what the best good is. Perhaps, then, we shall find this if we first grasp the function of a human being. (*NE* I, 7 1097b 22-25)

---

[1] The main text of this article has been translated from German by Stephen Lake (Australia).

Aristotle's ethics is likewise rightly regarded as an ethics of virtue, as in NE I,7, the achievable human good is understood as the "activity of the soul in accordance with virtue" (1098a 17), which is then explored in most of Books II-VI in the form of virtues of character and of intellect. A third, equally appropriate characterisation of Aristotelian ethics as "ethics of desire" or "aspiration-based ethics" has, however, found less acceptance.[2] Yet, on the basis of the text and its systematic interpretation, this last approach seems justified and in relation to questions of values, knowledge of them, their motivating force and their implementation, the motif of aspiration is particularly significant.

The basic concept of o)/recij / orexis is difficult to render into English with its range of meaning, because it is rooted in natural philosophy and can also be applied to unconscious tendencies, it includes human instincts and especially pathe, affects or emotions (which Aristotle discusses in his works On the Soul, the Ethics, and the Rhetoric), but equally, the desire for knowledge: "All men naturally desire knowledge".[3] The term "desire" does not fully reflect this range of meaning; in the following, therefore, orexis is for the most part not translated, or it is rendered as "aspiration". It should become apparent that the integrating character of the Aristotelian model of ethics is grounded precisely in orexis, that the phenomena of aspiration, in particular the affects, provide the immediate fundamental evaluation and the motivation for the realisation of the good.

Aristotle has been regarded to the present as the founder of a scientific, i.e. rational ethics. In the modern period, however, a dichotomy between rationality and emotionality has developed which, from the fourteenth to the twentieth centuries, has complicated our interpretation of Aristotle's views on the soul, aspiration, and the emotions.[4] Currently, there is nonetheless a renaissance of the idea of an ethics of virtue and aspiration, and de-

---

[2] The only English monograph about *Aristotle on Desire* assumes that "Aristotle's views on desire have yet to receive the attention they deserve" (Pearson 2012, 1). While this assessment is not wrong, it is still easier to maintain it by completely ignoring non-English research literature. The same holds true (with one exception) for Moss 2014. The extensive *Companion to Aristotle* (Anagnostopoulos 2009) does not pay sufficient attention to ὄρεξις – only three very general pages (Modrak 2009, 318-321), while Leighton (2009, 597-611) is limited to the context of the *Rhetorics*.

[3] Πάντες ἄνθρωποι τοῦ εἰδέναι ὀρέγονται φύσει (*Met.* I,1 980a 21; cf. *Rhet.* I,1 1355a 15). Compare in more detail Riedenauer (2000, 279-289).

[4] David Charles states that Aristotle's theory of aspiration as motivation "is not one of the familiar options of post-Cartesian philosophy... It should be seen rather as offering a radical alternative" (Charles 2011, 76). Nussbaum criticises a widespread ignoring of classical theories of the emotions: "Today, however, the accounts are almost always ignored in philosophical writing on emotion, which, therefore, has to reinvent laboriously (and usually falls well short of) what was clear there." (Nussbaum 1994; 508)

velopments in the psychological research of emotions once more render the Aristotelian model of ethics of the greatest interest.

The "cognitive turn" in psychology in the second half of the twentieth century, despite its anti-naturalist tendency supported by neurobiological research, and the associated proliferation of cognitive philosophies of the affects, displays structural parallels to the discourse in Antiquity, above all in relation to the cognitive and motivational dimensions. The understanding of particular feelings as cognitive phenomena seems to have been confirmed by neurobiology.[5]

The renaissance of theories of emotion is indebted not typically to a neo-Romantic or an anti-rational tendency, and rarely to a radical critique of *logos*, but rather to the characteristic of affects, which, in a sense to be specified, is designated as "cognitive". Recent discussion of the question in how far this means intentionality, propositions, judgements or some form of perception, has changed nothing in the prevailing cognitive approach.

> It is then the thesis that emotions can be epistemically rational that is essentially responsible for the renaissance of interest in the emotions in current philosophy.[6]

Anthony Kenny provided impetus within the analytical tradition for this renewed interest when, in 1963, he criticised theories of emotion based upon Cartesianism, and against this developed a plausible concept of the affects in relation to behaviour with the assistance of the concept of intentionality and the attribution of formal objects to affects (1963, 187-198). Ernst Tugendhat acknowledged in 1979:

> That this cognitive act of judgement belongs to the concept of the affects is today generally accepted in analytical philosophy.[7]

Kenny appealed to Aristotle and Thomas Aquinas, while within the phenomenological tradition, Martin Heidegger had achieved something structurally comparable already in 1927 with his book *Sein und Zeit*.

Affectivity as one form of aspiration with cognitive and/or evaluative components is a characteristic foundation for the integrative character of Aristotle's model of ethics. It combines natural philosophy, anthropology, psychology, ethics, and basic metaphysical

---

[5] For a summary, see Goller (1995, 36-49).
[6] "Es ist also die These, daß Emotionen epistemisch rational sein können, die für die Renaissance des Gefühls in der Gegenwartsphilosophie wesentlich verantwortlich ist." (Döring 2005, 26). The concept of epistemic rationality is opposed to strategic rationality, as in de Sousa.
[7] "Daß dieses kognitive, urteilsmäßige Moment zum Begriff eines Affektes gehört, wird heute in der analytischen Philosophie allgemein akzeptiert" (Tugendhat 1979, 201). Nussbaum summarises: "1. Emotions are forms of intentional awareness (...) 2. Emotions have a very intimate relationship to beliefs" (Nussbaum 1994, 80).

concepts. It is conceivable that there is still potential here for modern interest in and discussion around the formulation of a new ethics of aspiration. In this paper, the principal elements of the integrative Aristotelian ethics against the background of its multi-dimensional anthropology will be reconstructed.

I propose first to outline the basic structure of the theory of action based on the treatises *On the Soul* and the *Ethics*: self-movement through *orexis*. In the second and third sections, we will be concerned with the structure of the non-rational powers of the soul, in particular the emotions (*pathe*). The fourth and fifth sections will show that virtue results from the mediation of aspiration and reason, before we conclude with an assessment of the systematic findings.

1. The Basic Structure of Action Theory: Self-Movement through *orexis*

The Aristotelian approach to psychology and theory of action on the basis of his natural philosophy examines the phenomenon of the movement of living organisms – not merely bodily movement, but also the processes of growth and shrinkage, metabolism and reproduction etc. Living organisms have the origin of such movement within themselves – they have ψυχή as the principle of their self-movement (*DA* II,1 412b 17f). As the ἀρχή, it is the principle of becoming, of activity, and of self-development (*DA* I,1 402a 7f). While each individual being exists complete within itself and as a unified whole, the philosopher distinguishes various powers or δύναμεις of the soul. (I generally prefer to use the Greek terminology, because translations often entail problematic connotations.) Various powers are attributed to the vegetative, the sensible, and the cognitive life. That *dynamis*, which is the origin of self-movement, is called by Aristotle *orexis*; every movement is a manifestation of either aspiration or flight. It is associated with sensuality, the αἰσθητικόν, and yet should still be perceived as an independent essential power. According to Aristotle, aspiration is active *in* all other powers, it is bound with the vegetative life, with sensible perception, and with knowledge (*DA* III, 9 432b 3-8; cf. *EE* VIII,2 1247b 18f. and *MM* 1187b 36ff). I therefore designate it as a "transcendental" essential power; it transcends the limits of the received division of psychological powers and, driving these, establishes a relation to the environment that lends a specific relevance to that which is perceived (and thus also to that which is remembered, imagined, hoped).

Human souls, however, do not have various powers beside or over one another (as in an hierarchical model), but rather unite vegetative and sensible powers with the rational. According to my interpretation, the affects are central concretisations of *orexis*; emotionality demonstrates this integration. For ethics, they are more important than those desires which are concerned with metabolism, nutrition etc. The *pathe* are specific forms of aspiration (and avoidance) of concrete objects within the context of self-movement, which, however, are determined by each given situation. With this passive moment, a primary objectivity of the relationship to the world, to situations and objects, is guaranteed. The fundamental aspiration towards something is then not a diffuse appetitive movement in pursuit of something, but rather a dynamic relationship to something specific.[8] This means that these objects in one way or another will always be aspired to (or avoided) as evaluated objects, that they will be judged as beneficial or harmful in axiological categories.

An affective aspiration is always a total answer to something concrete that appears to be good: φαινόμενον ἀγαθόν (*NE* III,4 1113a 23-25). The concept of the good is understood here in terms of psychological and behaviour theory, that is, as pre-moral.[9] Affectivity allows good and bad to appear as such for the individual living organism. This evaluation is fundamental, because it is only on this basis that it can be distinguished whether that which *appears* to be good is indeed good or only *seems* to be so, and to what extent that which appears as bad really is so after rational examination.

The ethical writings of Aristotle, the leading focus of which is the teaching of successful living or happiness (*eudaimonia*), show another psychological approach. The distinction between psychological powers based on natural philosophy given above is not identical with the simplified division of human powers into those which possess *logos*, and those which are *alogos*:[10]

One [part] of the soul is non-rational, while one has reason (*NE* I,13 1102a 29f).[11]

In order to avoid misinterpreting this in the sense of a disjunction, it is important to take into account Aristotle's anthropology. On that basis, the question, which in the next stage of

---

[8] The relationship includes a passive and an active moment, the balance of which is discussed below in section 6.

[9] Here I agree with Moss that φαινόμενον in the first instance means "subjective experience" (Moss 2014, 4); likewise with her judgement that the primary appearance of the good is more fundamental for the psychology and ethics of Aristotle than is usually recognised. Nonetheless, her interpretation of "appearing" "in a narrow, technical sense", "quasi-perceptually" (Moss 2014, 5), because it depends on empirical experience, seems to be an unnecessary reductionism. This "practical empiricism" underestimates the role of *orexis* as a special power of the soul and cannot explain the normative dimension – what the moral good should be beyond the pleasant or agreeable.

[10] *DA* III, 9 432a 15-b 8 discusses the relationship between these two divisions.

[11] The translation by Rackham "the soul consists of two parts, one irrational and the other capable of reason" seems unfortunate because "irrational" sounds like the contradictory opposite of "rational". To talk of "parts of the soul" can hardly be evaded in English, but should be bracketed in light of the following sentence quoted above.

his argument Aristotle leaves open because it is not relevant to ethics in the narrower sense, can be answered:

> Whether these [two parts] are really distinct in the sense that the parts of the body or of any other divisible whole are distinct, or whether though distinguishable in thought as two they are inseparable in reality, like the convex and concave sides of a curve, is a question of no importance for the matter in hand. (1102a 30-33)

The result of the considerations in *DA* II,2 413b 13-32 is that the powers of the soul are to be differentiated only conceptually (cf. *DA* III,10 433a 31-b 13).

The *orexis* of man distinguishes itself from that of animals: the concept is applied to both only by analogy. The reason for this is the unity of the human form, i.e. because man as a whole exists in a state of openness to *logos*: ἄνθρωπος ζῷον λόγον ἔχων (cf. *Pol.* I, 2 1253a 9f). Man lives in a sphere of accessibility to the *logos*, as a total entity. All of his powers of the soul within which aspiration operates therefore have another character, namely, a specifically human, including the powers called *alogon*. The interesting question here is that of the precise, differentiated relationship between *orexis* and *logos*. First, though, we must address, in addition to the transcendental and the analogical character of *orexis*, its teleological function.

Human self-realisation occurs in action, to which affectivity disposes and impels. "Doing well is the End, and it is at this that desire aims."[12] To do what is morally good on the basis of *orexis* at the same time achieves the good of one's own being. In this dynamic final paradigm, a teleological aspiration of the *physis* towards the appropriate perfection of each organism is manifest. *Orexis* is the concrete manifestation of the disposition of man to the good. The goodness of action can be measured by the concordance with that perfection, as is demonstrated by the question of specific human activity, the ἔργον-argumentation in *NE* I, 7 (from 1097b 25). Central here is 1098a 7f: "The performance that is distinctive to man is the active exercise of the soul's faculties according to the *logos* or not without *logos*."[13] The formulation of Aristotle that the specifically human activity is that of reason "or not without reason", embraces exactly the emotionality with its participating rationality. In the next section we shall examine this further. Here, we should note that the affects are not particular events, but rather concretisations of a movement towards self-realisation. They are only fully understandable within a comprehensive teleological concept that includes the

---

[12] ἡ γὰρ εὐπραξία τέλος, ἡ δ'ὄρεξις τούτου (*NE* VI,2 1139b 4f.).

[13] ἔστιν ἔργον ἀνθρώπου ψυχῆς ἐνέργεια κατὰ λόγον ἢ μὴ ἄνευ λόγου. Again, I find Rackham's translation less convincing: "the function of man is the active exercise of the soul's faculties in conformity with rational principle, or at all events not in dissociation from rational principle".

human entelechy. Only a fully developed theory of aspiration (as presented in Riedenauer 2000) affords the correct hermeneutical parameters for a deeper comprehension of the relationship of Aristotelian psychology and theory of behaviour, and thereby, of the foundation of ethics.

2. The Specific Rationality of the *alogon*

The human psychological division of Aristotle's ethics distinguishes between τὸ λόγον ἔχων, the *logos*-possessing self, from ἄλογον, which is addressed in Book VI as a criterion of categorisation:

> We said that there are two parts of the soul, one that has reason and one non-rational"
> (NE VI, 1, 1139a 5).14

The being that possesses *logos* has the ability to understand, to recognise and to think (the *theoretikon* and the *logistikon*), whereas the *alogon* seems at first sight to be what *De Anima* attributes to the vegetative and sensible powers. However, this simplistic parallel allows no place for the phenomenon that concerns us here: would the emotions, for example, merely be the exercise of sensory powers? Or would they be directly attributable to cognitive powers? Apart from the fact that neither alternative resolves the problem, such a parallel also fails to recognise the analogical character of psychological powers, on the basis of which human sensibility differs from that of animals. Therefore, it is not correct to translate *alogon* with "irrational", which would suggest the contradictory opposite to "rational" – "pre-rational" is to be preferred.

The *alogon* can certainly participate in the *logos* (*NE* I,13 1102b 26-30), and for this reason I denote it as pre-rational. A cognitive turn did not occur only with the psychology of the emotions in the twentieth century.[15] *NE* I,13 concludes, almost provocatively: the *alogon* also has *logos* – as obeying.

> The non-rational [part] then, as well [as the whole soul] apparently has two parts. For while the plant-like [part] shares in reason not at all, the [part] with appetites and in general desires shares in reason in a way, insofar as it both listens to reason and obeys it. This is the way in which we are said to 'listen to reason' from father or friends (NE I, 13, 1102b 29-33).

---

[14] Rackham's translation again coarsens to "two parts, one rational and the other irrational."
[15] This development is explained in Brüderl and al. (see Brüderl/Halsig/Schröder 1988). Richard Lazarus, founder of the cognitive-relational-motivational emotion theory, ultimately saw an astonishing parallel to the concept of *pathos* in the *Rhethoric* (Lazarus 1993, 17).

This decisive affirmation of the participation of affectivity in reason is in my opinion often under-appreciated. There is a concordance, a harmony of the entire person including his affectivity with the *logos*.[16] Ultimately, it lies in the tendency of the teleological *orexis* itself that practical reason "takes over" the pre-rational movement and achieves a fully human activity.

The reason for this lies in the pre-rational evaluation of goals within the affective relationship to the world. Every aspiration already presents a provisional answer to that which shows and offers itself in a situation, it is respectively determined by the apparent good, the φαινόμενον ἀγαθόν. Human affectivity is then an openness to the possible meaning of specific objects, which is also influenced by the *ethos* of the respective cultural community. How, precisely, this occurs, is demonstrated by the structure of *pathos,* that integrates the essential dimensions of our humanity.

3. The Dimensions of *pathos*

The most extensive treatment of *pathos* by Aristotle is preserved in the *Rhetoric*, especially in the second book. This seems astonishing, but it contains insight that has long been overlooked (cf. the standard commentary Cope 1970, 117). Conley has even spoken of an "apparent boycott of II, 2-11" by interpreters (1982, 300). In fact, the *Rhetoric* displays an essential inter-relationship between affect (*pathos*), rationality and language (*logos*), community (*polis*) and the customs they preserve (*ethos*). These are dimensions of human existence, which, strictly speaking, implies that inter-relationship. Thus, this multi-dimensional theory of affects exposes the connection of the anthropological definitions in the *Politics*: man is the ζῷον λόγον ἔχων *as* ζῷον πολιτικὸν, and associated with both is the third definition (the significance of which is often under-valued) as the kind of animal which alone is capable of recognising moral qualities and thus of living within a community. *Logos* is "designed to indicate the advantageous and the harmful, and therefore also the right and the wrong; for it is the special property of man in distinction from the other animals that he alone has perception of good and bad and right and wrong and the other moral qualities, and it is partnership in these things that makes a household and a city-state." (*Pol.* I,1 1253a 14-18)

In this way, Aristotle lays the foundation for a possible, comprehensive, rational conduct of life, in which individual and communal decisions are reflected upon and dis-

---

[16] συμφωνεῖν τῷ λόγῳ (*NE* III,12 1119b 16); ὁμοφωνεῖ τῷ λόγῳ; κοινωνεῖ λόγου (*NE* I,13 1102b 28-30). The particular way in which Moss reinterprets these passages is significant (Moss 2014, 110, 119, 188).

succeed, that which is to be done is evaluated and the good is realised. Accordingly, the *Rhetoric* analyses each *pathos* phenomenologically in its threefold relation to circumstances, to (also bodily) disposition, and to other people. In this structural analysis, we find the cognitive, bodily, motivational and social dimensions of affectivity, each of which will be briefly presented in the following.

a) The Cognitive Dimension

Many scholars have now rejected earlier misunderstandings, which tended to see in the *Rhetoric* a technique for the manipulation of feelings (Fortenbaugh 1975, Conley 1982, Leighton 1982 and 2009, Wörner 1990). In such a mistaken interpretation, it was assumed that rationality and emotionality functioned in fundamental opposition to one another, so that every appeal to affects immediately posed the risk of manipulation. This view more closely describes the older critique of affects, against which Aristotle argued: that of Gorgias[17], Democritus ("wisdom cures *pathe* like medicine cures illness", fragment B31), Zenon (emotion as "irrational and contrary to nature"[18]), or certain writings by Plato[19]. In opposition to this, Aristotle proposed that the *pathe* already possess within themselves a specific rationality – a cognitive centre, namely, the spontaneous evaluation of whatever is encountered in a given situation. In my opinion, the most important and until now essential and fundamental achievement of the Aristotelian psychology of the affects is its clarification of the constitutive role of specific evaluative assumptions. The origin of any emotion lies – in distinction from sensory perceptions (e.g. of heat), pain, and somatically conditioned desires (e.g. hunger) – in a cognitive act that responds to something in the world (not only within the agent), that is, the spontaneous evaluation of whatever is encountered in a given situation as an affective 'object'[20]. Here lies also the 'added value' in contrast to simple per-

---

[17] *Helenes enkomion* excuses Helena by denouncing emotional motivation as a kind of sickness or drug (among other excuses) [cf. Euripides, *Medea* 446-450].
[18] τὸ πάθος ... ἄλογος καὶ παρὰ φύσιν ψυχῆς κίνησις (Zenon: SVF I; n. 205; "sickness of the soul"). For Zenon, wrong judgements constitute affects, while Chrysippos identifies both (Diog. Laert. VII; 110 f.).
[19] See mainly *Phaedo* (64d - 65c; 66b - 67a; 82d - 83d) and *Gorgias* (492d - 494b) in the context of the body-soul-dualism. Cf. the image of the soul as a carriage (*Phaidros* 247b 3-6) and the metaphors in *Politeia* IX 588 c-e, *Timaios* (69c5 - d4). A greater appreciation and different view of emotions and lust shows *Philebos* 21ff. and 32 ff.
[20] See *Topics* (IV,6 127b 30-32; VI,13 151a 16f.; VIII,1 156a 32f.; cf. *DA* III,3 427b 21-24). Aristotle further elaborates the view of the *Philebos*, that emotions arise "with" opinions (μετά), and replaces it with a causal connection; διά. In *Rhethoric* (Rhet. I, 11) he differentiates irrational desires (mostly

ceptions – therefore, perception theories of the emotions ought to become evaluation theories. Affects assess the significance of what is real and also what is possible in a given situation, immediately and in a totality, as useful or damaging, as things to pursue or to avoid, as a good or an evil. The general affective openness for significance is determined by each object under specific formal criteria, and through this the world in its meaningfulness becomes accessible in a nuanced fashion.

The example of anger is illuminating; it has routinely been examined as a paradigmatic basic affect (cf. Lazarus 1991, 217). Aristotle defines *orge* as "a longing, accompanied by pain, for a real or apparent revenge for a real or apparent slight, affecting a man himself or one of his friends, when such a slight is undeserved" (*Rhet.* II,2 1378a 30 f.). We can see how many assumptions specify and concretise a general desire for a recognition of my person or my concerns so that precisely this affect is formed. Now, I emphasize merely the central moment: something always appears *as* something to the person experiencing an emotion, and this is the origin of this feeling. Some fact is interpreted by the angered individual *as* an irritation, by a fearful individual *as* a threat, by a shamed individual *as* dishonouring etc. Such assumptions differentiate the various *pathe* from one another. They entail a provisional, but fundamental assessment of that which is for me in this moment good or bad. I designate this as the primary evaluation of a situation.

On the basis of the example of anger, an additional moment of anticipating evaluation is evident, insofar as this affect contains the hope of satisfaction (*Rhet.* II,2 1378b 2f.; II, 2 1379a 23f. and *DA* I,1 403a 30f). The imagination even assesses future possibilities, the evaluation of which is included in anger.

The affective hermeneutics of a situation is essential in the sphere of action, which is generally determined by the contingent, where theoretical knowledge is insufficient and the best way to act cannot be deduced by rationality unaided by affectivity.

b) The Social Dimension

People always react to comparable situations in somewhat different fashion, because what appears to any affectively affected individual of existential significance is already coloured by their specific character and experience. This disposition is influenced by both their physical constitution and the constellation of their social environment, by their position within their community and their particular self-image. For example, the above-

---

originating in the body) from desires which are rational in so far as they are experienced on the basis of a conviction (1370a 18-32).

mentioned definition of anger includes the seemingly undeserved slight. *Rhet.* II, 12-17 summarises in which existential situations people are particularly susceptible for specific affects.

The belonging to others (e.g. in the family) likewise determines their affective openness (cf. *Rhet.* 1379b 2-4). Aristotle concretised the respective social aspects accordingly in the psychology of the *Rhetoric*, while feelings that are independent of one's belonging to others scarcely play any role. Thus, in the case of anger, its public nature is significant for the irritation experienced (φαινομένη; *Rhet.* II,2 1378a 31). On the other hand, it has a positive, restorative function for the community: κατάστασις (II, 3 1380a 9). I interpret the rhetorical context of the Aristotelian psychology of emotions thus, that only within the sphere of an *ethos* of a community of communication does affectivity unfold its entire power of manifesting situational relevance within the framework of a verbal consensus about the respective good, the necessary or useful, and their opposites. The *pathos* unites the individual with the communal *ethos* and its *logos*. The spontaneous affective reaction of a child is always formed by the value system of the community and the parents – which, of course, can change – through its upbringing. From a contemporary perspective, this context of the respectively dominant *ethos* is the basis for the historical and cultural differences in evaluations. This is already reflected in the *Rhetoric* itself, which classifies anger as the answer to perceived injustice, unlike the account we find in Homer, according to which anger is more strongly grounded in the idea of honour; to this extent, Achilles' anger was of a different kind.[21]

c) The Bodily Dimension

The physiological foundation of the multi-dimensional emotion theory of Aristotle remains the starting point for classical theories of the affects, and similarly, the modern beginnings of the scientific study of psychology. Emotions are conditioned by age and physical circumstances, such as an illness, and the likelihood of their manifestation can be enormously strengthened or weakened. The brief definition of affect in *De anima* as "incarnated *logos*" emphasizes its physicality in union with their participation in *logos*: τὰ πάθη

---

[21] Konstan elaborates this cultural variability, which seems explicable on the basis of an Aristotelian theory of evaluation: "It is at the level of evaluation that cultural differences in the determination of the emotions are most salient... such an appraisal will involve a whole range of socially conditioned values and expectations." (Konstan 2006, 24)

λόγοι ἔνυλοί εἰσιν (*DA* I,1 403a 25 f.).[22] Accordingly, any emotion can also be considered in physical terms, because "all *pathe* of the soul are physical"[23] and inseparable from physical matter[24]. Despite having only minimal empirical knowledge of the somatic processes, Aristotle ascribed the greatest significance to this physiological dimension of emotionality, without, however, reducing the respective significance of the other three dimensions. It is conceivable that he would readily have integrated the findings of neurobiology in their relative importance into his theory. The emotional characteristic of feelings or experiences, often emphasized in psychology since the nineteenth century, which is combined with an inescapable sense of being personally affected, is implicit in the physical dimension. If somebody said, "I am very afraid, but it doesn't bother me!", we would not be able to understand him. This element of feeling was perhaps in Antiquity not a prominent topic, because it is a natural and self-evident phenomenon that was not yet compromised by a Cartesian abstraction of the self from the body, and hence from the world, as a result of which polarisation the perceived proximate relationship between 'subject' and 'object' was seen to require an explanation.

From a teleological perspective, the reason for the significance of the somatic phenomena is to be seen in the fact that behaviour ultimately also necessitates the mobilisation of physical powers – which is included in the concept of motivation, properly understood: to bring to movement. With this observation, we come to our fourth structural moment of *pathos*.

d) The Motivational Dimension

Emotions combine cognition and motivation, in that they dynamically situate us within a context that is understood pre-rationally, and they evaluate its significance. They impel to conscious, rational, moral decisions (προαίρεσις) by means of the motivating tension between pleasure and pain (ἡδονή, λυπή)[25]. In this way, they dispose and motivate man to a full and intentional *actus humanus*. This is a unified, felt reaction to that

---

[22] Hett's translation "formulae expressed in matter" is misleading, therefore better translations from *DA* are proposed.

[23] The *Rhet.* does not intend to treat the *causa materialis* of affects, but the *causa efficiens* and often also the *causa finalis* (*DA* 403a 17; cf. *MA* 7 701b 23f).

[24] τὰ πάθη τῆς ψυχῆς ἀχώριστα τῆς φυσικῆς ὕλης τῶν ζῴων (*DA* I,1 403b 17f.). Further Aristotle discerns the fundamentally different perspectives of the dialectician and of the researcher of nature (DA 403 a29ff.).

[25] Hence the component of "feeling" an emotion as a whole being, which is placed in the foreground by Jamie Dow's interpretation of emotions "as pleasures and pains." (Dow 2011)

which appears to be good or bad within its respective context, and constitutes the beginning of goal-oriented self-movement, which in turn forms the foundation of virtue ethics.

Emotion's specifically human significance is achieved in the rationally guided perfection of the individual's spontaneous reaction, i.e. a free and conscious cultivation of the affects that adapts each primary response to the response given by practical reason to specific situations, and that improves its long-term 'appropriateness'.

4. Rational Aspiration and Aspiring Reason

Προαίρεσις: The central concept of Aristotle's theory of behaviour, that of moral decision, cannot and need not be explored here. I wish merely to emphasize one aspect, the significance of which only becomes apparent in relation to the treatment of *orexis*: the dynamic unity of desire and rationality in its implementation. Aristotle defines decision-making as "aspiring reason or rational aspiration": ἢ ὀρεκτικὸς νοῦς ἡ προαίρεσις ἢ ὄρεξις διανοητική (*NE* VI,2 1139b 5f).[26] *Orexis* achieves here its moral purpose; it becomes effective, decisive willing, and reveals the extent to which Aristotle understood action as aspiring movement. *Proairesis* is not simply to be construed as a sub-category of aspiration, but rather as its highest form of realisation in his analogous-dynamic theory of action. Not only is the origin of decision-making "desire and reasoning directed to some end"[27], but *proairesis* is itself reflective *orexis*.

The decision realises the aspiration as teleological power, its finality towards fully human activity, and thereby the self-realisation of man. Decision-making also establishes a new and higher relationship of the agent himself: he determines *himself* – he actively assumes his existence.

There are phenomena in the face of which the conceptual differentiation between individual powers, in this case, between reason and aspiration, fails. In *proairesis*, a unity is operative – it is a complete act of human correspondence. Man as aspiring and *logos*-endowed determines himself. For a good *proairesis*, says Aristotle, "both the *logos* must be true and the aspiration right" (*NE* VI,2 1139a 25). The combination of this requirement – true and right – could already indicate that the *logos*-character of self-determination is not limited to finding the appropriate means in goal-oriented rational calculation. Aristotle emphasizes that practice is also called to realise the human power to bring forth truth: ἀληθεύει (*NE* VI,3 1139b 15); he speaks explicitly of practical truth: ἀλήθεια πρακ-

---

[26] Rackham's translation "thought related to desire or desire related to thought" unduly weakens the grammatical construction in Aristotle's text.
[27] "Purpose partakes both of intellect and of desire." (*NE* VI,2 1139a 32; cf. *MA* 6, 700b 23)

τική (NE VI,2 1139a 27). The capacity of man to realise the truth is absolutely not restricted to theoretical knowledge. The philosopher stipulates that truth in relation to practical reason consists in "conformity to the right aspiration": ὁμολόγως (ibid. a 31). This means in turn that without *orexis*, there are no human 'truths' in the sphere of action.

The basis of this capacity to respond, of the moral capacity to conform, is that the self finds itself as a being that aspires. The affective experience of being in pursuit of something opens the world first for self-determination in the *logos*.

5. Virtue as the Balance of Affective Responses

Aristotelian ethics is characterised by the central role assumed by virtue (ἀρετή). It is the habitually good evaluation of a situation, aiming at the rationally determined balance, the "middle" between an excess and a deficiency of affective responses to the given situation. Here, we are concerned merely to indicate its relationship to *pathos* and *orexis*. Human life is meaningful and successful through good actions (εὐπραξία). Both aspects are already contained within the meaning of the Greek word: on the one hand, good actions, and on the other, happiness, well-being, fortunate success. *Eupraxia* as constant virtuous action is possible if there are established dispositions to act well: good habits, ἕξεις. These dispositions stabilise the being in pursuit of the good, and strengthen the appropriateness of concrete desires. They contribute essentially to the mediation of aspiration with rationality.

The receptivity of man for objects of action which appear as good or bad can be malleably shaped within certain parameters. The affective susceptibility can be too high or too low – as the example of anger shows: Neither the individual disposed to become angry very often or very strongly, nor the opposite type, who lacks sufficient aggression and an ability to assert himself, is able to respond appropriately to situations of conflict. However, the sense of a good balance of reactions cannot be replaced with the application of general rules. As useful as practical principles may be, which may commonly apply, and which preserve useful experiences of successful and failed conduct, they can never perfectly and accurately grasp the contingent situations (see *NE* II, 2).

The evaluative response to situations by *pathos* is therefore essential. The ἕξεις mediate the concrete affective level of response with the balance determined by the *logos*, and ensure that the primary reaction of the individual will ordinarily be appropriate. The virtuous individual loves that which is good for him and abhors that which is genuinely damaging (*NE* II, 3 1104b 10-16). His emotions dispose him in such a manner that within his circumstances, he is always in a balanced appropriate state and in an optimal relation to everything. He is affectively oriented "at the right time, on the right occasion, towards the right people, for the right purpose and in the right manner" (*NE* II,6 1106b 21f). The measure of the good becomes apparent in broad openness and affective susceptibility for appearing possibilities to act. It manifests itself in so far as the virtuous individual habitually situates himself in the right balance and actively adapts to the respective reference points of that environment.

Virtue thus not only disposes to the best decision, but also already forms affective susceptibility. Insofar as emotionality is indirectly malleable, man has a responsibility for the way in which the world appears to him and affects him (cf. *NE* II, 2 1104a 19-27). The claim in the *Magna Moralia* is then reasonable "that, contrary to the opinion of other [moralists], it is not the *logos* which originally points the way to Virtue, but rather the passions" (*MM* II, 7 1206b 17-19). I can here only indicate a particularly important consequence of this: insofar as each affect is co-formed through the behaviour provoked by previous, similar situations, the emotions mediate the past of our life history to our future potential conduct.

It follows from this that the horizon of reason is not first revealed in a conscious resolve, rather, that its objectivity is facilitated and prefigured in the well-balanced affective evaluation. To live rationally (κατὰ λόγον) implies fundamentally the disclosure of the relevance of a situation through the emotions – not least because in quotidian circumstances, human behaviour remains uncompleted, i.e. without conscious, rational decisions. Rapid reaction often demands an impulse reliably determined by habit (see *NE* III,6 1115b 1ff. for the example of fortitude). To not allow one's responses to be dominated alone by *pathos*, i.e. not allowing one's self to be emotionally determined, means (in normal cases) not a struggle of reason against feelings, but consists in the total teleology of human affectivity as pre-rational and as co-operating with reason. Inversely, it can also be said with Aristotle that exclusively rationally controlled behaviour without affectivity (ἀπάθεια) would no longer be good conduct (*euprattein*) – apart from the fact that it would be an illusory ideal. Such an individual would also thereby be deprived of pleasure in such activity.

6. Affective Disclosure of the Integral Responding Relationship to the World

Man as a physical, reasoning and social being is always in pursuit of something. The world is accessible to him in its meaning and value profile, because he is engaged and aspires, while ultimately he is concerned with himself, with his own being. Emotions like anger manifest personal aspirations like the need for respect for oneself, one's relatives or friends, one's values or achievements. Other emotions like fear manifest natural needs for nourishment and protection, as do non-emotional phenomena of desire directed at survival like hunger or thirst. Although somewhat malleable, they show a natural teleology which Thomas Aquinas subsumes under *inclinationes naturales* (cf. *Summa theologiae* I-II 94, 2; 94,3-4; cf. 91,2 and 91,6).

On the basis of the human being in pursuit of something, the affects first grasp reality in a manner that involves one sensibly and completely in an irreducible value dimension: that of the good (or bad).[28] Ronald de Sousa calls this cognitive dimension of human affectivity "axiological rationality" and speaks of the essential "semantics of the affects", which are learned by every individual (constituting the foundation for a certain variability in meanings[29]).

The grasping of the axiological dimension of reality in relation to which the individual finds himself through affectivity is, in psychological models, usually not recognised in its irreducible uniqueness. It is more than research on coping strategies is able to reveal and to define, which describes emotions as a process of control and adaptation. The pre-rational evaluation of the existential and normatively relevant aspects of a situation through affective susceptibility and spontaneous evaluation unfolds the situation's potential axiological significance. The relationship with the conscious interpretations explains, moreover, the multiple possibilities of false interpretations, distortions of affective evaluation through to self-manipulation (see de Sousa 1997, chap. 9). The affective experience of a situation implies a provisional interpretation in reference to its existential significance, of whatever good or evil is important to the individual:

The relationship of man to the world is thus configured as dynamic. It is characterised through the four specified dimensions of the affects, as a physically incarnated, motivational, intentional-cognitive, and socially embedded relation. This understanding of the essential affective disclosure goes ultimately beyond the "cognitive-relational-motivational theory of emotions" of the pioneer of cognitive affect psychology, Richard Lazarus, who recognised the relational aspect as one of the three structural moments, but not as the basis of all other moments.

---

[28] "Affectivity is ... constitutive for the interestingly reflective relation of the person and everything else, for the fact that everything has a meaning for the life of the person, the background being that the person cares for her own life and how she lives. Therefore, it could be said that it is exactly in affectivity that an integral relation to one's own life is founded." (Wolf 1994, 115). See also Hastedt (2005, 141 ff.) and Solomon, for whom feelings – somewhat simplified – are simply the meaning of life (Solomon 2000, XII).

[29] De Sousa argues that emotional semantics are derived from "paradigm scenarios" which allow the individual to learn a repertoire of feelings and to define the formal objects of emotions (De Sousa 1997, 284).

The obvious vagueness of the concept of cognition, indiscriminately used by psychologists, can be eliminated by a clarification of the relational dimension of affectivity as a differentiated structure of challenge and response. Thus, the psychological concept of "emotional response" and the principle of relational meaning (Lazarus[30]) are understood on a fundamental, philosophical-anthropological level. The human capacity to respond is graded between unconscious, instinct-analogous goal-orientation, cognitive activity in the sense of pre-rational but conscious, and rationality in its fullest sense, on the basis of the active openness of the human condition as being concerned with meaning. Affects, so understood, do not exclude freedom and rationality.

According to my interpretation of emotions as responses, they are initial answers, and not merely reactions in the literal sense of the word with their connotation of passivity and automatism. The typical state of affective passivity is an experience, a qualified type of enduring, that is at the same time the beginning of an answer, which is only appropriate to human beings as physical, sensitive, self-moving, social, speaking and thinking beings.

In the same way that the philosophy of emotions since Aristotle has argued against an over-emphasis of the pathetic element, so the interpretation of the emotions as cognitive in twentieth-century psychology has opposed the modern tendency to denigrate emotions as "passions" juxtaposed against rationality. De Sousa designates this fundamental problem of the theory of feelings, that has been present since Antiquity, the antinomy of passivity and activity (De Sousa 1997, 21 f. and 35 f.). The response interpretation of the formulation of a relationship to the world by the affects avoids this dichotomy, and integrates passive and active aspects: the passivity of emotions enables a primary objectivity of the responses and is biologically based. This is not incompatible with the view that they are subject to cultural modifications. For at the same time, the active and activating aspects of the primary evaluation of a situation are accorded their appropriate place. Furthermore, the one-sidedness of the judgement theory of the emotions is eliminated, which overlooks the pathetic aspect of being affected and the capacity to be affected. If man is understood as an aspiring and responding being, who is in all situations concerned with himself (from his physical self-preservation to the necessary conditions of living together in a community), then even less specific, less intentional phenomena of feelings, such as moods, can be interpreted meaningfully, which purely representational theories have difficulty in doing. Neither one's relation to one's self, which is fundamental in all affectivity, nor its irreducible relation with the

---

[30] "This principle states that each emotion is defined by a unique and specifiable relational meaning... constructed by the process of appraisal, which is the central construct of the theory." (Lazarus 1991, 39) Speaking of "constructing" meaning should probably not be misunderstood in a technical sense, and I therefore prefer to speak of a responsive formation.

world, is excluded. In order to nurture its openness and thereby also its essential disclosing capacity, even more seems necessary than Aristotle's treatment of the cultivation of the concrete affects to virtues (which, certainly, constitutes an essential counter position against the Stoic ideal of *apatheia*): a kind of self-care and self-formation which aims to preserve my ability to feel on all levels, so that the world is of concern to me, to ensure that people, things, real and possible situations affect me, gain relevance and value, and can motivate me to act. Only for a being who can be moved by the affects is the world accessible and valuable, so that he can engage with it.

In this manner, man is first addressed and challenged (the philosophical interpretation of the relational dimension); second, he experiences this engagement in a totality and inescapably (the physical dimension and component of feeling); third, he evaluates this spontaneously in terms of the good and the bad (the cognitive dimension); which, fourth, is influenced by diverse factors from social interaction to cultural norms (the social dimension); and finally, he finds himself moved to provide his answer in action (the philosophical interpretation of the motivational dimension). What follows is the critical review or reappraisal of the spontaneous, pre-rational evaluation by practical reason.

The elaboration of *orexis* as the underlying constitution of aspiration allows us to view human existence as the implementation of a naturally grounded state of pursuit that is attracted to the good. Intentionality already on the level of affectivity is grounded in a finality that is not a metaphysical postulate, but rather concretely experienced and that is receptive to the hermeneutic of a philosophical psychology and anthropology.

The Aristotelian conception of *orexis* also has far-reaching consequences for the self-understanding of human reason, which here can only be briefly mentioned. Aspiration is the basis of the theoretical relation to the world, as the first sentence of Aristotle's *Metaphysics* emphasizes, which has not been taken with sufficient seriousness: "All men naturally desire knowledge" (quoted already in footnote 3). We should avoid interpreting human understanding and practical reason as restricted to the rational faculty. The aspiration-ethical approach avoids an aporetic dualism between an abstractly conceived rationality, and the phenomena of volition. Aristotle, however, regards willing in its concrete decision-making as the highest rational form of aspiration. Reason is not somehow applied to *praxis*, but as the rational capacity of orientation of a self-moving being, it always already exists within the realm of praxis. We humans find ourselves always already in a pre-evaluated world that affects us. Affectivity with its specific participation in *logos* achieves a primary comprehension that lies beneath the differentiation between rational and volitional faculties. *Orexis* constitutes a fundamental positioning of man in the world before the distinction between active and passive, in a characteristic susceptibility and responsiveness that underpins all *praxis*.

Prof. Dr. Markus Riedenauer, Institut für Christliche Philosophie,
Katholisch-Theologische Fakultät, Universität Wien,
markus.riedenauer[at]univie.ac.at

References

Aristotle. *On the Soul* [abr. *DA*]. (Aristotle Vol. VIII, The Loeb Classical Library No. 288). English Transl. by W. S. Hett. Cambridge and London: Harvard University Press, 1986.
Aristotle. *Eudemian Ethics*, in idem. *Athenian Constitution. Eudemian Ethics. Virtues and Vices* [abr. *EE*] (Aristotle Vol. XX, The Loeb Classical Library No. 285) English Transl. by H. Rackham. Cambridge and London: Harvard University Press, 1935.
Aristotle. *Parts of Animals. Movement of Animals. Progression of Animals* [abr. *MA*]. (Aristotle Vol. XII, The Loeb Classical Library No. 323). English Transl. by E. S. Forster. Cambridge and London: Harvard University Press, 1937.
Aristotle. *Metaphysics* [abr. *Met.*] (Aristotle Vol. XVII and Vol. XVIII, The Loeb Classical Library No. 271 and No. 287). English Transl. by H. Tredennick. Cambridge and London: Harvard University Press, 1956 (books I-XIX) and 1969 (books X-XIV).
Aristotle. *Magna Moralia*, in idem. *Metaphysics X-XIV. Oeconomica. Magna Moralia* [abr. *MM*] (Aristotle Vol. XVIII, The Loeb Classical Library No. 287). English Transl. by G. C. Armstrong. Cambridge and London: Harvard University Press, 1969.
Aristotle. *Nichomachean Ethics* [abr. *NE*] (Aristotle Vol. XIX, The Loeb Classical Library No. 73). English Transl. by H. Rackham. Cambridge and London: Harvard University Press, 1990.
Aristotle. *Politics* [abr. *Pol.*]. (Aristotle Vol. XXI, The Loeb Classical Library No. 26). English Transl. by H. Rackham. Cambridge and London: Harvard University Press, 1998.
Aristotle. *Art of Rhetoric* [abr. *Rhet.*] (Aristotle Vol. XXII, The Loeb Classical Library 193). English Transl. by J. H. Freese. Cambridge and London: Harvard University Press, 1975.
Arnim, Hans von (ed.). *Stoicorum Veterum Fragmenta* I [abr. *SVF*]. Leipzig: Teubner 1905.
Brüderl, Leokadia, Norbert Halsig, and Annette Schröder. "Historischer Hintergrund, Theorien und Entwicklungstendenzen der Bewältigungsforschung", in Leokadia Brüderl (ed.). *Theorien und Methoden der Bewältigungsforschung*. München: Juventa, 1988. 25-45.
Charles, David. "Desire in Action: Aristotle's Move." in Michael Pakaluk, and Giles Pearson (eds.). *Moral Psychology and Human Action in Aristotle*. Oxford, 2011. 75-94.
Conley, Thomas. "Pathe and Pisteis: Aristotle Rhet. II, 2–11." *Hermes* Vol. 110 (1982): 300-315.
Cope, Edward. *An Introduction to Aristotlés Rhetoric*. Hildesheim–New York: Olms, 1970.
De Sousa, Ronald. *Die Rationalität der Gefühle*. Frankfurt: Suhrkamp, 1997.
Döring, Sabine. "Die Renaissance des Gefühls in der Gegenwartsphilosophie." *Information Philosophie* Vol. XX n. 4 (2005): 14-27.

Dow, Jamie. "Aristotle's Theory of the Emotions: Emotions as Pleasures and Pains." in Michael Pakaluk, and Giles Pearson (eds.). *Moral Psychology and Human Action in Aristotle* Oxford, 2011. 47-74.
Euripides. *Medea*, in idem. *Cyclops. Alcestis. Medea.* Edited and translated by David Kovacs (Loeb Classical Library 12). Cambridge and London: Harvard University Press, 1994.
Fortenbaugh, William W. *Aristotle on Emotion.* London, 1975.
Fortenbaugh, William W. "Aristotle's Rhetoric on Emotion." in Jonathan Barnes, Michael Schofield, and Richard Sorabji (eds.). *Articles on Aristotle.* Vol. 4. London: Duckworth, 1979. 133-153.
Goller, Hans. *Psychologie. Emotion, Motivation, Verhalten.* Stuttgart: Kohlhammer, 1995.
Hastedt, Heiner. *Gefühle. Philosophische Bemerkungen.* Stuttgart: Reclam, 2005.
Kenny, Anthony. *Action, Emotion and Will.* Bristol: Thoemmes, 1963.
Knuuttila, Simon. *Emotions in Ancient and Medieval Philosophy.* Oxford: Clarendon, 2004.
Konstan, David. *The Emotions of the Ancient Greeks.* Toronto: University Press, 2006.
Lazarus, Richard. *Emotion and Adaptation.* New York–Oxford: Oxford University Press, 1991.
Lazarus, Richard. "From Psychological Stress to the Emotions." *Annual Review of Psychology* Vol. 44 (1993): 1-21.
Leighton, Stephen. "Aristotle and the Emotions." *Phronesis* Vol. 27 (1982). 144–174.
Leighton, Stephen. "Passions and Persuasion." in Georgios Anagostopoulos (ed.). *A Companion to Aristotle.* Chichester: Wiley-Blackwell, 2009. 597-611.
Modrak, Deborah K.W. "Sensation and Desire." in Georgios Anagostopoulos (ed.). *A Companion to Aristotle.* Chichester: Wiley-Blackwell, 2009. 310-321.
Moss, Jessica. *Aristotle on the apparent good: perception, phantasia, thought, and desire.* Oxford: University Press, 2014.
Nussbaum, Martha. *The Therapy of Desire. Theory and Practice in Hellenistic Ethics.* Princeton: University Press, 1994.
Pakaluk, Michael, and Giles Pearson (eds.). *Moral Psychology and Human Action in Aristotle.* Oxford, 2011.
Pearson, Giles. *Aristotle on Desire.* Cambridge: University Press, 2012.
Pearson, Giles. "Aristotle and Scanlon on Desire and Motivation." in Michael Pakaluk, and Giles Pearson (eds.). *Moral Psychology and Human Action in Aristotle.* Oxford, 2011. 95-118.
Riedenauer, Markus. *OREXIS & EUPRAXIA. Ethikbegründung im Streben bei Aristoteles.* Würzburg: Königshausen & Neumann, 2000.
Rorty, Amélie. *Explaining emotions.* Berkeley, Calif.: University Press, 1980.
Rorty, Amélie. "Aristotle on the Metaphysical Status of Pathe." *Review of Metaphysics* Vol. 84 (1984): 521-546.
Solomon, Robert C. *Gefühle und der Sinn des Lebens.* Frankfurt: Zweitausendeins, 2000.
Tugendhat, Ernst. *Selbstbewußtsein und Selbstbestimmung. Sprachanalytische Interpretationen.* Frankfurt: Suhrkamp, 1979.
Wolf, Ursula. "Gefühle im Leben und in der Philosophie." in Hinrich Fink-Eitel, and Georg Lohmann (eds.) *Zur Philosophie der Gefühle.* Frankfurt: Suhrkamp, 1994. 112-135.
Wörner, Markus. *Das Ethische in der Rhetorik des Aristoteles.* Freiburg–München: Alber, 1990.

OLAV EIKELAND (Oslo)

If *phrónêsis* does not develop and define virtue as its own deliberative goal – what does?

Abstract

The article discusses relationships and contexts for "reason", "knowledge", and virtue in Aristotle, based on and elaborating some results from Eikeland (2008). It positions Eikeland (2008) in relation to Moss (2011, 2012, 2014) but with a side view to Cammack (2013), Kristjansson (2014), and Taylor (2016). These all seem to disagree among themselves but still agree partly in different ways with Eikeland. The text focuses on two questions: 1) the role or tasks of "reason", "knowledge", and "virtue" respectively in setting the end or goal for ethical deliberation, and more generally, 2) the role of dialogue or dialectics in Aristotle's philosophy, including its role concerning question one. The author argues that phrónêsis needs to be interpreted in the context of the totality of Aristotle's philosophy, and explains how this totality is fundamentally dialectical.

Keywords: deliberation, dialectics, habit, imagination, phrónêsis, virtue

Introduction

The purpose of this text is limited, pretending neither to be exhaustive nor complete concerning its subjects nor in relation to the texts it discusses, nor will I be able to refer to the broader discussions on almost every aspect of Aristotle's philosophy. I will discuss relationships and context for "reason", "knowledge", and virtue in Aristotle, based on and elaborating some results from Eikeland (2008)[1]. "Reason" is, of course, a rather imprecise expression, since it could translate several different Greek expressions used by Aristotle and Plato (*noûs, diánoia, phrónêsis, boúleusis, lógos,* and more). The same goes for "knowledge". I will position Eikeland (2008) in relation to a few recent texts, mainly Moss (2011, 2012, 2014), but with a side view to Cammack (2013), Kristjansson (2014), and Taylor (2016). They all seem to disagree among themselves but still agree partly but in different ways with Eikeland. I will not be able to do full justice to these texts either. What

---

[1] Although I am the author of this book, I have chosen to refer to it in the third person in this text. For further references to secondary literature, see the references in Eikeland (2008).

follows will suggest how the perspectives presented in Eikeland (2008) elaborate, unite, and transcend the apparently different perspectives of the other texts considered.

I focus on two questions, 1) the role or tasks of "reason", "knowledge", and "virtue" respectively in setting the end or goal (*télos* or *skopós*) for ethical deliberation, and more generally, 2) the role of dialogue or dialectics in Aristotle's philosophy, including its role concerning question one. Concerning the first question, then, the dominant view – succinctly summarized by Moss (2011) and Taylor (2016) – has for several decades been that, in Aristotle, *phrónêsis* grasps not only the means but *also* the ends of practical deliberation, i.e. that we deliberate about both ends and means. This has recently been challenged by Moss (Moss 2011, 2012, 2014). Concerning the second question, the role of dialectics or dialogue in Aristotle is generally contested but often based on a restricted conception of dialectics as formal "reasoning" from generally accepted opinions (*éndoxa*). Since Owen (1961), dialectics has gradually received increased attention. Its central role has also been increasingly recognized (cf. Aubenque 1962; Wieland 1962; de Pater 1965; Owen 1968; Evans 1977; Irwin 1988; Sim 1999; Berti 2004; Schramm 2004; Eikeland 1997, 190-194, idem. 2008, 217ff). In addition, both questions are parts of a larger context concerning the relationship between theoretical and practical knowing and reasoning in Aristotle. The theoretical and the practical in Aristotle, are often seen as totally separate domains. According to Aristotle, they differ concerning ends pursued, the theoretical being merely concerned with discerning differences and similarities and truth and falsity by affirming and denying (*katáphasis* – *apóphasis*), while the practical is concerned with what to do (NE1139a21-b6; OtS 432b27-433a30; OtS 407a4-31; Ots 429a23-24; Top 141a5-10; Cat17a1-8; cf. Eikeland 2008, 35, fn.35)[2].

Eikeland (2008) starts as an interpretation of *phrónêsis*, based on a comprehensive reading of the whole *Corpus Aristotelicum*. It criticizes the tendency to isolate *phrónêsis* as a putatively independent alternative to *tékhnê* and *epistêmê*, and to use only the ethical works and mostly Book VI of the Nicomachean Ethics, as the interpretive base (Eikeland 2008, 23ff.). *Phrónêsis* needs to be interpreted in the context of the totality of Aristotle's philosophy. Eikeland's claim (ibid., 212ff.), to which the last half of his book is dedicated, is that this totality is fundamentally dialectical. After summarizing some mostly uncontroversial understandings of *phrónêsis*, explaining and discussing the ethical and intellectual virtues, and delimiting *phrónêsis* from rhetoric, practical syllogisms, and technical reasoning or calculation (ibid., 51-114), Eikeland focuses on two controversial issues concerning

---

[2] The concepts "theoretical" and "practical" are also too imprecise but cannot be discussed any further here (cf. Eikeland 2008, 79-96 and 301-327).

phrónêsis, the relationship between ends and means in ethical deliberation (ibid., 115-137) and the relationship between general knowledge and knowledge of particulars (ibid., 138-180).

Moss (2011, 2012, 2014) discusses the first question above. Her main claim is that, contrary to the current dominant view, *phrónêsis* or ethical deliberation tells us neither what ends are, nor what ends to pursue. It only considers how to pursue given ends or goals[3]. The ends in ethics are set by our ethical characters. Bad characters seek bad goals or goals which merely appear good to them, good characters seek truly good goals (Eikeland 2008, 116-121). Preferably, ends are defined by virtue, since virtue makes the goal right in Aristotle's thinking, but apparently without *phrónêsis* or deliberation. Truly virtuous individuals see truth and seek what is truly good, others merely apparent goods (NE 1113a23-b2, 1114a31-b25, 1140b17-20, 1144a31-36; EE1229b26, 1236b34-1237a9; Pol 1332a22-25). Deliberation, however, is only about the means, or what contributes to the end (*tà sumphéronta pros tò télos*) (Eikeland 2008, 194). Moss invokes several unequivocal quotes from Aristotle to prove her point that Aristotle meant exactly what he wrote many times, i.e. that virtue makes the goal right, *phrónêsis* only the things towards the goal (NE 1144a7-9, 1145a5-7, 1151a15-19; EE 1227b23-25)[4]. Eikeland (2008, 104ff, 133, 210, 224) and Moss agree on this and in their refutation of the dominant view that despite the textual evidence against it in Aristotle, phronetic deliberation somehow concerns the choice and clarification of ends as well[5]. The motive for the dominant view seems to have been that if we take what Moss's evidence says literally, Aristotle's viewpoint becomes indistinguishable from the reduced and instrumental conception of reason found in Hume (1978) where reason is "the slave of the passions", and "passions" are preferences given as natural facts (data). It also conflates *phrónêsis* with cleverness (*deinótês*), the ability to deliberate about any goal, good or bad (NE 1144a23-29; cf. Eikeland 2008, 103). Hence, the possibility of distinguishing between true and apparent goods as ends is decisive in the thinking of Aristotle. Somehow, saving some form of rationality in deciding ends – i.e. the role of knowledge and reason in defining the virtues – seems necessary even for saving *phrónêsis* as different from mere cleverness.

---

[3] Eikeland (2008, 22-131) discusses and distinguishes between *télos* (end, *causa formalis*, connected to *praxis* and *enérgeia*) and *skopós* (aim, causa finalis, connected to *poíêsis* and *kínêsis*). These distinctions are not pursued by Moss, although they are quite important. They cannot be pursued here either.
[4] Eikeland (2008, fn. 92) has many more references in support of this.
[5] Hämäläinen (2015) defends an intellectualist view against Moss, in line with the dominant view but without really engaging with Moss's arguments and evidence.

Since Eikeland and Moss agree in restricting *phrónêsis* to "the means", I will not use space to argue the case but move straight to the question about the rationality or reasonability of ends, or rather, how do we clarify and define ends, including the virtues, and how do we become virtuous, according to Aristotle. How does Moss think ends are set? She concludes: "it is character, *not* intellect, that gives us our goal" (Moss 2011, 256), neither the discursive or argumentative intellect, consisting in *lógos*, nor the intuitive (*nous*), supposedly lacking *lógos*[6]. Ends are not established intellectually, she claims, although virtue as a result of "good upbringing", establishes habits that are still "cognitive" by providing imagination (*phantasía*) with perceptual images of ends desired because they seem good to us. Even contemplators get their ultimate goals through "correct" ethical habituation (Moss 2011, 259). Moss's presentation of how this happens (ibid., 251-259) is in several ways close to Eikeland's (2008, 181-299). For example, when Moss says:

> My claim – call it Practical Empiricism – is that habituation can furnish starting points because it is a very close analogue of the first stages of induction. Through habituation in virtuous activity one repeatedly perceives or experiences such activity; the perception in question is pleasurable perception, which amounts to perception of such activity as good. (Moss 2011, 255)

Still, there are important aspects missing from Moss's presentation, which makes it misrepresent Aristotle's position. How are habits cognitive? The discussion requires clarification of what Moss means not only by "virtue" but also by "reason" and "rational" when claiming that "reason does not give us our goals" (Moss 2014, 240). What is virtue? What is reason? What is "correct ethical habituation"? These questions are decisive. Aristotle, of course, does not talk about "reason" but about many kinds of *lógos* and different uses of *lógos* connected to *nous*, *diànoia*, *boúleusis*, rhetoric, dialectic, *apódeixis*, etc. (Eikeland 2008, 214). As indicated, he also talks about apparent and true virtues, modified virtue and absolute virtue. In addition, he talks about bad and good habits and characters. So, who or what distinguishes them and how?

If questions like these are not discussed, essential challenges remain. The first is the mentioned instrumentalisation of reason. The other is how to avoid reducing the aims, ends, or goals to *either* irrationality, arbitrariness, or naturally given passion, *or* to habitual conventionalism, localism, traditionalism, and consequently, relativism. Despite restricting the task of *phrónêsis* to deliberating means, Moss has an ambition "to save Aristotle from the charge of Humeanism" (Moss 2014, 240). The same goes for Eikeland (2008, 103). Moss's

---

[6] Somehow, in Aristotle's discussions, *nous* seems to be sometimes *with lógos* and sometimes *without*. Se the discussion in Eikeland (2008, 212-271).

interpretation may be able to avoid the pitfall of irrationality. But her solution hardly escapes neither instrumentalising reason nor relativizing goals. Ultimately, of course, the question at stake, is to what degree we as human beings are mere "products", extraneously determined by biological, psychological, social, and other causes from which habit alone cannot save us.

Comparing Moss's position to Eikeland's also provokes other questions. First, what is the role of knowledge or knowing (*gnôsis*, *epistêmê*) in acquiring ethical virtue and acting virtuously? Second, Aristotle's ban on *lógos* concerning goals, presupposes a certain context (Eikeland 2008, 132-137), not considered by Moss. Third, how does her position relate to Aristotle's statements (a) that *lógos* and *nous* are the *télos* for human development (Pol 1334b14-28; EE 1220a3), (b) that we need to mobilize all the following to become good and virtuous (*agathoí kaì spoudaioí*): *phúsis* (nature), *éthos* (habit), and *lógos* (reason) (Pol 1332a36-b7), and (c) that the goodness of individuals depends on both the part of the soul having *lógos* and the part able to follow *lógos* (Pol 1333a16-20)? Fourth, Moss suggests a connection between induction and habituation but does not discuss the role of dialogue or dialectics, so central for the discussion in Eikeland (2008) and made explicit through the title of his Chapter 6.2.1 "*Nóêsis* as Dialogue, or, the Reason Why Aristotle Insists on Letting *Phrónêsis* Deliberate about Means Only."

Cammack (2013) and Taylor (2016) have picked up on the challenge from Moss, neither one accepting her dismissal of reasoning concerning ends of deliberation. Cammack (2013) recognizes that there are many forms of *lógos*, deliberation is not the only one, she refers to the "professional setting" for deliberations, and she mentions "theoretical reasoning" as a potential, at least raising the question of the relationship between ethical virtues and theoretical reason. She hardly elaborates, specifies, or utilizes these possibilities, however, in challenging Moss's main point, that virtue, or mere habit, provides the end.

Taylor (2016) considers three accounts of how the end of deliberation is acquired: (a) by virtue of character, (b) by dialectic, i.e. critical reasoning concerning authoritative beliefs, and (c) by induction from data of experience. In his view, dialectic and experience are required for grasping virtuous ends for deliberation by the intellect. He agrees with Moss that ends are not subject to deliberation but does not thereby exclude the possibility that they are acquired as the result of some process of intellectual enquiry. Although he distinguishes between *poíêsis-tékhnê* and *praxis-phrónêsis*, he seems to conflate them, and thereby calculation (*logismós*) and deliberation (*boúleusis*), as merely two forms of practical reasoning (Eikeland 2008, 68ff). He points to the two different ways of being rational in Aristotle but seems to think the rational part (*tò lógon ekhon*) "instructs" the part not fully rational (*tò álogon*). As the following will indicate, Taylor also works with too simple accounts of dialectics as reasoning from accepted opinions, and of induction and experience as well, and this I think leads him off track in his discussion about ends and aims for deliberation.

1. What is the role of knowledge or knowing in virtue and virtuous action?

Aristotle describes virtue or *aretê* as a *héxis* or habitus, which means an acquired ability, skill, habit, or incorporated disposition and inclination for acting and feeling in certain ways, resulting from practice, exercise, or habituation (Cat 8b25-9a13, 12a26-13a37; NE 1103a16-26, 1103b22, 1114a10; EE 1220b1 and 18-20). A *habitus* can be either bad or good, but virtue is the best *habitus* within its field or kind of activity. Generally, virtue means what makes any "thing" or activity work at its best (*áristos*) (NE 1120a6). It renders (*apotelei*) both something in a good general state, *and* (*apodídôsin*) its activity and work good (NE 1106a14-26). Ethical virtues are excellences of character (*êthos*) in contrast to excellences of the intellect (*nous / diánoia*). Character (*êthos*) springs from habit (*éthos*) (NE 1103a14-30). *Every* virtue is the result of a process of perfection (*teleíôsis*) from within a specific practice, starting inchoately, and resulting in a certain virtuous *habitus* (NE 1103a26; Ph246a10-248a9; Metaph 1021b21; EE 1220a22-b10). A virtue, then, is a potential or capacity (*dúnamis*). As a perfected, competent ability to act, it is an *entelékheia* or actuality of a fully developed potential.

The ethical virtues are called "*álogoi*" by Aristotle, a word sometimes translated as "irrational". But they are not irrational in opposition or contradiction to reason, or by being unattainable by reason. *Álogoi* means they do not *consist* in the use of *lógos* or reasoned speech like the intellectual virtues (*epistêmê, nous, phrónêsis, tékhnê*, and more) which *consist* in *lógos* in themselves (*kuríôs kaì en hautô*) (NE 1103a2-3; Pol1333a16-19). Their *lógos*-character makes these virtues *intellectual*. The ethical virtues are not necessarily "wordless" or tacit, however, but they cannot be *reduced* to reasoning words and speech, i.e. to intellectual virtues. Still, they can be influenced and must be guided by *lógos*, following recommendations or instructions it provides. The standard for choosing in the practical sphere is that the pleasures, pains, actions, and emotions of our non-lingual parts do not interfere with, but rather support and strengthen the ability of the soul to reason correctly and follow reason. To "act according to right reason (*katà tòn orthón lógon prattein*)" – as the contemporary saying went – is to act without letting those parts which *do not* consist in *lógos*, like habits, skills, emotions, desires, and actions, interfere with the correct functioning of the part consisting in *lógos*⁷. In one place (EE 1220b1-7), character (*êthos*) as such is even defined as the ability to follow reason. Thus, the ethical virtues do take part in *lógos* but in a different way from the intellectual virtues (NE 1102b13-1103a3; EE1219b26-1220a13). In being able to listen to and follow *lógos* without being *lógos* these tacit abilities differ *both* from clean-cut reason or mind (*nous, diánoia*), consisting in the use or activities of *lógos* on the one hand, *and* from pure corporeal nature (*sôma* or *sarx*), unable to become modified directly by *lógos* on the other. As *héxeis*, the ethical virtues occupy a middle ground as properties of the living "ensouled" body (*psukhê*), the mediator between the two extremes of mind and the corporeal body. Other forms of *álogoi*, i.e. irrationality really opposing or obstructing reason, Aristotle leaves out of his discussion (NE 1102b23-26; EE 1219b31).

This is an important reason why Aristotle insists on saying that the ethical virtues exist *with* good and articulated reasons or justifications (*metà lógou*), as an important modification of the saying about acting "according to right reason" (NE1103b33-35, 1144b16-30). Aristotle emphasizes that ethical virtues are not merely "in accordance with" right reason. Things can be done in a formally correct way – according to reason – by chance, technically, or under the influence of others as in mechanical rule-following, or in following orders (NE 1105a17-b9). On the other hand, ethical virtues are not in themselves reasons (*lógous*), or kinds of *epistêmê*, as Socrates argued (NE1145b21-31; EE1216b3-25), because they require right action and emotion, not just abstracted arguments; words or thoughts. The ethical virtues are *héxeis* of the embodied soul or ensouled body – converted into right action and right emotion – *with* correct reasoning or justification (*metà tou orthou lógou*).

Aristotle sets up criteria for ethically virtuous acts in several places (NE 1105a17-b12, 1109b35-1112a17, 1135a20-b11, 1144a13-23; MM 1197b37-1198a21). He mentions three qualities of an agent, necessary for his acts to count as virtuous. First, he has to act with knowledge of what he is doing (*eidôs*), secondly, his actions must spring from a deliberate choice (*prohaíresis*) (Eikeland 2008, 116-121), and they must be chosen for their own sake (*proairoúmenos di'autá*), without ulterior motives, merely as instruments for achieving something else (NE 1144a16), and thirdly, they must spring from a firm and unchanging character (NE 1105a26-b18, 1144a13-23; cf. NE 1135a20-b11). Finally, doers of virtuous acts must also enjoy doing them, since no one would call someone "just" if he did not like acting justly (NE 1099a18).

---

⁷ MM1208a5-21, NE1103b33-35, and 1138b34, which sets out to define the right reason or *orthòs lógos*, and its standard of excellence (*hóros*) in Book VI.

What, then, is the role of knowledge or knowing in developing virtue and acting virtuously in Aristotle? Does *lógos* participate merely in deliberating the means, or even in developing and defining the virtues as ends of deliberation? Virtue may not be *epistêmê*. But is *epistêmê* excluded? Although some form of knowledge or knowing is apparently included as a central criterion for calling anything virtuous, Book II of the *Nichomachean Ethics* (NE 1105b2-5) does say that knowing strengthens the ethical virtues little or nothing (*pros dè tò tàs aretàs tò mèn eidénai mikrón ê oudèn iskhúei*). Is he contradicting himself immediately after requiring virtuous acts to be done knowingly? Both the immediate and the wider contexts are important for understanding this. The paragraph (NE 1105a16-b18) is written to distinguish ethical from technical virtue (*tékhnê*) on the one hand, and from mere knowledge (*epistêmê*) on the other. The similarity between technical arts and ethical virtues is that they are acquired through practice (NE 1103b7-25, 1104a27-b3, 1105a13-b18). But works of art exist as separate products which can be evaluated in and by themselves (EE 1219a13-23; NE 1105a27-28), and when you have learnt either medicine, geometry, or house construction you are considered a professional in those fields (EE 1216b3-25). Ethical virtue, however, does not have a separate "product" apart from acting justly, friendly, truthfully etc. Also, in a technical art, a voluntary error is not as bad as an involuntary error. A voluntary error shows you are in control and know what you are doing as a master of the art, as when a virtuoso singer or pianist slips out of tune on purpose. In ethics, however, a voluntary mistake is worse than an involuntary mistake (NE 1140b23-24). A voluntary mistake would imply e.g. inflicting a premeditated injustice on somebody, or consciously not bothering to find out anything about the special background of someone or about the circumstances for an act before judging. Doing this is worse than doing the same "not-on-purpose". Knowing and understanding what justice is, does not automatically make you into a just person, and if you have a thorough knowledge and understanding of justice, but do not even attempt to act justly, it makes you more unethical than being inactive or a perpetrator without the knowledge or understanding (MM 1183b8-17, 1199a19-29). Injustice is not the same as ignorance (Top 114b9-13) the way amateurism is in the technical arts. The injustice increases when unjust acts are done *with* knowledge, and just acts can be done even *without* knowledge. In ways like this, distinguishing similarities and differences, Aristotle establishes the field of ethics apart from science and technical arts.

As for *phrónêsis*, it is an intellectual virtue but not only, as Aristotle points out. To forget something purely intellectually held, or merely technically performed, is not considered an ethical deficiency. But forgetting *phrónêsis* would be, as would also forgetting about justice. *Phrónêsis* is distinguished as a different form of knowledge from the other intellectual virtues (*génos állo gnôseôs*), having a truly ethical import in itself (EE

1246b36; MM 1183b8-17; Top 152b1-5). In addition, ethics does not allow a division of labour as in technical arts. In acting virtuously, personal responsibility cannot be delegated to any external instance. We cannot do in ethics as we do concerning health. We do not all study medicine to become healthy. Instead, we follow recommendations and get treatment from experts, since medicine is a technical art of making (*poíêsis*). In ethics, however, we cannot simply take orders from others possessing *phrónêsis*. Following advice or orders from others presumed competent is *not* sufficient in relation to the requirements for ethical virtue and acting virtuously (NE 1143b14-33).

What Aristotle says, then, is that apart from the criterion of knowledge (*plên autò tò eidénai*), the virtue criteria mentioned do not apply for technical virtues (NE 1105b1-3). Concerning knowledge, ethical and technical virtues are similar, but technical activity is not chosen for its own sake nor does it have to spring from a firm character. It does not even have to be deliberately chosen. Acting unwillingly or under command does not destroy the validity of technical performance. So, the apparent dismissal of the importance of knowledge for ethics, concerns knowledge in isolation. Knowledge *alone* qualifies you as a "scientist" and as a master artisan. Knowledge *alone* does not qualify you as an ethically good individual. The paragraph in Book II of the *Nichomachean Ethics* is polemically directed at people who think they become ethically good from merely discussing virtue without practising (NE 1105b9-18). Aristotle modifies but does not dismiss the Socratic requirement to know what virtue is, however (EE11216b3-39). So, in ethics, knowledge is insufficient. But is it really necessary?

As the *Magna Moralia* (MM 1198a15-21) explicates, it is possible to act "in accordance with right reason", i.e. formally correct (*orthôs*) in accordance with ethical virtue, merely from some irrational impulse (*hormê tini álogô*), without deliberate choice (*prohaíresis*), and without knowledge (*oudè gnôsei*), i.e. by accident. This would not deserve praise, however, and would not be counted as virtuous practice. You are not counted as virtuous for doing the right thing merely habitually, accidentally, or "hypocritically". Although anything done by inclination may be counted as part of a certain *habitus*, virtue as a habitus implies more. It is not like any habit you are drilled into.

Requirements for an act to be virtuous can also be gleaned from examples of imperfect, insufficient, or merely apparent virtue, e.g. courage (*andreía*). Aristotle lists, slightly differently in the three *Ethics* (EE 1228a27-1230a36; MM 1090b9-1191a35; NE1115a5-1117b22), five conditions sometimes called courage from similarity (*kath'homoiótêta, katà metaphorán*) without being true courage. They are 1) civic courage (*politikê*), based on shame in relation to current conventional standards, 2) military courage (*stratiôtikê*), based on experience and knowledge of how to encounter danger, 3) inexperienced courage (*di' apeirían kaì ágnoian*), based on lack of knowledge, 4) hopeful courage (*kat' elpida*), based on high expectations, and 5) unreasonably emotional courage (*dià páthos alógiston*). Truly courageous individuals follow reason and act because reason shows what is truly noble to do (EE1229b26). The truly courageous relate to the truth, and neither shame, technical knowledge, lack of knowledge, high hopes, nor passion, is enough to qualify an act as courageous. Courage, as virtue in general, is not knowledge alone, but *only* acting knowingly qualifies as virtuous acts.

Summing up, then, virtuous acts are distinguished from merely doing things a) *mechanically*, as in following a rule, an order, or habit, or b) *unknowingly*, meaning not knowing *whether* and *why* an act is an ethically good act, or c) *coincidentally*, by chance, meaning not deliberately chosen from an established virtuous disposition or *habitus*, or d) *for ulterior motives* and not for their own sake, reducing virtuous acts to instruments. Fulfilling these requirements takes more than imitation, repetition, obedience, and the uncritical establishment of any habit whatsoever through habituation. Explicit knowledge of and reasoning about the means is clearly necessary. But is it sufficient? Is knowledge of and reasoning about the ends – i.e. of *what* happiness, courage, wisdom, and other virtues *are* – necessary? The preceding discussion creates a suspicion that it is.

2. The context for the ban on deliberation about ends

Before continuing, the context for the strange restrictions Aristotle puts on deliberation must be clarified. As indicated, Aristotle states over and over that ethical virtue produces the right ends or objectives for ethical practice and that there is no reasoning or argument, no syllogism or *lógos* about these (NE1144a7-9, 1144a20-23, 1144a31-33, 1151a15-19; EE 1227b25, 1227b38, 1228a2). Ends are posited. We can wish for them and have opinions about them, but apparently not deliberate about them, discuss them, or even choose them (EE1226a16). *Nobody* chooses his end by deliberate choice, Aristotle claims, only the means (EE1226a8, 1226b10). The reason becomes clearer, however, when he presents examples of why "nobody" deliberates about or deliberately chooses their ends or objectives. Some ends or goals seem genuinely beyond reasoning and deliberate choice. It might seem unreasonable to say that we deliberately choose to be healthy or happy. Wanting this, we choose what we believe to be appropriate means for attaining it without having full control over the attainment itself. Banning other ends from deliberation seems more difficult to understand. Context explains, however.

A doctor does not deliberate about whether he should try to heal, an orator does not deliberate about whether to persuade or not, a politician does not deliberate about whether to produce good laws, and likewise no other artist or artisan deliberates about the ends of his art when performing professionally (NE 1112b12-16; EE 1227b23-1228a4). This is revealing. Here, Aristotle does not write existentially about "man as such" but about how trained professionals think who are already established within their professional horizons when they exercise their proper professional competence *qua* physician, orator, etc. Once inside a defined discipline – when you already are a doctor, or an orator, etc. – you take certain things for granted, i.e. the ends and objectives of the discipline, and presumably, you already know what it means to heal, to persuade, etc. These "professional" horizons are taken for granted, not only in the *Nicomachean* and *Eudemian Ethics*, talking about ethics. It pervades Aristotle's thinking, and he states the principles behind many times. It is well known that Aristotle insists that there is no demonstration (*apódeixis*) of first principles. This is part of the background for his view in the *Posterior Analytics* (PoA 72b19-32, 76a31-36, 77a36-b15, 84a29-33, 90b18-91a12, 99b15-19), in the *Physics* (Ph 184b26-185a21, 253a33-b6), in the *Topica* (Top 101a35-b4), in *Sophistical Refutations* (SR 170a20-b11), and in the *Magna Moralia* (MM 1182b23-1183a5) that neither a geometer, nor a physicist, nor any other professional, neither should nor has to account for the basic principles or ends of his own discipline *qua* performing professional (Metaph 1005a29-32). Whatever somebody says *qua* professional, presupposes the grasp of the proper disciplinary first principles and ends. This is also the proper context for why and how the virtues – both professional and ethical – presuppose ends and why ends are "laid down" (*keitai*) in a similar manner as hypotheses in theoretical sciences (NE1112b16, 1151a15-19, EE1222b15-1223a20, 1226a8-14, 1226b11, 1226b30, 1227a 7-10, 1227b25).

Properly contextualized, then, Aristotle does not say that no human being could ever discuss or clarify basic principles and ends, only that performing professionals do not. In every discipline, whether *tékhnê* or *epistêmê*, a certain kind or *genus* of being or activity has always already been chosen, clarified, and defined as the subject (Metaph 996b27-997a25, 1003b22, 1004a3-7, 1025b8, 1063b36; PoA75a38, 87a38-b4, 90b30-91a12; NE 1094b25; Pol 1288b11-12). As professional *performers*, we are defined in relation to specific subjects, fields, and contexts as frameworks. Professional practice reasons and deliberates *from* presupposed primary principles and ends. This is how Aristotle formulates it. For Aristotle (NE 1095a31-b8), there is an important difference between arguments (*lógoi*) leading *to* (*epì*) ends and principles, and arguments leading *from* (*apò*) them. Deliberation moves not *to* the end but *from* it (*apò toû télous*) (EE 1227a16), or *from* a principle and *from* a certain defined form (*apò tês arkhês kaì toû eídous*) (Metaph 1032b16). The argument is that since the forms, ends, and basic principles are clear, this and that is what we must do, and we deliberate until we have brought the starting point of the generation of the end, back to something we can do, here and now (EE 1226b13-14). Searching for or questioning basic principles and objectives of an activity or discipline is not something we do *as* professionals performing within defined disciplinary subjects. But, of course, professional deliberation does need a true conception or assumption (*hupólêpsis*) of the ends pursued. *Phrónêsis* presupposes a true conception of ends (NE 1142b31-33, 1151a19, 1142b16-22)[8]. This does not mean, however, that *phrónêsis* is responsible for developing virtue, or the corresponding insights, defining the ends.

Hence, "demonstration" too is called *apó-deixis* (*de*-duction or *de*-monstration), showing or pointing out what follows *from* (*apó-* / *de-*) some principle being as it is (OtS 407a27), contrasted to *epi-agôgê* (induction). In this respect, then, deliberation resembles demonstration, starting *from* ends and basic principles as given (EE 1227a6-20, 1227b20-1228a5), although deduction and deliberation move in quite different ways towards their conclusions. What leads *to* the ends and basic principles of the disciplines, however, is a different process. Moving "up" (*ánô*, PoA 82a21-24) belongs to a different capacity (*allês dunámeôs*) (MM 1182b23-31).

Accordingly, the context for discussing deliberation, deliberate choice, and *phrónêsis*, is not how we *become* virtuous. It is not the development of virtue. Nor is it how ends are defined. The context is how we think and act, once we have become ethically virtuous, i.e. how "professional", highly competent, ethical actors do it. The context is the *performance* of virtue. A *phrónimos* has to be ethically virtuous and good already. *Phrónêsis* as a reasoning power is essential for being able to act virtuously in practice, here-and-now. Hence, the contextualisation of the ban on providing and discussing ends through deliberation, makes the ban peculiar to professional performance. Neither deliberation nor demonstration as specific forms of *lógos*, provides ends and principles. There is no general ban against involving other forms of *lógos* in their development and definition, however. Arguments (*lógoi*) do exist, leading *to* (*epì*) ends and principles (NE 1095a31-b8). As Cammack (2013) indicates, there are other forms of *lógos* than deliberation, and these many different forms are starting points for Eikeland's suggested way out of the impasse (Eikeland 2008, 212-214).

---

[8] *Hupólêpsis* is generally any assumption on the same level as *dóxa*, which may be either true or false (see EN 1139b17; MM1197a30-31; OtS427b7-428b5; Top119b4; Ph 227b12-14). Hence, EN 1142b31-33 hardly says more than *orthodoxía* in EN 1151a19.

3. From imagination (*phantasía*) to dialogical gatherings (*dialektikai sunódoi*)

After effectively dethroning *phrónêsis* as provider of goals for deliberation, Moss (2011, 252ff.) mobilizes *phantasía* or imagination to help explain how habituated character (*éthos, héxis, êthos, aretê*) provides deliberators with ends. She uses *On the Soul* and the *Movement of Animals* to characterize this ability of character to provide images of ends as a non-rational, perceptive cognitive faculty (Moss 2011, 252; idem. 2014, 222). To support this, she invokes what Aristotle says in the *Nicomachean Ethics* (EN1098b2-6) about habituation generating practical ends as analogous to induction generating theoretical principles. In *De Anima* (433b11-13) Aristotle talks about the end or aim of practical deliberation being set by either thought or imagination (*noêthênai ê phantasthênai*). If we take this seriously, then, there must be a connection and even overlap between not merely *phantasía* and habituated character but even between *nous* and character, including virtuous character. By focusing on imagination alone, however, Moss conflates the important distinction Aristotle makes between apparent and true goods (Eikeland 2008, 118, 361-371).

On the Soul divides the soul differently from how it is done in the *Nicomachean Ethics*. The major division in *On the Soul* cuts across the division in the *Ethics* between the two parts taking part in *lógos* in different ways, the one *being lógos* (*tò lógon ekhon*), the other being able to listen to and follow *lógos* (*tò álogon*). The division in *On the Soul* is between 1) a part, generating knowledge (*tò gnôristikón* or *theôrêtikón*), whose task it is to think (*noein*), distinguish (*krinein*), and perceive (*aisthánesthai*), and 2) another part concerned with the individual's movement (*kinêtikón*) (MA700b19-21, OtS404b28-29, 427a17-20, 432a15-20, cf. 411a26-b1)[9]. *Phantasía* is placed with *aísthêsis* (perception), *doxa* (opinion), *epistêmê* (knowledge), and *nous* (mind) in the first category whereby we distinguish and are cognitively right or wrong (*kath' hên krinoumen kaì alêtheúomen ê pseudómetha*) (OtS 428a1-5, 427a17-22, 427b9-15, 432a15-17). This division creates wider and more reasonable categories than Book VI of the *Nicomachean Ethics*, especially concerning the first. While *praxis-phrónêsis* and *poíêsis-tékhnê* and the whole *logistikón* department in the *Ethics* fall within the *kinêtikón* department of *On the Soul*, the *gnôristikón*, *kritikón*, or *theôrêtikón*, is more diverse than the *epistêmonikón* part in the *Ethics*. Strictly speaking, the *epistemonikón* contains only *epistêmê* or science in an extreme form (NE 1139b19) dealing only with things completely stable and universal, which also exist by

---

[9] The mind (*nous*), as self-consciously judging and distinguishing, is self-identical across all activities, "departments", and different perceptive faculties of the soul (OtS407a7, 408b19-31, 411b7-11, 426b8-427a15, 430b6).

necessity and have received a deductive formulation[10]. The wider distinguishing or theoretical part in *On the Soul* (432a16) deals descriptively and analytically with all existing things, permanent and general, or changing and particular, thought of, imagined, or perceived. Hence, the *theoretical* spans wider than the *epistemic* (OtS 407a24-31) and contains *more* than *epistêmê*. The *epistemonikón* of the *Nicomachean Ethics* is one part of a wider *theoretikón* in *On the Soul* (Eikeland, 2008, 75f, 98f). Even *súnesis*, or the concrete understanding of particulars, "orphaned" as part of *neither* the *epistemonikón* nor the *logistikón* in the *Ethics*, clearly belongs in the *theôrêtikón* of *On the Soul*, being merely distinguishing (*kritikê mónon*) concerning particulars (NE 1143a10 and 30). *Súnesis* is an intellectual virtue *with lógos* created by using the faculty of opinion (*tò doxastikón*) in distinguishing well or correctly (NE 1143a14-17). Neither *súnesis* nor opinion is *epistêmê*, however.

Like opinion, imagination (*phantasía*) can be right or wrong, true or false, and mostly, imagination is false according to Aristotle (OtS428a1-18, 428a12, 428b18-26, 429a5-9, 432a8-14, 433a10-13, 433b30, 434a6-22). Men live by imagination when *nous* is lacking (OtS 429a5-9). As with perception, even animals have *phantasía* (OtS 428a20-25). But both perception and imagination exist *both* as a primitive ability to distinguish (*dúnamis kritikê*) hardly touched by *lógos* (PoA99b35-100a3), *and* as a more advanced version becoming immersed in *lógos* as soon as perceptions and images start being qualified as having either this or that characteristic. So, the *gnôristikón* or *kritikón*, or, with Moss, the cognitive part of *On the Soul*, contains *aísthêsis* (perception), *doxa* (opinion), *phantasía* (imagination), *súnesis* (understanding), *epistêmê* (scientific knowledge), and *nous*. But although cognitive, they are not all strictly theoretical, since some of them also belong to animals without *lógos*. Some of them belong to the *álogon* part in the *Ethics*, able to listen to and follow *lógos*. There are even a few other faculties or activities not listed, however, which must be categorised as cognitive and part of *tò gnôristikón*.

First, in the same way as with perception and imagination, practically acquired experience (*empeiría*) belongs in the *gnôristikón* department of the soul, partly independent of *lógos* and partly immersed in *lógos*. As argued and shown in Eikeland (1997, 2008), and despite the expositions in *Metaphysics* (980a22-982a3) and *Posterior Analytics* (99b15-100b17), experience as *empeiría* is never just passive, suffering receptivity (*páthos*) with Aristotle. It is not reducible to sense perception (*aísthêsis*). It produces the ability (*dúnamis*) to act in certain ways (Metaph 981a14, 980b26-981b6; NE1116b9-12, 1141b15-22, 1142a14-15, 1180b16-25; EE1217a4; SR164a23-b28). As with habits and skills, its acquisition takes time and practice. Like both habits and skills, *empeiría* is both embodied, gen-

---

[10] There are other, "milder" forms of *epistêmê* as well (cf. Eikeland 2008, 69ff).

eral, and generative. We accumulate them, carry them with us, and enact and apply them in new situations. As Aristotle's discussions reveal (Eikeland 2008, 153), experience and habit are produced in similar ways, but experience extracts and retains the cognitive content of habit and habitus without the habitual inclination to act in a particular way. Experience creates know-how and knowledge, inexperience indicates a lack of both. As Aristotle says (Metaph 980a28-b27; PoA 99b34-100a4), many other animals share in perception, memory, and imagination, even without *lógos*, but in acquired practical experience (*empeiría*) only very little. Animals lacking *lógos* share only to a small degree in acquired and accumulated experience (*metékhei mikrón empeirías*). *Empeiría*, then, requires more *lógos* than animals normally have. Still, it is the basis for *epistêmê*. The formulation from the *Magna Moralia* (MM 1190b30) suggests this process succinctly and better than *Metaphysics* (Metaph 980a22-982a3) and *Posterior Analytics* (PoA 99b15-100b17), because it is more consistent with how *empeiría* is used by both Plato and Aristotle (Eikeland 1998). *Epistêmê* becomes just that – *epistêmê* – from grasping the experience based on habit (*hê epistêmê ex éthous tên empeirían labousa epistêmê gínetai*). Even in the *Prior Analytics* (PrA 46a3-30), summarizing preceding chapters (PrA 43a20-46a2) on how to seize hold of primary and other premises, Aristotle ends up saying that it belongs to acquired practical experience (*empeiría*) to deliver the basic principles (*arkhai*) for each of the disciplines (NE 1142a12-21). The fact, then, is that perception (*aísthêsis*), opinion (*doxa*), imagination (*phantasía*), understanding (*súnesis*), scientific knowledge (*epistêmê*), "intuitive reason" (*nous*), and in addition experience (*empeiría*) all "cover the same cognitive ground (*tên autên khôran ekhousin*)", as he formulates it in the *Movement of Animals* (MA 700b20).

A similar process from opinion to *epistêmê* in the *Posterior Analytics* (PoA 89a17-23, cf. 75b31-33) goes through the process of definition (*horismós*), and the second faculty or activity of the soul belonging in the *gnôristikón* department of the soul, and clearly to its theoretical part consisting in *lógos* activity, is this process of defining (*horismós*). Aristotle (OtS 407a24-31) states explicitly that the theoretical "department" consists in *lógos*, and that it has two parts, demonstration (*apódeixis*) and definition (*horismòs*) (cf. Top 141a5-10). *Epistêmê* is characterised as a *héxis apodeiktikê* (demonstrative habitus) by Aristotle (NE 1139b32; cf. PoA 71b18). There is no *apódeixis* of primary principles or ends, however (PoA 76a31). Hence, in the *Posterior Analytics* (PoA 99b19, 85a1), Aristotle searches for what kind of *habitus* (*héxis*) that familiarises us (*gnôrízousa*) with the primary and basic principles. His answer is *nous* both here and elsewhere (NE 1142a24-30, 1143a35-b6) but it is also induction (*epagôgê*) (PoA 72b30, 81a38-b9, 87b28-88a8). There is in fact an extensive overlap between many faculties and activities providing us with principles and ends[11]. There is *nous* in the *Nicomachean Ethics* (1141a8) and *Posterior Analytics* (100b5-16), *empeiría* in the *Nicomachean Ethics* (NE 1142a15-23) and in the *Prior Analytics* (PrA 46a3-30), where we are referred to the *Topica* for elaboration, *dialectics* in the *Topica* (Top 101a36-b4), induction, perception, and habituation again in the *Ethics* (NE 1098b1-6), definition in several places (NE 1098b6; EE1214b6-14, 1218b16-24; PoA 89a17-23; MM1182b30-31), induction and definition in the *Magna Moralia* (MM 1182b17-18), definition again in the *Physics* (Ph 200a34-b9) and, of course, virtue in the *Eudemian* and *Nicomachean Ethics*. In the *Ethics* (NE 1098b1-6; EE1214b6-27), however, Aristotle reminds us that these apparently different ways of engendering ends and principles, still demand the work of definition to be done carefully. The process of definition overarches and encompasses them all. Hence, as revealed in the *Eudemian Ethics* (EE1218b16-24), teachers do not prove or deliberate ends, they *define* ends.

As argued extensively in Eikeland (2008, 214-224), it would be reasonable if Aristotle had called *nous* a *héxis horistikê* (defining habitus) or a *héxis epaktikê* (inductive habitus), and as he furthermore points out (ibid., 216, 262), it could just as well be called a *héxis dialektikê* (dialogical habitus) complementary to how he calls *epistêmê* a *héxis apodeiktikê*, since everything in the *Topica*, Aristotle's work on dialectics, also deals with definitions directly or indirectly (Top102b27-103a4). Dialectics is not necessarily conversational, however. It is a "different" thought process. As Eikeland suggests that *nóêsis* – the process of thought and activity of *nous* – should be read as synonymous with dialectics or dialogue in many places (Eikeland 2008, 212ff.). Induction (*epagôgê*), engendering universals from particulars, is also categorized specifically as a form of dialectical argument (*lógos dialektikós*) (Top 105a10-19, 164a13-16, 157a18-21). In *On the Soul* (DA 413a11-21, 402a11-22; cf. Ph 184a10-b14) the process of engendering universals from particulars is called *lógos horistikós*, a defining argumentation (cf. Metaph 1063b8-15; Top101a38-b2; PrA43a36-39; Ph200a34-b9), starting from vague but more apparent things, gradually clarifying and revealing, connecting to important distinctions between what is more knowable to us and in itself (PoA 71b35-72a5) (Eikeland 1997, 2008, 83-84). Almost all Aristotle's inquiries start in this way from what is more knowable to us (Ph184a10-b14 and more), a process he calls a different but not absolute form of proof (*hetéra apódeixis*) (PoA 72b32). It certainly is where to start in ethics (NE1095b1-4, 1098b9-12; EE1216b26-40). As argued extensively

---

[11] Although Aristotle finds it reasonable to talk about separate parts of the soul and mind according to their different functions, activities, ends, and results, he concludes that they are very difficult and even absurd (*átopon*) to hold separate in OtS432a23-b7, 411b5-31, NE1102a30-34, and EE1219b32-1220a3 (see also OtS426b23-427a15, 430b5-6, 433a22, and 433b10-12).

in Eikeland (2008, 205-299), this "different way" of clarifying ends and principles is clearly dialectical, not by merely reasoning syllogistically from accepted opinions (*ex éndoxa*) but by going critically through them (*dià endoxôn*) sorting differences and similarities (*tàs dóxas episkopein / exetázein*) (NE1095a28, EE1214b28, 1215a6, 1217b16, Top101b4). The most important and proper task of dialectics, or dialogue, is said explicitly to be apprehending the primary principles of each discipline and each kind of activity. Dialogue is called *the way* (*hê hodós*) to arrive at basic principles in *all* inquiries (Top 101a37-b4, PoA84b24). Dialectics discusses and defines ends (*télê*) and aims (*skopoí*). Aristotle gives one among several summaries of this dialectical way towards ends and principles at the beginning of Book III (B) in the *Metaphysics* (Metaph 995a24-b4; cf. Eikeland 2008, 255f). The gradual and dialectical task of defining, then, transforms, grasps, and guides conceptually by means of *lógos*, what gets formed and moulded into patterns subconsciously through repetitions by the part of soul able to listen and follow reason (*tò álogon*), i.e. by habits, skills, emotions, desires, and actions. As the *Ethics* states, the form and content of the *álogon* part of the soul, the middle ground between mind and matter, can be modified by *lógos*. Dialogue does it.

The real virtue question, then, concerns what must be an overlap of habit and *habitus* with elements in this cognitive capacity. The relationship between *héxis* and *empeiría* is a key. *Empeiría* extracts the cognitive content from *héxis without* the habitual inclination as indicated in the *Nicomachean Ethics* (NE 1116b3-23). As indicated above, and in contrast to most other concepts of experience, the practically acquired concept of *empeiría* is not merely a perceptual confrontation with particulars. It results in a general ability to act, a general pattern in itself, even before it is elaborated by *lógos*, which even animals take part in to a small extent. The process of defining transforms both *empeiría* and opinion into *epistêmê*. Experience may be said to be the basis for *epistêmê*, *tékhnê*, *and* virtue. But virtue is even less than the two others, reducible to mere cognitive *empeiría*. This is why it needs to be established as a firm *habitus* (NE 1100b11-17), i.e. as a spontaneous inclination to act in a certain way e.g. courageously with conviction and understanding, not merely as a trained and experienced, but still possibly egotistical and cowardly ability to *recognize* danger approaching, and then run away. Even more than the others, ethical virtue needs a deep understanding and conviction. It must know, understand, and be able to justify the ethical correctness of its own acts. Virtue is right and adequate skill, attitude, will, and understanding united. As indicated, *every* virtue is the result of a process of perfection (*teleíôsis*) from within a specific practice, starting inchoately, and resulting in a certain virtuous habitus. According to the *Metaphysics* (Metaph 1051a24-33), *nóêsis*, i.e. critical dialogue, always accompanies and guides the actualizing development from *dúnamis* to *enérgeia*. This is the way virtues are developed. Dialogue mediates between the partly rational and completely rational parts, bringing them into the realm of *lógos*. Modernised, we might say that critical dialogue "theorizes" the pre-rational but still cognitive patterns generated "inductively" through repetitious activity as habit and experience. Hence, as Aristotle says, there is no deliberation (*boúleusis*) about ends and principles as there is no demonstration (*apódeixis*) but there certainly is a *lógos* of a different kind, a dialectical, defining *lógos* (*horistikós*). *Phrónêsis presupposes* the other ethical virtues as inclinations to do good. It is part of the "*Ausübung*" of virtue. Dialogue does not *presuppose* them, however, but fosters, cultivates, and defines them as based in and springing from the *álogon* part of the soul. Dialectics is part of their "*Einübung*".

As the evidence above makes plausible and indicated by Eikeland's further discussion (2008, 287-290) of how Book VII of the *Nicomachean Ethics* provides even inferior states like self-control and unrestraint with *nous*, virtue or even imperfect characters *cannot* be merely non-rational, perceptive cognitive faculties of the soul, the way Moss concludes (Moss 2011, 252; idem 2014, 222). Virtue as the result of a "non-rational upbringing and character" (Moss 2014, 234) is insufficient. This becomes even more clear from Aristotle's discussion of how the personal acquisition of *epistêmê* as a power or potential (*dúnamis*) with *lógos* is the basis for freedom and autonomy by distinguishing this from non-rational potentials (*álogoi dunámeis*) and habituated inclinations (*héxeis*) as powers *without lógos* on the other (Metaph 1046a36-b28, 1050b28-35, 1051a4-22, 1047b31-1048a24; NE1129a12-23; EE 1227a23-b5). Non-rational potentials without *lógos* can only produce one kind of result or calculable, one-dimensional results with limited variation, and habituation without some form of guidance can go in any direction. Potentials having *lógos* can produce opposite and contrary effects (in medicine, both health and unhealth). They thereby create space for desire and deliberate choice (*órexin ê prohaíresin*), i.e. freedom (Metaph1048a8-11). *Lógos* brings out and articulates the diverse potentials of things, and can rationally and by choice produce opposite results *from the same* basic principles (*apò tês autês arkhês / mia gàr arkhê periékhetai*) (Metaph 1046b7-28, 1065b23-1066a7; Ph 201a30-b15; EE 1222b41-42). For rational potentials to be realised, then, ethical virtues, desire, deliberation, and deliberate choice – what moves us – become *necessary*. Epistemic knowing liberates the knower and makes autonomy possible (OtS 429b3-10).

The *Movement of Animals* (700b25, OtS433a11-13) states explicitly that the end for *praxeis* (*tò tôn praktôn télos*) is provided by the objects of desire and thought (*tò orektòn kaì tò dianoêtón*). The challenge of deliberate choice (*prohaíresis*) is to make them coincide (Eikeland 2008, 115-121). For Aristotle, the virtues coincide with the *pragmata* (*die Sachen*) as "ideal" standards attracting us erotically (Eikeland 2008, 196-205). The gradually developed and acquired *praxis* or performance of a *pragma* is identical to the *praxis* of virtue. its specific virtue (NE 1098a8-17; EE 1219a18-23) And any activity, "thing", or *habitus* is perfected when it achieves its proper virtue through a process of perfection (Ph 246a10-b2). We all start out in life as inchoate and undefined (*aóristoi*) (Eikeland 2008, 178, 246f.). The personal acquisition of skill and virtue – gradually better adjusted to different *pragmata* – is the process of definition. In this process, theoretical reason and practical reason are united. The process of habituation (*ethismós*) resembles not only induction but also the process of defining (*horismós*), sorting similarities and differences. For Aristotle (NE 1170a16-25; EE 1244b35-1245a11), to take part personally in what is truly and pragmadequately defined (*hôrisménon*), is to arrive at what is good, i.e. at a life perfectly or optimally adjusted to the *pragmata* as they really are (Prot26b-d). Thus, to be personally defined is not at all to be arbitrarily "framed" or determined from the outside. It is to reach perfection from the inside at the end of the way of *praxis*. It is to enter the figure of virtue (*arêtes skhêma*) (MM 1183b25-27; Metaph 1050a8-b6).

My conclusion here, then, is that the *gnôristikón* or *kritikón* – the cognitive or distinguishing – part of the soul clearly provides deliberation with ends (*télê*) and aims (*skopoi*). This far Moss and I seem to agree. But this it is not provided merely by the part without *lógos*, and hardly at all, or only as starting points, without the involvement of *lógos*. Definition elaborates, transforms, extracts, and articulates the pre-theoretical and pre-linguistic patterns of the cognitive soul into powers with *lógos*, i.e. *epistêmê*, *tékhnê*, and ethical virtue. Habituation as the process of engendering a virtuous habitus through repetitions and practice, then, needs guidance in order to aim well (NE 1103b13; EE 1220b2). It needs teachers. But neither teachers nor anyone else prove or deliberate ends. They do not instruct ends and principles didactically. They define them (EE 1218b16-24), and dialectics defines.

Finally, this becomes even more obvious when we see what Aristotle himself does in his ethical writings. Aristotle is a teacher, and the theoretical task of defining ends and principles – the what it is (*tì estin, ti ên einai*) of happiness and all the virtues – is clearly what Aristotle is doing in the *Ethics*. Although the purpose of the *Ethics* is to promote ethical excellence, this is done by providing knowledge (*gnôsis*) of the target (*skopós*) to aim at (NE 1094a23-27). Aristotle discusses the question of "what-it-is" (*ti estin*) concerning virtues (NE1105b19, 1107a7-8, 1117b21-22), a necessary theoretical task in order to find the *télos* of *praxis* (NE 1094a19; EE 1216b35-40). Hence, after the discussion with the technical arts, Aristotle starts directly with the theoretical task of defining virtue (NE 1105b19, 1106a13, 1107a1-8, 1109b20-22, 1109b3, 1114b26-30; cf. Pol 1332a22), and he does it as an ethical "architect" or constructor of principles (NE 1094a6-b12, 1152b1-5) and as a teacher (Eikeland 2008, 292-298).

Clearly, then, Kristjansson (2014), attacking the question of ethics from a totally different angle, is right in claiming that dialogue is not merely a Socratic method of moral education abandoned by Aristotle. It is equally and essentially Aristotelian. But Kristjansson (2014, 343-347) uses only what we might call "external" and indirect evidence from how the *Ethics* describe tasks of friendship. Eikeland (2008, 399ff.) uses the same evidence in conjunction with the internal, theoretical and methodological evidence outlined above, and the evidence from the *Topica* (Top 159a25-38, 161a20-27 and a36-b10, 163a29; cf. SR171b3-172a2) to show how what Aristotle calls dialogical gatherings or *dialektikai sunódoi* play a most central role in both ethics and politics (*paideía*). Different purposes are distinguished. Rhetorical or eristic gatherings for fighting and competing (*agônos khárin*) are clearly different from properly dialectical gatherings for the sake of training and experimentation (*gumnasías kaì peíras héneka*), experience and inquiry (*peíras kaì sképseôs khárin*), exercise and study (*gumnasían kaì melétên*), or teaching and learning (*didaskalía kaì máthêsis*). Dialectical gatherings are constituted by a common task (*koinón érgon*) of better understanding, deeper insight, and shared truth, where no one wins while others lose, but all win better understanding, etc. or all lose by not achieving it. According to the *Nichomachean Ethics* (NE 1100b19-20, cf. NE1179b1-4, PrA43a20-24), the happy individual (*ho eudaímôn*) spends all or most of her time alternately performing and studying (*práxei kaì theôrêsei*) the activities according to virtue or excellence, placing the dialogical way (*hodós*) towards a virtuous life individually and collectively, presumably in dialectical gatherings, at the centre of practical ethics and politics. Kristjansson (ibid.) argues against others who find it necessary to use non-Aristotelian sources to supplement Aristotle with dialogue. My comment is that the internal evidence for Aristotle as a dialectician is much stronger than Kristjansson presents.

My claim then is, that what I have outlined above – the way or *hê hodós* from *dúnamis* to *entelékheia* and *enérgeia* through *praxis*, *empeiría*, and dialogue – is what Aristotle aims at when he says that *lógos* and *nous* are the *télos* for human development (Pol1334b14-28); it is how and why we need *phúsis*, *éthos*, and *lógos* to become virtuous (*spoudaíos*) (Pol1332a36-b7), and why the goodness of individuals is judged according to both the part of the soul having *lógos* and the part able to follow *lógos* (Pol 1333a16-20). The whole process outlined above is what Aristotle calls "the principle, or starting point, of science", *arkhê epistêmês* (PoA 72b25, 100b15), "the way towards the principles in every investigation" (*hê pròs tàs hapasôn tôn methódôn hódos*).

This is also, why even Jessica Moss, despite her fruitful starting points and effective refutation of the dominant view's overburdening of *phrónêsis*, ends up as misrepresenting Aristotle. In spite of her final discouragement of any further inquiry from where her discussion stops then, halfway to the finishing line; "if this is not enough to save Aristotle from the charge of Humeanism, then we should not bother trying to save him from that charge" (Moss 2014, 240), I think, to really save Aristotle from Hume, we need to go all the way to the end (as Eikeland 2008 does), to where the way itself (*hê hodós*) appears to us as the ultimate virtuous end.

Prof. Dr. Olav Eikeland, Oslo and Akershus University,
College of Applied Sciences, olav.eikeland[at]hioa.no

References

Aristotle. *Categories. On Interpretation. Prior Analytics* [abr. Cat and PrA]. (Aristotle Vol. I, Loeb Classical Library no. 325). Cambridge, MA: Harvard University Press, 1938.

Aristotle. *Posterior Analytics. Topica* [abr. PoA and Top]. (Aristotle Vol. II, Loeb Classical Library No. 391). Cambridge, MA: Harvard University Press, 1960.

Aristotle. *On Sophistical Refutations. On Coming-to-be and Passing Away. On the Cosmos* [abr. SR]. (Aristotle Vol. III, Loeb Classical Library No. 400). Cambridge, MA: Harvard University Press, 1955.

Aristotle. *On the Soul. Parva Naturalia. On Breath* [abr. OtS]. (Aristotle Vol. VIII, Loeb Classical Library No. 288). Cambridge, MA: Harvard University Press, 1957.

Aristotle. *Metaphysics, Books I-IX* [abr. Metaph.]. (Aristotle Vol. XVII, Loeb Classical Library No. 271). Cambridge, MA: Harvard University Press, 1933.

Aristotle. *Metaphysics, Books X-XIV. Oeconomica. Magna Moralia* [abr. Metaph. and MM]. (Aristotle Vol. XVIII, Loeb Classical Library No. 287). Cambridge, MA: Harvard University Press, 1935.

Aristotle. *Physics*, Vol. I, Books 1-4, and vol II, Books 5-8 [abr. Ph]. (Aristotle Vol. IV and Vol. V, Loeb Classical Library No. 228 and No. 255), Cambridge, MA: Harvard University Press, 1957.

Aristotle. *Nicomachean Ethics* [abr. NE]. (Aristotle Vol. XIX, Loeb Classical Library). Cambridge, MA: Harvard University Press, 1934.

Aristotle. *Athenian Constitution. Eudemian Ethics. Virtues and Vices* [abr. EE]. (Aristotle Vol. XX, Loeb Classical Library No. 285). Cambridge, MA: Harvard University Press, 1935.

Aristotle. *Politics* [abr. Pol.]. (Aristotle Vol. XXI, Loeb Classical Library No. 264). Cambridge, MA: Harvard University Press, 1932.

Aristotle. *Parts of Animals. Movement of Animals. Progression of Animals* [abr. *MA*]. (Aristotle Vol. XII, The Loeb Classical Library No. 323). English Transl. by E. S. Forster. Cambridge and London: Harvard University Press, 1937.

Aristoteles. *Protreptikos – Hinführung zur Philosophie* [abr. Prot]. Rekonstruiert, übersetzt und kommentiert von Gerhart Schneeweiss. Darmstadt: Wissenschaftliche Buchgesellschaft, 2005.

Aubenque, Pierre. *Le problème de l'être chez Aristote: essai sur la problématique aristotélicienne.* Paris: PUF, 1962.

Berti, Enrico. "Does Aristotle's conception of dialectic develop?" in William Robert Wians (ed.). *Aristotle's Philosophical Development: Problems and Prospects.* Lanham, MD: Rowman & Littlefield Publishers, 1996. 105–30.

Cammack, Daniela. "Aristotle's Denial of Deliberation about Ends." *Polis.* Vol. 30, Nr. 2 (2013): 228-250.

De Pater, Wilhelmus Antonius. *Les Topiques d'Aristote et la dialectique platonicienne. Méthodologie de la définition.* Fribourg: Editions St. Paul, 1965.

Eikeland, Olav. *Erfaring, dialogikk og politikk – den antikke dialogfilosofiens betydning for rekonstruksjonen av moderne empirisk samfunnsvitenskap. Et begrepshistorisk og filosofisk bidrag.* Oslo: Universitetsforlaget, 1997.

Eikeland, Olav. "Anámnêsis – dialogisk erindringsarbeid som empirisk forskningsmetode", in Eikeland, Olav, and Knut Fossestøl (eds.). *Kunnskapsproduksjon i endring – Nye erfarings- og organisasjonsformer.* (AFIs skriftserie nr. 4.). Oslo: Work Research Institute, 1998. 95-136.

Eikeland, Olav. *The Ways of Aristotle. Aristotelian Phrónêsis, Aristotelian Philosophy of Dialogue, and Action Research.* Bern: Peter Lang, 2008.

Evans, John D.G. *Aristotle's Concept of Dialectic*, Cambridge, UK: Cambridge University Press, 1977.

Hämäläinen, Hasse. "Aristotle on the Cognition of Value". *Journal of Ancient Philosophy* Vol. 9, Nr.1 (2015): 88-114.

Hume, David. *A Treatise of Human Nature.* Oxford: Oxford University Press, 1978.

Irwin, Terence Henry. *Aristotle's First Principles.* Oxford: Clarendon Press, 1988.

Kristjánsson, Kristjan (2014). "On the old saw that dialogue is a Socratic but not an Aristotelian method of moral education." *Educational Theory* Vol. 64, Nr.4 (2014): 333-348.

Moss, Jessica. "Virtue Makes the Goal Right: Virtue and Phrónêsis in Aristotle's Ethics." *Phrónêsis* Vol. 56, Nr. 3 (2011): 204-261.

Moss, Jessica. *Aristotle on the Apparent Good. Perception, Phantasia, Thought, & Desire.* Oxford: Oxford University Press, 2012.

Moss, Jessica. "Was Aristotle a Humean? A Partisan Guide to the Debate" in Roland Polansky (ed.). *The Cambridge Companion to Aristotle's Nicomachean Ethics.* Cambridge: Cambridge University Press, 2014. 221–241.

Owen, Gwilym Ellis Lane. "Tithénai tà phainómena", in Suzanne Mansion (ed.). *Aristote et les problèmes de méthode.* Louvain: Publications Universitaires, 1961. 83-103.

Owen, Gwilym Ellis Lane (ed.). *Aristotle on dialectic – proceedings of the Third Symposium Aristotelicum.* Oxford: The Clarendon Press, 1968.

Reeve, C.D.C. *Practices of Reason – Aristotle's Nicomachean Ethic.* Oxford: Oxford University Press, 1995.

Schramm, Michael. *Die Prinzipien der Aristotelischen Topik.* München – Leipzig: K. G. Saur, 2004.

Sim, May (ed.). *From Puzzles to Principles? Essays on Aristotle's Dialectic.* Lanham: Lexington Books, 1999.

Taylor, Christopher C. W. "Aristotle on Practical Reason." *Oxford Handbooks Online*, 2016 (online: http://www.oxfordhandbooks.com/view/10.1093/oxfordhb/9780199935314.001.0001/oxfordhb-9780199935314-e-52).

Wieland, Wolfgang. *Die aristotelische Physik – Untersuchungen über die Grundlegung der Naturwissenschaft und die sprachlichen Bedingungen der Prinzipienforschung bei Aristoteles*. Göttingen: Vandehoeck & Ruprecht, 1962.

WEI LIU (Beijing)

Aristotle on *Prohairesis*

Abstract

Prohairesis plays a central role in Aristotle's moral psychology. It is prohairesis that determines an action to be rational, that provides the proximate efficient or moving cause of rational action, and that better reveals one's character than the action itself. This paper will discuss (1) Aristotle's shifted emphases when speaking of prohairesis in different ethical treatises; (2) Aristotle's pursuit of the nature of prohairesis and his special argumentative strategy in dealing with prohairesis; (3) the structure, i.e., the desiderative and deliberative components of prohairesis; and will conclude with some remarks about the significance of prohairesis.

Keywords: *prohairesis* (decision); *boulēsis* (wish); *bouleusis* (deliberation)

Prohairesis plays a central role in Aristotle's moral psychology. It is *prohairesis* that determines an action to be rational, that provides the proximate efficient or moving cause of rational action, and that better reveals one's character than the action itself. Aristotle also defines ethical virtue as *hexis prohairetikē*, a state that issues in decision. But the proper meaning of *prohairesis*, its nature and its structure are all far from clear. In this paper, I will make some observations in these aspects, and will pay special attention to the desiderative component of *prohairesis*, i.e., *boulēsis*.

I. *Prohairesis* as "πρὸ ἑτέρων αἱρετόν"

The most common starting point to understand Aristotle's *prohairesis* is his own etymological remark in the *Nicomachean Ethics* (*NE*):

[T1] Then perhaps *to prohaireton* is what has been deliberated before (τὸ προβεβουλευμένον). For *prohairesis* is with reason and thought. Even the name seems to indicate that *it is chosen before other things* (πρὸ ἑτέρων αἱρετόν). (*NE* III.2.1112a15-17)[1]

But there is a general division among scholars about how to interpret this "*pro*" or "before." Ross, in his famous translation of the *NE*, says, "the etymological meaning is 'preferential choice'." (Ross 1925, 52) Influential as it is, this etymological remark seems far from certain, and scholars are still debating about whether we should take this *pro* in preferential or temporal sense. Those who favor the preferential sense tend to translate *prohairesis* into "choice" (e.g., Ross 1925, Nussbaum 1978, Woods 1982, Price 1995, 2011, 2016, Taylor 2006, Pearson 2012, Simpson 2013, Kenny 2013), "deliberate choice" (e.g., Stewart 1894, Reeve 2014), "preferential choice" (e.g., Charles 2007, 2009, 2011), "rational choice" (Crisp 2004); whereas those who favor the temporal sense tend to translate *prohairesis* into "decision" (Joachim 1951, Irwin 1999, Lorenz 2009, Inwood and Woolf 2013, Müller 2016).[2] There is still a third group of scholars who simply indicate both possibilities and the difficulty of translating this word, without taking side between the preferential or temporal sense.[3]

This division seems to be rooted in Aristotle's own texts. For the text we just quoted from the *NE* shows quite clearly that this *pro* should be taken in the temporal sense, for the perfect participle *probebouleumenon* ("what has been deliberated before") in the previous clause is obviously temporal. And as we survey all the other appearances of *prohairesis* in the *NE*, we do not see any example going against this temporal sense. Furthermore, several other passages also favor this temporal sense. For example, when speaking of the difference between an unjust action and an unjust character, Aristotle comments, "for someone might lie with a woman and know who she is, but the starting-point might be affections rather than *prohairesis*" (*NE* V.6.1134b19-21). And in his discussion of the incontinent person (*akratēs*), Aristotle says,

> **[T2]** He [i.e., the incontinent person] is not base, since his prohairesis is decent (ἡ γὰρ προαίρεσις ἐπιεικής); hence he is half base...For one type of incontinent person [i.e., the weak] does not abide by what he has deliberated (οὐκ ἐμμενετικὸς οἷς ἂν βουλεύσηται), while the volatile person is not even prone to deliberate at all (NE VII.10.1152a15-19; see VII.9.1151a29-b4 for more extensive discussion).

---

[1] Translations of the *NE* are from Irwin 1999, with amendments.
[2] The earliest commentator of Aristotle's ethics, Aspasius, is the strongest supporter of this temporal understanding (see Aspasius 2006, 70.31-71.2).
[3] Such as Rowe and Broadie 2002, Ross and Brown 2009, p. 220. Taylor interestingly remarks: "Aristotle plays on the ambiguity of the preposition to support his account of preferential choice as choice resulting from prior deliberation" (Taylor 2006, 155).

It seems clear that in these passages *prohairesis* is taken to mean the "decision" made *before* the actual action takes place.[4]

But if we turn to the parallel passages from *Eudemian Ethics* (*EE*), we see that it is less decisive than the *NE* passage, but points more toward the preferential sense:

> [T3] *Prohairesis* is *hairesis* [choice or taking], but not *hairesis* without qualification, but *hairesis* of *something before something* (ἀλλ' ἑτέρου πρὸ ἑτέρου), and this is not possible without inquiry and council (τοῦτο δὲ οὐχ οἷόν τε ἄνευ σκέψεως καὶ βουλῆς). That is why *prohairesis* is from deliberative belief (ἐκ δόξης βουλευτικῆς). (*EE* II.2.1226b6-9)[5]

In this passage, given the alternative between *heterou* and *heterou*, *prohairesis* is more likely in the preferential sense, i.e., making choice between different alternatives.[6] The parallel passage from the *Magna Moralia* (*MM*) favors the preferential sense still more clearly:

> [T4] But *prohairesis* seems to be what the name suggests, for example we *prohairoumetha* one thing instead of another (προαιρούμεθα τόδε ἀντὶ τοῦδε), for example *the better instead of the worse*" (τὸ βέλτιον ἀντὶ τοῦ χείρονος). (*MM* I.17.1189a12-16).

The proposition *anti* (instead of *pro*), and the examples between this and that, better and worse, makes it beyond any doubt that *prohairesis* is in preferential sense here. This is thus taken by some scholar as decisive evidence to determine the meaning of *prohairesis*, and to settle the debate about *pro*.[7] If we examine the other passages containing *prohairesis* in the *EE*, we will see that none of them goes against the preferential sense. Furthermore, there are several occasions the contexts clearly favor or even force us to take the preferential sense. For example, when he lists three different kinds of life, Aristotle says, "we see also that there are three lives, *prohairountai* by all who have the means to do so, i.e., political, philosophical, and that of gratification" (*EE* I.4.1215a35-b1).[8] When he speaks of *homo-*

---

[4] Although I will not step into the controversy about the attribution of the "common books," it seems that these two examples from the common books, given the similar usage of *prohairesis* with the *NE*, may lend some weight to the view that even if the common books were originally written for the *Eudemian Ethics*, they were nevertheless reworked by Aristotle to fit into the context of the *NE*.
[5] Translations of the *EE* are from Inwood and Woolf 2013, with amendments.
[6] Lorenz 2009 is one of few interpreters who insist that this is also in the temporal sense.
[7] For example, Woods 1982, 155, and Price 2016.
[8] This is clearly a choice between three candidates, so it is appropriate to translate it into "choose." But in the parallel passage in the *NE*, Aristotle does not mention "*prohairesthai*" in the context of three kinds of lives, but only mentions this word in his comments on the people who choose the life of gratification:

noia [like-mindedness, or concord], Aristotle says that among the likeminded people, "the same *prohairesis* is made about ruling and being ruled, not each for himself, but all for the same one" (*EE* VII.7.1241a30-33).⁹ And when he talks about the markers (*horoi*) of friendship, Aristotle says,

> [T5] Here are several markers (ὅροι) and each of them seems, though in fact does not, to belong to friendship as a unity; for example, the *prohairesis* about the other person's existence (ἡ τοῦ εἶναι προαίρεσις). (*NE* VII.11.1244a27-28).

We can only favor, or "choose" to certain extent, our friend's life and existence, but certainly cannot decide on it, for it is not up to us (*eph' hēmin*).¹⁰ Since *MM* follows *EE* much more closely in both its terminology and doctrine than *NE*, it is not surprising that *MM* also defines *prohairesis* in this preferential sense.¹¹

After this survey, we may conclude that even if Aristotle's general doctrine of *prohairesis* remains the same in the two ethical treatises, as will be shown in the following sections, there seems to be a shift of emphases concerning the meaning of *prohairesis*, from the preferential sense in the *EE* to the temporal sense in the *NE*. If we compare the discussions of deliberation in the *EE* and *NE*, we may find some theoretical consideration behind this shift:

> [T6] One deliberates not about end, since that is given for everyone, but about what leads to the end, *whether this or that is conducive* (πότερον τόδε ἢ τόδε συντείνει), and when one has a view about that, how it will come about. (*EE* II.10.1226b10-12)

> [T7] We lay down the end, and then examine the ways and means to achieve it. If it appears that any of several means will reach it, we examine, which of them will reach it most easily and most nobly; and *if only one means reaches it, we examine how that means will reach it, and how the means itself is reached* (δι' ἑνὸς δ' ἐπιτελουμένου πῶς διὰ τούτου ἔσται κἀκεῖνο διὰ τίνος), until we come to the first cause, the last thing to be discovered. (*NE* III.3.1112b15-20)

"the life they *prohairoumenoi* is a life for grazing animals" (I.5.1095b20-21). Although the context is somewhat similar to that of the *EE*, it is nevertheless possible to translate it as "decide on," since this is about the result of their "decision," rather than the "choice" among three candidates.

⁹ In this case the *prohairesis* is surely concerned with different candidates, and thus preferential. So it is perfect to translate it into "choice" or "preferential choice" here. Interestingly, in the parallel passage about *homonoia* in the *NE*, Aristotle does not use *prohairesthai*, but only says the common and the decent have the same mind (*homonein*) to let the best people rule (*NE* IX.6.1167a34-b1).

¹⁰ Admittedly, given the existence of a friend is not (completely) up to us, the *prohairesis* used here is not in the strict sense of the word. This passage has no clear parallel in the *NE*.

¹¹ Given the more disputable status of the authenticity of the *MM*, I will leave it aside in this paper.

In the *EE* passage Aristotle only considers the deliberation between alternative means ("this or that"); whereas in the *NE* Aristotle clearly allows deliberation to be *not* about alternatives, but about only one means and the relevant facts or elements about this one single means, just like there being only one way to solve a mathematical problem. So it seems that Aristotle's shift of emphases from the preferential sense to the temporal sense does have some theoretical consideration. But even if Aristotle makes this shift of emphases, the preferential sense is still there, and is incorporated into the temporal sense, for even in [T7] the preferential sense is mentioned first ("if...any of several means"), and the non-alternative and non-preferential case is treated as a special case ("*if only one means...*"). Therefore, Aristotle might have realized the limitation of the preferential sense of *prohairesis*, and then shifted to the safer and broader temporal sense of this term.[12] As for the translation of *prohairesis*, I think in most cases "decision" is better than "choice," since the latter is too general, and will also make *hairesis* difficult to translate.

II. The Nature of *Prohairesis* and Aristotle's Argumentative Strategy

As Aristotle indicates at the beginning of his discussion of *prohairesis*, the nature of *prohairesis* seems to be a complicated and difficult topic, with a number of *aporiai* to be solved:

> [T8] One might be unsure in what genus it naturally belongs, what kind of thing one should place it under, and whether or not what is voluntary (τὸ ἑκούσιον) and *to prohaireton* are the same thing. In particular there are some who claim, and it might seem so on inquiry, that *prohairesis* is one or other of two things, either belief or desire (ἤτοι δόξα ἢ ὄρεξις), since both of these appear to follow along with it (παρακολουθοῦντα). (*EE* II.10.1225b19-24; see also *NE* III.2.1111b10-12 for a less extensive version of the *aporiai*)

Accordingly, in both treatises Aristotle proceeds to articulate the nature of *prohairesis* through a series of distinctions, distinguishing it (1) from what is voluntary (*to hekousion*), (2) from different kinds of desire (*orexis*), i.e., appetite (*epithumia*), spirit (*thumos*), and wish (*boulēsis*), and (3) from simple thought (*dianoia*) or belief (*doxa*).

The difference between *prohairesis* and the voluntary is clear. For *prohairesis* is said to be a sub-set of the voluntary, and the difference lies in the rational component or element in *prohairesis*:

---

[12] Without argument, I assume, together with most of the scholars, that *NE* is a later and more mature work than *EE*. But if my argument about the reasonableness of this shift is correct, it may shed some light on the relative dates between *NE* and *EE*.

[T9] *Prohairesis*, then, seems to be voluntary, but not the same; the voluntary extends more widely. For children and the other animals share in voluntary action, but not in *prohairesis*; and the actions we do on the spur of the moment are said to be voluntary, but not in accord with *prohairesis*. (*NE* III.2.1111b6-10; see also *EE* II.10.1226b34-36)

Therefore, *prohairesis* is reserved for adult human beings whose rational capacity is (fully) developed.[13] But Aristotle does not require that these adults, with rational capacity, are good men in order to have *prohairesis*, for the strictly vicious person acts in accord with his *prohairesis* and without regret, and this is in fact an important difference between the vicious and the akratic (*NE* VII.8.1150b29-36). Therefore, the rational element or reason in *prohairesis* is not in its normative sense, but in the descriptive sense. These two senses correspond well with *phronēsis* (prudence) and *deinotēs* (cleverness), the former only looking for the morally best way to achieve the morally good ends, whereas the latter discovering whatever means to fulfill whatever ends (see *NE* VI.121144a23-b1).

This rational element also provides the first reason to distinguish *prohairesis* from *epithumia* and *thumos*, the two kinds of desire that both human being and other animals possess (*NE* III.2.1111b12-13; *EE* II.10.1225b26-27). A second difference is based on the famous "principle of contradiction," which is used by both Plato and Aristotle to distinguish different parts of the soul (see *Republic* IV.436a-437b and *NE* I.13.1102b13-25), for both *epithumia* and *thumos* may be contrary to *prohairesis* (*NE* III.2.1111b13-19). A third difference lies in the fact that many *prohaireseis* arise without the contribution of *epithuumia* or *thumos*, and thus without pain (*EE* II.10.1225b27-32).[14]

What distinguishes *boulēsis* from *prohairesis* is the fact that we may wish for the impossible, such as immortality or ruler of all mankind; we may also wish for something that is completely beyond our agency, such as the victory of certain actor or athlete. But we only *prohairesthai* what is possible and what is up to us (*EE* II.10.1225b32-37; *NE* III.2.1111b19-26). Another difference, which will play more important role below, is that "wish is more [or "rather"] for the end, whereas *prohairesis* for the things that promote the end (ἡ μὲν βούλησις τοῦ τέλους ἐστὶ μᾶλλον, ἡ δὲ προαίρεσις τῶν πρὸς τὸ τέλος)" (*NE*

---

[13] Aristotle clearly thinks that small children do not have reason, but it is less easy to determine whether the youth, whose rational capacity is still developing through habituation, have *prohairesis* or not. Perhaps Aristotle would say, with his typical vocabulary, that they do, but not without qualification.

[14] As Müller 2016 correctly indicates, Aristotle's comment "many decisions are made with no contribution from spirit or appetite (πολλὰ καὶ ἄνευ θυμοῦ καὶ ἐπιθυμίας προαιροῦνται)" makes it clear that either spirit or appetite contributes at least to some decisions.

III.2.1111b26-27; see also *EE* II.10.1226a7-17, where Aristotle says "wish and belief are *above all* about the end" [μάλιστα τοῦ τέλους]).

Whether the object is impossible or up to us (*eph' hēmin*) also distinguishes *prohairesis* and simple thought or belief, for a number of beliefs have nothing to do with possibility or our own agency, such as our beliefs about scientific facts (*EE* II.10.1226a2-4; *NE* III.2.1111b31-33). The second difference is that we use true or false to describe belief, but good or bad to describe *prohairesis* (*EE* II.10.1226a4; *NE* III.2.1111b31-33, 1112a5-8). The third difference is that *prohairesis* is from what kind of people we are, but belief does not depend on our character (*NE* III.2.1112a1-11). The fourth and last difference is that mere belief or thought has nothing to do with pursuing and avoiding, but *prohairesis* directs us to pursue and avoid (*EE* 10.1226a4-6; *NE* III.2.1112a3-5).

After all these distinctions, Aristotle reaches the first formulation (F1) of the nature of *prohairesis*, as shown in **[T1]** ("*to prohaireton* is what has been deliberated before. For *prohairesis* is with reason and thought. Even the name seems to indicate that *it is chosen before other things*") and **[T3]** (*prohairesis* "is not possible without inquiry and council. That is why *prohairesis* is from deliberative belief"). The emphasis of this first series of formulation lies in the *rational elements*, i.e. deliberation, reason, thought, inquiry, council, and deliberative belief.

Judging from this first formulation, *prohairesis* seems above all a rational process, the result of deliberation. But it turns out that this formulation is only half way, or less than half way, to the true nature of *prohairesis*.

Following the series of distinctions between *prohairesis* and different kinds of desire and belief, and following the formulation, which emphasizes the rational element in *prohairesis*, Aristotle goes on to analyze the rational element in it, i.e., deliberation (*bouleusis*). It is at the end of this analysis that Aristotle reintroduces the desiderative element, and provides the second formulation (F2) of the nature of *prohairesis*:

> **[T10]** What we *prohairetou* to do is, among those up to us, what we deliberate about and desire to do. Hence also *prohairesis* would be *deliberative desire* of what is up to us (ἡ προαίρεσις ἂν εἴη βουλευτικὴ ὄρεξις τῶν ἐφ' ἡμῖν). When we judge as a result of deliberation, we desire to do it in accord with our deliberation/wish (βούλευσιν/βούλησιν). (*NE* III.3.1113a9-12)

> **[T11]** It is clear that *prohairesis* is *deliberative desire* for things that are up to oneself (ὄρεξις τῶν ἐφ' αὑτῷ βουλευτική). For we all deliberate about/wish for (βουλευόμεθα/βουλόμεθα) the things we *prohairoumetha*, but it is not the case that we *prohairoumetha* all things we deliberate about/wish for (βουλευόμεθα/βουλόμεθα). By *deliberative desire* I mean one whose starting point and cause is

deliberation; the desire arises through one's having deliberated (λέγω δὲ βουλευτικήν, ἧς ἀρχὴ καὶ αἰτία βούλευσίς ἐστι, καὶ ὀρέγεται διὰ τὸ βουλεύσασθαι). (*EE* II.10.1226b16-20)

There is more to be commented on these two passages in the next section. What is clear for the present purpose is that Aristotle calls *prohairesis* "deliberative desire," and thus clearly attributes desire (*orexis*) as the genus of *prohairesis*. This formulation seems to be the final conclusion of his analysis of *prohairesis* in *NE* III and *EE* II. It admits both the desiderative and the rational element in *prohairesis*, and clearly classifies it into the category of desire.

But if we keep this formulation in mind, we will be surprised when we see Aristotle's third formulation (F3). When he comes back to the topic of the origin of rational action in the context of intellectual virtue, Aristotle offers some seemingly uncertain remarks about the nature of *prohairesis*:

> [T12] The principle of an action (πράξεως...ἀρχὴ), i.e., the source of motion, not the goal, is prohairesis; the principle of prohairesis is desire and goal-directed reason (ὄρεξις καὶ λόγος ὁ ἕνεκά τινος). That is why prohairesis requires intellect and thought (οὔτ' ἄνευ νοῦ καὶ διανοίας), and also a state of character (οὔτ' ἄνευ ἠθικῆς)...Thought by itself moves nothing (διάνοια δ' αὐτὴ οὐθὲν κινεῖ); what moves us is goal-directed and practical thought (ἀλλ' ἡ ἕνεκά του καὶ πρακτική)...That is why prohairesis is either desiring intellect or thinking desire (ἢ ὀρεκτικὸς νοῦς ἡ προαίρεσις ἢ ὄρεξις διανοητική), and this is the sort of principle that a human being is. (NE VI.2.1139a31-b5)

According to this formulation, it matters nothing or very little whether we say *prohairesis'* genus is desire or intellect, because it is a harmonious combination of both elements. So it makes the distinction neither necessary nor important. This almost undistinguishable harmony reminds us of the metaphor Aristotle uses to describe the difference between rational and non-rational parts of the soul as "concave" and "convex." *Prohairesis* is the best representative of this two-in-one relationship between desire and reason.

> [T13] It makes no difference if the soul is or is not divisible into parts; it still has different capacities, including those we have mentioned—just as the convex is not separable in a curve from the concave. (*EE* II.1.1219b32-34; see also *NE* I.13.1102a28-32)

And it is also reaffirmed by Aristotle's remark in the *De anima*,

> [T14] That which moves therefore is a single faculty, i.e., the faculty of desire, for if there were two sources of movement, intellect and desire, they would produce

movement *in virtue of some common form* (κατὰ κοινὸν ἄν τι ἐκίνουν εἶδος). (*DA* III.10.433a21-22)[15]

If we take a fresh look at the complicated nature of *prohairesis* from this final verdict, and from Aristotle's overall doctrine, it seems that the first set ([T1] and [T3]), and the second set ([T10] and [T11]) of formulations of the nature of *prohairesis* may be called temporal and partial. To emphasize either the rational or desiderative aspects of *prohairesis* is certainly not wrong (given the remark at *DA* III.10.433a21-22, to call it a kind of "desire" is probably more correct), but still not comprehensive enough. They may serve as landmarks toward the final conclusion about the nature of *prohairesis*, but still not the final destination. *Prohairesis* in its nature is so *sui generis* that we can even hardly assign a proper genus to it.

III. The Structure of *Prohairesis*

Now let us take a closer look at the two components of *prohairesis* in turn. The rational component, i.e., deliberation, is relatively clear; whereas there are considerable controversies about the desiderative component of *prohairesis*. Let us start from the clearer one.

1. Rational Component: Deliberation (*bouleusis*)

The role of deliberation is fairly clear. As Aristotle repeatedly emphasizes, "we deliberate not about ends, but about what promotes ends (περὶ τῶν πρὸς τὰ τέλη)" (*NE* III.3.1112b11-12; see also 1112b33-34); "we lay down the end, and then examine how and through what to achieve it (τὸ πῶς καὶ διὰ τίνων ἔσται σκοποῦσι)" (*NE* III.3.1112b15-16); "one deliberates not about the end, since *that is given for everyone* (τοῦτο κεῖται πᾶσι), but about what leads to the end (περὶ δὲ τῶν εἰς τοῦτο τεινόντων)" (*EE* II.10.1226b10-11); "everyone's deliberation, technical or nontechnical, investigates what promotes the end (πρὸς τὸ τέλος)" (*EE* II.10.1227a11-12).

So the general picture is as follows: first, an unspecific and indeterminate end or goal is set by wish (*boulēsis*), which is "given for everyone." Of course for different people the end may be different, for example, a doctor's given end is to cure, a rhetor's given end is to persuade, a politician's given end is good order (these are the examples from *NE* III.3.1112b12-14); or more generally, health or happiness may simply be the ends for human being as such (see *NE* III.2.1111b27-30; *EE* II.10.1226a7-15). Then deliberation

---

[15] Translations of *DA* are from Smith's translation in Barnes 1984, with amendments.

comes into play, looks for the best means to achieve the end, and at the same time makes the end more specific, more determinate, and more practicable. To illustrate it with Aristotle's famous doctrine of the mean: it is the wish of the virtuous person to achieve the mean in particular circumstances, and it is the task of deliberation to find "the right time," "the right things," "the right people," "the right end,"[16] and "the right way" (*NE* II.6.1106b21-22). Deliberation, therefore, is a kind of inquiry (*zētēsis*) and analysis, and results in *prohairesis*.

As a component of *prohairesis*, deliberation is about what is within our own agency, that is to say, about thing that we can make it otherwise. Accordingly, it is not about what is eternal, what is necessary, what varies all the time, what results from fortune, what is far away (*NE* III.3.1112a21-31). It is the calculative capacity (*logistikon*) of our rational part of the soul, and the "goal-directed" reason mentioned in **[T12]**. Aristotle calls it "analysis," the capacity to go backward from the end or goal to the action or movement one can immediately perform to achieve this goal:

> **[T15]** For a deliberator would seem to inquire and analyze in the way described, as though analyzing a diagram…The last thing in the analysis would seem to be the first that comes into being (τὸ ἔσχατον ἐν τῇ ἀναλύσει πρῶτον εἶναι ἐν τῇ γενέσει). (*NE* III.3.1112b20-23)

After examining the rational component in *prohairesis*, let us now turn to the much more problematic desiderative component of it.

2. The Desiderative Component: Wish (*boulēsis*)

Boulēsis was not yet a philosophical term in Plato, and it is a non-technical word for both what we want in general, and what we want in a more rational sense. This ambiguity remains in Aristotle even if he generally takes it as a philosophical term and uses it, in most cases, to refer to the so-called "rational desire," but I will argue in what follows that to call it "rational" may not be as appropriate as the majority of commentators think. Furthermore, I will argue that there is an ambiguity in *boulēsis*, i.e., between the *boulēsis* that sets the end for deliberation (I will call it *boulēsis$_{[e]}$*), and the *boulēsis* that results from deliberation (I will call it *boulēsis$_{[r]}$*), and the latter sense seems to be the same as *prohairesis* itself.

---

[16] Here it is the more restricted sense of "end" as components of the more general end given to the agent.

2.1 Boulēsis[e]

Just as he repeatedly emphasizes that deliberation is not about the end, Aristotle also repeatedly says that wish is for/about the end, such as "wish is more [or "rather"] about the end (ἡ μὲν βούλησις τοῦ τέλους ἐστὶ μᾶλλον)" (*NE* III.3.1111b26; III.4.1113a15); "we wish for the end, and deliberate and decide about the things that promote it" (*NE* III.5.1113b3-4); "what one wishes for is above all the end (βούλεται δέ γε μάλιστα τὸ τέλος)" (*EE* II.10.1226a13). As mentioned above, the proper ends for deliberation are "given to everyone," such as to cure, to persuade, to produce good order, to be healthy or to be happy. What is wished for is what one takes to be good. Different people may see different goals as good, and thus take different things as their end. The virtuous person wishes for the good without qualification or in truth (ἁπλῶς μὲν καὶ κατ' ἀλήθειαν), whereas the other people only wish for the apparent good (τὸ φαινόμενον ἀγαθὸν), i.e., what they take to be good (*NE* III.4.1113a21-24; see also *EE* II.10.1227a28-30 where the two kinds of *boulēsis* are qualified as "by nature" [*phusei*] and "contrary to nature" [*para phusin*]). Thus an intemperate or unjust person would wish what is unjust or intemperate (*NE* III.5.1114a11-12).

Based on the above remarks, it seems only natural to understand wish as setting the end, which comes first, and then deliberation comes into play, and turns what is general, unspecific and indeterminate into something particular, specific and determinate. This particular, specific and determinate conclusion is *prohairesis*, and this is an action to be done at the moment, for "what is deliberated is the same as *to prohaireton*, except that *to prohaireton* is determinate (ἀφωρισμένον), for what *to prohaireton* is what we have judged from council (ἐκ τῆς βουλῆς κριθὲν)" (*NE* III.3.1113a2-5). I call this *prohairesis* that sets the end *boulēsis[e]*. For example, a virtuous person may set the end as "I want to be just," then examines the circumstances, deliberates about what to do to realize justice, and eventually reaches the *prohairesis* to distribute the money in front of him equally to the five people in need.

Now we need to pause, and tackle a central controversy about *boulēsis[e]*, i.e., whether it is a kind of desire that is generated or produced by reason itself, or located in reason, and a related question, i.e., whether Aristotle holds a similar view as Plato on this point, for Plato clearly says that reason has its own desire (see *Republic* IX. 580d-581b). Most scholars takes it to be the case that Aristotle's *boulēsis[e]* is located in reason, so Aristotle's view is similar to Plato's.[17]

---

[17] For example, Aspasius 2006, 68.28, Mele 1984, Cooper 1988/1999, Lorenz 2009, Grönroos 2015, and Müller 2016. For a few examples for the opposite view, see Price 1995, Moss 2011, 2014, and Pearson 2012.

I tend to disagree with this general view about *boulēsis*[e], and even think that *boulēsis*[e] is *not* generated by the rational part of the soul is an important departure of Aristotle's moral psychology from Plato's, and related to his objection of Socratic or Platonic intellectualism. If the goal is set by reason itself, and the deliberation is also done by reason, then there is very little room left for desiderative part of the soul. For Aristotle, the motivational function of desire is explicitly distinguished from the non-motivational function of reason as we have seen from **[T12]** ("thought by itself moves nothing; what moves us is goal-directed and practical thought"), and as we can also see this from the following statement, "reason does not seem to move without desire (for *boulēsis* is a kind of desire, and whenever something is moved in accordance with reasoning, it is also moved in accordance with *boulēsis*)" (*DA* III.10.433a23-25).

I cannot solve all the problems about *boulēsis* here. What I would like to do is to gather some pieces of evidence, which, *when put together*, may give us strong reasons to reconsider the common view.

First of all, according to Aristotle's basic theory of desire in his ethical works, appetite (*epithumia*), spirit (*thumos*), and wish (*boulēsis*) are different species of desire (*orexis*), and they all belong to the desiderative part of the soul (*orektikon*), instead of the rational part. And this desiderative part of the soul is said to share in reason, or be able to obey reason, but not having reason in itself. This is a basic distinction made in Aristotle's moral psychology:

> **[T16]** The nonrational part, then, also seems to have two parts. For while the plantlike part [i.e., nutritive] does not shares in reason at all, the appetitive part, and *in general desiderative part* (ὅλως ὀρεκτικὸν), shares in reason in a way, insofar as it both listens to reason and obeys it. (*NE* I.13.1102b28-32; see also *EE* II.4.1221b27-32).

Here Aristotle mentions both the appetitive and the desiderative part in general, and classifies the "desiderative part in general" into the nonrational part of the soul, without singling out any kind of desire (*boulēsis*) as located in the rational part of the soul. The way the *desiderative part in general* shares in reason is to listen to and obey reason, not belongs to reason.[18]

---

[18] Lorenz 2009 underplays the importance of this passage by pointing out that in some cases Aristotle uses *orexis* to refer to non-rational desire, i.e., appetite and spirit. But for one thing Aristotle does not do this in his ethical treatises, and for another, Aristotle never adds *holōs* when he uses *orexis* to refer to non-rational desire.

Second, the two series of virtues are distinguished in accordance with the two "parts" of the soul, and ethical virtue (*aretē ēthikē*) is precisely the excellence of the desiderative part of the soul (*NE* I.13.1103a5-10; *EE* II.1.1220a8-11).[19] Aristotle makes it clear that it is ethical virtue that makes the goal right (*EE* II.11.1227b22-28; *NE* VI.12.1144a7-9, VI.13.1145a5-6). Furthermore, it is the task of *boulēsis*$_{[e]}$ to set the goal for deliberation, and character, be it virtuous or vicious, determines what kind of *boulēsis*$_{[e]}$ one has: "For the excellent person, what is wished for will be what is in truth, while for the base person, what is wished for is random" (*NE* III.4.1113a21-24; *EE* II.11.1127b34-1228a4). Aristotle also explicitly says that the end is not the result of calculation or inference, but like the principle of mathematics, which is grasped directly by virtue: "we affirm that it [virtue] makes the goal correct, since the goal is not arrived at by deduction or reasoning" (*EE* II.11.1227b23-25), and more elaborately,

> **[T17]** For virtue preserves the starting point, whereas vice corrupts it; and in action the end we act for is the starting point, as the assumptions are the starting point in mathematics. Reason does not teach the starting point either in mathematics or in action (οὔτε δὴ ἐκεῖ ὁ λόγος διδασκαλικὸς τῶν ἀρχῶν οὔτε ἐνταῦθα); it is virtue, either natural or habituated, that teaches correct belief about the starting point (ἀλλ' ἀρετὴ ἢ φυσικὴ ἢ ἐθιστὴ τοῦ ὀρθοδοξεῖν περὶ τὴν ἀρχήν). (*NE* VII.9.1151a15-19)

Another two famous passages from *NE* VI also confirm the goal-setting role of ethical virtue: "virtue makes the goal correct, and prudence the things promoting the goal" (*NE* VI.12.1144a7-9); "*prohairesis* will not be correct without prudence or without virtue, for the latter makes us do the end, whereas the former makes us do the things promoting the end" (*NE* VI.13.1145a4-6).

Third, a passage at *DA* III.9.432b5-6, which is often taken as the decisive textual evidence for the view that wish belongs to the rational part (for Aristotle seems to say explicitly "wish is found in the calculative part and appetite and spirit in the irrational"), upon scrutiny in its context, may not do the service as most commentators think. I put this passage in its larger context first:

> **[T18]** The problem at once presents itself, in what sense we are to speak of parts of the soul, or how many we should distinguish. For in a sense there is an infinity of

---

[19] Lorenz 2009 argues that *EE* regards the ethical virtue to belong to the desiderative part of the soul, while *NE* does not do so, because *NE* only says that the distinction of the two series of virtues is in accordance with (*kata*) the two parts of the soul, not that the two series of virtues "belong to" (genitive) the two parts of the soul. But it is important to note that at *EE* II.4.1221b28-29, Aristotle uses the same words as he uses in the *NE* and says that "the virtues are classified in accordance with (*kata*) these." It seems, then, that Aristotle's "belong to" has the same meaning as "in accord with."

parts: it is not enough to distinguish, with some thinkers, the calculative, the spirited, and the appetitive, or with others the rational and the irrational; for if we take the dividing lines followed by these thinkers we shall find parts far more distinctly separated from one another than these, namely those we have just mentioned: the nutritive, which belongs both to plants and to all animals, and the sensitive, which cannot easily be classed as either irrational or rational; further the imaginative, which is, in its being, different from all, while it is very hard to say with, which of the others it is the same or not the same, supposing we determine to posit separate parts in the soul; and lastly the desiderative, which would seem to be distinct both in definition and in power from all hitherto enumerated. *It is absurd to break up the last-mentioned faculty: for wish is found in the calculative part and appetite and spirit in the irrational; and if the soul is tripartite desire will be found in all three parts* (καὶ ἄτοπον δὴ τὸ τοῦτο διασπᾶν· ἔν τε τῷ λογιστικῷ γὰρ ἡ βούλησις γίνεται, καὶ ἐν τῷ ἀλόγῳ ἡ ἐπιθυμία καὶ ὁ θυμός· εἰ δὲ τρία ἡ ψυχή, ἐν ἑκάστῳ ἔσται ὄρεξις). (*DA* III.9.432a22-b7)

This passage is to raise difficulties (*aporiai*) toward the view that the soul has separate parts and about what these parts are. Aristotle especially singles out two models of dividing the soul, tripartition (*to logistikon, to thumikon,* and *to epithumētikon*), and bipartition (*to logon* and *to alogon*), and then he very briefly mentions some "soul-parts" according to his own classification, i.e., the nutritive (*to threptikon*), the sensitive (*aisthētikon*), the imaginative (*phantastikon*), and the desiderative (*orektikon*), as problematic cases if we take the bipartite or tripartite models. Aristotle considers two lines of objections:

(1) There will be some "parts" that are as well qualified as the other "parts" mentioned by his opponents, but that are not included in his opponent's view, so the number of the "parts" of the soul is unlike what his opponents say;

(2) There will be some "parts" that are difficult to fit in his opponents' bipartite or tripartite models, so to divide the soul into separate parts is false.

According to Aristotle, (1) is true for the all the four "parts" he mentions, i.e., the nutritive, the sensitive, the imaginative, and the desiderative, for they all have distinctive functions, corresponding to different objects and having different mechanisms. (2) is especially true in the cases of the sensitive and the imaginative, for they can hardly fit into the bipartite (explicitly said) or the tripartite (presumably so) models. Aristotle takes sensation as informed or used by reason, and speaks of two different kinds of imagination, i.e., *phantasia aisthētikē* and *phantasia logistikē* (or *phantasia bouleutikē*).

As for the last "part," the desiderative, Aristotle is not as clear as the previous three. What is clear is that Aristotle takes it as "absurd" (*atopon*) to tear apart (*diaspan*) this faculty or "part." According to my interpretation, Aristotle discusses two kinds of absurdities, in accordance with the bipartite and the tripartite models respectively. According to the former, wish will be classified into the rational part, whereas appetite and spirit into the nonrational part; and according to the latter, wish, spirit, and appetite will belong to rational, spirited, and appetitive parts of the soul respectively. But both cases are "absurd," because they both mean to divide the soul into separate parts. It seems that in the case of "desiderative part," Aristotle is not speaking of the *difficulties* of distributing different kinds of desire into different "part," like in the cases of the sensitive and the imaginative parts, but speaking of the *impossibility* to divide this faculty into different part, and objecting two attempts to introduce divisions to it, so in the end the desiderative faculty should be kept intact, somewhat like the nutritive faculty of the soul. So it seems that only (1), not (2) is applied to desiderative part of the soul. Therefore, Aristotle does not take *boulēsis* as belonging to the rational part of the soul, but rather take the entire desiderative part of the soul in some sense as a whole (of course he agrees there are different kinds of desires), somewhat like the nutritive part, without trying to fit the desiderative part into the bipartite or tripartite model.[20] And this is precisely in the same line as in **[T16]**.

Fourth, Aristotle explicitly says that children whose reason is not yet developed have wish, and this also shows that wish does not belong to the rational part of the soul:

> **[T19]** Just as soul and body are two, so we see that the soul has two parts as well, one that is nonrational and one that has reason. Their states are also two in number, desire and intellect. And just as the development of the body is prior to that of the soul, so the nonrational part is prior to the rational. This too is evident. For *spirit, wish, and also appetite are present in children right from birth* (θυμὸς γὰρ καὶ βούλησις, ἔτι δὲ ἐπιθυμία, καὶ γενομένοις εὐθὺς ὑπάρχει τοῖς παιδίοις), whereas reasoning and understanding naturally develop as they grow older. (*Politics* VII.15.1334b22-25)[21]

---

[20] Whether Aristotle's distinction of desire is consistent throughout his corpus, such as *Topics*, *Rhetoric*, *DA*, *NE*, *EE*, *Politics*, and so forth, is another question. But so far as I am aware, only in the *Topics* and *Rhetoric* I.10, generally agreed to be early works, Aristotle unmistakably says "wish is always found *in the reasoning faculty* (*pasa gar boulēsis en tōi logistikōi*)" (*Topics* IV.5.126a12-13), and "wish is rational desire (*logistikēn orexsin*)" and spirit (here "anger") and appetite are "nonrational desire (*alogoi orexeis*)" (*Rhetoric* I.10.1369a1-4). All the rest discussions do not necessarily support this kind of "Platonic" understanding of wish.

[21] Quotation from the *Politics* is from Reeve 1997, with amendments.

This passage both confirms that *boulēsis* belongs to the nonrational part of the soul as we mentioned in the first point, and makes it clear that children who have no reason also have *boulēsis* in its strict sense, because Aristotle lists all three kinds of desire here.[22]

Fifth, some may object and argue that since the particular object of wish is "good," be it real or apparent, and since the "good" can only be grasped by reason, wish can only be produced by reason.[23] But it seems that the second premise is not granted by Aristotle, because, on the one hand, nonrational animals may also grasp the "good," and on the other hand, the object of appetite may also appear good to the agent. The following two passages show these two aspects clearly. When speaking of the three factors in *all animal movements*, Aristotle says,

> **[T20]** All movement involves three factors, (1) that which originates the movement (τὸ κινοῦν), (2) that by means of which it originates it (ᾧ κινεῖ), and (3) that which is moved (τὸ κινούμενον). "That which originates the movement" has two meanings: it may mean either something, which itself is unmoved or that which at once moved and is moved. Here *that which moves without itself being moved is the realizable good* (τὸ μὲν ἀκίνητον τὸ πρακτὸν ἀγαθόν), that which at once moves and is moved is the faculty of desire...that which is in motion is the animal. The instrument, which desire employs to produce movement is bodily. (*DA* III.10.433b13-19; see also *De motu animalium* [*DMA*] 6.700b25-29)

And in his discussion of the object of wish, Aristotle says,

> **[T21]** The excellent person is far superior because he sees what is true in each case, being himself a sort of standard and measure. In the many, however, pleasure would seem to cause deception, since *it appears good when it is not* (οὐ γὰρ οὖσα ἀγαθὸν φαίνεται). Certainly, *they choose what is pleasant as good*, and avoid pain as bad (αἱροῦνται οὖν τὸ ἡδὺ ὡς ἀγαθόν, τὴν δὲ λύπην ὡς κακὸν φεύγουσιν). (*NE* III.4.1113a32-b2; see also *EE* VII.2.1235b18-1236a10)

This is important, because this is to say that wish is *not generated by reason*, but more like *recognized by reason* as something good. Unlike the good or virtuous person, who wishes for the real good, the base or the common people only wish for the apparent good, just like a sick person might not be able to tell accurately a given flavor because his taste is misled by, say, the high temperature of his tongue (*NE* III.4.1113a22-31).

---

[22] Grönroos takes this remarks to mean "even the as-yet non-rational infant has the propensity for wish" (Grönroos 2015, 68), but this is not persuasive given the context, for it is clear that Aristotle does not speak of "propensity" here, but something already actualized in infant.

[23] Cooper 1996/1999 argues for the different objects of desire most emphatically.

Last of all, as we have seen above, we may wish impossible and irrational things, even like immortality, and this does not seem to be something generated or produced by reason.

2.2 *Boulēsis[r]* and *Prohairesis*

As we have seen above in **[F2]**, Aristotle calls *prohairesis* "deliberative desire," but curiously, this "desire" is not the desire we just discussed, i.e., *boulēsis[e]*. Here we have to take a closer look at **[T10]** and **[T11]**. Still more curiously, there are parallel textual problems in these two passages. In the majority of the manuscripts, **[T10]** has βούλευσιν and this is also the choice of most of the editors and translators (e.g., Ross 1925, Rowe and Broadie 2002, Crisp 2004, Taylor 2006, Reeve 2014). Only M^b in Bywater's list has *boulēsin* (this variation was noted by Aspasius 2006, 75.1-11); Gauthier/Jolif 1970 and Irwin 1999 follow this line of reading. The situation of **[T11]** is similar. Most of the MSS have βουλευόμεθα, and this is also the choice in Susemihl's text, and followed by Woods 1982, Solomon in Barnes 1984, Kenny 2013, Simpson 2013. But in OCT, the editors follow some manuscripts (V, Λ^1), Dirlmeier and Rowe, choose βουλόμεθα, and this is followed by Inwood and Woolf 2013.

Besides the fact that the majority of the MSS support the "deliberation" reading, which makes perfect senses in these contexts. We also have strong philosophical reasons to favor this reading. In **[T10]**, the context shows clearly that what we desire is the *result* of deliberation, but so far all the discussion of *boulēsis* in the *NE* is about its role of setting the goal, and thus provides the starting point of deliberation, rather than the result of deliberation. Furthermore, this *boulēsis[e]* is unspecified as we have seen above, and thus cannot become action immediately, but what is indicated in **[T10]** is a specific desire for immediate action.

This also sheds important light on how to understand the parallel case in **[T11]**. Furthermore, we can make two more observations in **[T11]**. First, the context of **[T11]** is about "deliberative desire," and if we accept βουλόμεθα, it will become a discussion that both starts and ends with deliberation, but the middle and explanatory part ("*gar*" at 1226b18) has nothing to do with deliberation. Second, if we take the "wish" readings in both places, we have to accept that Aristotle speaks of two different senses of wish and introduces some strange vocabulary in this very short passage, for the "wish" in "we all *wish for* the things we *prohairoumetha*" can only be the desire in accordance with *prohairesis*, and this will be strange since *prohairesis* itself is the desire to do certain action; whereas the "wish" in "it is not the case that we *prohairoumetha* all things we *wish for*" can only be the desire that sets the end for deliberation.

In these passages Aristotle calls *prohairesis* "deliberative desire," i.e., desire in accordance with deliberation. Given Aristotle's exhaustive tripartition of desire into appetites, spirit, and *boulēsis*,[24] this desire that follows from deliberation cannot be otherwise than *boulēsis*. Therefore, I call it *boulēsis$_{[r]}$*, a desire resulting from deliberation.[25] But interestingly Aristotle never calls this kind of desire *boulēsis* in his ethical treatises (except we accept the "wish" reading in [T10] and [T11]), and whenever he mentions *boulēsis*, he means *boulēsis$_{[e]}$*, i.e., the one that sets the goal. And so far as I am aware, the only undoubtful reference to *boulēsis$_{[r]}$* is in the *DA* III.10.433a23-24 as we quoted above: "*boulēsis* is desire, and when movement is produced in accordance with calculation, it is also in accordance with *boulēsis*."

Given the standard use of *boulēsis* as the desire for the goal of deliberation or *prohairesis*, Aristotle probably should not have called this desire "*boulēsis*," and thus introduce an unnecessary ambiguity, for this *boulēsis* in the sense of the result of rational calculation, is the same as the "deliberative desire" in [T10] and [T11], and this is precisely *prohairesis*.

2.3 Success and failure of *prohairesis* to motivate action

According to the above pictures, we may reach the following diagram [D1] to describe the basic structure of *prohairesis*:

[D1] Normal cases
                    Deliberation
    Boulēsis$_{[e]}$ ⎯⎯⎯⎯⎯⎯⟶   *Prohairesis* or *Boulēsis$_{[r]}$*   and Action

In this diagram, there is no gap between *prohairesis* and action, for Aristotle says in [T15], "the last thing in the analysis would seem to be the first that comes into being." And in the famous discussion of "practical syllogism," the actual procedure of deliberation, in *DMA*, Aristotle also says that *the conclusion of practical syllogism is action*, such as the following example:

---

[24] *EE* II.10.1225b24-26 provides the clearest support for the exhaustiveness of this division; see also *DA* II.3.414b2, *DMA* 6.700b22, 7.701a36-b1, *EE* II.7.1223a26-27, *Rhet*. I.10.1369a1-7.
[25] Some commentators take this as the standard meaning of *boulēsis*, for example, Irwin (1980) and Cooper (1988/1999). According to this interpretation, *boulēsis* is not only a rational desire, but also *a reasoned desire*. Grönroos (2015), pp. 65-67 provides a good criticism of this view.

(a) I need a covering.
(b) A coat is a covering.
(c) I need a coat.
(d) What I need I ought to make.
(e) I make a coat.

The goal or first premise of this syllogism, i.e., "I need a covering," is hardly something produced or generated by reason, but more likely from a direct sense of chilliness, and then *recognized by reason* as an appropriate goal to be achieved. And (b)-(e) represent a deliberative process, and when I reach the conclusion or *prohairesis* in (e), I will start making a coat immediately. This is indeed the *normal* case. When we reach a *prohairesis* about what particular action should be done to promote the goal set by our *boulēsis*, we naturally follow this *prohairesis* and do the action, which is immediately practicable. This is also the sense when Aristotle says the decision and action are the same (*Met.* VI.1.1025b23-24).

But in the above context of *DMA*, Aristotle also raises a restriction, "if there is no hindrance or necessity" (ἂν μή τι κωλύῃ ἢ ἀναγκάζῃ, 7.701a16), and in the *NE* account of "practical syllogism," similar restriction is also at place: "it is necessary for someone who is able and unhindered to act on this at the same time (ἀνάγκη τὸν δυνάμενον καὶ μὴ κωλυόμενον ἅμα τοῦτο καὶ πράττειν)" (*NE* VII.3.1147a30-31). These hindrances or necessities may be something external that intervenes, such as someone stops me from doing the things I decide to do. Furthermore, there is another sense of hindrance, which explains certain *abnormal* cases, when our *prohairesis* is not realized due to some internal hindrance.[26] The most obvious abnormal case is weak *akrasia* in, which the agent forms a correct *prohairesis*, but fails to perform the action in accordance with this *prohairesis*, because he is weak, and easily overcome by appetite or emotion (see [T2]). So for this kind of akratic person, he reaches the correct *prohairesis* or practical conclusion, but fails to turn this conclusion into action. And the following diagram [D2] shows the mechanism of this abnormal case:

[D2] Abnormal cases

                Deliberation   Appetite or Emotion

Boulēsis$_{[e]}$ ⟶ *Prohairesis* or *Boulēsis$_{[r]}$*   Action$_2$ ⟶ of Action$_1$

---

[26] This is the way Charles 2009 understands "hindrance." See Müller 2015, 26-27, for an objection of this reading from more philological point of view. But as Müller shows in n.90, Aristotle uses *kōluein* to mean the prohibition that reason imposes to stop the agent from following certain desires or emotions, if so, there seems to be nothing to prevent the opposite process, i.e., appetite imposes some prohibition to stop the result of reasoning, i.e., *prohairesis*, to be carried out.

In this diagram, *boulēsis[e]* is what we take to be good, and sets the goal for a *prohairesis*. It is unspecified, such as "I want to be courageous," or 'I want to be healthy," or "I would like to enjoy some good music as relaxation."[27] With this end set, our reason or deliberation comes into play and does the analysis, and it reaches a *prohairesis* concerning the action, which can be done immediately, and which can best promotes the goal. This *prohairesis* may be something like "(in order to be courageous) I should hold my position," "(in order to be healthy) I should take a walk," or "(in order to enjoy music) I should go to the National Theater." In *normal* cases, this *prohairesis* or *boulēsis[r]* will be actualized in action, so the result of practical syllogism will be action. In these cases, while *boulēsis[e]* and *boulēsis[r]* are not the same, they are closely related, for *boulēsis[r]*, the immediate moving cause or motivation of action, is a direct transmission from *boulēsis[e]*, the more remote moving cause or motivation, and is a specification and determination of *boulēsis[e]*. But in *abnormal* cases, *boulēsis[r]* is overcome by the impact or hindrance of emotion and/or appetite, so the agent fails to actualize his *prohairesis*. In our examples, the agent may be too afraid to hold his position, too greedy to stop eating another big chunk of cake, or too lazy to go to the National Theater.

IV. Significance of *Prohairesis*

I will conclude by briefly commenting on some of the significances of *prohairesis* in Aristotle's moral psychology.

1. Borderline of Rational Action

It is well-known that Aristotle uses the world "action" (*praxis*) in various ways. The broadest sense is whatever is done by an agent, both voluntary and involuntary. The second broadest sense is voluntary action, i.e., "what has its principle in the agent himself, knowing the particulars that constitute the action" (*NE* III.1.1111a20-21). Both rational and nonrational actions (nonrational actions are those from appetite, spirit, or from an episode of emotion) can be voluntary, and bear praise and blame, thus moral responsibility, for the agent. Aristotle is even happy to call animals and children to have these two kinds of ac-

---

[27] Therefore, unlike Müller 2016, I think unharmful pleasure can be the object of *boulēsis[e]*, since it can be recognized or taken as something good. So, his case is actually not an example that challenges the scope of *prohairesis*.

tions (*NE* III.2.1111b6-10). The third sense is *praxis prohairetikē* i.e., the action based on *prohairesis*. This may be called "rational action," narrowly human, and more narrowly reserved for adults who have rational capacity. *Praxis prohairetikē*, as we have discussed above, is action whose starting point is wish and brought about through rational calculation or deliberation. It is a sub-set of voluntary action, and *prohairesis* provides the efficient cause for rational action. The most narrow and most strict sense is rational action, which has the action itself as end, not serving any further end. It is more narrow than the third both in the sense that it has to be correct rational action, thus distinguished from bad ones, and in the sense that it is its own end, thus distinguished from productive actions (see *NE* I.1.1094a3-6, VI.2.1139b1-4).

Prohairesis, thus understood, provides a threshold for distinguishing rational and non-rational actions, and further pins down the moral responsibility of the agent to his reason, and his fully developed character (since we at least "co-responsible [*sunaition*] for our own character"; *NE* III.5.1114b21-24), as we will see in the next point.

2. *Prohairesis* Better Reveals One's Character

Aristotle always emphasizes the difference between one's action and character. It is precisely this salient feature of his ethical perspective that justifies the gap between ancient character-based ethics and modern action-based moral philosophy. A good action, say a just distribution of goods, may be done by chance, compulsion, someone else's instruction, or even out of hypocrisy; and an unjust action may also be done by chance, compulsion, out of ignorance, neglect, or an outburst of anger or *thumos* (see *EE* II.11.1228a11-17; *NE* II.4.1105a21-26, V.8.1135b11-25). It is only action out of *prohairesis*, i.e., out of rational deliberation, that reveals one's true character, and thus is more subject to praise and blame than the action itself. It is from one's *prohairesis*, i.e., from what things he takes into consideration and how he reaches the action he actually performs, that we can fully judge his character. Aristotle's distinction between an unjust person and an unjust action makes this clear enough, "if *prohairesis* causes him to inflict the harm, he does injustice, and this is the sort of act of injustice that makes an agent unjust...a person is just if his *prohairesis* causes him to do justice; one does justice if one merely does it voluntarily" (*NE* V.8.1136a1-5), and more generally, *prohairesis* "is thought to be most closely bound up with virtue and discriminate character better than actions do" (*NE* III.2.1111b5-6; see also IV.7.1127b14-15, *Topics* IV.5.126a30-126b3; *Rhetoric* I.2.1355b18-21). This is certainly in line with Aristotle's famous definition of ethical virtue as a "*hexis prohairetikē*" ("state that issue in decision"; *NE* II.6.1106b36-1107a3).

On the other hand, Aristotle also realizes that it is difficult to judge one's decision, and that in most cases we have to judge one's character through action, so he does not downplay the importance of action and simply values good intention, because he nevertheless holds that activity (*energeia*) is more important than mere state (*hexis*) or possession (*ktēsis*) (see *NE* I.8.1098b31-1099a7). Therefore, he says, "it is because of the difficulty of discerning the quality of *prohairesis* that we are compelled to judge what someone is like on the basis of his deeds. So *activity is more choiceworthy but prohairesis is more praiseworthy* (αἱρετώτερον μὲν οὖν ἡ ἐνέργεια, ἐπαινετώτερον δ' ἡ προαίρεσις)" (*EE* II.11.1228a15-18).

But when he comes to rhetoric and poetic composition, Aristotle instructs the rhetorician or poet to overcome this difficulty. In epideictic rhetoric, to establish the goodness of one's character, the rhetorician "should try to show that his actions are in accordance with *prohairesis*. It is useful for him to have acted often. Therefore, one should make coincidences and accidents as *prohairesis* (διὸ καὶ τὰ συμπτώματα καὶ τὰ ἀπὸ τύχης ὡς ἐν προαιρέσει ληπτέον). For many similar examples seem to be a sign of virtue and *prohairesis*" (*Rhet.* I.9.1367b23-27).[28] And the way to establish the goodness of a dramatic personage is to compose some lines of speech or actions to reveal his or her *prohairesis*, and by doing this to reveal his good character (*Poet.* 15.1454a17-19).

3. A New Psychology of Action

In Plato, the relation between reason and desire is usually a picture of division and suppression, even for the virtuous person. We only need to remind ourselves of the allocation of appetite, spirit and reason into different parts of the body in the *Republic* and *Timaeus*, the image of multiform beast for the appetitive part in the *Republic*, the interesting function of liver in the *Timaeus*, and the famous metaphor of charioteer and the two horses in the *Phaedrus*. But moral psychology is developed into a new stage in Aristotle, where desire and reason can be perfectly harmonious, even hardly distinguishable. This is especially clearly revealed in the ambiguous status of *prohairesis* as either "desiring intellect" or "thinking desire," and this ambiguity, in turn, best shows Aristotle's deep insight into the nature of human soul and human action. In transforming a non-philosophical word into an important philosophical term, Aristotle also formed a new moral psychology.

But somewhat curiously and unfortunately, when Hellenistic and Neoplatonic philosophy took over the stage, we see a backward step toward the Socratic/Platonic suppressive model of desire in moral psychology, and this more balanced Aristotelian insight was

---

[28] Translation of the *Rhetoric* is Roberts in Barnes 1984, with amendments.

somehow lost from sight. Therefore, it is worthwhile to take a fresh look at this rather unique Aristotelian heritage, especially from the perspective of *prohairesis*.[29]

Assoc. Prof. Wei Liu, School of Philosophy,
Renmin University of China (Beijing), weiliu18[at]gmail.com

References

Aristotle. [*Aristotelis Eudemica Ethica*] *Eudemii Rhodii Ethica*. Edited by Franz Susemihl. Leipzig: Teubner, 1884.
Aristotle. *Ethica Nicomachea*. (ed.) I. Bywater, Oxford: Oxford University Press, 1894.
Aristotle. *De anima*. Edited by Sir David Ross. Oxford: Oxford University Press, 1956.
Aristotle. *Politica*. Edited by Sir David Ross. Oxford: Oxford University Press, 1957.
Aristotle. *Rhetorica*. Edited by Sir David Ross. Oxford: Oxford University Press, 1959.
Aristotle. *Ethica Eudemia*. Edited by Richard R. Walzer et al. Oxford: Oxford University Press, 1991.
Aspasius. *On Aristotle Nicomachean Ethics 1-4, 7-8*. (ed. and trans.) David Konstan, London: Bloomsbury Academic, 2006.
Barnes, Jonathan (ed.) *The Complete Works of Aristotle*, Princeton: Princeton University Press, 1984.
Charles, David. "Aristotle's Weak Akrates: What does her Ignorance Consist in?" in Christopher Bobonich and Pierre Destrée (eds.) *Akrasia in Greek Philosophy*, Leiden: Brill, 2007. 193-214.
Charles, David. "*Nicomachean Ethics* VII.3: Varieties of *Akrasia*." in Carlo Natali (ed.) *Aristotle's Nicomachean Ethics, Book VII*, Oxford: Oxford University Press, 2009. 41-71.
Charles, David. "Desire in Action: Aristotle's Move." in Michael Pakaluk and Giles Pearson (eds.) *Moral Psychology and Human Action in Aristotle*, Oxford: Oxford University Press, 2011. 75-93.
Cooper, John M. "Some Remarks on Aristotle's Moral Psychology." *Southern Journal of Philosophy*, vol. 27 (1988): 25-42, reprinted in John M. Cooper, *Reason and Emotion: Essays on Ancient Moral Psychology and Ethical Theory*, Princeton: Princeton University Press, 1999. 237-252.
Cooper, John M. "Reason, Moral Virtue, and Moral Value," in Michael Frede and Gisela Striker (eds.) *Rationality in Greek Thought*, Oxford: Clarendon Press, 1996. 81-114; reprinted in John M.

---

[29] The draft of this paper was read in the first RUC-PU-LMU Conference on Ancient Greek Philosophy, and LMU-Berkeley Workshop on Ancient Moral Psychology. I would like to thank helpful comments and criticisms from Jozef Müller, Susan Sauvé Meyer, Benjamin Morison, Hendrik Lorenz, Katja Vogt, Wei Chen, Wei Cheng, Chirstoph Rapp, Klaus Corsilius, and Vasilis Politis.

Cooper, *Reason and Emotion: Essays on Ancient Moral Psychology and Ethical Theory*, Princeton: Princeton University Press, 1999. 253-280.

Crisp, Roger (trans.) *Aristotle: Nicomachean Ethics*, Cambridge: Cambridge University Press, 2004.

Dirlmeier, Franz. (trans. and comm.) *Aristoteles. Nikomachische Ethik*, Darmstadt: Wissenschaftliche Buchgesellschaft, 1956.

Dirlmeier, Franz. (trans. and comm.) *Aristoteles. Eudemische Ethik*, Darmstadt: Wissenschaftliche Buchgesellschaft, 1963.

Gauthier, René A. and Jolif, Jean Y. (trans. and comm.) *Aristote: L'Éthique à Nicomaque*, 2nd ed., Louvain: Publications Universitaires, 1970.

Grönroos, Gösta. "Wish, Motivation and the Human Good in Aristotle." *Phronesis*, vol. 60 (2015): 60-87.

Inwood, Brad and Raphael Woolf (trans.) *Eudemian Ethics*, Cambridge: Cambridge University Press, 2013.

Irwin, Terence. "First Principles in Aristotle's Ethics." in P. French, T. E. Uehling, and H. K. Wettstein (eds.) *Midwest Studies in Philosophy, vol. 3: Studies in Ethical Theory*, Minneapolis: University of Minnesota, 1980. 252-272.

Irwin, Terence. (trans. & comm.) *Nicomachean Ethics*, 2nd ed., Indianapolis: Hackett, 1999.

Joachim, Harold H. *Aristotle: Nicomachean Ethics: A Commentary*, ed., D. A. Rees, Oxford: Oxford University Press, 1951.

Kenny, Anthony. (trans.) *Eudemian Ethics*, Oxford: Oxford University Press, 2013.

Lorenz, Hendrik. "Virtue of Character in Aristotle's *Nicomachean Ethics*." *Oxford Studies in Ancient Philosophy*, vol. 37 (2009): 177-212.

Mele, Alfred R. "Aristotle's Wish." *Journal of the History of Philosophy*, vol. 22 (1984): 139-156.

Moss, Jessica. *Aristotle on the Apparent Good*, Oxford: Oxford University Press, 2012.

Moss, Jessica. "Was Aristotle a Humean? A Partisan Guide to the Debate," in Ronald Polansky (ed.) *The Cambridge Companion to Aristotle's Nicomachean Ethics*, Cambridge: Cambridge University Press, 2014. 221-241.

Müller, Jozef. "Aristotle on Actions from Lack of Control," *Philosophers' Imprint*, vol. 15.8 (2015): 1-35.

Müller, Jozef. "What Aristotelian Decision Cannot Be," Ancient Philosophy, vol. 36 (2016): 173-195.

Nussbaum, Martha. *Aristotle's De motu animalium*, Princeton: Princeton University Press, 1978.

Pearson, Giles. *Aristotle on Desire*, Cambridge: Cambridge University Press, 2012.

Price, Anthony *Mental Conflict*, London: Routledge, 1995.

Price, Anthony. "Aristotle on the Ends of Deliberation," in Michael Pakaluk and Giles Pearson (eds.) *Moral Psychology and Human Action in Aristotle*, Oxford: Oxford University Press, 2011. 135-158.

Price, Anthony. "Choice and Action in Aristotle," *Phronesis*, vol. 61 (2016): 435-462.

Reeve, C. D. C. (trans.) *Aristotle: Politics*, Indianapolis: Hackett, 1997.

Reeve, C. D. C. (trans.) *Aristotle: Nicomachean Ethics*, Indianapolis: Hackett, 2014.

Rowe, Christopher and Sarah Broadie (trans. and comm.) *Nicomachean Ethics*, Oxford: Oxford University Press, 2002.

Ross, W. D. (trans.) *Nicomachean Ethics*, Oxford: Clarendon Press, 1925.

Ross, W. D. (trans.) and Lesley Brown (rev.) *Aristotle: Nicomachean Ethics*, Oxford: Oxford University Press, 2009.

Simpson, Peter (trans. and comm.) *The Eudemian Ethics of Aristotle*, New Brunswick: Transaction Publishers, 2013.

Stewart, John A. *Notes on the Nicomachean Ethics*, 2 vols. Oxford: Clarendon Press, 1892.

Taylor, Christopher. (trans. and comm.) *Aristotle: Nicomachean Ethics, Books II-IV*, Oxford: Clarendon Press, 2006.

Woods, Michael. (trans. and comm.) *Aristotle: Eudemian Ethics Books I, II & VIII*, Oxford: Clarendon Press, 1982.

AUDREY L. ANTON (Bowling Green, KY)

Sculpting Character: Aristotle's Voluntary as Affectability[1]

Abstract

I argue that the two criteria traditionally identified as jointly sufficient for voluntary behavior according to Aristotle require qualification. Without such qualification, they admit troubling exceptions (i.e., they are not sufficient). Through minding these difficult examples, I conclude that a third condition mentioned by Aristotle – the eph' hēmin – is key to qualifying the original two criteria. What is eph' hēmin is that which is efficiently caused by appetite and teleologically caused by reason such that the agent could have, in theory, acted differently. I propose that praise and blame are justified only when 1: the behavior is voluntary and 2: the agent is susceptible (at least in principle) to the positive influences of appropriate praise and blame to help form, improve, or strengthen a good character. Through concentrating on the agent's affectability in morally salient situations, we may better understand the qualified criteria's role in voluntary human behavior in general.

Keywords: voluntary, involuntary, character, eph' hēmin, praise, blame

1. Introduction

At *Nicomachean Ethics* (*NE*) III.i, Aristotle declares that an inquiry into the voluntary (*to hekousion*) is necessary:

> Since excellence is concerned with passions and actions, and on voluntary passions and actions praise and blame are bestowed, on those that are involuntary forgiveness, and sometimes also pity... (*NE* III.i.1109b30-33).[2]

Here Aristotle suggests we consider virtue, feelings, and action in light of what we praise and blame. Virtue is a character type, and all other character types are classified according to dispositions to feel and act as well. In addition, Aristotle indicates that what-

---

[1] I am very grateful to Alan Silverman, Paula Gottlieb, and Larry Jost for their helpful comments and suggestions on earlier versions of this paper.

[2] The translations used in this paper come from W. D. Ross's translations (revised by J. O. Urmson), from *The Complete Works of Aristotle*, ed. Jonathan Barnes (Princeton: Princeton University Press, 1984).

ever is an appropriate object of praise and blame is voluntary, and when behavior is involuntary, it is an appropriate object of pardon or forgiveness. Therefore, we must take care to understand the voluntary so that we may praise and blame people well and fairly for their relevant voluntary behavior.

Before proceeding, a few caveats are in order. First, the class of what is voluntary extends beyond the behaviors Aristotle focuses on immediately after this passage. For example, animals and very young children behave voluntarily. However, we do not praise or blame animals and young children as we do adult humans. We might do so in efforts to encourage good behavior and discourage bad behavior, but we do not necessarily praise and blame them because we believe the animal or child deserves it. For instance, when we praise and blame small children we take their development into account, and we may praise and blame them *so that* they develop reason and become the kinds of beings worthy of praise and blame later on in life (*NE* X.i 1172a21).

Second, while we are considering actions and passions that we praise or blame, we should acknowledge that some actions and passions are voluntary and deserving of neither praise nor blame. Some simple behaviors might also satisfy this description. For example, stretching one's arms to relieve muscle aches, under normal circumstances, is hardly the type of behavior calling for third-party evaluation. While Aristotle would likely agree, he eschews discussion of such behaviors, as he seems to be primarily concerned with the kinds of behavior eligible for moral assessment.

Third, as Aristotle discusses the virtuous person (or, rather, how to become one), we may presume that the actions and passions we are to praise or blame are truly *worthy* of praise or blame.[3] Indeed, we are trying to avoid praising and blaming people incorrectly, as such responses can be detrimental to becoming (and helping others become) virtuous.[4]

Let us be clear that the universe of discourse up for discussion satisfies the following proposition where P stands for "The agent's behavior is praiseworthy," B stands for "The agent's behavior is blameworthy," and V stands for "The agent's behavior is voluntary":

$$((P \lor B) \rightarrow V)$$

---

[3] Aristotle states clearly that what is morally correct is what the virtuous person would do (*NE* III.iv 1113a30-35). Therefore, we are entitled to infer from this text that we investigate the voluntary *so that* we will be good judges of how to act, which should make us good judges of how to respond to the behavior of others. For a compelling account of what it means to be so good at judging the behavior of others that one can recognize mitigating circumstances and even exceptions to rules, see Phillips-Garrett 2016.

[4] We might imagine that blaming the innocent could inspire resentment and even steer them towards the wrong behavior, since they will be blamed for such behavior regardless of whether or not they exhibit it.

At the very least, whenever human behavior is deserving of praise or blame, that behavior must be voluntary.

This description alone does not fully satisfy Aristotle's inquiry. After all, we might need assistance in conceptualizing when such behavior is deserving of praise or blame. We aim to praise and blame others aptly, and a study of the voluntary should shed light on what it means to deserve praise or blame. Indeed, the antecedent of the conditional above may be unknown to us. After all, Aristotle's audience consists of people interested in becoming virtuous; as such people have yet to achieve a virtuous state, they may not have sufficiently keen moral perception to detect the praiseworthy and the blameworthy in every scenario.5 Further inquiry into the voluntary may be necessary to avoid begging the question given Aristotle's audience.

Describing the voluntary to Aristotle's audience will prove difficult. Instead, Aristotle offers a description of *involuntary* behavior that is intuitive and suggests two conditions for voluntary behavior by negating the ways in which behavior qualifies as involuntary:

> Since that which is done under compulsion or by reason of ignorance is involuntary, the voluntary would seem to be that of which the moving principle is in the agent himself, he being aware of the particular circumstances of the action (*NE* III.i 1111a 22-24).

First, the agent must be the source (*archē*) of the behavior in question. Second, the agent must have sufficient awareness and understanding of relevant particular details and facts concerning the situation in which she acts.

In this paper, I explore the possibility that these two criteria are suggestions for how to evaluate an agent's behavior based on a more-fundamental feature of the voluntary *for a human*. While nonhuman animals act voluntarily, just as the good of a cow is distinct from the good of a human, the structure of voluntary behavior for a cow will be distinct from that of an adult human. I argue that there is a third consideration Aristotle had in mind concerning the behavior of human agents that is both more fundamental and less identifiable than the two conditions noted above. Human voluntary behavior stems from the aspects of the soul that are *most* human: 1. Reason and 2. Appetite (insofar as it may listen to reason). I

---

[5] Aristotle tells us that the purpose of reading *Nicomachean Ethics* is not merely to know the good in a theoretical and detached sense, but also (and more importantly) to *become good* (II.ii1103b26-30; X.ix 1179a33-79b4). Therefore, since Aristotle's audience wants to become good, we may surmise: 1. That the audience may not yet be good and 2. That the audience must at least be interested in becoming good (which seems to exclude vicious people). For interesting discussions of Aristotle's audience in *Nicomachean Ethics* and how taking that audience into account affects our reading of Aristotle, see Tessitore 1996 and Burnyeat 1980.

suggest that whenever human behavior is up to us (*eph' hēmin*), it is efficiently and teleologically caused by the aspects of the soul that constitute dispositions to feel and act (reason and appetite, respectively). For convenience's sake, I shall refer to the complex of reason and appetite as the *character center* of the human soul. The character center precedes any character a person develops[6] (as no one is born with a character, but rather a capacity to develop character), and it is that upon which an acquired character supervenes.[7]

Aristotle distinguishes one's character (what we commonly refer to as *second nature*) from one's human nature.[8] One significant difference between our human nature and our second nature is that only the latter can be changed (*NE* II.i 1103a17-26). The fact that the nature of the character center can change (it can develop into something else, change course, or become stronger) is very important to understanding the voluntary whenever voluntary behavior has a moral context.

As previously noted, Aristotle's discussions of the voluntary are predominantly concerned with voluntary behaviors that have moral import. Of course, there are voluntary behaviors of no moral consequence. However, the behaviors worth distinguishing from involuntary behaviors are of some moral concern. For this reason, I suggest a litmus test for discerning whether a behavior of moral import is voluntary. Such behavior is voluntary when the agent's character may be *in principle* positively affected by justified praise or blame. That is, human voluntary behavior of moral consequence is that which, if praised or blamed appropriately, could positively contribute to the development, improvement, or strengthening of character.

The two criteria – sourcehood and knowledge – considered outside of the context I suggest, admit exceptions or counterintuitive evaluations. For example, it is difficult to comprehend how we might deal with nutritive actions of which we are conscious, merely

---

[6] Since infants lack choice, we might conclude that they also lack reason. Indeed, Aristotle tells us that reason develops as we grow. Therefore, the *character center* for young children either includes a bud of reason or it is distinct from that of animals at least insofar as it has potential to be joined by reason.

[7] I believe Aristotle maintained that we are responsible for actions that lead to and issue from character, and one of the reasons why we are responsible for our character is that it is a product of prior behavior that was voluntary. After all, we can perform the same action with the same or similar motive prior to developing virtue as well as through our virtue once it is attained. For an interesting account to the contrary, see Meyer 2006. Meyer argues that, 'Aristotle thinks character is praiseworthy in virtue of the actions it causes, not because of anything about the process by which it comes into being' (2006, 139).

[8] I use the phrase 'human nature' here to refer to the universal, which is predicated of all human beings. I reserve the term *first nature* for those natural characteristics individuals are born displaying (e.g., proclivities, innate talents and strengths, etc.), which, though native, can be altered by practice. For instance, one child might be naturally more spirited than others. However, it is not impossible for the child to grow up to be a coward, just as it is possible for a naturally skittish child to someday become courageous.

non-voluntary behavior of moral consequence, and bad actions performed as a result of pressures that overstrain human nature. Given my suggestions, we shall have reasons to exclude behaviors issuing from the nutritive aspect of our souls from the class of the voluntary, we can better handle the perplexing instances of the merely non-voluntary actions of moral consequence, and we can better understand justified mercy in instances where humans behave poorly but understandably.

In order to illustrate these claims, we shall first re-acquaint ourselves with the nature of character in Aristotle's virtue ethics. I shall focus on the acquisition, efficacy, and evaluation of character states, foreshadowing my reasons for considering the voluntary that which is caused by the character center and identifying the affectability of character as the main focal point of the category of human voluntary behavior of moral consequence.

2. Character

Character is a quality of a human being's soul (*Categories,* Ch. 8). The human soul has three parts or aspects: nutritive, appetite, and reason. All living beings have a nutritive soul, which is responsible for digestion, growth, and other such bodily functions. All animals have appetite, which is responsible for desires, feelings, mobility, etc. Only the rational animals (humans) have reason. Reason behaves theoretically (when contemplating first principles, or learning something new) as well as practically (identifying ends and calculating how to achieve them). Reason rules over appetite. Though appetite is itself irrational, it can behave rationally vicariously by listening to and obeying reason (*NE* I.xiii and VI.ii; *De Anima* (*DA*) II.ii and III.ix). All human characters are explained in virtue of the behavior of this rational-appetitive team, the *character center*.

Character states are relatively fixed dispositions to feel and act in certain ways. There are six types of character according to Aristotle – four or which are human. Human characters one may develop include: virtue (*aretē*), continence (*enkrasia*), incontinence (*akrasia*), and vice (*kakia*). The person of virtuous character knows the good, behaves in accordance with the good, and feels appropriately about the good. The continent person both knows and behaves in accordance with the good; however, she may not feel appropriately about the good. The incontinent person knows the good, but fails to act in accordance with the good. Therefore, the incontinent person cannot feel appropriately towards the good, or else she would be sufficiently motivated by the good to behave appropriately. The vicious person does not know the good. In fact, this is the root of her blameworthy existence. She fails to have basic universal knowledge of moral truths. Because of her moral ignorance, what she believes is good is unlikely to be good. As every person aims at the apparent good in action (*NE* I.i), the vicious is unlikely to behave in accordance with what is in fact good (or, if ever she does, it is purely by coincidence (*NE* II.iv 1105a23)). Since the vicious person fails to know the good, she neither acts in accordance with it voluntarily nor does she feel appropriately towards the good.

Aristotle designates two character types, which, while beyond those of the four human types, are sometimes (though rarely (*NE* VII.i 1145a25-27)) found among humans. The first is the sub-human type. The bestial character (*thēreotēs*) is found in mentally underdeveloped, emotionally stunted humans. We imagine such a character to resemble the legendary "wild child," and Aristotle surmises that either extreme abuse at an early age or some sort of disease cause this condition (*NE* VII.i 1145a30-32). The person displaying such a character may resemble humans in physique, but she resembles animals more in her behavior. As reason is the human's distinguishing mark and the root of human function and flourishing, such people are deprived of both that which makes them human and that which makes happiness possible. Therefore, we do not hold such people accountable for their behaviors any more than we might hold a pig responsible for its behavior (*NE* VII.i1145a25-26). We pity the bestial character. While it may behave voluntarily, the lack of sophistication in their voluntary behavior renders such behavior beneath moral assessment.

The second kind of non-human character rarely found amongst humans is above human nature. The godlike character (*tēn huper hēmas aretēn* (virtue above that of ours (human)); *hēroïkēn tina kai theían* ([goodness] on a heroic or divine scale)) is that which is beyond even the goodness of the virtuous character. While the two are likely to behave similarly, the godlike character transcends the greatness of the virtuous human. Aristotle's example is taken from Homer, where Priam described Hector as having had such a character on account of his surpassing valor (*NE* VII.i 1145a20-22). I imagine that one who is godlike surpasses the virtuous in wisdom, courage, and strength (*qua* fortitude[9]). This is not to say that the virtuous may lack wisdom, courage, or even strength. The virtuous merely have these capacities developed insofar as it is reasonable to expect a human to develop them. However, on occasion, individuals manage to transcend even human greatness, and for this reason, they are beyond human nature.

According to Aristotle, characters are acquired by doing the kinds of acts characteristic of a particular character state repeatedly until a habit for doing such acts is formed (*NE* 1103a33; 1105b9-10). For example, one becomes virtuous by doing the types of actions

---

[9] I separate courage and fortitude here with the special qualification that fortitude might involve an endurance to withstand pressure and suffering. This specific characteristic will be very important in discussing actions performed in response to pressures that typically overstrain human nature (e.g., divulging or keeping a secret under extreme torture).

that virtuous people do repeatedly and over time. Oftentimes, we do certain types of acts repeatedly because we experience pleasure in doing them; others we avoid because of previous experiences of painful consequences. As a disposition to act in a particular way develops, the individual acquiring the character begins to take pleasure in doing the acts that accord with this habit (*NE* 1099a19-20). By taking pleasure in the good, for instance, an agent identifies something that is actually good as good. On the other hand, when a person does the types of acts repeatedly that a vicious person might do, that person will eventually take pleasure in those acts. The more we behave a certain way, the more comfortable we are with such behavior. We are pleased by the comfortable and familiar. Without any pain associated with such acts (i.e., let us pretend our imaginary agent is not punished for her behaviors and finds no reason to be discouraged in repeating them), the agent easily behaves similarly in the future. As vicious acts become familiar and easy, the agent performing them takes delight in so doing. Therefore, just as was the case with the agent performing good acts consistently, she who behaves badly consistently begins to identify her own ends as good and choiceworthy. However, unlike the agent who behaves well, the agent who behaves badly is *not* correct in her identification of the good. When others blame her, they communicate their disapproval of the behavior, and the agent might reconsider her previous judgment of choiceworthy ends. However, this may depend on how entrenched her character already is.

Once acquired, a character state perpetuates itself.[10] That is, the agent's moral perception is informed by the character that she has. Vicious people view bad ends as good ones, while virtuous people have keen moral perception (*NE* 1113a 31-34, 1114b 2, 1114b 21-24). Since, ultimately, every human acts towards some apparent good (*NE* 1110b11), what is viewed as the good by a given individual is what she pursues as well as that in

---

[10] I use the term 'perpetuate' here loosely. As I argue in Anton 2014, if given sufficient time and consistent expression, both the continent and the incontinent character states may undo themselves. Hopefully, one who acts continently consistently over time will eventually become virtuous. Unfortunately, one who behaves incontinently consistently and over time may slide into viciousness. Still, as it is rare that anyone behave incontinently across the board and without qualification, we can imagine one who is mostly incontinent remaining that way throughout a lifetime so long as she behaves sufficiently occasionally continent that it prevents vice. Indeed, we might imagine that a basically continent person 'slips up' and behaves more as an incontinent person would often enough to protract her moral development sufficiently that she never reaches full virtue. Therefore, there is a sense in which both the continent and the incontinent perpetuate themselves; each perpetuates itself for a time and, when a person waffles between the two, neither takes full hold. However, I maintain my position that continence and incontinence do, *in principle* and eventually, undo themselves. Vice and Virtue are distinctly more self-perpetuating in this regard.

which she delights when she achieves it. Therefore, a character state moves an agent towards doing the kinds of acts that led to the formation of that character[11] in the first place.[12]

Since, characters are dispositions to feel and act certain ways, characters can be identified and assessed by analyzing their effects: types of actions done and accompanying feelings. The ends a person selects and what a person enjoys are determined by the type of character that she has (*NE* 1099a19-20, 1115b21-22). Therefore, if we witness someone intentionally harming an innocent with great amusement, we might conclude that she is vicious. Likewise, if it is evident that it pains an agent to do the right thing, though she brings herself to do it nevertheless, we believe that she is continent, though not yet virtuous.

3. The Notion of the Voluntary from Sourcehood and Knowledge

Recall the two ways Aristotle distinguishes the voluntary from the involuntary: the agent has knowledge of the relevant particular facts of the behavior, and she is the origin or source of the action. It is common to consider these two criteria for the voluntary jointly sufficient. Let us call this position **2C** (for *two criteria*) and let 'K' stand for "The agent has the relevant particular knowledge" and 'S' stand for "The agent is the source of the behavior." **2C** maintains:

$$((K \& S) \rightarrow V)$$

There is a natural way to read the passage cited above from *NE* III.i 1111a 22-24 as stating the joint sufficiency of the two criteria (**2C**). After all, Aristotle does conclude "…the voluntary would seem to be that of which the moving principle is in the agent him-

---

[11] There is a wealth of literature on this consequence of Aristotelian character concerning the possibility of character change. Brickhouse suggests that one cannot alter one's character because once sufficiently fixed, it would be impossible to act contrary to that character (which is what is required to develop a contrary state). Bondeson suggests that Aristotle did believe in character change, but that it was difficult given the proclivities of the agent and the types of ends towards which she acts. Ott discusses the argument Aristotle develops for our being responsible for our character, arguing that Aristotle jumps to his conclusion. While we might be responsible for individual acts, it does not follow, says Ott, that we are responsible for our character. Di Muzio argues that character can be altered only if a vicious person were to happen to imitate a virtuous person's actions by chance in pursuit of some other goal (e.g., avoiding misery). In another paper (Anton 2006), I argue that fixed characters can be altered, but only if the change is initiated from without (i.e. external). If a person is influenced by others to act contrary to character (that is, others select her ends for her and manipulate her into pursuing them), the fixed habit can be weakened.

[12] This is, in part, due to the fact that, for Aristotle, reason alone does not act (1112b13). Therefore, while an incontinent person might know what is better, she might not be able to do what is better based on this knowledge. Her character is attracted to the worse, and for this reason it selects worse ends for action. Also, see Tuozzo (1991) for a convincing discussion of why, for Aristotle, we do not deliberate about our ends.

self, he being aware of the particular circumstances of the action." Nevertheless, we might not be entitled to draw this conclusion, as the "definition" describes what *seems to be* (*doxeien an enai*) voluntary. For this and other reasons that will soon become apparent, I believe this description is a description *for the most part*. We might describe birds as feathered winged bipedal animals. Usually, they are. But we can imagine a man in a bird costume meeting this description, and we can imagine a bird that's lost a wing or its feathers is still a bird. In a similar vein, I think that it is reasonable to consider these two criteria a *sign* of voluntary behavior. However, as I shall now argue, they are hardly sufficient.

I believe **2C** is false; it is not the case that the two criteria alone are sufficient for voluntary action in humans. Surprisingly, it should require little imagination to find a counterexample to this view. Simply consider any nutritive action of which the agent is aware. For instance, my heart is beating right now. I can concentrate on the pulses if I apply pressure to a specific place on my wrist or neck. I know why the pulse is happening. I am familiar with the relevant particulars. It also originates from within me. I am the source of my nutritive behaviors.

One might object that such action is not really *mine*; it is *my body's*. Such an objection would work for just about anyone else's account (Plato's, for instance). Yet, Aristotle's view of the human *psyche* obviates this concern. As was described earlier, for Aristotle, a human soul has three parts: reason, appetite, and a "life force" often referred to as the nutritive part. The nutritive part tends to all autonomic behaviors such as blood flow, breathing (when we're not doing it intentionally), nervous reactions, growth, digestion, etc. Therefore, *my soul* is the source of the behavior and, as Aristotle aptly notes, a human is most its form, which is its soul.[13] Furthermore, we cannot consider such behaviors acceptable "exceptions," as they are abundant. Any rule that admits such a plethora of exceptions ought not be considered a rule.

In no way do I wish to suggest that Aristotle foolishly considered digestion and blood flow voluntary actions. On the contrary, I am certain that he would not, and for this reason, we ought to abandon **2C** as a conclusive description of the voluntary.

Perhaps some may prefer to consider the two criteria negatively; perhaps the lack of either criterion is sufficient to consider a behavior *involuntary*. Let us call this position **2I**, where *I* stands for "The agent's behavior is involuntary":

---

[13] In *Categories*, Aristotle introduces secondary substance (Ch. IV, V), which is the kind of thing a substance is (in the example of a person, this is *human*. Cf *Physics* (*Phys.*) 194a-195b 30 (secondary substance as a cause); *Metaphysics* (*Meta.*) IV 1029b14-15 (being one's essence). For humans, the mind is the form of the hylomorphic compound, which is its actuality (*De Anima* (*DA*) ii 1, 412b5–6).

$$(I \rightarrow (\sim K \vee \sim S))$$

Alas, proposition **2I** is also false. If it were true, then behaviors caused by ignorance of the particular facts of the situation would always be involuntary. Aristotle explicitly denies this possibility when he introduces the class of behaviors I shall call *merely non-voluntary* (*ouk hekousion*). Aristotle tells us that behaviors caused by the innocent ignorance of particulars are non-voluntary, but only those that one regrets are involuntary (*NE* III.i 1110b19-21). This exception renders moral assessment mysterious. Any such non-voluntary act must be neither praiseworthy nor blameworthy (by definition and as stipulated above). However, as it is not involuntary either, this act ought not be pardoned. Still, there are instances whereby some reactive attitude seems appropriate.

In order to illustrate this problem, consider the following example. Terry dislikes children. One day, while out for a drive, Terry hits a child with his car, and the child dies. Terry did not see the child running through the parked cars. Let us presume that he had no reason to suspect that a child would pop out from between the cars (so Terry is not guilty of any negligence that might have caused his ignorance of the child's presence). However, when Terry realizes what he has done, he is slightly amused: "One less brat in the world! I did the world a favor!" he thinks to himself.

Terry feels no regret. From what we can tell about the two criteria and the nature of praise, blame, and pardon, we have no idea how to handle Terry. There seems to be no appropriate response given Aristotle's account if we rely on *NE* III.i exclusively. And yet, I want to blame Terry. Of course, I do not want to blame Terry for the act of running over the child. I concur with Aristotle that under no interpretation did Terry commit that act voluntarily. But his amusement suggests some kind of psychological consent to the state of affairs that is morally troubling (to say the least). We shall return to the terrible case of Terry in our analysis of the proposed interpretation.

Why might Aristotle have introduced this class of behaviors? I contend that his reasons are related to the fact that **2C** and **2I** are false. I believe that the merely non-voluntary will help to illustrate a proposition concerning the voluntary that is true.

Instead of conceptualizing the voluntary as that which is the opposite of the involuntary (as Aristotle seems to at *NE* III.i 1111a21-22) perhaps we ought to broaden **2I** to encompass all non-voluntary behavior. Once we arrive at such a proposition, perhaps we need only to negate that proposition to identify the voluntary (as nothing is both voluntary and non-voluntary). For argument's sake, let us see where this takes us. Let 'N' stand for "The behavior is non-voluntary." Let us call this proposition **NV** (*non-voluntary*):

$$(N \rightarrow (\sim K \vee \sim S))$$

Let us now consider what happens when we assume the negation of **NV**:

1. ~(N→(~K v ~S))   premise
2. N & ~(~K v ~S))   conditional equivalence, 1
3. ~(~K v ~S))   & elimination 2
4. (~~K & ~~S)   DeMorgan's
5.   K & ~~S   double negation elimination 8
6.   K & S   double negation elimination 9

The result is the converse of **2C** (let us call it '**CV**' (for consequent of V)): V→(K & S)
This proposition is likely true; however, it only tells us two necessary conditions for the voluntary. It does not give us a complete account. We already saw how **2C** is false *because* it claimed K & S were jointly sufficient conditions for voluntary behavior. Therefore, we must continue our search for a more complete understanding of the voluntary according to Aristotle than the description offered at *NE* III.i.

It seems that, at the very least, we need to add a third criterion or, at most, we need to supplant these two entirely. Readers should decide for themselves, which I have done.[14] I maintain that, with a loose understanding of the requisite "knowledge" of the particulars, a limited scope of *sourcehood,* and an adequacy condition of remaining firmly in the realm of what is most human about the agents in question, our understanding of the voluntary will be complete. Introducing the *eph' hēmin* helps make these qualifications.

4. Eph' Hēmin

At this point, some might interject that Aristotle already gave us a third criterion – that which is voluntary is *eph' hēmin*, or "up to us." Aristotle tells us that whenever behavior is voluntary, we may do it or not do it: "For where it is in our power to act it is also in our power not to act, and *vice versa*" (*NE* III.i 1113b9-13; *Cf NE* III.i 1110a17-18, III.iv 1113b6-13). This statement reminds contemporary scholars of a common incompatibilist notion of free will and moral responsibility: the Principle of Alternate Possibilities (PAP), which holds that in order to be morally responsible for φ-ing, it must have been possible to refrain from φ-ing. Let us call this position **3C**, which maintains that a behavior is voluntary

---

[14] If my qualifications of knowledge, sourcehood, and human nature strike the reader as too revisionary to resemble the standard interpretation of K and S, then perhaps the reader would prefer to consider my proposal a complete overhaul of the standard account. As long as I have argued convincingly that what follows is supported by Aristotle's texts and compatible with his overall anthropology and ethics, the reader and I shall be in agreement regarding what matters most.

if the agent has sufficient knowledge of the particulars, she is the source of her behavior, and she has free will (F):

$$((K \& S) \& F) \rightarrow V$$

When *freedom* is understood as *eph' hēmin*, the above proposition is likely true. However, freedom in the metaphysical sense of the term (the one implied in discussions of PAP) is not the missing criteria.[15] While it may be sufficient, this kind of freedom is not necessary. The relevant sense of freedom involves a kind of control that can only be explained in reference to the character center.

I say that what is *eph' hēmin* is in reference to the character center for the following reasons. First, nutritive behavior is not *eph' hēmin*; even if we are aware of the nutritive acts we perform, it is not possible (nor was it ever possible) that we perform them differently (*NE* III.v 1113b25-30).

Another reason why behavior that is *eph' hēmin* must issue from the character center is that the character center (insofar as appetite is part of it) is responsible for the efficient causation of voluntary acts, and what it means to be the origin of such behaviors is (among other things) to be the efficient cause (*Phys.* 194b29-30, 195a11), which includes omissions (*Phys*.195a11-14). Therefore, in being the efficient cause, the character center is able to perform an act or refrain from performing the act.

Third, what is *eph' hēmin* is sensitive to what reason knows insofar as its options are concerned, as reason is the efficient cause of behavior through choice (*NE* VI.ii 1139a31-32). Barring reason's ignorance of general moral truths (which is more often than not a flaw voluntarily acquired), when reason is ignorant of the particular facts of the case, reason is also ignorant of all of the options that are truly available to it. Reason cannot choose what it does not know is available. Therefore, when reason "refrains" from choosing an unknown option that is unknown due to ignorance of particulars, reason could not have chosen otherwise. For this reason, it is not *eph 'hēmin* for reason to neglect such options.

5. Human Nature and Natural Impulse

The voluntary is also discussed in *Eudemian Ethics (EE)*. While this account is often deemed the earlier account and the account of *NE* the refined version, an examination into this account may provide insight into any additional requirements of voluntary behavior.[16]

---

[15] For convincing explanations of why this is the case, see Everson 1990, Klimchuk 2002, and Meyer 2006, 138.

[16] Meyer 2006 argues that the *Eudemian* account is the beginning of a dialectical exercise in describing the voluntary that is taken up again in *Nicomachean Ethics* (i.e., as such, it is consistent with that in

Aristotle proposes that the voluntary is that which accords with impulse and the involuntary is that which is contrary to impulse (*EE* 1225b 1-2). It would seem that Aristotle is considering action exclusively here; for every emotion that an agent has is in accordance with impulse at least insofar as it is in accordance with itself.[17] Additionally, insofar as action is concerned, this proposal will not work. Aristotle recognizes that he will have strange results in the cases of the incontinent and the continent persons, who have multiple opposing impulses. They would seem to act both voluntarily and involuntarily (which Aristotle explicitly declares impossible (*EE* 1223b9-10)). In order to reconcile these problems, Aristotle discusses the voluntary as that which is a "natural motion" and the involuntary as that which is a "forced" or "violent motion" (*EE* 1223a 24-26 and 1224a 4-5). The conclusion of this section is that contrariety to impulse is always external to the agent (*EE* 1224a 19-22). That is, for an agent's action to be involuntary, the action must go against the agent's impulse and also be external to the agent.[18] This sounds similar to the description of the first criterion offered at the beginning of *NE* III.i – that the agent be the source of that which is voluntary. Indeed, in *NE*, Aristotle distinguishes voluntary behavior from the involuntary thusly:

> Those things, then, are thought involuntary, which take place under compulsion or owing to ignorance; and that is compulsory of which the moving principle is outside, being a principle in which nothing is contributed by the person who acts or is acted upon, e.g. if he were to be carried somewhere by a wind, or by men who had him in their power (NE III.i 1110 a 1-4).

Like in EE, here it is suggested that the involuntary involves an external principle. More clearly, the act is involuntary if the agent or victim contributes nothing. This would seem to suggest that if the agent contributes anything at all to the act, the act is not involuntary. However, I contend that the account in *EE* is not merely an earlier version of the source condition. By focusing on impulse, the *EE* account excludes the nutritive aspect of

---

Nicomachean Ethics). I follow Meyer in this regard. What this account provides that is useful is a notion of something being in accordance with the internal and natural impulse of the agent. While this notion requires some refining to explain blameworthy incontinent behavior, it has its intuitive value in understanding how an agent must be the source of her voluntary behavior.

[17] Of course, if Aristotle is not limiting the discussion to actions, then this passage would suggest Aristotle considers all emotions voluntary. I do not think this a trivial point. It is hard to imagine how emotion might be contrary to impulse. The only way that it could is to be contrary to another impulse. But then the person would behave both voluntarily and involuntarily at the same time, which is not possible according to Aristotle. I suggest that we keep an open mind at this point as to what constitutes an impulse. In addition, there is groundwork laid for a discussion of praising and blaming emotion in *EE* (1223 b 18-29) and this issue is echoed in *NE* III.i.

[18] See Heinaman 1988.

the soul, limiting our attention to the character center. In addition, it appears to suggest that some motions exhibited by humans are *natural*, while others are *violent* as if they are happening more to the person than being done by the person. An agent's body might move in ways that feel foreign to the agent (as when swept away by a violent wind), and for this reason, the agent is not considered to voluntarily act on such occasions.

At this juncture, it is clear that the semantics of K, S, and F matter a great deal. Let us consider how we may refine these notions so that we may better see what links them all together as features of voluntary behavior.

6. Knowledge Qualified

Here would be the standard place to remind readers how Aristotle qualifies *knowledge* to mean knowledge of the particulars only, and not general knowledge of moral truths. While this qualification will matter a great deal for my account, it is not the qualification I wish to illuminate in this section. Instead, I shall explain how the scope of this criterion may require more or less qualification.

Recall how at the outset of our inquiry, we reminded ourselves that the voluntary is broader than that of the kind of actions Aristotle proceeds to describe. Indeed, Aristotle tells us that animals and small children have a share in the voluntary (*NE* 1111b 6-9). While I do believe that the voluntary manifests differently in a cow than it does in an adult human, it might not be the case that I can dismiss the knowledge requirement for the former.

In addition to including animals and small children in the voluntary, Aristotle makes reference to them when considering the types of actions adult humans undertake that may be considered voluntary. Aristotle considers whether human voluntary behavior is in accordance with desire (*orexis*) choice (*prohairesis*) or thought (*daionoia*) (*EE* II.vii 1223a24-27).

Desire is further divided into three types: wish (*boulesis*), spirit (*thumos*), and sensual appetite (*epithumos*). Wish is too specific to be present in all voluntary behavior, for the incontinent person acts against her wish (and, on some occasions, her choice (*prohairesis*) as well). But these are the kinds of behaviors for which she regularly deserves blame. And as we already noted at the beginning of our inquiry, if a behavior deserves blame, it is voluntary. Therefore, if we are correct in blaming incontinent behavior (and I believe that we are), it cannot be the case that all voluntary behavior issues from wish.

However, it cannot be the case that all voluntary behavior issues from choice either. First, we often act quickly with little thought and even from habit (*NE* III.ii-v). Such behaviors can be blameworthy. Imagine a parent leaves an infant in a bathtub as it fills up to answer the phone. Imagine that same parent becomes engaged in a conversation about trivial matters, and she completely forgets she had left the infant in the tub. Imagine that the infant sadly drowns. Clearly the parent did not *intentionally* drown the child. Therefore, the parent did not choose to drown the child, as choice, for Aristotle, involves deliberation. As the parent's behavior was not deliberate, it is difficult to see how she may have deliberated. Still, such negligent behavior would seem to be the kind for which one deserves blame.

We also behave voluntarily under time-constraints. Imagine a parent arrives home to find her babysitter alone and outside her home ablaze. Imagine she rushes into the home, finds her child, and rescues it from the fire. Imagine she does so without deliberation or choice.[19] After all, there wasn't time for such things. This parent behaved from habit and love – not choice. Still, I consider her praiseworthy.

These two examples of parenting illustrate that choice is too specific to qualify as the standard and universal cause of all voluntary behavior. In addition, Aristotle reminds us that animals and children have a share in the voluntary, but neither has the capacity of choice (*prohairesis*). Aristotle's use of animals and small children as counterexamples to the claim that all that is voluntary is chosen is puzzling. By pointing to animals and small children's lack of reason as an indicator that *choice* may not be necessary for the voluntary behavior we praise and blame, Aristotle seems to suggest that the relevant voluntary behavior of adult humans also need not require reason. However, Aristotle concludes that voluntary behavior *is* in accordance with thought (*daionoia*) (*EE* II.viii 1223b39-1224a8). For this reason we might need to qualify the knowledge requirement. It is apparent that in his discussion of the voluntary in *NE* Aristotle is considering behaviors of adult humans. After all, his examples are all human adults. And yet, Aristotle's descriptions of *knowledge* throughout his corpus seem to consider knowledge to rest firmly with the rational part of the soul (*NE* VI.iii-xi). The rational part of the soul *just is* reason. However, as we just saw, animals lack reason entirely, and young children have yet to develop it; still, both have a share in the voluntary where the scope of *the voluntary* in play is one where discussions of particular knowledge are relevant.

Animals *never* have knowledge in the sense that Aristotle frequently discusses. Children have reason the way they have reproductive capacities – as potentialities. Children's reason is dormant and underdeveloped, and it is not clear at what age a child's reason is fully developed (modern science might put it somewhere in the mid-twenties, which seems far too late to justify praising and blaming them). Therefore, the *knowledge* they employ when behaving voluntarily would seem to be quite weak. Animals and children

---

[19] Aristotle states clearly that such behavior is possible at *NE* III.ii 1112a14-16.

must have something *like* knowledge. For example, animals might respond to appearances (*phantasma*). But the "knowledge" employed in each instance must be more like *awareness*.

Indeed, I believe the same must be true for adult humans when they are acting quickly under pressure. Consider the example of the parent returning home to find it ablaze. The parent didn't have to confirm with the babysitter that the child was inside. Noticing the child was absent was sufficient to motivate her heroism. Naturally, if the child had been at the neighbor's house, her behavior would be quite unfortunate (especially if any harm came to the parent). What this example shows us is that the knowledge may be minimal (and minimally justified) provided it is accurate.

Aristotle lists six kinds of ignorance of the particulars that might excuse behavior. First, the agent might not be aware of who she is. This ignorance is likely rare and probably applies to people with mental illness or head trauma. Second, the agent might be ignorant of what he or she is doing. The agent might not realize she is leaning on a button that, if pushed, executes a damaging command. Third, one might be ignorant of who or what is affected. For instance, imagine that I turn the knob of a door and push it open. I have no reason to suspect anyone would be affected by my action. However, unbeknownst to me, a maintenance person is working on the knob of the door at the other side. I inadvertently shove the doorknob into her nose, thus breaking it. I was ignorant that anyone would be affected by my behavior. Fourth, one might be ignorant of the means one is using. For instance, a hostess might serve a guest food containing an ingredient neither of them is aware will aggravate the guest's allergy. The hostess (and her guest) believes she is nourishing the guest. She does not realize that the means she uses is also a means to making the guest ill. Fifth, one might be ignorant of the result intended by one's action. For instance, imagine a waitress serves a customer a drink that was poisoned by the customer's worst enemy just before it was placed on the service counter. The waitress did poison the customer. But the waitress did not realize that she was a pawn in the enemy's dastardly plot. She thought she was merely fulfilling the customer's order. Sixth, one might be ignorant of the manner in which they act. For instance, imagine a friend embraces another friend tightly upon a joyful reunion. Imagine the embracer did not know that the friend just recently injured her back. Under normal circumstances, such an embrace would be suitable. Under the current circumstances, the embrace is not sufficiently gentle. Therefore, the first friend is unaware that she embraces her friend too harshly, since such embraces have never caused the friend pain before and she has no reason to question the strength she exerts at the present moment (*NE* III.i 1110b 33-1111a 1-15).

None of these instances of ignorance of the facts resemble the kind of situation typically requiring considered investigation, cognitive calculation, or even deliberation between options. Indeed, we might imagine that we are often merely *aware* of such facts on a day-to-day basis. When such awareness is accurate, we perform the behaviors we mean to perform. The fact that we may be merely mildly justified in our thoughts on the situation is irrelevant. We cannot possibly investigate every behavior thoroughly prior to exhibiting it. For this reason, I suggest that the kind of knowledge that is required is more like a perceptive awareness of the conditions in which we act. For the most part, such awareness is easily justified by past experience and even subconscious inductive "reasoning." It is only when the particulars are not as one would expect that excuses are warranted.

There are many instances that might defy such excuses. These include instances when the agent should expect to take such matters into consideration as well as instances when the agent has personal special obligations to be certain about the particulars. Let's consider an example of each kind in turn. An instance of the first type might involve driving a vehicle behind a school bus. When the bus halts, a "Stop" sign protrudes from the street side of the vehicle. Imagine that Terry (from the previous example) decides to pass the bus anyway, since he cannot see anyone crossing the street. Once again, Terry runs over a child, thus killing the child. Terry may have been ignorant of the fact that a child was about to cross the street. Terry may have been ignorant of the fact that the child might cross his path so quickly that he'd have no time to apply his break. But Terry's ignorance is not an excuse. Terry should know that the "Stop" signs on the sides of buses are there to prevent accidents just like this one, which just occurred. Terry might exclaim defensively, "But I thought that child lived on the other side of the street!" However, this explanation gets Terry nowhere. Terry should know of the possibility that a child will dart across the road. His ignorance of the particulars was no excuse.

Imagine the scenario were slightly different. Imagine the child did live on that side of the street, the child did not cross the street, and Terry did not hit any children. A nearby police car sees Terry's traffic violation, pulls Terry over, and issues him a citation. Imagine Terry offers the officer the same excuse as above concerning where the child lives. The officer is not persuaded. Terry deserves blame (and a ticket) because Terry should know not to risk harming any child. It is true that Terry is not to blame for hitting any children simply because Terry did not hit any children. However, Terry got lucky. Therefore, it is not sufficient that Terry is correct in his awareness and anticipation of the particular circumstances. It appears that the knowledge requirement concerns reasonable guesses. The agent need not *know* in the strongest sense of the term all of the relevant particulars. But the agent must be aware of particulars insofar as the agent can be expected to imagine them, and that perception must be sufficiently accurate (according to the conditions listed by Aristotle).

Finally, certain special obligations raise the threshold for the degree of justifiable certainty required for an agent to be excused when ignorance of the particulars causes the agent to behave badly. Physicians are expected to take and consider a patient's vital signs prior to administering any treatment. Imagine Dr. Smith neglects to take a patient's blood pressure prior to administering to that patient a blood thinner. When the patient's blood pressure drops drastically to a medically dangerous level, Dr. Smith is not excused for being ignorant of the patient's already low blood pressure. It is Dr. Smith's job to investigate the patient's condition thoroughly prior to administering any medication.

Now, we are in a position to reconsider the knowledge of particulars required for the voluntary. In most instances, this knowledge need only be an accurate general awareness of the facts as anyone in that position could be reasonably expected to imagine them. That is why we might not fault a watchdog that barks aggressively at a noise in the backyard in the middle of the night, not realizing its owner slipped outside to reset the sprinklers. There's no reason the dog would suspect the owner would be prowling about her own property after dark. The dog imagined it was alerting its owner of a prowler, not that it was barking aggressively *at* its owner. However, had the dog been alerting its owner to an actual threat, the owner would not be wrong to praise the animal. Similarly, a child who steals a friend's toy because it is identical to one the child has at home (so, she mistakes it for her own) might be forgiven because the child may not have developed any understanding of object permanence. Perhaps the child cannot yet reason that if the toy was left behind at home, it could not have miraculously appeared at the friend's house. The child is aware of which toys it has and whether it has permission to play with those toys. But the child cannot rationalize the degree of awareness it would take to recognize that the toy is more likely a duplicate than that it travelled through a wormhole independently. Such a scenario is very different from an older child who steals a toy from her friend simply because she likes it. Imagine that child was rational enough to hide the toy in her backpack and stealthily remove it when her parents weren't looking, storing it safely in her closet. That child is blameworthy for stealing her friend's toy. The first child is not. The first child cannot be expected to have the degree of awareness required to know of the unique likeness of the particular toys. The second child most certainly knew exactly what she was doing. She believed the toy was not hers, she was correct in that belief, and yet she stole it anyway.

As long as we are comfortable qualifying the type of knowledge of the particulars necessary, I am happy to continue to endorse the knowledge requirement. This knowledge can be a mere perceptual awareness or an animalistic "judgment" based on such awareness.

There are conditions that could raise the threshold of cognition and certainty required to consider any cognitive excuses. The threshold and kind of cognition should be sensitive to the kind of cognition of which the agent is both capable and morally obligated to employ. For this reason, the ignorance of the particulars of our watchdog's situation excuse the animal's unfriendly treatment of its owner, whereas the ignorance of Dr. Smith's patient's blood pressure hardly excuses Dr. Smith's endangering that patient's health.

7. Qualifying Sourcehood

Aristotle takes care to distinguish agency from influence in *NE* III.i, and he concludes that influence is rarely exculpatory. For Aristotle, the agent is the source of her behavior unless the agent contributes nothing to the behavior (*NE* III.i 1110a2, 1110b17). In other words, compulsion (an excusing condition) must be external to the agent. Agents are not compelled from within. Aristotle makes this clear in a discussion of several specific scenarios. Perhaps the most informative is that of the so-called "mixed actions."

A mixed action is one that, in the abstract, is undesirable, but in the particular circumstance, is desirable. Aristotle gives two compelling examples. First, he imagines we do something undesirable because a tyrant has control over our family and will harm them if we do not perform the ordered task. We might imagine instances like the following: a bank teller assists dangerous robbers in robbing a bank because they have taken her family hostage and they threatened to harm her family if she does not comply. Second, he describes a scenario where a ship is in a dangerous storm. It is essential to saving the lives of those on board to throw cargo overboard to lighten the weight of the ship. Normally, no one would voluntarily discard the cargo whose transport was the entire point of the journey. However, under these unusually bad circumstances, such an act is desirable (*NE* III.i 1110a9-12).

Aristotle describes how the *endoxa* would have it that there are some actions that are involuntary because the action considered by itself is fundamentally undesirable, and no one would naturally want to perform such an action. Therefore, the conditions that impose the necessity of such behavior must disqualify that behavior from moral assessment. After all, we do not want to blame people on such occasions. If one does such an act, one does it from fear of greater evils or for some noble object (*NE* III.i 1110a 5). However, Aristotle distinguishes the situation from the act in order to determine whether it is voluntary, and then reconsiders the act in light of the situation to determine praise or blame. First, he notes that if we ignore the situation and the type of act that is done (i.e. that it is a discarding of property), it is undeniable that the agent is the source of motion and knows the particulars, suggesting that his action is voluntary. Reconsidered in light of the situation, we can see that discarding property was *the best action available*, and therefore desirable at the time of acting (*NE* III.i 1110a 14-18). The *endoxa* is correct that we ought not to blame such an agent. However, the reason our agent is exempt from blame is not because the behavior was sufficiently coerced to render it *involuntary*. On the contrary, the agent performs the act because it is the morally best course of action. Therefore, the agent ought to be praised for doing the right thing and saving lives. Blame is out of the question because the unusual particular circumstances render a typically bad act a good one. Since we only ever act in particular situations and under specific circumstances, and since we never act *in general*, so-called mixed actions are voluntary. The only reason to be tempted to call them involuntary is their inherently general undesirability. But no one ever acts *in general*. Instead, we act at specific times and places and with limited options (and even fewer if we are innocently unaware of some of those options).

We act voluntarily under sub-optimal conditions often. The fact that we may not like our options is not enough to make our choosing one involuntary. We could imagine any action with foreseeable unpleasant consequences satisfying this description. We do not say that we purchase milk "involuntarily" because we paid for it, and we would prefer to take it for free. We do not say that we exercise "involuntarily" because we are "compelled" to do so by the knowledge that a failure to exercise makes one unhealthy, which is more painful than exercise (as if any painful predictable outcome renders an action undesirable, "mixed," or a matter of fear from "great" evils).

Likewise, claims Aristotle, no one is "compelled" (in the sense that renders behavior involuntary) to behave well. While there is a sense in which the virtuous are psychologically incapable of voluntarily performing base acts, the reason for their apparent compulsion is their good nature. The fact that the virtuous *will not* behave otherwise voluntarily does not mean their behavior fails to be *eph' hēmin*. Their behavior remains contingent; they are the kinds of creatures that could have behaved differently (despite the fact that they will not). The virtuous (as well as the vicious) are responsible for their characters (*NE* III.v). Aristotle is a proponent of *tracing*, the notion that we can be responsible for behaviors we cannot help but to exhibit when this inflexibility is a consequence of earlier behaviors for which we were responsible. Virtue and vice are like this. It would be ridiculous to claim the virtuous person does not act voluntarily (and therefore deserves no praise) for her good acts because she no longer can voluntarily behave differently. She is so good as a result of performing the kinds of acts that made her virtuous repeatedly. When performing *those* acts, the agent could have failed to do so. In this sense, her actions were *eph' hēmin* (up to her) in that she could have done them or refrained from doing them. Just as it would be ridiculous to disclaim responsibility for the death of a person one intentionally shoots on the basis that the shooter did not kill the person, the bullet did, it is ridiculous to claim that a virtuous person does not voluntarily perform her good actions, her character does.

Interestingly, there is a way in which Aristotle speaks of non-voluntary behavior that mirrors such distancing tactics. For instance, recall that Aristotle distinguishes acting *due to* ignorance (*agnoian prattein*) and acting *in* ignorance (*agnoounta poiein*). Indeed, even in English the distinct agencies are implied. When one acts unwittingly involuntarily, the behavior (described as a bad act) is more a result of her ignorance than her character center. Much like how only eyes can be blind (and not hands or feet), our ignorance is only a deficiency *of ours* if we, by nature, are supposed to have knowledge in its place according to our function. A perfectly well functioning human being can be said to be "ignorant" of the precise moment the sun will rise in a city in China, and such "ignorance" is like the "blindness" of one's hand. It is no more the work of a human to know exhaustive bits of trivia of no particular significance than it is the work of a hand to see. When our ignorance is not our fault, *it* causes our behavior. When our ignorance is blameworthy, we are said to act *in* that ignorance much like one might act *in* a fit of rage. Our anger (and its consequences) is as much ours as our culpable ignorance (and its consequences) are. While our merely non-voluntary actions do, in a way, issue from the character center (as we often intend to do *something* when we act), the causal connection between the character center and the *telos* achieved by the action is sufficiently interrupted to disconnect the agent from the effects of her action.

Today's reader might lament Aristotle's language concerning the causes of involuntary behavior done by force as well. In his example of one being carried away by a strong wind, readers complain that the "action" isn't really one of the agent's at all. Instead, it is something done *to* the agent. Modern speakers would prefer to say, "I was blown away by a gust of wind" to "I blew away by a gust of wind." The latter invokes images of one riding a gust of wind as a surfer rides a wave. But Aristotle is not suggesting anything intentional. Indeed, the point of the example is that the agent did not cause the event. Aristotle tells us that involuntary actions done by force are those whereby the agent *contributes nothing*. But if the agent contributes nothing, how can the event be one of the agent's behaviors?

The answer is made clear by attention to the character center's role in voluntary behavior. When we are blown away by a gust of wind, our appetite is not the efficient cause. Similarly, when we act due to ignorance, our reason is not the cause of our behavior, its misfortune is. Aristotle not only distinguishes forced acts as having *external* causes, he distinguishes unwitting acts as having a *foreign* cause (ignorance) in a way that disassociates the agent from responsibility for the act.

Limiting the scope of *sourcehood* on Aristotle's account of the voluntary to the character center separates *foreign* causes according to our considered intuitions. First, nutritive acts of which we are aware would be disqualified outright. They do not issue from the character center. This is convenient because we intuitively view such behaviors as non-voluntary. More importantly nutritive behaviors are not *eph' hēmin*. Even if I am aware of my tummy rumbling, and even if I understand the digestion process well, I cannot voluntarily refrain from making the noise. Therefore, while I do understand the particulars of the situation in which I exhibit such behavior, and while it is true that the behavior emanates from within me, I am not its *source* in the relevant sense because I am not *causing* my behavior via the efficient-teleological powers of my character center. We saw how the two criteria alone could not get us this result, since nutritive acts issue from the nutritive soul. Since only the behaviors for which our character center is the source can be *eph' hēmin*, we may take the mental shortcut in limiting the scope of sourcehood in this way.

My suggestion of limiting our scope of sourcehood to the character center also helps us make sense of our intuitions concerning certain merely non-voluntary behavior. Whenever one accidentally performs a bad act and does not respond appropriately, that agent is demonstrating something important about her character (or characteristics of her character center in instances prior to character acquisition). The aspect demonstrated is a character flaw. Since good people do not want to behave badly, it pains them to learn that they have done something wrong. This is true even if they recognize that they weren't at fault, since someone who wants to be good doesn't want to be even associated with the bad. One who is already good simply doesn't want unwarranted harm to come to anyone. Strangely, it might be morally appropriate to feel pain and regret for behavior for which one deserves no pain or reproach. The good person who acts badly non-voluntarily does not deserve to feel regret, but she will if she is a decent person.

Aristotle makes it clear that all involuntary actions are painful. If Terry is not pained by accidentally killing a child, something in Terry's character center has failed to appreciate the moral import of the situation. As Aristotle aptly notes, ignorance of moral truths is never an excuse – it is, in fact, something blameworthy itself. What's worse in Terry's case, delighting in the misfortune almost suggests a retroactive consent to the behavior and outcomes.[20] Reactions can be separate bits of behavior to evaluate (See Kosman 1980). There-

---

[20] Meyer (1989 and 2006 143-4) argues that regret is a sign that the action is one that goes 'against the grain of the agent.' I prefer Meyer's characterization to the common impulse to consider pain and regret signs that the agent would not have done the act had she knowledge of the particulars. I prefer Meyer's use of *going against the grain of the agent* because we can imagine an akratic agent acting due to ignorance of the particulars in a way she regrets even though her weak will may have led her to behave

fore, while it is absolutely true that Terry did not voluntarily kill the child (since the voluntary requires knowledge of relevant particulars), it is not clear that Terry does not voluntarily assess the outcome as favorable.

Merely non-voluntary actions give us an opportunity to delineate actions and their effects separately. Indeed, Terry acted non-voluntarily. We should not blame him for his action. His action was not *eph' hēmin* because he was not even aware of the action he was performing. He may have been the efficient cause of the tragedy, but his lack of cognitive grasp of the particulars that rendered the act of driving also an act of manslaughter precludes Terry from being the teleological cause. In driving, Terry was not pursuing any child-ridding goals; Terry could not have been aware of the fact that ridding the world of a child was a possibility.

Nevertheless, Aristotle did not have to stop here. Aristotle could have given us an example like Terry's to show that we can blame a reaction to a non-voluntary action. Since Terry's reaction is a true expression of his character and assessment of the event as it happened, we are justified in blaming Terry for that reaction.

One might argue that it is not up to Terry how he reacts to such situations, but this objection is misguided. Perhaps Terry cannot resist being gleeful about the result the same way that a virtuous person cannot resist spreading joy intentionally. But such behaviors are impulsive – *not compulsive*. As we learned from the account in *EE*, only involuntary behaviors go against the agent's impulse in the sense relevant to our inquiry.[21]

8. Human Nature and the Character Center

Qualifying the knowledge and sourcehood conditions through the lens of the *eph' hēmin* allows us to exclude nutritive behavior and merely non-voluntary actions from the voluntary while making better sense of our distaste for and reluctance to pity and forgive merely non-voluntary acts with morally unfavorable outcomes.[22] Behavior for which the

---

similarly with the relevant knowledge. There remains an important difference between acting due to ignorance and acting due to weak will that Meyer's phrasing captures well.

[21] One might also argue that we would not be justified in blaming Terry at all had he not shared with us his delight in the outcome, and this would be correct. However, the lack of justification in this scenario stems from our ignorance of Terry's internal reaction and not Terry's blameworthiness. *We* are not justified in blaming others when we do not know whether they deserve blame. But Terry does, in fact, deserve blame.

[22] We may eschew discussions of merely non-voluntary behaviors that are innocuous or even good. For instance, imagine I go outside to fetch the mail just in time to startle a cat that was terrorizing a nest of baby birds atop my porch. I did not harm the cat by startling it, but I did cause it to abandon its plan to snatch the birds just in time for the mama bird to return. The neighbor calls the cat, and it obediently runs

knowledge and sourcehood requirements are qualified by the *'eph hēmin* considered in light of human nature also allows us to make sense of occasions when mercy is appropriate.

Aristotle exempts agents from blame when they fail to meet superhuman standards. He writes:

> On some actions praise indeed is not bestowed, but forgiveness (*sungnōmē*) is, when one does what he ought not under pressure which overstrains human nature and which no one could withstand. (*NE* III.1 1110a 23-25)

A possible example might be if one were to divulge a secret under extreme torture, or make a false confession under torturous circumstances.[23] Given Aristotle's suggestion here of forgiveness, might he consider such acts involuntary?[24]

Unlike the so-called "mixed actions," Aristotle does not say whether these acts are voluntary. On the one hand, they satisfy the sourcehood and the knowledge requirements – even the qualified versions we have created. For this reason, we might be tempted to consider them voluntary. However, they do not pass the *eph' hēmin* test. A typical human under torture who is trying her best not to reveal a secret will eventually divulge the information. A typical human lacks the strength necessary to hold out indefinitely. Therefore, the agent did a bad thing and it was *not* true that she could both divulge the secret and refrain from divulging it. Therefore, in the instance of a typical human who tries to resist the temptation to perform the bad act but fails, the agent does not act voluntarily.

Interestingly, if a superhuman agent were to succeed in keeping the secret, we might want to praise her. After all, this feat is difficult. This may be appropriate provided the *godlike* character is similar enough to us to be an object of our praise. However, Aristotle makes it clear that we do not praise gods. We do not do so (presumably) because 1. Gods are above us (and virtue *NE* VII.i) and praise suggests we are in a position to judge she whom we praise as though we were equals and 2. The gods are happy and have an

---

home. I non-voluntarily saved the birds. I imagine I also non-voluntarily spared the cat a bird attack from the parent birds. I do not regret this. In fact, I am pleased by the outcome. I do not deserve praise for having done anything. But as my reaction is appropriate, I do not deserve blame either.

[23] While it is not impossible to keep a secret or tell the truth under such conditions, contemporary psychology and sociological research suggests that the vast majority of people are susceptible to such pressure. People who are able to withstand the torment and maintain their moral commitments might be considered exceptional human beings who exhibit the *godlike* character that Aristotle mentions, which is more aptly considered superhuman (i.e., beyond human nature).

[24] I grant that in saying we bestow pardon or pity on involuntary behavior, Aristotle is not committed to the idea that *we only* bestow pardon or pity on involuntary behavior. However, I believe we have more reason to consider behavior like that mentioned in the above passage involuntary than voluntary.

achievement in this regard (*NE* I.xii). We may congratulate others on achievements; yet praise seems inappropriate.

While the superhuman who withstands torture probably does so voluntarily, she does so as a superhuman. Just as the voluntary for a cow is different from that of a human, it is likely that superhuman or godlike voluntary behavior is in a class of its own. Furthermore, it is possible that superhumans are not as susceptible to praise and blame. First, being praised by an inferior is likely to matter little to them. Second, we might imagine that in *being* superhuman, the agent won't backslide and needs no external encouragement to develop, alter, or strengthen her character. If a godlike person performs a superhuman act, it is likely that she acts *eph' hēmin* and satisfies the human conditions of the voluntary. However, she is practically no longer human; she is *super*human. Therefore, the voluntary nature of her behavior is beyond the scope of our inquiry.

On the other hand, such instances help us to understand justified mercy when some humans perform bad acts under extreme pressure. Any human who resists the bad act initially will eventually give in. Perhaps it is better to consider divulging a secret under such circumstances a failure to sustain keeping it (and not a separate act). As noted above, since this human is not able to refrain from the bad act, the bad behavior is not *eph' hēmin*. Certainly, the human can *try* to keep the secret or *refrain from* even trying to keep the secret. What the human cannot do (successfully) is *keep the secret*. For this reason I consider her behavior involuntary. Her behavior only meets the original two requirements before we qualified them. Understood in light of the *eph' hēmin* requirement, such bad acts cannot be voluntary.

Even if the sourcehood and knowledge requirements were sufficient in themselves, the fact that human nature and not the character center causes the behavior is also excusing. The first thesis of this paper was that voluntary behavior is efficiently and teleologically caused by the character center, and our qualifications of the first two criteria are indicative of this adequacy condition. However, a failure to resist doing a bad act due to pressures overstraining human nature is a failure of human nature and not a failure of the individual in the situation. Just as ignorance of the particulars intercepts legitimate teleological causation, human nature can usurp efficient causation from the character center. Furthermore, as such behavior is caused by human nature and not the character center, no amount of blame could motivate a typical human to behave more heroically in the future.

9. Affectability

Praise and blame must be fitting and must have the potential to make their target better. Aristotle's view is not purely consequentialist. He does not suggest spreading false praise or blaming the innocent to steer them in the right direction. Indeed, I am confident that Aristotle doubted the potential success of such methods. Falsely praising others who do not deserve it leads to an inflated ego; falsely blaming others makes them either resentful or psychologically powerless. Either way, falsely blaming someone pushes them to the extremes of rage and meekness (coupled with a sense of hopelessness and lack of ambition).

Whether a character center *is in fact* improved is not essential to whether the assessed behavior is voluntary. We should expect to have to praise good behaviors frequently to yield any results, and we must be prepared for these results to be delayed. We must also expect that moral encouragement is never sufficient; agents must follow the suggestions of accurate praise and blame to improve morally.

Affectability, or the human capacity to be positively affected by apt praise and blame, is often indicated in human voluntary behavior. When behavior is morally significant, whether one can be affected is a sign of whether or not the behavior issued from the character center, as the character center should be susceptible to praise and blame. The parts of the soul that constitute the character center are, in principle, subject to moral growth and improvement: reason and appetite. That is to say, if the behavior issues from an agent's rational and appetitive aspects of soul, the behavior is voluntary. However, a lack of factual knowledge disqualifies behavior from having issued from these two aspects of the soul, as reason cannot choose what it does not grasp.

Similarly, praise and blame are otiose when applied to unwitting behavior. Imagine that Kyle accidentally knocks a vase from Kim's grasp because neither person was aware that the other was standing so closely behind them. Imagine they came from different directions, passed each other, and without realizing that the other would behave similarly, they both paused for a few seconds. Kim stopped to grasp the vase with the opposite hand; Kyle stopped to read the sign that indicated his destination was in the opposite direction. The collision occurs when Kyle turns around inadvertently bumping Kim. If Kim were to exclaim, "Watch where you're going!" Kyle wouldn't be wrong to respond sarcastically, "Yeah, I'll try to remember that the next time someone hides directly behind me." What could Kyle have done differently? Even if Kyle were to turn to look and see whether someone happened to suddenly materialize behind him, given Kim's proximity, *that* movement alone (the movement that constituted watching where Kyle was about to go) might have been sufficient to launch the vase. Neither person knew that the other was directly behind them. Blaming either one will not improve their character, because that requires making efforts towards goals contrary to their character. The innocent ignorance of what is immediately behind one (an ignorance that is, quite literally, often impossible to avoid) is not the kind of thing that could be encouraged or discouraged. It is not as though one's reason could "take it into account" in the future (or ever). Therefore, it is not possible that Kyle's collision (in the described instance) could have come from Kyle's rational part.

As I suggested earlier, we may be justified in blaming the reaction of morally significant merely non-voluntary behavior lacking regret. In addition to the attractiveness of distinguishing the status of an action (as non-voluntary) and the status of a separate behavior, the reaction (as voluntary), this solution supports my claim concerning affectability. It would do us no good to scold Terry (in the first scenario) for hitting the child. Like Kyle's example, no amount of blame could prevent future occurrences of unintentional acts. However, we do not want to *pardon* Terry. That seems to be going too far, and his callous reaction to the whole scenario seems wildly inappropriate. Even though we may not blame the non-voluntary act, in blaming the sincere reaction that belies Terry's underlying moral flaws, we may positively affect his character. Nothing will prevent Terry's future innocent accidental behavior. However, blame of his reaction might help Terry to reconsider his attitude towards children (and their right to live). If he can develop compassion for child victims, Terry's character will have improved.

Similarly, there is an important way in which affectability can explain Aristotle's distinction between the excusing power of ignorance of the particulars and the culpability of general moral ignorance. One's general moral knowledge is an aspect of one's moral character. If an agent fails to recognize that torturing others for amusement is wrong, that failure of knowledge is the very thing grounding her blameworthiness. After all, Aristotle is not concerned with merely knowing how to be good, but also actually becoming good. No one can become good with ignorance of moral knowledge. Therefore, general moral knowledge is something we should consider a duty of each person to develop. Furthermore, everyone believes his or her perspective is correct. Terry has no reason to doubt his judgment concerning children until others challenge it. It is difficult to see how someone like Terry could improve without some questioning of his general moral positions. Left unchecked, Terry may be aware of contrary positions, but he need not consider them superior to his own.

10. Conclusion

In this paper, I have argued two main points. First, I argued that human voluntary behavior issues from the character center whereby appetite is the efficient cause and reason is the teleological cause. This origin of voluntary behavior is unique to humans. In order to understand the causal role of the character center, we considered apparent exceptions to the original unqualified two criteria offered by Aristotle at *NE* III.i. These exceptions (coupled with Aristotle's comments concerning the voluntary behavior of animals, children, and unreflective acts) illuminated why the scope of sourcehood had to be narrowed to exclude the nutritive aspect of the soul and why the scope of knowledge had to be broadened to include justified true thoughts, beliefs, and perceptions.

After considering the character center as the source of which Aristotle spoke, we saw that what justifies our qualification of the original two criteria is a specific understanding of what is *eph' hēmin*. When the character center is able to perform the behavior it does *or* refrain from so doing, the agent is the proper cause of her behavior. Otherwise, the behavior would be caused by something external to the agent (*qua* character center), and that would not constitute voluntary behavior.

Behaviors that are *eph' hēmin* are up to us because we are not necessitated to perform them. When acting in morally charged scenarios, we *ought to* exercise volition as the virtuous person would (thus refraining from behaving otherwise). However, we may not fully grasp the ends of the virtuous person. For this reason, humans benefit developmentally from appropriate praise and blame; we can and should φ, it is possible that we not φ, and we can become more prone to behave well with practice. Unfortunately, poor practice makes us prone to behave poorly when it is possible for us to behave well. The character center's susceptibility to change grounds both the contingency of voluntary behavior issuing from it and the importance of being held accountable when voluntarily behaving well or poorly. The self-perpetuating nature of character states renders external challenges to and affirmations of an agent's ends welcome vehicles for steering moral improvement. If fair moral assessment can, in theory, inspire good voluntary behavior in the future, then the agent may be affected for the better.

Assist. Prof. Dr. Audrey Anton, Philosophy Faculty of
Western Kentucky University, audrey.anton@wku.edu

References

Anton, Audrey L. "Fixed and Flexible Characters: Aristotle on the permanence and mutability of distinct types of character." *Society for Ancient Greek Philosophy Newsletter* Vol. 15, Nr 1 (2014): 22-28.
Anton, Audrey L. "Breaking the Habit: Aristotle on recidivism and how a thoroughly vicious person might begin to improve." *Dialogue with Ancient Philosophy*, a special issue of *Philosophy in the Contemporary World* Vol. 13, Nr. 2 (2006): 58-66.

Aristotle. *The Complete Works of Aristotle: the Revised Oxford Translation*, ed. Jonathan Barnes, Princeton, NJ: Princeton University Press, 1984.

Bondeson, William. "Aristotle on Responsibility for One's Character and the Possibility of Character Change." *Phronesis*. Vol. 19 (1974): 59-65.

Brickhouse, Thomas C. "A Contradiction in Aristotle's Doctrines Concerning the Alterability of "Hexeis" and the Role of "Hexeis" in the Explanation of Action." *Southern Journal of Philosophy*. Vol. 14 (1976): 401-411.

Burnyeat, Myles F. "Aristotle on Learning to Be Good" in *Essays on Aristotle's Ethics*. In Amélie Oksenberg Rorty (ed.). Berkeley: University of California Press, 1980: 69-92.

Di Muzio, Gianluca. "Aristotle on Improving One's Character." *Phronesis*. Vol. 45, Nr. 3 (2000): 205-219.

Everson, Stephen. "Aristotle's Compatibilism in the *Nicomachean Ethics*." *Ancient Philosophy*. Vol. 10, Nr. 1 (1990): 81-103.

Heinaman, Robert. "Compulsion and Voluntary Action in the Eudemian Ethics." *Nous*. Vol. 22, Nr. 2 (1988): 253-281.

Klimchuk, Dennis. "Aristotle on Necessity and Voluntariness." *History of Philosophy Quarterly*. Vol. 19, Nr. 1 (2002): 1-19.

Kosman, L. A. "Being Properly Affected: Virtues and Feelings in Aristotle's Ethics," in *Essays on Aristotle's Ethics*. Amélie Oksenberg Rorty (ed.). Berkeley: University of California Press (1980): 103-116.

Meyer, Susan Sauvé. "Aristotle on the Voluntary." in *The Blackwell Guide to Aristotle's* Nicomachean Ethics, Richard Kraut (ed.). London: Wiley-Blackwell, 2006: 137-157.

Meyer, Susan Sauvé. "Why Involuntary Actions are Painful," in *Spindel Conference 1988: Aristotle's Ethics*. T.D. Roche (ed.). *Southern Journal of Philosophy supplement*. London, Wiley-Blackwell, 1989.

Ott, Walter. "A Troublesome Passage in Aristotle's *Nicomachean Ethics* iii 5." *Ancient Philosophy*. Vol. 20, Nr.1 (2000): 99-107.

Phillips-Garrett, Carissa. "Sungnōmē in Aristotle." *Apeiron: Journal for Ancient Philosophy and Science*. Vol. 49, Nr. 5. DOI 10.1515/apeiron-2016-0030.

Tessitore, Aristide. *Reading Aristotle's Ethics: Virtue, Rhetoric, and Political Philosophy*. Albany, NY: State University of New York Press, 1996.

Tuozzo, Thomas M. "Aristotelian Deliberation Is Not Of Ends," in *Essays in Ancient Greek Philosophy IV: Aristotle's Ethics*. Anton, J.P. and A. Preus. (eds.). Albany, NY: State University of New York Press, 1991.

DIMKA GICHEVA-GOCHEVA (Sofia)

The Influence of Herodotus on the Practical Philosophy of Aristotle

Abstract

The approach of this paper is a retrospective one. It is an attempt to show that many important ideas of Herodotus, a great ancestor of Aristotle, have influenced his practical philosophy. The paper focuses specially on several topics from the Histories of Herodotus, which have found a resonance in the Nicomachean ethics and in the Politics of Aristotle. The main ones in respect of the ethical theory are: the different forms of justice and the just as for example the super-human justice, the just in the family relations, the judicial just and the just in the polis or the larger human community. Book Epsilon of the Nicomachean Ethics is indebted to Herodotus in several points. In respect of Aristotles' political theory, there are two topics in the History of Herodotus which deserve a special interest: firstly, the conversation of the three noble Persians, who discuss the six basic types of political order and organization of power-and-submission in a state or city-state (in book III, 80-82); this becomes a paradigm for the next typologies of Plato (in the Republic and the Statesman) and Aristotle (in the Politics); secondly, the importance of personal freedom, the equity of the speaking (discussing?) men on the agora, and the supremacy of law for the well-being of any community and its peaceful future. The legacy of Herodotus is obvious in many anthropological and ethical concepts of Aristotle, especially in his most read and quoted ethical writing and in his Politics.

Keywords: Aristotle, Herodotus, justice, the just, anthropology, ethics, political theory, freedom, equity, law

1. Contextual introduction

The *History* (or *The Histories* in some translations) of Herodotus (484-425 BC) is an encyclopedic source for the later anthropology and the practical philosophy of Aristotle. Its value is immeasurable and of utmost importance as a source for the Greek-Persian conflict in the 5th century BC and for its pre-history. However, the text is much more than the alpha of historiography. The immediate narrative of the warfare begins just in the last quarter of the work and in the other three preceding quarters Herodotus narrates about many different historical persons, powerful families, important dynasties and significant events. In detail and very attentively, he describes all possible aspects of the way of life of dozens of human communities. Some of them are Hellenic (Athenians, Euboeians, Spartans, Corinthians), others are not (Lydians, Medians, Persians, Egyptians, Phoenicians, Massagetae, Pelasgians, Scythians, Thracians). He describes without any cultural predilections and prejudices their dietary habits and/or the men's hairdresser-fashion and the clothes they wear. Even more precious than these life-style descriptions are his accounts of the customs and the habits, the mythological beliefs and the images of the gods they worship. In short, he provides voluminous material for all major peculiarities in the worldviews and the everyday practices of tens of communities in the decades, contemporary with the rise and decline of the Persian Empire.

Another remark is to be added: The father of the idea of history has to be respected as the founder of anthropology, as well. The nine books of his work, called by him after the nine Muses, are labeled *History* much later, and even their translation in English as *The Histories*, in the plural, by George Rawlinson, is quite indicative[1]. In addition to the abundant historical material and the accurate insights into the multiple dimensions of human existence, they are an extraordinary encyclopedia of the origin of the Greek knowledge of geography, zoology and of everything related to Egypt.

Last, but not least, the method of the historiographer is the weaving of the 'great' political history with the hundreds of smaller personal, family and/or dynasty stories – countless narratives mainly not of full biographies, but of telling episodes of fatal importance for the destinies of the humans, engendering the fabric of the 'great' history. Thus, the writing acquires depth and value not only as anthropological and historical chef-d-oeuvre but also as a sketch of the ancient philosophy of life and philosophy of history.[2]

Why it is worth looking back at Herodotus as an ancestor of some ethical ideas in Plato and Aristotle?

The influence of Herodotus on Plato and on the practical philosophy of Aristotle, conceived as inseparable unity of political, ethical and anthropological thinking is obvious, although in different facets. Its traces are more visible and explicit in Aristotle, and somewhat hidden in the delicate texture of the Platonic dialogues. In contrast to the *De anima*, whose book Alpha abolishes with devastating criticism absolutely everything, proposed by the previous thinkers on the soul-body problems, the practical philosophy of Aristotle is indebted to many of his predecessors, mainly to Herodotus, Thucydides, Sophocles and

---

[1] This text quotes his translation. Herodotus. *The Histories*. Translated by George Rawlinson (1858) with an Introduction by Rosalind Thomas. London: David Campbell Publishers, 1997.

[2] More on this point in Karl Reinhart's *Vermächtnis der Antike* (see Reinhart 1960) and Richard Winton's "Herodotus" (see Winton 2000)

Plato. Maybe the most impressive concept in the heritage, left by Herodotus for both Plato and Aristotle is the differentiation between ἡ δικαιοσύνη and τὸ δίκαιον: ἡ δικαιοσύνη is justice, the individual autonomous self-sufficient *virtue*, whereas τὸ δίκαιον is the *correlational* ethical, juridical or political *result* of interpersonal interaction between at least two agents[3].

Two great ideas from the thesaurus of Herodotus are cherished only by Plato and neglected by Aristotle: the first one is the causal theonomy in the course of the historical events and the second is the relativity of the human narration of the past. The latter is easier to explain, because it is stated clearly in the very first pages of the *History*: the Hellenes, the Persians and the Phoenicians have three completely different versions for the causes, the origin, the happening and the development of the same events. Herodotus stays at a distance from the epic and mythology. For him the real events and the real persons are unmasked in their deeds and *"human happiness never continues long in one stay"* (I, 5).

The causal theonomy mentioned above is striking in the instructive stories of the rise and fall of the greatest Lydian and Persian kings: Croesus the Lydian, Cyrus the Great, his son and successor Cambyses; Darius and Xerxes. Herodotus summarizes the moral of them in the sentence:

ὡς τῶν μεγάλων ἀδικημάτων μεγάλαι εἰσὶ καὶ αἱ τιμωρίαι παρὰ τῶν θεῶν. *When great wrongs are done, the gods will surely visit them with great punishments* (II, 120, 10).

It is not difficult to see how these stories of the fall of rulers, who are punished for their cruel atrocities, and even for the deeds of their far remote predecessors, are echoed in the final myths of the *Republic* (614b-621d) and the *Gorgias* (522e-527a). Indeed, Plato mirrors the moral of Herodotus' stories of the severely punished rulers with a greater emphasis on the deserved retribution, provoked by their own wickedness, rather than on the family guiltiness.

As a distinguished mark of this causal theonomy-framework of the stories, especially of the rulers, the reader of the masterpiece encounters several astonishing examples of the power of the providence and its prophecy in dreams, oracles and signs. The credo of Herodotus is expressed in the famous: "ἐν τῇ γὰρ ἀνθρωπηίῃ φύσι οὐκ ἐνῆν ἄρα τὸ μέλλον γίγνεσθαι ἀποτρέπειν. *It is impossible for men to turn aside the coming fate* (III, 65, 10-11). Some examples are to be mentioned: (1) The death of the son of Croesus (I, 34-45); (2) The failed attempt of Astyages to change his destiny (after a dream of a sexual intercourse with

---

[3] The largest possible mapping of the wider context of the Greek thinking of justice and the just is available in the several volumes of Erik Wolf's. *Griechisches Rechtsdenken*. (see Wolf 1950-1970).

his daughter; which was a prophecy that his grandson will run over Asia, but will deprive him of the power as well. (I, 107, 108); (3) Cambyses, frightened by a dream, also tried to escape from the predicted future; (4) Also, the unveiling of the future through the bird-prophecy for the new-coming dynasty: the seven pairs of hawks tearing the two pairs of vultures (III, 76).

This part of the paper should be finished, however, by pointing out that Plato and Aristotle remained indifferent to some admirable sparks of humanism, expressed by the sophists and Herodotus, who was a close friend at least with one of them, Protagoras. These ideas, unfortunately neglected by Plato and Aristotle, are Herodotus' convictions and statements that there is *one and universal human nature*, which is inherent in all human beings, irrespectively of their origin and tongue. The readers find the relevant passages on the human nature in plenty of stories:

a) to begin with, in the conversation between Solon and Croesus (I, 29-33);

b) in the conversations and the letters, exchanged between the tyrant Periander and his son Lycophron, and between Lycophron and his anonymous sister (III, 52): the passionate appeal of the anonymous sister brings the message that the fatal feuds in a family must be ended, because *we are all just mortal humans*;

c) in the conversations between Xerxes and his uncle Artabanus (VII, 45) and between Xerxes and Demaratus (VII, 101-104);

d) in the unbelievable reversals in the life of the Egyptian Amasis and his golden sink(II, 172); and,

e) the letter of the same Amasis to the tyrant Polycrates (III, 40). Although his personal story is one of the very few examples in the *Histories* for the generosity of the benevolent fate, the happy vicissitudes have not deprived him of the sober wisdom concerning not only the uncertainty of power, but also the fragility of human beings in every aspect of their existence. πᾶν ἐστι ἄνθρωπος συμφορή. *Hence man is wholly accident* (I, 32)[4]

2. Fundamentals of the thinking of ἡ δικαιοσύνη and τὸ δίκαιον in the *Histories*

For the sake of conciseness, in this paper several fundamental ideas of Herodotus, adopted later by Aristotle, will be sketched as follows. Let's begin with the unjust as *casus belli gerendi*, with which the chain of the great conflict is conceived: one unjust deed was followed by another, by a third and then by one more unjust deed (I, 2, 1-3). Herodotus is positive: the sequence of unjust events and the sequel of reciprocal acts of revenge do not

---

[4] Compare with Pindar, VIIIth Pythian Ode.

lead to a just solution and do not resolve any conflict righteously. See (in I, 2) the report of the successive kidnappings of Io and Europe, of Medea and Helen. This message sounds already as conviction in the second book, where Herodotus proposes an alternative to the epic of Homer with his version of the real and true story of the beautiful Helen. It is worth comparing Herodotus' apology of Helen in this alternative story (II, 113-115) with the *Enkomion for Helen* by Gorgias (Diels-Kranz 1934, 288, 294).

3. The just as a result of subjective human judgment

There are at least three examples in the *Histories*, which might be read as the foundation of the Greek juridical and philosophical thinking of the subjective role of the person who judges properly (or not) for the attainment (or the failure) of a justified decision: a)The verdict of the judge Proteus in Egypt, reported in the true history of Helen and Menelaus; Proteus issued what is to be done after the awful crime, committed by Alexander in Egypt; b) the story of the gradual rise of Deioces from a humble judge to the power of authoritarian ruler (I, 100); c) the depiction of the merciful Egyptian ruler Mycerinus, son of Cheops (II, 129).

If we remove all the details from these stories, we will see that beneath them lies an important idea, later developed by Aristotle in book Epsilon of the *Nicomachean Ethics* as one of the forms of the just. The just in the decision of any judge is a possibility, which might be actualized, but also might not be.(II, 31) NE, E: ὁ γὰρ δικαστὴς βούλεται εἶναι οἷον δίκαιον ἔμψυχον (1132a 21-22). *A judge is meant to be, as it were, justice personified*[5], sums up Aristotle. The readers familiar with Herodotus are reminded at this point of the prototypes or the impressive personifications of the embodiment of the just, portrayed by Herodotus.

There are also shocking pages in the *Histories* of quite the opposite. Let's recall this horrifying episode: Cambysus punishes cruelly the corrupt judge Sisamnes, but puts his son Otanes in his place(V, 25): *Therefore Cambyses slew and flayed Sisamnes, and cutting his skin into strips, stretched them across the seat of the throne whereon he had been wont to sit when he heard causes. Having so done Cambyses appointed the son of Sisamnes to be judge in his father's room, and bade him never forget in what way his seat was cushioned.*

Another similar, but not analogical example is the punishment, imposed by Darius, who ordered the crucifixion of Sandoces, but later interrupted the torture (VII, 194) because the punishment must be commeasurable with the crime. The commensurability of the crime

---

[5] Here and elsewhere in the paper the translation of Roger Crisp is quoted (see Aristotle 2000).

(or in milder cases of the unjust deed, the wrong doing with the punishment becomes one of the milestones in the NE, book Epsilon. The just solution of any case is in the middle between the wrong or the unjust deed and becoming a victim of wrong or unjust judgment.[6]

4. The just in the family

Earlier in this text, in the mapping of the relevant passages with regard to the idea of the (universal) human nature in the *Histories*, the correspondence between Lycophron, the son of Periander, and his anonymous sister was mentioned. A passage from her appeal is worth quoting:

> παῦσαι σεωυτὸν ζημιῶν. φιλοτιμίη κτῆμα σκαιόν. μὴ τῷ κακῷ το κακὸν ἰῶ. πολλοὶ τῶν δικαίων τὰ ἐπιεικέστερα προτιθεῖσι. πολλοὶ δὲ ἤδε τὰ μητρώια διζήμενοι τὰ πατρώια ἀπέβαλον.[7] ... *cease to punish thyself. It is scant gain, this obstinacy. Why seek to cure evil by evil? Mercy, remember, is by many set above justice. Many, also, while pushing their mother's claims have forfeited their father's fortune* (III, 53, transl. by Rawlinson).

The message of the compassionate sister, who remains unnamed, deserves very attentive inspection, because in these several lines it sketches the prototype of two conceptions, later enriched by Aristotle. One of them is the appraisal of the merciful just, the indulgent, τὸ ἐπιεικές, as the supreme form of the just in the *NE*. In the English translations of the NE (see Rackham 1996, Chase 1934, Crisp 2000) *the equitable* prevails as a rendering of τὸ ἐπιεικές. The same Latin root is seen in the term, used in the French translation by sister Pascale-Dominique Nau: *l'équitable*[8]. The translation in German by Franz Dirlmeier uses *das Gütige* for τὸ ἐπιεικές and *das Gerechte* for τὸ δίκαιον (Dirlmeier 1979).

In the newest translation in English, done by Sarah Broadie and Christopher Rowe τὸ ἐπιεικές is translated as *the reasonable* (Broadie and Rowe 2002). Other possible options, suggested by the context might be *the indulgent, the merciful, the milder just, the temperate*. In the address of the anonymous sister to her brother it is said that *mercy is*

---

[6] ἡ δικαιοπραγία μέσον ἐστι τοῦ ἀδικεῖν καὶ ἀδικεῖσθαι (1133b 29-30) *Acting justly is a mean between committing injustice and suffering it* (transl. by Crisp); this is the conclusion of an argument from a previous chapter.

[7] τὰ ἐπιεικέστερα in the *Histories* is reflected in the Nicomachean Ethcs (NE, E, ch. 14) as the more abstract concept τὸ ἐπιεικές: the supreme form of the just is the indulgent, which is not the proper and the commeasurable judgment, but the merciful and milder one (NE 1137a 30-1138a2).

[8] Available on the internet (see https://fr.wikisource.org/wiki/%C3%89thique_%C3%A0_Nicomaque, accessed on the 8th of January 2017).

above justice, as quoted above. Precisely this is the point of Aristotle's reasoning in a very long chapter in book Epsilon of the *Nicomachean Ethics* (NE 1137a 31-1138a3), in which he discusses τὸ ἐπιεικές. The essence of his understanding is that the supreme, the best, the unsurpassable form of the just is the milder, the merciful, the indulgent just.

> κρεῖττον τὸ ἐπιεικές. διὸ δίκαιον μέν ἐστι, καὶ βέλτιόν τινος δικαίου, οὐ τοῦ ἁπλῶς δὲ ἀλλὰ τοῦ διὰ τὸ ἁπλῶς ἁμαρτήματος. καὶ ἔστιν αὕτη ἡ φύσις ἡ τοῦ ἐπιεικοῦς, ἐπανόρθωμα νόμου, ᾗ ἐλλείπει διὰ το καθόλου (1137 b 24-27). *What is equitable, therefore, is just, and better than one kind of justice. But it is not better than unqualified justice, only better than the error that results from its lacking qualification. And this is the very nature of what is equitable – a correction of law, where it is deficient on account of its universality.* (trans. by Roger Crisp)

The other remarkable idea in the appeal of the anonymous sister is the supremacy of the rights and the power of the man-and-the-father in the family. This idea is exposed briefly as consideration about τὸ πατρικὸν δίκαιον in the NE (book E, ch. 6) and at a considerable length in book Alpha of the *Politics* (book A, ch.12) as one of the unquestionable principles of the political science according to Aristotle.

Another tricky question from the thematic circle of the just in the family, found in the *Histories,* concerns the heir of the throne: when a ruler has a polygamous family and many spouses, which one of his sons, born of different mothers, has the right to inherit the father? The eldest of all the children or the first one born after the father's ascension to the throne? The just solution of this question has triggered feuds and bloodshed in many dynasties throughout the millennia. Herodotus reports reservedly, without any partial comments, that the decision was taken according to the following definition, borrowed from Spartan law: the son, who was born after his father had become the actual king, should be heir to the empire, rather than the sons, born before him by the other spouses, because at their birth the father still was a private person and did not rule the state (VII, 2-4).

5. The just in the human community

The real foundation of the political thinking on the different types of the self-organization of a community is discussed on several significant pages of the *Histories* (III, 80-82), in the famous trialogue, in which collocutors are Otanes, Megabyzus and Darius.

The first to speak is Otanes, the unhappy child, who has witnessed the terrible death of his corrupt father: it is no wonder that after such a shocking experience in his childhood the first speaker should glorify τὸ πλῆθος opposed to μουναρχίη. Indeed, we cannot expect argumentation and concepts, clarified by definitions in Herodotus. He narrates short rather suggestive stories, bearing sense, which will later engender political or ethical concepts. It is not by chance that the speech in favour of the rule of the many should be delivered not by anyone else but by Otanes. This reveals the talent of the historiographer, who is a writer as well. Otanes is the judge who has inherited the position of his corrupt and severely punished father. His accusation of the excesses of the unbounded monarchic power is to be expected and the motives for it are both negative and psychological. The power of the one is detrimental to himself, because it is the source of arrogance, cruelty and disdain. In the speech of Otanes the accent is laid on the psychological degradation of the ruler, who enjoys absolute power. Its devastating effects fall much more on himself, than the arbitrariness and the atrocities, which destroy the lives of his victims. Of course, Otanes combines the denial of the one form with a praise of another and offers a positive enumeration of the five essential merits of the opposite to the monarchy: the rule of the many.

> The rule of the many, on the other hand, has, in the first place, the fairest of names, to wit, isonomy; and further it is free from all those outrages which a king is wont to commit. There, places are given by lot, the magistrate is answerable for what he does, and measures rest with the commonalty. I vote, therefore, that we do away with monarchy, and raise the people to power. For the people are all in all. (III, 80)

After him, Megabyzus praises the rule of ἀρίστων δὲ ἀνδρῶν, opposed to ὀλιγαρχίη. The speech of the second noble collocutor provides a real example of dialectical *Aufhebung*, because it partially preserves and partially discards what has been already said: the monarchy is bad, he agrees, but at the same time he disagrees that the supreme power should be concentrated in the majority.

> For there is nothing so void of understanding, nothing so full of wantonness, as the unwieldy rabble. It were folly not to be borne, for men, while seeking to escape the wantonness of a tyrant, to give themselves up to the wantonness of a rude unbridled mob… Let the enemies of the Persians be ruled by democracies; but let us choose out from the citizens a certain number of the worthiest, and put the government into their hands. (III, 81)

Darius is the last to speak in the trialogue and his speech is also dialectical development of the previous statements: he supports the negative evaluation of the rule of the many, proposed by Megabyzus, but rejects the appraisal of the aristocracy as the best form of political governance. On the day after, he will become the new king with treachery and falsification, because he convinces the other four participants who remain silent in the dispute, but are entirely persuaded by him and vote in favour of his opinion: thus the champion in the debate is Darius, who proclaims the monarchy as the best form of governance, opposed to the power of the people/demos (III, 85).

The third opinion is also much more psychologically grounded than politically elaborated. Like the first speaker Otanes, the third one Darius emphasizes the personal degradation of the ruling figures, who inevitably become the first victims of the concentration of power not only in the hands of a minority, but even in the rule of the many. The disastrous consequences of the oligarchic and the democratic political orders likewise according to Darius, tooq are much more detrimental to the ones, who rule than to the human community governed by them.

> In oligarchies, where men vie with each other in the service of the commonwealth, fierce enmities are apt to arise between man and man, each wishing to be a leader, and to carry his own measures; whence violent quarrels come, which lead to open strife, often ending with bloodshed… Again, in a democracy, it is impossible but that there will be malpractices: these malpractices however do not lead to enmities, but to close friendships, which are formed among those engaged in them, who must hold well together to carry on their villainies. (III, 82)

The closer inspection of the precise words, used by the three noble Persians in this political debate on the best form of governance, supports more decisive observations and conclusions: the six basic political forms – the three good ones and their three opposites, later laid down as fundamental by Aristotle, are sketched in this conversation. The speech of Otanes points out the advantages in the rule of the majority, τὸ πλῆθος - the rule of the many, later called democracy, and to the enormous dangers in its contrary, which he labels μουναρχίη, but in fact means its distorted form, the tyranny. Megabyzus advocates the rule of ἀρίστων δὲ ἀνδρῶν – the aristocracy and blames the power of the unbridled mob, later labelled the bad or the deviated democracy. Darius properly describes the psychological mechanisms in the group of the ruling men, which in his view transforms any aristocracy into oligarchy, and declares that monarchy is the best.

The conversation of the three Persians is reflected with some variations and new arrangements by Plato in the *Republic* (in the VIIIth book, with the addition of timocracy to the forms of the political orders) and in the *Statesman* (291d-292e), but there is no complete coincidence, because in the *Republic* one more type is added, whereas in the *Statesman* one form (not surprisingly the good form of the rule of the many) is missing. These six forms, sketched by Herodotus in the trialogue of three Persian noblemen, are the focal points of Aristotle's meticulous analysis, developed at length in the *Politics* from the middle of the third book to the end of the sixth.

6. The just in the rule of the majority

The Aristotelean account of the great advantages of democracy, the rule of the many, called *politeia* in his typology in the *Politics*, is greatly influenced by Herodotus: 1. In the view of Otanes the inherent feature of the rule of majority is stated to be ἰσονομίη – literally, the equity of all in respect of the requirements of the laws; the germane idea of the rule of law; 2. What a monarch does, never occurs under the rule of the many. The bitter experience of Otanes and his childhood trauma obviously influenced him to insist on this, but in tens of other stories in the *Histories* Herodotus narrates that there are perilous consequences of the unlimited power of a person first on himself. The boundless power of a ruler leads him to madness and disaster. 3. Another valuable characteristic in the rule of the many, according to Otanes, is the distribution of many public duties, positions and responsibilities by the lot - πάλῳ μὲν γὰρ ἀρχὰς ἄρχει. 4. Even more important is the responsibility for these responsibilities, or translated into our modern parlance, the accountability of the persons, who have been in charge: ὑπεύθυνον δὲ ἀρχὴν ἔχει – the power is held into account, it is responsible. 5. Last in the speech of Otanes is the mode of decision-taking: all problems are discussed and resolved in common βουλεύματα δὲ πάντα ἐς κοινὸν ἀναφέρει. This might be read as the first advocacy of the deliberative democracy.

Later on in the fifth book of the *Histories,* two other important factors for the democratic developments in Athens and its subsequent leadership among the city-states are mentioned: ἡ ἰσηγορίη ὡς ἐστὶ χρῆμα σπουδαῖον... ἀπαλλαχθέντες δὲ τυράννων μακρῷ πρῶτοι ἐγένοντο (V, 78)[9]. Firstly, ἡ ἰσηγορίη, the equity-and-equality of the citizens on the agora, the participation of the citizens in the arguing and the decision-making of the public matters; and, secondly, the abolishment of the tyrants' regime, the hostility and the resistance to many despotic authoritarian practices - these are the healthy strengths of the Athenians, which lead their city-state not only to the economic prosperity, but also to the military and the political supremacy among the Greek communities.

The abolishment of the tyranny, which is the worst of all political orders, made Athens the mightiest Greek polis in the military aspect. The freedom of the citizens and the chances they received to work for the fulfillment of their private entrepreneurships enhanced the economic prosperity of the city as well. The work for the family property and the personal household, and not for the tyrant, who would expropriate the gain, became the

---

[9] See the pertinent commentaries of Robert W. Wallace and Paul Cartledge on this subject in *The Origins of Democracy in Ancient Greece.* (Raaflaub, Kurt A., Josiah Ober, and Robert W. Wallace 2007).

basis of the Athenian polis. Another meaning of the concept ἡ ἰσηγορίη is to be pointed out. It means not only *equity of the free men on the agora*, the *right to be equally eligible and to elect* like all the rest free citizens. It signifies also *the equity to participate and to cooperate* in the exertion of the political power. Last, but not least it means *freedom of speech*, the equity of all deliberative positions of all free citizens, expressed in the public debates, in the discussions and the taking of decisions, especially the ones, passed by the assembly.

All of them are marked as the inner engines of the glory and the positive changes in the polis by Aristotle in *The politeia of the Athenians*. Once more we see how brilliant examples of stories, used as instruments by the narrative method in the *History* of Herodotus, become implicit concepts in an Aristotelian text. In the institutional history and the constitutional stages in the development of Athens, the warfare is just mentioned: the Greek-Persian wars and the Peloponnesian war are just referred to, because *The politeia of the Athenians* was meant to be a sketch of the successive forms of the institutional self-governance of the city-state and not a political history. In this brief survey of the constitutional progressive development of Athens many of the explanations of the political evolution of the city-state are in harmony with the ones, proclaimed as the most influential ones by Herodotus.

7. Conclusion

Herodotus is a true anthropologist, political and ethical thinker, and philosopher of history. He is not just a modest historiographer of chronicles, because in all the stories he looks for the real understanding of man and the causes of the events. His main concern always is the answer to the question "why did it happen", and not just "what and how did it happen". He is confident in the answers for the causes of the victory (VII 138-139): the Athenians saved the whole Hellas, because they were free. Earlier in the same book (VII 102) he writes that in contrast to the enormous wealth and territory of the empire of the invaders 10, poverty was always a neighbor to Hellas, but nevertheless the virtue of the Greeks was firm and invincible. However, the liberty of the majority of the Greek city-states, and the resistance to the despotic and authoritarian rules in the bigger part of them 11

---

[10] The number of the invaders is exactly 5 283 220 (VII, 186).
[11] "Surely the heaven will soon be below, and the earth above, and men will henceforth live in the sea, and fish take their place upon the dry land, since you, Lacedaemonians, propose to put down free governments in the cities of Greece, and to set up tyrannies in their room. There is nothing in the whole world so unjust, nothing so bloody, as a tyranny" (V, 92). There are 'small' exemplary stories (of some deeds) of more than 50 tyrants in more than 50 Greek polices in the *History*.

never was a source of anarchy, because the master which all of them obeyed unconditionally was the law (104). The divided and competing city-states reached some form of unity not only because they were threatened by the mighty enemy, but also because of the underlying bonds between them. For the shaping out of the united Hellas VII (136), the engendering prerequisite was that all those formerly conflicting city-states were inhabited by people, who have the same blood, the same tongue, the same sanctuaries and temples devoted to the same gods; the same habits, rituals and traditions (VIII, 144; see also Fritz 1967, 243 and Jäger 1973, XV). However, his most important moral is:

> There was nothing they had so much at heart as the salvation of Greece, and they knew that, if they quarreled among themselves among the command, Greece would be brought to ruin. (VIII, 3)[12].

*Assoc. Prof. Dr. Dimka Guicheva-Gocheva, Faculty of Philosophy,
Sofia University St. Kliment Ohridski,* gichevagoc[at]phls.uni-sofia.bg

References

Aristotelis *Ethica Nicomachea*, Bywater, Ingram (transl.) Oxonii, 1890.

Susemihl, Franciscus and Otto Appelt (ed.). Aristotelis *Ethica Nicomachea*, . Lipsiae: in aedibus B. G. Teubneri, 1903.

Aristoteles. *Die Nikomachische Ethik*. Eingeleitet und Übertragen von Olof Gigon. Zürich: Artemis Verlag, 1951.

Dirlmeier, Franz (transl.). Aristoteles. *Die Nikomachische Ethik*. Übertragen von Franz Dirlmeier. Berlin: Reclam, 1979.

Chase, Drummond Percy. *The Nicomachean Ethics* of Aristotle. Translated by D.P. Chase. London & Toronto: M. Dent & Sons Ltd. 1911, 1934.

Rackham, Harris (transl.). Aristotle. *The Nicomachean Ethics*. Wordsworth Classics of World Literature. Ware, Hertfordshire: Wordsworth Editions, 1996.

Aristotle. *The Nicomachean Ethics*. Translated and edited by Roger Crisp. Cambridge: Cambridge University Press, 2000.

---

[12] See also Christopher Pelling on *Le Miroir d'Hérodote* (Pelling 1988).

Aristotle. *Nicomachean Ethics*. Translation, Introduction and Commentary Sarah Broadie and Christopher Rowe. Oxford: Oxford University Press, 2002.

Aristote. *L'Éthique a Nicomaque*. Introduction, traduction et commentaire par R.A. Gauthier (op.p.) et Jean Yves Jolif (op.p.). Louvain: Publications universitaires de Louvain, 1958.

Hérodote. *Histoires*. Texte établi et traduit par P.E. Legrand, 9 vol. Paris: Les Belles Lettres, 1:1932; 2:1930; 3:1939; 4 (3rd edn.):1960; 5:1946; 6:1948; 7:1951; 8:1953; 9:1954 (repr. 1:1970; 2:1963; 3:1967; 5:1968; 6:1963; 7:1963; 8:1964; 9:1968):

Crisp, Roger and Trevor J. Saunders. "Aristotle: Ethics and politics", in Furley, David (ed.) *Routledge History of Philosophy. Vol. II. From Aristotle to Augustine*. London: Routledge, 1997, 109-146.

Fritz, Kurt von. *Die griechische Geschichtsschreibung*. Band I : *Von den Anfängen bis Thukydides*. Berli:, De Gruyter, 1967.

Furley, David (ed.) *Routledge History of Philosophy. Vol. II. From Aristotle to Augustine*. London and New York: Routledge, 1997.

Herodotus. *The Histories*. Translated by George Rawlinson (1858) with an Introduction by Rosalind Thomas. London: David Campbell Publishers, 1997.

Jäger, Werner. *PAIDEIA. The Ideals of Greek culture*. Vol. I: *Archaic Greece. The Mind of Athens*. Oxford University Press, 1965.

Kraut, Richard. *Aristotle. Political Philosophy*. Oxford: Oxford University Press, 2002.

Pelling, Christopher. *The Mirror of Herodotus* (1988) [online: http://www.dur.ac.uk/Classics/histos/1997/pelling.html]

Platonis Dialogi secundum Thrasylli Tetralogias dispositi ex recognitione Caroli Friderici Hermanni. Vol. IV, Lipsiae, in aedibus B. G. Teubneri. MDCCCLXXXIII.

Raaflaub, Kurt, A. Josiah Ober and Robert W. Wallace. *Origins of Democracy in Ancient Greece*. Berkeley: University of California Press, 2007.

Reinhardt, Karl." Herodots Persergeschichten, Gyges und sein Ring", in idem, *Vermäechtnis der Antike. Gesammelte Essays zur Philosophie und Geschichtsschreibung*. Göttingen: Vandenhoeck und Ruprecht, 1960,133 – 183.

Rowe, Christopher (ed.). *The Cambridge History of Greek and Roman Political Thought*, , Cambridge: Cambridge University Press, 2000.

Wolf, Erik. *Griechisches Rechtsdenken*. Bd. I-IV, Frankfurt am Main: Vittorio Klostermann.1950-1970.

Receptions of the Aristotelian Ethics and Practical Philosophy

MARTIN HUTH (Vienna)

Humans, Animals, and Aristotle. Aristotelian Traces in the Current Critique of *Moral Individualism*

Abstract

The concept of moral individualism is part of the foundational structure of most prominent modern moral philosophies. It rests on the assumption that moral obligations towards a respective individual are constituted solely by her or his capacities. Hence, these obligations are independent of any ἔθος (ethos), of any shared ethical sense and social significations. The moral agent and the individual with moral status (who is the target of a respective action) are construed as subjects outside of any social relation or lifeworld significations. This assumption has been contested in the last decades by diverse authors with very different approaches to moral philosophy. In the last years, an increasing number of philosophers like Cora Diamond and Alice Crary (with a Wittgensteinian background), but also phenomenologists like Paul Ricœur, Klaus Held, and Bernhard Waldenfels question the presupposition that individual capacities are the agent-neutral and context-neutral ground of moral considerations. This critique of moral individualism in different contemporary discourses shows a striking similarity between Wittgensteinian and phenomenological philosophers as their critical inquiry of prominent theories like the ones by Immanuel Kant, John Rawls, Peter Singer or Tom Regan is derived from mostly implicitly efficacious Aristotelian theorems. Telling examples are the ἔθος (ethos) as pre-given normative infrastructure, the ἕξις (hexis) as individual internalization of the ethos, the φρόνησις (phronesis) described as a specific practical know-how in contrast to scientific knowledge, and not at least the definition of the human being as ζῷον πολιτικόν (zoon politikon). However, the Aristotelian sources of this movement have not yet been scrutinized systematically. This paper aims, first, to reveal the significance of these sources to make them visible and, second, to contribute to the notion of the topicality of Aristotelian philosophy in current debates on ethics.

Keywords: Aristotle, Cora Diamond, Alice Crary, phenomenology, ethos, hexis, phronèsis

1. Introduction

Modern theories in moral philosophy (contractualism, deontology, utilitarianism) are often relying on assumptions that can be subsumed under the concept of *moral individual-*

ism[1]. Individual capacities like rationality, self-awareness or the alleged ability to suffer are supposed to build the agent-neutral and context-neutral ground of moral obligations towards the individual. But this presupposition has been contested in the recent years from different perspectives like feminist ethics, post-structuralism, the discourse after Wittgenstein, and current phenomenology, because the reduction of the ground of the moral status to mostly cognitive abilities leads potentially to counterintuitive consequences in regard of the obligations towards embryos, infants, cognitively impaired humans, or animals. To underpin their critique, this is the underlying thesis of this article, all these theories go back to Aristotelian sources of moral philosophy. However, these keystones of the criticism are often implicit and have not yet been analysed systematically.

This paper aims to provide an investigation in the Aristotelian sources of the current critique of moral individualism focussing on "Wittgensteinian" authors like Cora Diamond and Alice Crary and on current phenomenology exemplified by Paul Ricœur, Klaus Held or Bernhard Waldenfels. Philosophers of both discourses refer implicitly and explicitly to crucial Aristotelian concepts. This paper will focus among them on four crucially important concepts: (a) the ἔθος (*ethos*) as the lived moral sense (NE 1094 a26-b1) as ground and horizon of moral decision-making and ethical reflection; (b) the ἕξις (hexis), the morally relevant habituation of perceiving and acting (ibid., 1142 a27); (c) connected to the practical know-how that is coined φρόνησις (*phronesis*) (ibid., book VI), the practical wisdom that is considered a specific practical know-how in comparison to the scientific knowledge of the ἐπιστήμη (*episteme*); and (d) not at least to the definition of the human being as ζῷον πολιτικόν (*zoon politikon*) (ibid., 1094 b5-10; 1097 b8-12; Politics 1253 a1-5) who is "by nature" dependent on social relations – also in regard of developing moral skills.

The following section provides a description of the basic structures and the pitfalls of moral individualism. The contractualism by Thomas Hobbes or more recently of John Rawls is an important example for modern ethical theories qua *moral individualism* that refer to *individual cognitive abilities* as the only source of moral obligations. Hobbes presupposes the equality of intellectual capacities without any further clarification – infants, impaired humans or living animals do not occur in the *Leviathan* (Hobbes 2011). In Rawls, impaired humans as well as nonhuman beings are explicitly excluded from his theory since they cannot partici-

---

[1] The concept of *moral individualism* is used explicitly in Crary 2010. But it occurs more or less implicitly in Diamond 1978, in Ricoeur 1990, in Held 2007 as well as in theoretical frameworks that would be beyond the scope of this paper like the feminist ethics (Iris Marion Young, Catriona Mackenzie, Martha Nussbaum) or poststructuralist theories like the one by Judith Butler.

pate in the initial deliberation to determine the basic structure of society (that is defined as reciprocal cooperation to contribute to mutual advantage) (Rawls 1971, 4).

This account is also visible in Kant's *Groundwork for the Metaphysics of Morals* (Kant 1977) where he proceeds from an autonomous being that is capable of being aware of the universal moral law, the Categorical Imperative, by virtue of her/his reasonability. This autonomy (that relies etymologically on the Greek terminology for self-legislation) is also the sine qua non for existing as a being with dignity (an absolute value) that calls for moral respect (ibid., 429). This dignity serves as a criterion for inclusion (of reasonable beings) and exclusion (of animals and potentially of infants or impaired humans) in regard of ethical consideration.

Similarly, the utilitarianism of John Stuart Mill or, more recently Peter Singer, provides a selectivity of moral consideration. Here, the keystone is the degree of rationality or self-awareness that determines the quality of interests that are weighed in the utilitarian calculation of harms and benefits.

The third section proceeds from Cora Diamond's lapidary statement that it is extremely strange to interpret severely impaired humans as outside of fundamental moral and political considerations (cf. Diamond 1991, 44f.). In contrast, Diamond and Alice Crary who draws on Diamond, refer (a) to *a lived, communal ethical sense* as fundamental basis of moral deliberation. This ethical sense is indeed concerned with the significance of being human independently of showing average intellectual capacities; on the contrary, an infant or a cognitively impaired person are usually seen as particularly vulnerable beings who deserve special moral respect. Hence, the application of clear and strict principles of respect appears as significant only against the background, and not in opposition, to this lived ethical sense. This could be brought very easily in a connection with Aristotle's broadly elaborated concept of ἔθος (*ethos*) as well as (b) the ἕξις (hexis) as a habituated pattern of perceiving, judging and acting. Moreover, this refers to the (c) φρόνησις (*phronesis*), the specific kind of know-how that informs our praxis and constitutes our ability for moral judgment. Lived morality and its inner logic is accordingly not to be considered as working by (independent) principles that are applied with mathematical accuracy but by sensitivity for the situation, the person who we treat, and other features that are minded in the broad consideration of actions (e.g. Aristotle, Nicomachean Ethics 1104 b20-25). Finally, this has to be seen against the background of an inevitable relationality between actor, context and the respective via-à-vis. The actor is not an entirely independent subject from social normalities and approbations, the context, the situation – a *zoon politikon*.

The fourth section is also concerned with the four cornerstones of the Aristotelian ethics – first of all once more with the shared structures of (a) the lived ἔθος (*ethos*) - as they are of importance in the phenomenological discourse. Phenomenologists like Paul Ricœur, Klaus Held or Bernhard Waldenfels analyze morality in terms of lifeworld significations. These significations arise from the lived sociality and build the basis for ethical considerations that are always relying on the already existing "normative normality". This normality is (b) incorporated through embodied habits of acting and perceiving (this refers also clearly to Aristotle's ἕξις [*hexis*]). As in Diamond's and Crary's accounts, – but even more explicit and elaborated, we find (c) a quasi-Aristotelian *hermeneutics of the praxis and its normalities from within the praxis in regard of informing this praxis itself* (kind of a hermeneutical circle, Gadamer 2010, 270-295; cf. also Ricœur 1990, Held 2010, Waldenfels 2006). Moreover, the phenomenological discourse is very aware of the fact that the self is a socially dependent being (d). Here, the role of socialization and education beginning with the early childhood is extremely important for incorporating shared values and for the constitution of the responsible self as such (Ricœur 1990, section 7-10) – a consideration similar to reflections by Aristotle in the first two books of the *Nicomachean Ethics*.

The final conclusion will provide a synopsis of the paper referring to the four fundamental keystones of the Aristotelian sources of the critique of moral individualism. Moreover, it will point out the topicality of Aristotle's ethics particularly in approaches that are more and more present in the current academic discourses.

2. The "Moral Individualism" and its Pitfalls

Starting from Hobbes, but not at all ending with John Rawls, the different accounts within contractualism proceed from the idea that morality is constituted by a primal agreement between rational agents. Hence, they share one crucial presupposition: Any social and/or political community is understood within the model of association (cf. Young 2005, 19f.). According to this model, we constitute or enter communities intentionally to free us from a "solitary, poor, nasty, brutish, and short" (Hobbes 2011, 78) existence. In the previous natural state, we are confronted with a war all against all because we live outside of any moral order or agreement. In giving up the (natural) right for everything – that makes us to enemies for each other – we gain the higher or second order freedom from being in peril of death by any other human because everyone can claim the same right for everything and no-one is protected by morality or laws. The somewhat strange presupposition here is that all human beings are equal in their intellectual capacities. This is supposedly proven by the fact that they are all proud about their intelligence (Hobbes 2011, 42). According to Hobbes, this equality is the reason why we socialize with each other. Since we all share the same abilities there will never be a situation of subordination in the natural state – the competition or war will last forever. Hence, we are as primarily independent, however, we are endangered beings in need of protection. It is our rational and selfish interest to associate with others. Infants, impaired humans as well as non-human beings do not occur as addressees of moral or political concerns.

In John Rawls, things turn out to be in a way quite similar. In his work *A Theory of Justice* (1999) he assumes that the agents participating in the "original position"[2] are equally rational and "that they are cooperating on terms to which they would agree if they were free and equal persons whose relations with respect to one another were fair". (ibid., 12; cf. also xii, 26, 131). Like Hobbes, Rawls presupposes that the individual as such is free, in the possession of average rational capacities and is basically not dependent or connected to others. Here, the ζῷον λόγον ἔχον (the *zoon logon echon* qua reasonable being) is not inevitably but only "later" a ζῷον πολιτικόν (the *zoon politikon* qua social being) and by no means a dependent and ontologically social being that is influenced by and socialized in the sociocultural world in which (s)he is living and growing up. The association with others is motivated by a selfish concern for the mutual benefit by reciprocal efforts. Only within an already intentionally constituted association that is considered fair, the development of a sense of justice is predisposed (cf. ibid., e.g. 177f.). Moreover, the moral obligations towards individuals lacking the same level of rational capacities (and not considered a part of reciprocal mutual cooperation) are either only derived from the obligation towards "average rational agents" or different by nature. One has to conclude that we have indirect, restricted or lower moral obligations towards infants, mentally severely disabled individuals or humans with psychiatric diseases, and further, animals must be put aside completely (ibid., 15). This appears as counterintuitive and outside of the *normative normality* we are living in, in which

---

[2] The original position denotes a famous thought experiment in *A Theory of Justice*: Free and equal participants in a deliberation consider themselves under the "veil of ignorance". Without any knowledge about their position in society, virtually before they enter this society, they decide about the principles that should govern the basic structures and institutions that determine the co-existence. The famous outcomes of this virtual deliberation are the principle of equality (equal chances for all) and the principle of difference (differences are legitimized if they provide a benefit for the whole society).

infants as well as mentally impaired adults usually appear as beings with special needs that generate special obligations.[3]

As a second example, one can take the Kantian approach to involve a commitment to moral individualism. In the second Categorical Imperative the reciprocity of mental capacities becomes most visible – at least at second glance: "Act in such a way that you treat humanity, whether in your own person or in the person of any other, never merely as a means to an end, but always at the same time as an end" (Kant 1977a, 429). Humanity does not represent the characteristics of the species Homo Sapiens but the capacity of reason, but at the same time morality. The ones who have to be defended against any kind of instrumentalization or abuse are the ones who are autonomous[4]; they are persons with dignity (an absolute value) in contrast to mere things with a price (see Kant 1977a, 434-436) – *tertium non datur*. Obligations towards non-autonomous beings are either non-existent, or, if they are considered vulnerable beings, they have to be conceived as obligations *in regard of e.g. animals* – but *towards ourselves* as Kant states in the famous section *On an Amphiboly in Moral Concepts of Reflection, Taking What Is Man's Duty to Himself for a Duty on Other Beings* (Kant 1977b, §16). This seems to be particularly problematic if we think of infants or severely disabled humans but could also play a role in the moral consideration of animals. In humans, one can counter this conclusion with the argument of potentiality (that is used by many Kantians), but even in Kant himself we find an indication that in turn counter the argument of potentiality. In the *Doctrine of Morals* section of the *Metaphysics of Morals*, we find *Doctrine of Morals* a passage where Kant suggests treating the drunken person like an animal rather than a human since (s)he has inhibited her/his intellectual capacity and has therefore failed humanity qua morality (see Kant 1977b, 80).

---

[3] In the following I will try to construe the critique of moral individualism as an in a way Aristotelian enterprise. This happens admittedly from a particular perspective and aims to make the similarities visible. However, in Aristotle the exclusion of infants, women and others who are not regarded as citizens of the polis (cf. Aristotle, Nicomachean Ethics 1134 b16f.) is an often criticized feature of his practical philosophy. The connection to Cora Diamond, Alice Crary, Paul Ricœur, Klaus Held or Bernhard Waldenfels is in some respects closer related to the methodology and the structure of argumentation than to the respective conclusions. Particularly in this case, one has to mind the differences between the ancient and the modern ethical common sense.

[4] The concept of autonomy is to be understood closely related to the etymology: Construed as the capacity of self-legislation, it describes a certain capacity that is not necessarily tied to the membership to the species Homo Sapiens.

In animal ethics, in the following exemplified by Peter Singer's utilitarian approach and Tom Regan's deontological approach, we find kind a culmination point of moral individualism and its counterintuitive consequences. Particularly the afore-mentioned "normative normality", the lived traditional ethos, is the bogeyman of Peter Singer. In stating that the anchor of moral consideration is reducible to the ability to suffer and the level of (self-)awareness (Singer 2011, 64-66), he claims to take an absolute distance to the lived ethical sense from the point of view of morality (ibid., 13). Drawing on John Locke's concept of the person as a "bundle of experiences" with a diachronic identity[5], he questions both common practices like the use of animals and some moral intuition in regard of the sanctity of human life (ibid.). His most fundamental assumption might be summarized by James Rachels who gets particularly to the heart of moral individualism with the following statement: "The basic idea is that how an individual may be treated is to be determined, not by considering his group memberships, but by considering his own particular characteristics" (Rachels 1990, 173). The equal consideration of interests independently of any kind of species (in contrast to *speciesism* as fundamental kind of a discrimination similarly to sexism or racism) is Singer's core argument (ibid., 53-70). Basically, this approach seems sound and logically stringent. However, the public outcries after the first publication of the *Practical Ethics* in 1979 showed – although sometimes truly harsh and dependent more on an emotional response to Singer rather than on a critical inquiry in his thought – the discomfort that occurs if a theory enters our lifeworld as a foreign body. Particularly the claim that experiments on animals equal experiments on mentally impaired humans with the same cognitive abilities led to debates and protests. The crucial assumption is the one of being human as a mere biological fact without any further significance. Hence, in a utilitarian weighing of interests animals can potentially be preferred over humans (e.g. infants or impaired adults) according to the quality of their interests derived from individual mental capacities. This is most visible in the following quote: "If we make a distinction between animals and these humans, how can we do it, other than on the basis of a morally indefensible preference for members of our own species?" (Singer 2011, 52) Singer serves here as one telling example among others that show clearly the animal ethics discourse as a culmination point of moral individualism that counters common moral convictions as merely traditional, irrational, contestable, and in need of correction.

---

[5] Diachronic identity is the term that describes the self-awareness over time that enables us to have future preferences. In Singer, these future preferences build the basis for the weighing of interests that is crucial for any utilitarian approach.

We find striking similarities in Tom Regan's *deontological* animal ethics approach. The crucial criterion of moral consideration is the "subject-of-a-life-criterion" that is built upon "beliefs and desires; perception, memory, and a sense of a future, including their own future; an emotional life together with feelings of pleasure and pain; preference- and welfare interests; the ability to initiate action in pursuit of their desires and goals; a psychophysical identity over time; and an individual welfare in the sense that their experimental life fares well or ill for them, logically independent of their utility for others and logically independent of their being the object of anyone else's interests" (Regan 2004, 243). Any living being that meets this principle has an inherent value (ibid.) that equals the Kantian concept of dignity insofar as it is an absolute value qua basis for inalienable rights. The case of a collision of rights is exemplified by the famous thought experiment of the "lifeboat case". In this thought experiment, we imagine five persons (four humans and one dog) in a lifeboat that is made only for four persons, and – all passengers will drown if none of them is sacrificed for the other four persons. Regan claims that the dog should be sacrificed for the others because for an animal death has a minor significance – *if none of the human persons is severely impaired*. In such a case the impaired person would be the one to leave the lifeboat because now for the dog the drowning would be the greater harm (ibid., 324).

This does not seem to be rooted in the moral common sense we live in; on the contrary, it appears as a strange moral claim that is outside of our common convictions and practices. In contrast, Aristotle starts in his approach to moral philosophy from the assumption that this lived common sense, this rough ground of the lived and always-already known ἔθος (*ethos*) is the very starting point of any ethics and the basis for the validity and plausibility of moral claims (NE 1095 b3-8). This leads to another perspective on morality and moral philosophy that builds the basis for a present discourse that questions the assumptions of moral individualism that has been exemplified by contractualism, deontology and utilitarianism.

3. The shared ethical sense: Cora Diamond, Alice Crary, and Aristotle

In the following I proceed from Cora Diamond's lapidary statement that it appears extremely strange not to consider impaired humans as addressees of justice or other fundamental and general obligations (Diamond 1991, 44f.). With this claim, she is building on a critique of moral individualism that has been visible throughout her work since her early text *Eating Meat and Eating People* from 1978 (which was published one year before the first edition of Singer's *Practical Ethics*). The fundamental starting point of her criticism (influenced by Wittgenstein's *Philosophical Investigations*) is her reference back to an inevitable pre-determination of any moral thinking and of any practice to a lived ethical sense that is articulated in ordinary moral judgments (see also Alice Crary's comment on Diamond in Crary 2010, 22). This is made explicit by remarks like the following: "We can most naturally speak of a kind of action as morally wrong when we have some firm grasp of what *kind* of beings are involved." (Diamond 1978, 469; italics in the original text) This is fully understandable only against the backdrop of the fact that she does not consider any kind of being solely according to her/his biological categorization but according to a presupposed common notion of humans *as humans* and of *animals as animals*. This is particularly visible in the following quote:

> *We do not eat our dead*, even when they have died in automobile accidents or been struck by lightning, and their flesh might be first class. We do not eat them; or if we do, it is a matter of extreme need, there is a very great reluctance. We also do not eat amputated limbs. (…) [F]undamental features of our relationship to other human beings which are involved in our not eating them" (Diamond 1978, 467).

Hence, to express it with once more, this time using the words of Alice Crary, "we are necessarily guided by a conception of the kinds of things that matter in lives like ours" (Crary 2010, 26) without any possibility of justification or proof. To recognize a being as human or as animal has normative implications that are not expressed according to or even through principles, rights or obligations – and not fulfilled by a mere application of these principles, rights or obligations. Human beings are even pre-intentionally recognized as fellow humans (Diamond 1978, 474) without any consideration of their cognitive capacities. Moreover, we recognize a" special susceptibility" that leads us to the obligation of a "special solicitude" (Crary 2010, 21). For that fact no underlying reasons are given independently of having the orientation that has been described above (see ibid., 31). This refers clearly to an Aristotelian notion of moral significances that are summarized in the concept of the ἔθος (*ethos*). Any kind of moral significance is derived from a pre-knowledge that structures our patterns of recognition, patterns of action and the underlying social approbation.

It is not incidental that *recognition* bears a close etymological and phonetic proximity to cognition. The *ethos* turns out to be efficacious on the subtle level of perception and in our immediate experience. To grasp the nature of this orientation it is useful to draw on Wittgenstein's later philosophical writings, which build an important starting point for Diamond and Crary. According to him, perceptions of other humans (and nonhumans) are imbued with attitudes (that represent tacit recognition); to consider a being as a vulnerable living being, as someone who merits a certain form of respect, neither a conclusion nor evidence nor a mere opinion is required: "My attitude towards him is an attitude towards a soul. I am not of the *opinion* that he has a soul" (Wittgenstein 1986, 178). This shows heuristically, what is expressed clearly in Crary´s claim that our supposedly immediate perception is pre-determined by attitudes with ethical significances (Crary 2010, 24, 26, 28). It is a matter of course that this imbuement influences our relation to others on a pre-reflective level since our actions towards them are disposed by most fundamental significances. These perceptions are "intrinsically practical" and expose things (or: living beings) as "woven into the real fabric of our lives"(ibid., 30). The individual notion of humans and animals as fellow beings is derived from a pre-supposed socialization that is constitutive factor of a personal *hexis*, a *disposition* or *attitude* to perceive and conceive humans as humans and animals as animals with different significances. Since the development of such a disposition is analyzed much more in detail by the phenomenological tradition in close connection to Aristotle´s reflection, I will return to constitution of the *hexis* in the following section.

This attitude is to be understood as a kind of sensitivity and of tacit know-how (in contrast to explicit knowing-that; cf. Varela 1989), not as a matter of abstract knowledge. The most concrete *aistheta*, the most concrete contents of cognition, cannot refer to ἐπιστήμη (*episteme*), that is, to scientific or quasi-scientific knowledge – this goes us back to typically Aristotelian insights (NE 1142 a 27). According to Aristotle, in praxis nothing is totally stable so that a mere application of principles to cases does not suffice (NE 1103b-1104 a9). The individual case exceeds this application and is not sufficiently captured by procedures like the syllogism; the case is more than an example of the rule. Hence, ethics turns out to be a discipline that is not only concerned with the finding and application of principles (which is not necessarily futile when done in the proper context) but also a discipline that is concerned with the (hermeneutical) understanding of "one´s way of viewing things" (Diamond 2001, 118). This refers particularly to the famous sixth book of the *Nicomachean Ethics* that is concerned with the intellectual (dianoetical) virtues – these are the different kinds of knowledge that are of significance in regard to practice or theory. The central intellectual capacity with respect to praxis is the φρόνησις (*phronesis*) – in contrast to theoretical knowledge, the ἐπιστήμη (episteme), as well as in contrast to the τέχνη (*techne*) qua technical know-how that builds the basis for the ποίησις (*poiesis*, the production). The *phronesis* is a "practical wisdom" that is to be considered another kind of habitus than the ethical virtues (NE 1140 a24f.; see also Gadamer 1998, 20). This subtle, tacit habitus orients our actions and co-constitutes our perceptions (NE 1142 a27). To put it paradoxically, one could speak of a mediated immediacy – the experienced, well-trained *phronimos* person has a structured perception through which (s)he directly grasps moral significances. Aristotle indicates an inner relation between *phronesis* and *ethos* on the very level of perception (NE 1142 b30-32). This connects directly to Wittgenstein's concept of the *attitude towards others* that opens our eyes for their being human (or in case nonhuman) fellows.

This has also been visible in Diamond's reflections on the being affected by dead corpses in a morally non-neutral way. Although the dead body obviously is not able to suffer, lacks of course cognitive abilities and does not show any preferences, we are confronted with a representation of the vulnerability of humans that exceeds individual conscious experiences. Hence, one has to assume that the relation to the individual *as a human being* plays a crucial role.

In other words, and from a different perspective, the justification for treating animals in a particular way is not reducible to the equal consideration of interests or the recognition of a subject-of-a-life as such. Diamond says that "we are plainly not treating like cases alike" (Diamond 1978, 466) because this would appear as unfair, cruel (when preferring animals over humans) or simply weird because it would even "attack significance in human life" (ibid., 477). The following quote by Robert Musil shows that heuristically as well as ironically:

> And if someone were, from a pure vegetarian conviction, to say 'ma'am' to a cow (bearing in mind that one is much more likely to behave inconsiderately to a being that one addresses as 'hi, you!') he would be regarded as a prig, if not a madman – but not on account of his animal-loving or vegetarian convictions, which are considered highly humane, but on account of their being directly applied to reality. (Musil 1996, 249)

Now let us turn to two objections that apparently meet virtue ethics in Aristotle and beyond as well as the reflections by Diamond and Crary. *First*, the repeated accusation is vagueness. Without any clear principle, how can such an account inform us about the praxis? Isn't this a slippery slope to an arbitrary treatment of living beings? But Aristotle already responded to this demur with his distinction between *bios politikos* and *bios theoretikos*. In praxis, the reflection and the strictness of the normative claim should be adequate to their object also in terms of certainty and strictness (NE 1094 b 12-27; 1098 b26-34; 1101 a26). In the previous section, we dealt with the pitfalls of moral individualism. One of them is the fact that the application to any situation without considering the relevant circumstances might lead to counterintuitive consequences and maybe even to hard cases. The – at first glance – fuzzier logic of virtues and the soft knowledge represented by the concept of *phronesis* are, at second glance, helpful alternatives to a strict logic of either-or. By constituting *moral gestalts*, (instead of clear, but abstract principles) through the *phronesis* that is directed towards the general norm as well as the most concrete (NE 1142 b35f.), the corresponding practical know-how, the whole situation and the sensitivity for concrete circumstances become crucial (ibid., 1104 b20-25; 1109 b27-30). Aristotle's understanding of the logic of praxis is probably most visible in his famous discussion of the ἐπιείκεια (*epikieia*, translated as reasonableness) in the fifth book of the Nicomachean Ethics. This *epikieia* serves as a complement to justice[6]. However, the reasonableness is not entirely different from justice (NE 1137 b9f.), so obviously there is a complex relation between these two concepts: "The same thing, in that case, is just and reasonable, and while both are good the reasonable is superior." (NE 1137 b24-26) Since justice is a general concept with a universal aspect, there is a need for a rectification (NE 1137 b26f.) – otherwise the mentioned counterintuitive consequences and hard cases could arise. To express it using Wittgenstein, the underlying idea is that the "rough ground" (Wittgenstein 1996, 46) of praxis is in tension with the "crystalline clarity" (ibid.) of the moral principles and their unexceptional application.

Second, many philosophers would claim that the arguments for virtue ethics and the idea of a morally imbued perception rests on the fact that an orientation towards others as humans or vulnerable animals is always-already pre-given and cannot be questioned or criticized. Hence, according to the critique *by* moral individualists, ethical considerations rest on already presupposed orientations that are neither provable nor universal: "Their point is to persuade us that intrinsically practical properties cannot possibly achieve objective status by showing us that judgments about them are invariably characterized by this form of circularity." (Crary 2010, 29) This second objection against Aristotle and the described Wittgensteinian approach to ethics is derived from the epistemological assumption that any kind of circularity in argumentation represents a *circulus vitiosus*, an incorrect circular reasoning. But this can be countered with support from phenomenology that will be the subject of the following section. In *Truth and Method* (Gadamer 2010), we find a systematical analysis of what is only indicated, but not broadly considered in Crary. In the vein of Heidegger's *Being and Time*, Gadamer claims that tacit prejudices and fore-projections have a positive significance because they build the primal condition of the possibility of any kind of understanding (ibid., 271-273). "The recognition that all understanding inevitably involves some prejudice" (ibid., 274) leads us – with respect to practical philosophy – to the conclusion that ethical reflection must not neglect the shared lifeworld significances (nothing else but the ethos!) that build the basis for meaningful moral decision-making and the raising of moral claims. As a result, this does *not* lead to the absurd conclusion that we are basically trapped in long-lasting traditions – like slavery, racism, sexism, animal abuse, etc. Gadamer points out that we can deal with prejudices in a productive way and become aware of them to achieve a critical distance. This is not conceivable in moral individualism as part of a tradition of enlightenment that is stuck

---

[6] The finely detailed analysis of different layers of justice would be beyond the scope of this text.

in "prejudices against prejudices" (cf. Gadamer 2010, 275) and that believes that "moral thinking is exclusively or primarily a matter of applying principles to a world of non-moral facts" (Cordner/Gleeson 2016, 58). Hence, the claim that we should neglect the significance of being human (as construed e.g. in Diamond 1978 to criticize Peter Singer or Tom Regan) as a *mere, unjustifiable* traditional prejudice leads to logical stringency, a nagging moralistic tone (cf. Diamond 1978, 469) and a practical dead end.

To conclude this section, I want to point at the fourth keystone that builds the basis of this paper together with the *ethos*, the *hexis*, and the *phronesis*. The implicit starting point in Diamond and Crary is the understanding of humans as ζῷον πολιτικόν (*zoon politikon*) that is also crucially important in Aristotle. In moral individualism, rational capacities are not only a necessary feature for the moral patient or moral object (the other who is target of an action) but also constitute the independence of the moral agent. The moral actor is *independent of social structures and atmospheres and is able to emancipate her-/himself from any traditional normality*. This is, for instance, most visible in Kant's idea of autonomy by virtue of our reasonability (Kant 1977a, 431) or in Singer's idea that humans are (not as members of the species but as rational beings) able to take the point of view of the universe/of morality (Singer 2011, 13). This independence is not removed but is diminished against the backdrop of an understanding of an embedded actor that is dependent on (but not determined by) shared significances (and also prejudices and fore-projections) that build the basis for the social intelligibility of moral practice and moral claims. This is most visible in the Aristotelian idea of the importance of education to support and to orient the development of ethical and intellectual virtues through social approbation and education (e.g. Aristotle, Nicomachean Ethics 1105 a2f.; 1109 b19).

4. The embodied ethos – Phenomenological Ethics and Aristotle

In phenomenology, the starting point of ethical considerations in authors like Paul Ricœur, Klaus Held or Bernhard Waldenfels can be identified with the lived ethical sense that is already visible in Diamond and Crary – and of course Aristotle.[7]

---

[7] Phenomenology cannot be seen as a uniform tradition of thinking. There are extremely different accounts within phenomenology that cannot all be mentioned in this paper. Hence, the further investigation in phenomenological ethics concentrates on some authors who can easily be brought in a connection to each other due to similar starting points as regards ethics.

To understand the phenomenological enterprise as regards ethics it might be helpful to go back to one very basic cornerstone. With the following sentence, Husserl as founding father of phenomenology presents in his famous *Ideas I* the basis for a broad movement in continental philosophy:

> No conceivable theory can make us err with respect to the principle of all principles: that every originary presentive intuition is a legitimizing source of cognition, that everything originally (so to speak in its "personal" actuality) offered to us in "intuition" is to be accepted simply as what it is presented as being, but also within the limits in which it is presented there. (Husserl 1976, 44)

Drawing on this fundamental phenomenological "principle of all principles", Paul Ricœur and Klaus Held refer equally to the primacy of the *ethos* in relation to *morality* in terms of explicit rules (Held 2010, 15; see also Ricœur 1990, 227). The constitution of abstract principles like the Categorical Imperative is to be seen as a hypostatization that rests on a lived, fluid, contingent (although by no means arbitrary) *ethos* that constitutes a tacit pre-understanding. This is manifest in traditions, different forms of life with different normalities, social structures, and cultural characteristics in which and through which we live (Waldenfels 2006, 269). Principles like the Categorical Imperative are only understandable against the backdrop of this pre-understanding (as already seen in Diamond and Crary and supported by Gadamer); otherwise it would appear as foreign bodies and would not be helpful or applicable in our practice.

The individual takeover of the normative normality is neither a conscious decision nor an appropriate behavior. On the contrary, we are, from the phenomenological point of view, always-already immersed in a social context and learn the most basic sorts of conduct by being-with-others and by tacit rehearsal – we learn very subtly to be polite, tactful, but also not to do harm to each other or to mind special vulnerabilities (Waldenfels 2006, 48). This resembles strikingly the Aristotelian idea of a *hexis*, which is acquired through habituation from childhood on (Aristotle, Nicomachean Ethics 1105 a2f.). The constitution of different habits is then to be interpreted as an *incorporation of moral norms* that are not explicitly conscious; further, the actions in accordance with these norms are not always entirely explicit decisions. The *hexis* is always partly unconscious and turns out to be "operative"[8]; it builds a *tacit know-how* that constitutes us as *native actors* which equals the Aristotelian *phronimos* (Waldenfels 2006, 107). According to Held, the acquisition of the *hexis* is a habituation that evades regarding its status

---

[8] Eugen Fink describes operative concepts as condition of the possibility to be able to define and understand explicit concepts (see Fink, 1957).

as being a personal past (Held 2007, 25). Habituation is not to be interpreted as an event with a clear starting point and a clear end point. Our own moral standpoint is not the outcome of an intentional learning process but refers to a "past that never has been now". On the contrary, it goes back to a being immersed in a social world with normative normalities that serve as a kind of an element in which we are raised and socialized. Held points out that the ἔθος (*ethos*) as well as the latin translation of ἕξις (*hexis*), *habitus*, refer etymologically to habituation as well as habitation (Held 2010, 9f.). Our primal experience with the normative normality is not the conscious confrontation with moral norms and obligations but the growing into this normality. There is no doubt at all that this reflection draws in detail on Aristotle's explanations in the Nicomachean Ethics where the individual is always-already immersed in a lived sociality. The society and its institutions have the task to the development (the internalization of the ethos) of the children.[9]

In Kant's interpretation of the actor as autonomous being, habits represent a decrease of, or danger for, freedom. Freedom and moral practice are then considered as field of continuing conscious decisions. In Held (2007, 2010), but also in Waldenfels (2006), the habituation or incorporation of a normative normality is kind of an enablement for freedom. The routines or dispositions of behavior free us from long and difficult deliberations and are, to come to the second keystone, inscribed in our perceptions and immediate impulses of action. Moreover, they also constitute an affectability or emotional sensitivity to the particular situation because they are not strict principles to applied regardless of the who, the how, the when etc. (see NE 1104 b20-25). However, the downside is a finitude of morality that is disavowed in the Kantian approach (see Held 2007, 28). The conclusion has to be a perspective of moral consideration that is close to relativity – but that is not to be mistaken for a sheer relativism. The backdrop of this reflection is Husserl's enterprise of the rehabilitation of the δόξα (*doxa*, the supposedly mere opinion) (cf. Husserl 1962, 127 f., 135 f., 158, 465). As an ancestor of Gadamer, Husserl is concerned with the significations of the lifeworld that build the condition of the possibility of the intelligibility of abstract scientific insights. The same holds for abstract moral claims like the Categorical Imperative. If we connect this idea with some fundamental insights of the *Nicomachean Ethics*, we can see a striking similarity. Aristotle dismisses Plato's *idea of the good*

---

[9] The question how much coercion is connected to that task in the Aristotelian conception would be very interesting but lies beyond the scope of this paper. When Aristotle uses metaphors like the one of straightening a piece of wood (Aristotle, Nicomachean Ethics 1109 b6f.), one is inclined to assume that he would argue for a strict education. At the same time, he assures us that there is a "natural virtue", a common human predisposition to acquire ethical virtues as well as the *phronesis* (NE, 1103 a24f.).

as impractical and abstract and points at a πρακτον ἀγαθὸν (*prakton agathon*, a good that is to be achieved in existing horizons of practice and significances. (NE 1094 a16f.; 1097 a23).

Another important issue that is discussed by Held, Ricœur and Waldenfels is the one of Kant's "rigorism" (that builds so to say the backside of the objection of "vagueness" against Aristotelian moral philosophy). The interpretation of the entirely individual conscience as a *forum internum* (Kant 1977b, 438) is derived from a "morality" (Waldenfels 2006, 56). First, this rests on the assumption of a radical individuality of the responsible subject. The *forum internum* is a relation of the decision-maker to her-/himself and not connected to an external frame or shared horizon of normativity. Second, it is not incidental that the conception of a forum (that is basically religiously charged) brings up associations with jurisdiction. The relation to oneself is described as being observed by an inner judge (Kant 1997b, 438); lived morality then becomes a supervision by a strict conscience that leaves virtually no room for an εὐβουλία (euboulia, the good counsel, the seeking reflection) and a creative or sensitive decision-making as seen in Aristotle (NE 1112 b23-25). Third, this is also connected with the binary dichotomy of right or wrong in Kant's moral philosphy that is problematic not the least in terms of a common understanding of numerous actions not only as entirely right or wrong but as more or less permissible, respectively good and bad. This certainly refers to a core element of Aristotle's *Nicomachen Ethics*. In numerous passages, Aristotle puts the emphasis on the dichotomy of good/better and bad/worse in contrast to the strictly binary dichotomy of true and false. Moreover, this consideration is closely linked to Held's claim that graduation in the moral consciousness does not (as in Kant) represent indecision between duty and inclination (Kant 1977a, 399) that builds a flaw for the judge of the moral conscience. The mere fulfillment of duty is a borderline case of moral behavior. Like the *forum internum* this represents an example of the Kantian proceeding specifically *not* from the lived experience of being immersed in an *ethos* but rather from what is basically an alleged state of emergency. The basis is the assumption that morality rests on a need for coercion and that we might not trust any instance despite its independent a priori reasonability.

Moreover, one also might face the "problem" of circularity that has already been mentioned in the previous section referring to Diamond's reflections on the *significance of being human* (Diamond 1978) or to Crary's idea of *minding what already matters* (Crary 2010): Outside of regular *horizons of moral judgments* (Held uses the term "*Beurteilungshorizonte*" [Held 2010, 17]) abstract duties appear as counterintuitive, weird or even meaningless. This refers, for instance, to the ranking of animals over humans in Singer or Regan that has already been described. Sacrificing the impaired human instead of the animal appears even in an emergency case as strange if not entirely misguided. One can go one step further and interpret moral individualism as reductionism that potentially withdraws most basic significations. The background is a general tendency to strive for objectification and clear principles that excludes everything that seems not objectifiable as vague (Husserl 1962, 34). This is also visible in the (in)famous Kantian text *On a Supposed Right to Lie from Philanthroplogy* (Kant 1977c). Here, Kant refuses to accept that lying can be morally permissible at least in some extreme cases – even if one would save another's life by lying to the potential murderer. If a maxim has been refuted through the Categorical Imperative there is no situation that might build an exception. There is simply no white lie. This refers to two crucial theorems in his moral philosophy: First, the universalization of a maxim is meant to give us a criterion for acting independently of the particularities of a situation. This is certainly in clear opposition to the Aristotelian point of view. Aristotle refers in several passages of his text to the relativity and situationality of praxis. The culmination point of this line of argumentation might be once more the ἐπιείκεια (*epikieia*) that is meant to correct the generality of strict norms and to constitute sensitivity for the very situation. Second, the respective action is attributed clearly and exclusively to one autonomous, independent being. Hence, responsibility cannot be distributed through or shared between different actors. We are not acting together but only next to each other – this is clearly in contrast to our common understanding of praxis as something, in which others, communities or social atmospheres are usually involved (cf. NE 1112 b27f.).

Finally, the acceptability of judgments is never a matter of quasi-scientific proof. As this acceptability refers to the mentioned horizons of judgments, singular moral judgments and convictions have to build on a kind of plausibility that is also visible in the *Nicomachean Ethics*. In this paper, I referred several times to passages in which Aristotle emphasizes the nature of the *phronesis* as practical wisdom and as tacit sensitivity. This tacit know-how builds the basis for the fact that in Aristotle the kind of argumentation appropriate for ethics is particularly not the one of proof, syllogism and the like. According to Aristotle, in the field of ethics it suffices to show that it is so or so – "there will be no need to know in addition *why*" (NE 1095 b6-8; italics in the original text). Hence, moral philosophy that is inspired by Aristotle should be interpreted as building on the Gadamerian hermeneutical circle that presented in the previous section.

5. Conclusion

We have analyzed some fundamental concepts that build the foundations of Aristotle's *Nicomachean Ethics* and serve as keystones in variegated current theories that contest modern moral individualism. This has been exemplified by the Wittgensteinian tradition (represented by Cora Diamond and Alice Crary) and by the phenomenological tradition (represented by Paul Ricœur, Klaus Held, and Bernhard Waldenfels).

These foundations comprise, among others, four crucial concepts. First, the lived ethical sense that is close to Aristotle's analysis of the *ethos*. Significances that build the basis for moral concerns and moral claims are not derived from strict principles but from a being immersed in a broad horizon of meaning. The *application* of abstract principles is dependent on the socio-cultural context we are living in. Hence, there is no sheer opposition between argumentation or ethical reflection and tradition.

Second, the "normative normality" is not only manifest on the level of intentionality, but already efficacious on the tacit level of pre-intentional behavior and perception. The lived ethical sense is incorporated through education and socialization. This refers to Aristotle's crucially important concept of the *hexis*.

Third, the acknowledgment of the individuality of actor, situation and socio-cultural context leads to the conclusion that adequate moral knowledge differs from scientific knowledge. Drawing on Aristotle and his analysis of the *phronesis*, in both contemporary discourses that have been analyzed, an embodied moral know-how is a kind of a sensitivity that differs from the simple application of principles.

Fourth, the embedded actor is not only part of a social horizon of meanings but also in social relations that pre-determine actions and moral obligations. Thus, responsibility is always constituted, conditioned, and limited by the social world we are always-already immersed. This refers to Aristotle's definition of the human as *zoon politikon*.

These four fundamental concepts are striking examples of Aristotelian theorems that are still a valuable source of current debates in ethics – although protagonists of modern ethical theories often try to dismiss virtue ethics and its elements as vague or outdated. A relying on Aristotle is not only to be found in the Wittgensteinian and the phenomenological discourses but could also be seen in feminist ethics, post-structuralism, theories of recognition, and other contemporary approaches to practical philosophy. However, such a broad analysis for Aristotelian sources of present debates in ethics would go beyond the scope of a journal article.

Dr. Martin Huth, Messerli Forschungsinstitut Vetmed Universität Wien,
Institut für Philosophie - Universität Wien, martin.huth[at]univie.ac.at

References

Aristotle. *Politics*. Oxford: Oxford University Press, 2009.
Aristotle. *Nikomachean Ethics*. (abbr. NE), Oxford: Oxford University Press, 2002.
Crary, Alice. "Minding What Already Matters. A Critique of Moral Individualism." *Philosophical Topics* Vol. 38, Nr. 1 (2010): 17-49.
Diamond, Cora. "Eating Meat and Eating People." *Philosophy* Vol. 53, Nr. 206 (1978): 465-479.
Diamond, Cora. "The Importance of Being Human." in: Cockburn, David (ed.). *Human Beings*. Cambridge: Cambridge University Press, 1991. 35-62.
Diamond, Cora. "The Difficulty of Reality and the Difficulty of Philosophy," in: Cavell, Stanley et al. (eds.). *Philosophy and Animal Life*. New York: Columbia University Press. 43-90.
Fink, Eugen. "Operative Begriffe in Husserls Phänomenologie." *Zeitschrift für philosophische Forschung* Bd. 11 (1957): 321-337.
Gadamer, Hans-Georg. *Wahrheit und Methode. Grundzüge einer philosophischen Hermeneutik*. Tübingen: Mohr Siebeck, 2010.
Gadamer Hans-Georg. "Einführung," in: Aristoteles. *Nikomachische Ethik Buch VI*. Herausgegeben und übersetzt von Hans-Georg Gadamer. Frankfurt am Main: Klostermann, 1998.
Held, Klaus. "Lebenswelt und politische Urteilskraft," in: Leghissa, Giovanni, and Michael Staudigl. *Lebenswelt und Politik. Perspektiven der Phänomenologie nach Husserl*. Würzburg: Königshausen und Neumann, 2007.
Held, Klaus. "Zur phänomenologischen Rehabilitierung des Ethos." *Phainomena* XVI/60-61: 7-20.
Hobbes, Thomas. *Leviathan*. Lexington: Empire Books, 2011.
Husserl, Edmund. *Ideen zu einer reinen Phänomenologie und phänomenologischen Philosophie: Buch 1. Allgemeine Einführung in die reine Phänomenologie*. Dordrecht: Springer 1976.
Husserl, Edmund. *Die Krisis der europäischen Wissenschaften und die transzendentale Phänomenologie. Eine Einleitung in die phänomenologische Philosophie*. Dordrecht: Springer, 1962.
Kant, Immanuel. *Grundlegung zur Metaphysik der Sitten*. Frankfurt am Main: Suhrkamp, 1977a.
Kant, Immanuel. *Die Metaphysik der Sitten*. Frankfurt am Main: Suhrkamp, 1977b.
Kant, Immanuel. *Über ein vermeintes Recht aus Menschenliebe zu lügen*. Suhrkamp: Frankfurt am Main, 1977c.
Musil, Robert. *The Man Without Qualities*. London: Vintage, 1996.
Rachels, James. *Created from Animals. The Moral Implications of Darwinism*. Oxford University Press, Oxford, 1990.
Rawls, John. *A Theory of Justice*. Harvard: Harvard University Press, 1999.
Regan, Tom. *The Case for Animal Rights*. Berkeley: University of California Press, 2004.

Ricœur, Paul. *Soi-même comme un autre*. Paris: Gallimard, 1990.

Singer, Peter. *Practical Ethics*. Cambridge: Cambridge University Press, 2011.

Varela, Francisco. *Ethical Know-How. Action, Wisdom, and Cognition*. Stanford: Standford University Press, 1989.

Wittgenstein, Ludwig: *Philosophical Investigations*. Oxford: Basil Blackwell, 1996.

Young, Iris Marion: "Five faces of oppression," in: Cutt, Ann E., and Robin O. Andreasen (eds.). *Feminist Theory: A Philosophical Anthology*. Oxford: Blackwell Publishing. 2005. 91-104.

Waldenfels, Bernhard. *Schattenrisse der Moral*. Frankfurt am Main: Suhrkamp, 2006.

KATHI BEIER (Leuven)

The Soul, the Virtues, and the Human Good: Comments on Aristotle's Moral Psychology

Abstract

In modern moral philosophy, virtue ethics has developed into one of the major approaches to ethical inquiry. As it seems, however, it is faced with a kind of perplexity similar to the one that Elisabeth Anscombe has described in Modern moral philosophy with regard to ethics in general. For if we assume that Anscombe is right in claiming that virtue ethics ought to be grounded in a sound philosophy of psychology, modern virtue ethics seems to be baseless since it lacks or even avoids reflections on the human soul. To overcome this difficulty, the paper explores the conceptual connections between virtue and soul in Aristotle's ethics. It claims that the human soul is the principle of virtue since reflections on the soul help us to define the nature of virtue, to understand the different kinds of virtues, and to answer the question why human beings need the virtues at all.

Keywords: Elisabeth Anscombe, Alasdair MacIntyre, Aristotle, virtue, soul, modern virtue ethics, moral psychology

1. Introduction: The lack of the 'soul' in modern virtue ethics

Virtue ethics has regained a central position in modern moral philosophy. Over the last decades, it has been developed into one of the major approaches to ethical questions besides deontology and consequentialism. The reappearance of virtue-ethical thinking can be traced back to Elizabeth Anscombe's widely discussed essay *Modern moral philosophy* (1958). In this essay, Anscombe accuses both Kantian and consequentialist ethical theories of being reliant on what she calls 'a law conception of ethics', which, at the same time, lacks a well-grounded law-giving authority – such as God as the law-giver – and, hence, lacks justification at its foundation. As she writes, it is 'as if the notion "criminal" were to remain when criminal law and criminal courts had been abolished and forgotten' (Anscombe 1997, 31). For Anscombe, the only alternative is that the concepts of moral obligation and moral duty and of what is *morally* right and wrong 'ought to be jettisoned' because they are 'survivals (…) from an earlier conception of ethics, which no longer generally survives, and are only harmful without it' (Anscombe 1997, 26). I shall not attempt to determine whether this is a fair description of the pitfalls of Kantianism and consequentialism. Instead, I would like to turn to the more positive side of Anscombe's essay. Her suggestion is twofold. Firstly, she claims that it is more promising for ethics to evaluate a person's actions with reference to the 'thick', specific concepts of the virtues and vices known from Aristotle than to employ the highly abstract notions of being *morally* right or wrong. In this respect she writes:

> We should no longer ask whether doing something was 'wrong', passing directly from some description of an action to this notion; we should ask whether, e.g., it was unjust; and the answer would sometimes be clear at once. (Anscombe 1997, 34)

Secondly, Anscombe admits that turning to an ethics of the virtues is easier said than done. For in order to do so, we first need to develop a better understanding of virtue concepts; and this, according to her, presupposes what she calls a 'philosophy of psychology', i.e. reflections on basic psychological states connected to virtuous agency, such as an agent's motives or intentions. Therefore, she claims that reintroducing the Aristotelian virtues into ethical thinking cannot be done without analysing the psychological conditions of virtuous and vicious behaviour. She argues for this second claim in the following manner:

> In present-day philosophy an explanation is required how an unjust man is a bad man, or an unjust action a bad one; to give such an explanation belongs to ethics; but it cannot even be begun until we are equipped with a sound philosophy of psychology. For the proof that an unjust man is a bad man would require a positive account of justice as a 'virtue'. This part of the subject matter of ethics is, however, completely closed to us until we have an account of what *type of characteristic* a virtue is (…) and how it relates to the actions in, which it is instanced (…). For this we certainly need an account at least of what a human action is at all, and how its description as 'doing such-and-such' is affected by its motive and by the intention or intentions in it; and for this an account of such concepts is required. (Anscombe 1997, 29-30)

If we try to translate this into more Aristotelian terms, it can roughly be interpreted like this: the very concept of a virtue, and, with it, a sound analysis of virtuous and vicious actions, rests on a theory of the human *psychē*, i.e. the human soul. And if we want to understand the virtues and vices, we need to elaborate their psychological basis and thus to develop a rich account of the different powers residing in the human soul, of their structure and their order.

While the first of the two positive claims made by Anscombe has initiated a whole series of books promoting the idea of the virtues in modern ethics, the second has been widely ignored. Today, there are all kinds of modern virtue ethics, the main ones still neo-Aristotelian in style, yet there are also Platonic, neo-Stoic, utilitarian, Humean, Nietzschean, and explicitly pluralistic accounts of virtues. They all more or less subscribe to Anscombe's first claim by taking it for granted that our everyday moral life is in the end better described and analysed in terms of virtues and vices than in terms of duties, preferences, pleasure and pain, consequences, and the like. Almost none of the approaches, however, not even of the neo-Aristotelian ones, takes up Anscombe's second claim.

Thanks to Anscombe's own work, we have certainly gained a better understanding of human agency and of the issues connected to it, such as action causation, the difference between explanatory and justifying reasons, intentionality, and so on. This, however, belongs to action theory, which itself is only *part of* what Anscombe has called a 'philosophy of psychology'. Anscombe suggests that we need to ask questions such as 'what type of characteristic a virtue is', or how a virtue 'relates to the actions in, which it is instanced'. Put in Aristotelian terms again, this amounts to asking what the nature of virtue is, i.e. how virtue is to be defined, and whether the virtues are mere potencies to perform virtuous actions or rather something actual themselves. According to Aristotle, questions like these can only be answered on the background of an elaborated doctrine of the human soul. Yet this is what modern virtue ethics does *not* provide. There is little talk about the soul, and the proposed functional substitutes, if there are any, create difficulties for both defining virtue and exploring the link between the virtues and the overall theory of the human good. Let me give just two famous examples:

In his *After Virtue* (1981), Alasdair MacIntyre explicitly states that in order to reintroduce virtues into ethical thinking, we can no longer rely on what he calls Aristotle's 'metaphysical biology'; i.e. Aristotle's assumption that what is good for an individual living being will have to be defined in terms of its specific nature,, which is such that it moves a living being towards a specific *telos* (MacIntyre 2007, 148). The *telos* of a living being is in line with the order of its soul, and the latter corresponds to its specific nature, Aristotle claims. Therefore, the *telos* of a dog is different from the *telos* of a lion or a human being. Moreover, the order of the soul of a living being is not always in pre-established harmony with its nature but might sometimes be achieved in the very process of pursuing the *telos*. For human beings, the virtues are a result of such an ordering process. MacIntyre wants to preserve Aristotle's teleology but rejects his metaphysical biology, i.e. the grounding of virtues in the human soul (MacIntyre 2007, 162-63).[1] In effect, he replaces biology with social theory and comes to define virtue with respect to the concept of *practice*, that is, as 'an acquired human quality the possession and exercise of, which tends to enable us to achieve those goods, which are internal to practices and the lack of, which effectively prevents us from achieving any such

---

[1] Due to the fact that MacIntyre does not give any reasons for his rejection of Aristotle's metaphysical biology, some critics have argued that it is best understood as tracing back to MacIntyre's Marxist background (see Lutz 2012, chap. 1,150-160).

goods' (MacIntyre 2007, 191). Thus, the grounding of the virtues in a metaphysics of the human soul is replaced by a 'socially teleological account', as MacIntyre emphasizes (MacIntyre 2007, 197). The difficulties that stem from this replacement are obvious. MacIntyre himself recognizes the need for embedding his claims into a bigger story in order to exclude the possibility that a disposition can be called a virtue, which enables us to achieve the goods of, for example, the practice of torture (MacIntyre 2007, 199-200).[2]

A second kind of replacement can be found in Philippa Foot's *Natural Goodness* (2001). Foot seeks to elucidate the meaning of virtue terms by showing that they belong to a wider range of evaluative concepts, which denote natural norms. The underlying conception of natural normativity is based on the claim that all normative judgments about an individual living being share a common structure insofar as they are species-dependent. The life-form of the species sets the norms for evaluating individual members of that species. So, as oak trees need deep and sturdy roots in order to flourish, bees need stings. And just as an individual oak tree, which lacks deep and sturdy roots is a bad oak tree, i.e. an oak tree suffering from a natural defect, so a bee without a sting is a deficient bee. According to Foot, the same is true for human beings. In this respect, she agrees with Peter Geach in claiming that human beings need virtues as bees need stings (Foot 2001, 44). But how do we arrive at a full description of the life-form of a species that in turn helps to define the norm? Foot refers to Michael Thompson's essay *The representation of life* (1995) in, which he claims that the description of a life-form is a set of natural-historical judgements found, for example, in 'the voice-overs on public television nature programmes' or in field guides (Thompson 1995, 280). Thompson explicitly states: 'I think our question should not be: What is a life-form, a species, a *psychē*?, but: How is such a thing described?' (Thompson 1995, 279) Here, again, the study of the human soul is replaced by something else. Thompson means to reinforce the *ontological* study of the soul by way of approximating it *logically*, i.e. by an examination of how we talk about its performances. In effect, he substitutes philosophical psychology for a linguistic approach. This, in turn, creates difficulties for Foot's conception of the good human life. For if we want to follow Foot, we will certainly have to count reproduction among the norms defined by the human life-form, and, thus, will regard it as essential for the flourishing of human beings since it also belongs to the flourishing of plants and animals. Consequently, Foot cannot account for the fact that a human being who voluntarily refrains from reproduction, say for religious reasons, does not exhibit a natural defect but rather a virtue, i.e. chastity. If she insisted, however, that a life of chastity cannot be good, that would run against many intuitions.

---

[2] It should be added, however, that MacIntyre has changed his position and has come to reaffirm both a metaphysical and a biological grounding of the virtues (see MacIntyre 1999 and 2007, xi).

In modern virtue ethics, so it seems, we are faced with a similar kind of perplexity as Elisabeth Anscombe was 60 years ago. If we assume that Anscombe is right in claiming that virtue ethics ought to be grounded in a philosophical psychology, modern virtue ethics, so it seems, is baseless since it lacks a theory of the human soul. It is, we could say, as if the notion of "virtue" were to remain when thinking and talking about the human soul, as the enabling condition of all the virtues, had been abolished and forgotten.

Some authors, however, have in fact connected the virtues and the soul to each other, but apparently with rather destructive consequences. Philosophers like John Doris or Gilbert Harman have tried to show that, from the point of view of empirical psychology, the assumption that there are stable character traits globally influencing our behaviour is not warranted. The experimental record, they say, speaks for "situationism." It suggests, as Doris says, 'that situational factors are often better predictors of behavior than personal factors' (Doris 2002, 2; cf. Harman 2000). Hence, according to Doris and Harman, there is no room for thinking that the kinds of traits called virtues exist at all. This seems to be the most extreme attempt to get rid of philosophical psychology in the sense Anscombe has suggested. Simultaneously, it is meant to refute Aristotelian virtue ethics. If moral behaviour can be perfectly explained by referring to situational factors alone, Doris and Harman suggest, then we should better not assume the existence of dispositions such as virtues and vices. The experimental record, however, does *not* warrant the antecedens. As, for example, Lorraine Besser-Jones or Rachana Kamtekar have shown, the psychological studies the "situationists" invoke can just as well be interpreted in terms of virtue theory (Besser-Jones 2015, Kamtekar 2004). Nancy Snow has even pointed out that there are other studies, which explicitly support the attribution of virtues and vices to persons (Snow 2010 and 2013). So empirical psychology and virtue ethics do not contradict each other.

In what follows, however, I shall focus on what Anscombe has called a 'sound philosophy of psychology'. I shall argue that Anscombe is right in claiming that virtue ethics needs to be grounded in a philosophical psychology. To put things more straightforwardly, I shall defend the claim that the human soul is the principle of virtue. Reflecting on the human soul will not only help us to see 'what type of characteristic a virtue is' but also what kinds of virtues there are, and why we human beings need the virtues at all. In defending this claim, I am able to rely on Aristotle who has given a full account of the relation between virtue and soul. Aristotle's account, however, is not easily accessible in every respect. Although he explicitly links the different kinds of virtues to the different parts of the human soul, the details of the supposed connection are highly controversial. In the following chapter, I shall start with a recollection of the more uncontroversial parts of his theory, which at the same time aims at a first understanding of the nature of virtue. I shall then proceed to the more problematic aspects of the relation between virtue and soul in Aristotle. Finally, I hope to solve the most pressing problems by extending the focus and taking into consideration not only Aristotle's ethical writings but also his metaphysical and psychological reflections. In doing so, I wish to contribute to both the ongoing debate concerning Aristotle's moral psychology and contemporary neo-Aristotelian virtue ethics.

2. The general relation between virtue and soul in Aristotle's ethics

As Aristotle clearly indicates in the first two books of the *Nicomachean Ethics* (EN), virtue and soul are fundamentally inter-connected concepts. It is in these passages that Aristotle establishes the fundamental bond between virtue and soul. He does so in three steps: firstly, in introducing the concept of virtue in the context of the *ergon* argument (EN I 7); secondly, in defining the essence of virtue (EN II 5-6); and, finally, in distinguishing different kinds of virtue (EN I 13 and VI 2). In this chapter, I shall briefly summarize and explain the main ideas behind the three steps.

a) First step: how virtue is introduced in the ergon *argument (EN I 7)*

The *ergon* argument is built on the assumption that what it means for something to be good needs to be determined with regard to its *ergon*, i.e. its characteristic activity. Aristotle explains the underlying thought by drawing the following analogies: just as we call an eye a good eye if it perfectly actualizes its most salient potency, i.e. sight, and just as we call a harpist a good harpist if he perfectly actualizes his most salient potency qua harpist, i.e. if he plays the harp well, so a human being is called a good human being if it perfectly actualizes its most salient potency. Now, given that eyes or harpists have an *ergon* qua eyes and harpists, human beings, too, must have an *ergon* qua human being, which works as a standard of excellence for each of them. Like others, I do not consider this assumption to be unjustified from the outset (cf. Wilkes 1980, Whiting 1988, Gómez-Lobo 1991). On the contrary, it is well-grounded in our everyday practice of evaluating artefacts, bodily organs and persons with a particular profession or social function. Moreover, it is by no means dogmatic, since it does not take for granted that human beings have an *ergon* but, rather, invites us to search for one.

So, the question we should ask at this stage is what the *ergon* of human beings might be. In order to find a characteristic activity of human beings, Aristotle starts to reflect on the question what genus human beings belong to. That is, he starts by asking what is peculiar to us *as living beings*. This is an intelligible move given the general fact that we can learn more about the nature of some X, and hence about its characteristic activity, if we realize both the species and the genus X is a member of. Again, just as we come to see what is peculiar to eyes by realizing that an eye is a certain bodily organ, we presumably come to see what is peculiar to human beings by realizing what is special about them in comparison with other living beings. For Aristotle, living beings are different from non-living beings by having a soul. The soul is the principle of life, so he claims in *De Anima* (Aristotle, *De An.* 413b10). It is by being "ensouled" that living substances live, i.e. that they can actualize the capacities living things characteristically exhibit, such as nutrition, growth, perception, locomotion, or reason; and it is by lacking a soul that non-living substances cannot perform such activities.

Someone who does not accept that souls exist does not need to resign at this early stage. We can easily take Aristotle's claim to be merely terminological. Given that there is a difference between living things and non-living things, living things must have a special feature; there must be a cause for their peculiar life-activities. Others may call this cause whatever they like, Aristotle calls it 'psyche', soul.

Now, being ensouled is what human beings share with plants and animals. Therefore, in order to see if there is something peculiar to human beings, we have to compare the soul of human beings with the souls of animals and plants. In doing so, we shall discover how the human soul is by far more complex than the soul of plants and animals. Here is how Aristotle describes the differences:

> (…) living is apparently shared with plants, but what we are looking for is the *ergon* of a human being; hence we should set aside the life of nutrition and growth. The life next in order is some sort of life of sense perception; but this too is apparently shared with horse, ox, and every animal. The remaining possibility, then, is some sort of life of action of the part of the soul that has reason. One part of it has reason as obeying reason; the other has it as itself having reason and thinking. Moreover, life is also spoken of in two ways as capacity and as activity, and we must take a human being's *ergon* to be life as activity, since this seems to be called life more fully. We have found, then, that the human *ergon* is activity of the soul in accord with reason or requiring reason. (EN I 7: 1098a1-8)

Now if, as Aristotle states, the human *ergon* is an 'activity of the soul in accord with reason', how is virtue related to it? Aristotle continues by explaining that it is through virtue alone that we actualize the human *ergon* fully or perfectly. Consequently, if a human being is supposed to be a good human being, it needs to acquire the virtues and it needs to act according to them. This is the final premise of the *ergon* argument, which leads to the well-known conclusion that what is good for human beings is to live in accord with virtue.[3] Hence, it is

---

[3] As Aristotle puts it in EN I 7 (1098a14-18): '(…) we take the human *ergon* to be a certain kind of life, and take this life to be activity (*energeia*) and actions (*praxeis*) of the soul (*psyches*) that in-

through virtue that we come to act perfectly rationally. No virtue, no perfectly rational activity, and so no human good. It will be easier to see whether this is true once we have reached a better understanding of the nature of virtue.

b) Second step: how virtue is defined (EN II 5-6)

In book II of the *Nicomachean Ethics*, Aristotle defines human virtue in terms of an essential definition; he first identifies its genus term (*genus proximum*) and, after that, explores the specific difference (*differentia specifica*). As Aristotle holds, the genus term virtue needs to be subsumed under is *hexis*, that is, virtue is a habit or state.[4] He reaches this conclusion by way of elimination:

> Since there are three conditions arising in the soul – feelings (*pathē*), capacities (*dynameis*), and *hexeis* – virtue must be one of these. (...) If, then the virtues are neither feelings nor capacities, the remaining possibility is that they are *hexeis*. And so we have said what the genus of virtue is. (EN II 5: 1105b20-1106a13)

While it is rarely mentioned in the commentaries, Aristotle here apparently presupposes what he has elaborated in the *Categories*. Ontologically speaking, virtue is a quality. If we call someone temperate, for example, we predicate a property, i.e. being temperate, of a substance, i.e. a particular person; her being temperate characterizes the person *qualitatively*. For being temperate is neither a quantitative feature nor a relational, temporal, or local one, nor any of the other categories Aristotle distinguishes.

Quality, however, has a fourfold meaning (cf. Aristotle, *Cat.* 8: 8b24ff.) One of it pertains solely to the material side of a first substance. Being tall and thin as a rail, for example, are features of the body alone, of its shape and external form (*schēma, morphē*). Second, a quality can be a property of both body and soul jointly; such qualities are called affections (*pathē*). There are different kinds of affection, depending on the part of the soul that is chiefly involved. Some affections merely pertain to the body, e.g., the bleaching of light hair in the summer sun. In others, the different parts of the soul interact with the body. If, for instance, someone gets pale when being ill, his paleness is an affection of his body, which is caused by a disturbance of his vital functions, hence by some disorder in his vegetative soul. If, by con-

---

volve reason (*meta logou*); hence the *ergon* of the excellent man (*spoudaiou de andros*) is to do this well and finely. Now each *ergon* is completed well by being completed in accord with the virtue proper to that kind of thing (*kata tēn oikeian aretēn*). And so the human good proves to be activity of the soul (*energeia psychēs*) in accord with virtue (*kat'aretēn*).'

[4] Since the translations of *hexis* are diverse, I will stick to the Greek term throughout this paper, including quotations.

trast, he gets angry when talking to a stubborn person, a different kind of affection comes into play since in order to get angry, the mind is presupposed; hence, this is an affection of body and animal soul, which is caused by some intellectual activity. Natural capacities (*dynameis*), by contrast, are not qualities of the body but of the soul. Two persons may have the same bodily shape, yet one is by nature good in drawing whereas the other is not. The fourth meaning of quality is what Aristotle calls "hexis kai diathesis", usually translated as states and conditions (*Cat.* 8b26). The difference between the two, Aristotle claims, is a difference of perseverance. Conditions, on the one hand, are those qualities 'that are easily changed and quickly changing', like heat and chill, or sickness and health, for 'a man is in a certain condition in virtue of these but he changes quickly from hot to cold and from being healthy to being sick' (*Cat.* 8b35). These conditions are, as Thomas Aquinas explains, dependent on accidental or external factors that often vary (cf. Thomas Aquinas, *Sum. theol.* I-II, 49, 2, ad 3). *Hexeis*, on the other hand, differ from conditions in being more stable and long-lasting for they are caused by long-term formation. Aristotle mentions the virtues as examples since 'justice, temperance, and the rest seem to be not easily changed' (*Cat.* 8b33). A *hexis*, then, is a subcategory of *diathesis*; it is a condition but a stable and long-lasting one.

So, when Aristotle identifies the genus of virtue in book II of the *Nicomachean Ethics*, he can rely on what he has said in the *Categories*. Given that virtue terms denominate a person's qualities, and given that there are four kinds of quality, virtue must be one of these. Since we already know that virtue makes us realize our *ergon*, and that the human *ergon* is an activity of the soul, we can exclude shape and external form from the list of possible genus terms. What is left are affections, natural capacities, and *hexeis*. Now, neither virtues nor vices can be affections or feelings. For whereas affections arise involuntarily, virtues and vices do not; furthermore, we are praised for virtues and blamed for vices but we are neither praised nor blamed for having an affection. For much the same reasons virtues are not capacities either. We are born neither virtuously nor viciously, but we are born with certain natural capacities such as, for example, sense perception. If something arises in us by nature, Aristotle explains, we first have the capacity for it, and later perform the activity; virtues, by contrast, need to be acquired, and they can only be acquired by having learned to perform virtuous acts (Aristotle, EN II 1: 1103a26-b3). Furthermore, capacities are ethically neutral, we can use them either for good or for bad ends; virtues, by contrast, are not. If then, Aristotle concludes, virtue is neither an affection nor a capacity, it must be a *hexis*; so *hexis* is the genus term.

Before turning to the specific difference of virtue, let me pause here for a moment in order to give a more positive account of what it means that both virtues and vices are *hexeis*. In this respect, Thomas Aquinas can be of great help. No doubt, there are many differences between his own and Aristotle's theory of virtue.[5] However, the doctrine of virtue he develops in the *Summa theologiae* seems to be fundamentally Aristotelian.[6] For Thomas, as for Aristotle, every virtue is a habit or *habitus*, i.e. a *hexis*. Therefore, Thomas carefully examines the nature of habit before he deals with the virtues. This examination is quite illuminating. It gives us, first, a definition of *habitus* that helps to explain why it is that human beings need to acquire the virtues at all. According to Thomas Aquinas, a habit is a disposition or arrangement, something that brings order into what is not ordered or arranged yet (Thomas Aquinas, *Sum. theol.* I-II, 49, 3). Consequently, dispositions and habits reside in compound beings alone, i.e. in beings 'for whose natures and operations several things must concur, which may vary in their relative adjustability' (*Sum. theol.* I-II, 49, 4, in c). Human beings, as we have seen, are of such a complex nature. We are compounds of body and soul and we are endowed with different capacities, among them, not the least, the capacity of choice. If we did not acquire the virtues, we would not be disposed to live in accord with our specific nature as rational beings who act for reasons,, which entails acting voluntarily. Secondly, Thomas helps to explain the way we "have" the virtues or vices once we have acquired them. Unlike conditions such as being sick or cold, virtues and vices are stable and long-lasting qualities. They dispose and arrange us so profoundly that we cannot lose them easily. Rather, we have them as some sort of permanent possession. In this respect, the virtues and vices belong to what has been called "second nature." And thirdly, as something like a "second nature", we can see that virtues and vices are both something actual and something potential. As *acquired* habits, the virtues are actualizations of our potency to acquire them. In this respect, Aristotle holds that the virtues arise in us neither by nature nor against nature, rather that we are able by nature to acquire them (Aristotle, EN II 1: 1103a24). However, once we have acquired them, we have acquired stable *dispositions*, i.e. potencies, in this case potencies to act in accord with the virtue in question. Hence, insofar as virtues are subject to the logic of act and potency, the acquisition of virtues is not an end in itself, as Thomas emphasizes; we do not acquire virtues in order just to possess them, we acquire them in order to be able to *act* virtuously.

Regarding the specific difference of virtue, we need to determine what exactly we are disposed to when we have acquired the virtues. For this, Aristotle can once more refer to what has been said in the context of the *ergon* argument. Given that every virtue causes its possessor to be in a good state and to do well, his overall definition of human virtue is this: "(…) the virtue of a human being will (…) be the *hexis* that makes a human being good and

---

[5] The dissimilarities between Aristotle and Thomas Aquinas are emphasized by De Young/McClusky/Van Dyke (2009), Pinsent (2012), and Stump (see Stump 2011 and 2015).
[6] As, among others, Flannery (2001) and Te Velde (2015) try to show.

makes him perform his *ergon* well" (EN II 6: 1106a23). Both virtues and vices are *hexeis*, that is, human habits or states; whereas vices are *hexeis* that bring about something bad, virtues are *hexeis* that bring about something good. And what is good and bad for a human being is determined by the *ergon*. Virtues, then, make us act rationally, vices make us act irrationally. The claim that the virtues arrange or dispose our soul so as to enable us to act rationally can be fully grasped once we see how the human soul is in need of such an arrangement. Step three is supposed to elucidate this point.

c) Third step: how the different kinds of virtue are distinguished (EN I 13 and VI 2)

Virtue itself is a genus term covering different sorts of virtue. Aristotle distinguishes ethical from intellectual virtues; but he also distinguishes two different sorts of intellectual virtue, one concerned with practical thinking, the other with *theoria*, i.e. speculative thinking. The distinctions clearly refer to the different parts of the soul. Aristotle proceeds as follows. He first claims that one part of the soul is non-rational, while the other has reason (EN I 13: 1102a29). The non-rational part of the human soul is itself divided. One part of it is the bearer of those capacities we human beings share with plants; it is the cause of life-activities such as nutrition and growth. Yet in this respect the morally good and bad people are not distinct from each other; so, for Aristotle, the nutritive part of the human soul (*threptikon*) has no share in human virtue. There is, however, a second part of the non-rational soul, which is of a more complex nature, for it seems to partake in both the non-rational and the rational part. As proof of the existence of this part, Aristotle refers to weak-willed or acratic agents as well as to their more controlled or continent counterparts:

> Another nature in the soul would also seem to be non-rational, though in a way it shares in reason. For in the continent and the incontinent person we praise their reason, that is to say, the part of the soul that has reason, because it exhorts them correctly and toward what is best; but they evidently also have in them some other part that is by nature something apart from reason, clashing and struggling with reason. (…) However, this part appears, as we have seen, to share in reason. At any rate, in the continent person it obeys reason; and in the temperate and the brave person it presumably listens still better to reason, since there it agrees with reason in everything. The non-rational part, then, as well as the whole soul apparently has two parts. For while the plant-like part (*phytikon*) shares in reason not at all, the part with appetites (*epithymētikon*) and in general desires (*orektikon*) shares in reason in a way, insofar as it both listens to reason and obeys it. (EN I 13: 1102b14-32)

Whoever is familiar with weakness of will certainly would agree. For it is in being weak-willed or incontinent that we can experience the different parts of the soul Aristotle talks about here. On the one hand, there is our desire, say, to stay in bed; on the other hand, reason reminds us of the duties of the day. The continent person will finally get up, even though with an inner resistance; the weak-willed person will not, her desires win over. So, the part of the human soul, which is the cause of our desires and affections apparently is of a special nature. It belongs to the non-rational part insofar as it does not necessarily care for reason and even struggles against reason at times; yet it is also able to listen to and obey reason, hence it can partake in the rational part of soul. Consequently, the rational part of soul must also be twofold. One part has reason to the full extent, 'by having it within itself', as Aristotle says; the other one is the desiring part that has reason only insofar as it can listen to it (EN I 13: 1103a3).

The division between intellectual and ethical virtues accords with this difference. The *ethical virtues* dispose the non-rational part of the human soul; once we have acquired the ethical virtues, our desires and affections will no longer struggle against but obey reason. Hence the right way to acquire the ethical virtues is long-term habituation, through, which the desires and affections are adjusted to reason. The *intellectual virtues*, by contrast, dispose the fully rational part of the human soul; once we have acquired the intellectual virtues, the virtue of wisdom for instance, our rational capacities will be working perfectly. Since there are no desires in the rational part of the soul that need to be adjusted, the right way of acquiring the intellectual virtues is by teaching and learning. Yet, in book VI of the *Nicomachean Ethics*, Aristotle declares that the fully rational part of the human soul is also twofold:

> Now we should divide in the same way the part that has reason. Let us assume there are two parts that have reason: with one we study beings whose principles do not admit of being otherwise than they are, and with the other we study beings whose principles admit of being otherwise. For when the beings are of different kinds, the parts of the soul naturally suited to each of them are also of different kinds, since the parts possess knowledge by being somehow similar and appropriate to their objects. Let us call one of these the scientific part (*epistēmonikon*), and the other the rationally calculating part (*logistikon*). (EN VI 1: 1139a6-13)

Things whose principles admit of being otherwise are practical goods, most of all goods concerned with action. It might be good for you to φ here and now but not for me; and while it was good for you to φ then, it need not be good now, even though the situation may be similar. Thus, in practical thinking we have to deal with contingencies. Since this is a special *ergon*, the part of the rational soul that is concerned with practical truths, i.e. the calculating part (*logistikon*), has a special virtue. Aristotle calls it *phronesis*, that is, prudence or practical wisdom. In theoretical thinking, by contrast, we study things that cannot be otherwise. The virtue that makes us appropriate to that kind of activity by perfecting the scientific part (*epistēmonikon*) of the rational soul, is *sophia*, that is, wisdom.

So far, it should be obvious that for Aristotle virtue and soul are closely connected to each other. Without exploring the human soul, we neither understand the nature of virtue nor the different kinds of human virtue nor the reason for the necessity of acquiring the virtues at all. From the reflection on the human soul, however, we are also faced with the following question: Is the human soul a unity or rather an aggregate of many things? With this question, we enter the more controversial elements of Aristotle's moral psychology.

3. Does the human soul have unity?

In current debates, the question of the human soul's unity has been primarily addressed with respect to the virtue of *phronesis*. Where does *phronesis*, i.e. prudence or practical wisdom, belong to, to the rational or to the non-rational part of the human soul? The question emerges because, for Aristotle, *phronesis* and the ethical virtues can be conceptually distinguished but not separated from each other. As he claims, we cannot be prudent without being good, that is, without having the ethical virtues; likewise, we cannot have the ethical virtues without being prudent (Aristotle, EN VI 13). Prudence requires goodness of character because the prudent agent, in contrast to the clever one, deliberates his actions on the basis of willing to promote something good. Hence his practical inference about what to do here and now has a good principle. He asks himself, for instance, what it means to obey the demands of justice here and now, whereas the clever agent starts deliberating by asking how he can gain as much personal advantage as possible in the given situation. The good principle, Aristotle says, is present in the mind of the good agent but not in that of the vicious one, 'for vice perverts us and produces false views about the principles of action' (EN VI 12: 1144a35). Conversely, goodness of character requires prudence because we cannot know what to do here and now unless we have come to an adequate understanding of the situation we find ourselves in and to a wise decision on that basis; prudence is what enables us to deliberate and decide rationally. Given, for example, that it is good to fulfil the duties of the day, it will be good to get up early. While the good character provides the good end and, thus, the major premise of the practical deliberation, the intellectual virtue of prudence produces the minor premise and the right conclusion, i.e. the decision to get up sufficiently early.

So, again, the question is: Do the ethical virtues, on the one hand, and *phronesis*, on the other hand, belong to two distinct parts of the human soul? Or are they one and the same under two different descriptions, such as the convex and the concave? This is how Jennifer

Whiting puts the problem in a recent paper.[7] According to her, there are two ways of solving it. The first one is the more common and traditional reading among Aristotle scholars. Whiting calls it the "conservative solution"; I prefer to call it the *relational view* of ethical virtue for it tries to solve the problem by giving a relational account of the two parts of the human soul that are involved in ethically virtuous agency. Here is how Whiting describes it:

> What we have here is a single state that involves both the practical subpart of the rational part and that subpart of the non-rational part that is capable of obeying reason, so that this state does not belong exclusively to either of these parts but involves a certain *relation* of these two parts. (Whiting, 'Hylomorphic virtue', 10)

The second view is the one, which Whiting ascribes to John McDowell and, which she wishes to defend herself. She calls it the "radical solution"; I prefer to call it the *identity view* of ethical virtue for it tries to solve the problem by identifying the two parts of the human soul that are involved in acting ethically virtuously. Whiting describes it as follows:

> The alternative is to *identify* the relevant subparts with one another: McDowell could say of practical intellect and the desiring part that is capable of obeying reason that they are ultimately a single part of soul, which can however be described in two different ways. (Whiting, 'Hylomorphic virtue', 10)

Whiting, I think, is perfectly right in ascribing this view to John McDowell for in *Some Issues in Aristotle's Moral Psychology* McDowell claims: 'Practical wisdom *is* the properly moulded state of the motivational propensities in reflectively adjusted form; the sense in, which it is a state of the intellect does not interfere with its also being a state of the desiderative element (i.e. the desiring part of soul, K.B.).' (Mc Dowell 2002, section 11) So, what is the correct account of the human soul and its connection to ethical virtue in Aristotle? How can we determine whether the relational or the identity view is true?

Two points seem to speak for the *relational view*. First, Aristotle clearly relates the ethical virtues to the non-rational, desiring part of soul, and *phronesis* to the practical subpart of the rational part of soul; he then explains how both come together in ethically virtuous actions. This is what I have tried to show in the second part of this paper. Secondly, his description of the continent and the incontinent agent presupposes that the two parts of soul are distinct from one another. In the case of incontinent, or weak-willed, agency, reason wants us to φ while desire causes us not to φ; in acting continently, we φ but we still feel the desire not do so. As Jennifer Whiting claims, the whole second point is of minor concern. For neither the incontinent nor the continent agent exemplify virtuous action. Therefore, if we aim to

---

[7] This paper, called 'Hylomorphic virtue', has been presented at several workshops but is not yet published. It is to appear in *Body and Soul* (see Whiting 2018).

understand the relation between the ethical virtues and the soul, we can leave continence and incontinence aside. As it seems to me, however, the first point is not convincing either. For it seems to be too weak to say that, in acting ethically virtuously, the two parts of the soul happen to be related to each other. Such a relation could easily come about incidentally. Yet it is not by incident that reason and desire pursue the same good end in the case of the virtuous agent. Rather, it is in accordance with the human *ergon* that reason takes the lead and gets the desires to follow. Thus, it seems that the relational view cannot account for the *necessity* of the connection between the different parts of soul.

Do these arguments support the *identity view*? Concerning the virtue related to continence and incontinence, i.e. temperance, it may seem so. As Aristotle explains, in temperate action there is no conflict between reason and desire. He even claims that 'what reason asserts *is* what desire pursues' (Aristotle, EN VI 2: 1139a24). It seems tempting to read this as an identification of reason and desire in virtuous agency. Yet, they *are* not identical. They cannot, if it is true that *phronesis* is the virtue of the practically rational part of soul whereas the ethical virtues are the excellences of the desiring part of soul. This is what Aristotle holds. As we have seen, the different parts of the human soul each have their particular *ergon* or function, hence there have to be different virtues enabling the performance of these *erga*. And this is in fact the case, as Aristotle says at the end of book VI of the *Nicomachean Ethics*. It is here that we see how the different kinds of virtue are connected to the different parts of the human soul:

> First of all, let us state that both prudence (*phronesis*) and wisdom (*sophia*) must be worthy of choice in themselves, even if neither produces anything at all; for each is the virtue of one of the two rational parts of soul. Secondly, they do produce something. Wisdom produces happiness, not in the way that medical sciences produces health, but in the way health produces health. (...) Further, we fulfil our *ergon* insofar as we have prudence and virtue of character; for virtue makes the goal (*skopos*) correct, and prudence makes the things promoting the goal correct. The fourth part of the soul, the nutritive part, has no such virtue related to our *ergon*, since no action is up to it to do or not to do. (EN VI 13: 1144a1-12)

Here it is apparent that, contrary to Whiting's claim, the practical intellect and the desiring part that is capable of obeying reason are not identical. Of course, they need to converge in ethically virtuous agency; yet they do so precisely in virtue of being distinct from each other. The desiring part makes us pursue a good goal, and prudence enables us to make a good decision about how to reach the goal here and now. Hence, the identity view cannot account for the apparent *diversity* of the different parts of the human soul.

I therefore want to propose a third reading,, which I think comes closer to Aristotle. We might call it "the unity in diversity view." It takes into account not only Aristotle's ethical writings, but also his psychological considerations expressed in *De Anima* and the *Politics*. In the following chapter I will briefly sketch this view.

4. Virtue and soul: the unity in diversity view

According to Aristotle, human beings are composed of body and soul; yet the human soul is made up of heterogeneous components, as I have mentioned above. One of them is the non-rational soul comprising nutritive, perceptive and appetitive capacities. For Aristotle, this part of the soul is nothing but the form of the living human body; it is essentially linked to bodily organs and bodily functions. The other part is the rational soul or, as Aristotle calls it, the intellect or '*nous* as such'. Taken as such, the intellect has no connection with the body; it is neither linked to bodily organs, nor does it regulate bodily functions, at least not immediately. Furthermore, *nous* in the sense of the *nous poietikos*, i.e. the active intellect, seems to be ontologically different from the rest of the human capacities. This is at least one way of interpreting the notoriously difficult passage of *De Anima* III 5. Yet, at the same time, the intellect is the supreme element in human beings, as we learn from *Nicomachean Ethics*, book X. Aristotle takes it to be either itself divine or the most divine element in us; and he takes the objects of the intellectual activity to be the supreme objects of knowledge (EN X 7: 1177a15-22). So far, we can once again account for the diversity in the human soul. Diversity, however, does not preclude unity. Unity can obtain between different things if they are parts of a whole. But in order for parts to form a whole, there has to be a unifying principle that sets apart the ruling and the subjected element. Since we now deal with different kinds of governance, the relevant passage is in the *Politics*:

> At all events, we may firstly observe in living creatures both a despotical and a constitutional rule; for the soul rules the body with a despotical rule, whereas the intellect rules the appetites with a constitutional and royal rule. And it is clear that the rule of the soul over the body, and of the mind and the rational element over the passionate, is natural and expedient; whereas the equality of the two or the rule of the inferior is always hurtful. (*Pol.* I 5: 1254b3-10)

By ruling the body *despotically*, the soul is united with the body. A despotic regime, Aristotle claims, is a regime that prevails between elements of different kinds, i.e. elements that barely have anything in common. A resemblance (*homoiōma*) to it or a pattern (*paradeigma*) of it, so Aristotle holds, can be found in households (Aristotle, EN VIII 10: 1160b24-1161a9).[8] For him, the master governs over the slave despotically. This can be a natural and expedient kind of rule for both master and slave if the slave is by nature unable to govern himself.[9] At the same time, the master as the ruling element absolutely controls the activities of the ruled element. Regarding the relationship between body and soul, it follows that it is only through the reign of the soul that the body of a living being can do well; likewise, the living being's characteristic activities all emerge from the soul. The unifying principle of the rational and the non-rational part of the human soul, by contrast, is a *constitutional* or *royal* regime, that is, a regime between elements of similar kind. In the household, this corresponds, for example, to the community of a father and his children, 'since the father is concerned for his children' (Aristotle, EN VIII 10: 1160b26). Regarding the relationship between the rational and the non-rational soul, it follows that the interests, so to speak, of the desires and appetites residing in the non-rational part of the soul cannot be neglected by reason; they are important for the well-being of the whole living creature. The intellect needs to respect them even though it is the intellect that decides to what extent.

Hence, it is the intellect, i.e. the rational part of the human soul, which is responsible for its diversity but brings about its unity. Since the intellect is ontologically different from the rest of the soul, perhaps even a divine element in us, as Aristotle suggests, understanding the intellect allows us to explain why the human soul is of such a heterogeneous nature. At the same time, the intellect's activity is the ultimate *ergon* of human beings; thus, it is the key to understanding how the unity of the human soul is to be established. It needs to be established by unfolding the intellect's ruling power. And here virtue comes in, for the virtues help to execute the ruling power of the intellect. We human beings need to acquire the virtues because the unity of the human soul is neither given nor granted by nature. Rather, it is the acquired perfection of the human soul, that is, the result of a perfective process of unification. It is a twofold perfection, for both parts of the soul need to be perfected in order to bring about the perfect unity of the whole:

The *intellectual part* of the soul needs to be perfected in order to come into touch with the non-rational part. It needs the non-rational part in two different respects. Firstly, in order to develop theoretical excellence, i.e. wisdom, the intellect needs the *phantasmata*, i.e. the perceptual impressions and sensual representations of objects in the environment, as a start-

---

[8] "For master and slave have nothing in common, since a slave is a tool with a soul, while a tool is a slave without a soul. Insofar as he is a slave, then, there is no friendship with him. But there is friendship with him insofar as he is a human being." (EN VIII 11, 1161b)

[9] Note that this is not meant as a justification of Aristotle's claim in *Pol.* I 3-7 that there *are* slaves by nature.

ing point for forming true believes about the world. Secondly, in order to develop practical excellence, i.e. prudence, the intellect needs to reign over the body and the animal appetites to be able to bring about the practical good in the material world. The perfect qualities of the human intellect that are the result of the perfective process in question are the *intellectual virtues*.

The *non-rational part* of the soul needs to be perfected since it is unable to rule human conduct all on its own. Unlike non-rational animals, human beings lack natural instincts; there is no pre-established harmony between perceptions, affections and bodily movements in human beings. The non-rational part of the human soul, taken as such, lacks order. The positive side of this negative claim is that the non-rational soul is capable of listening to reason and of obeying its commands. But the sensual capacities of the soul do not conform with reason from the start. They have to receive this condition by a certain formative, perfective process. This process is the process of ethical habituation. If it is successful, the non-rational soul acquires qualities of perfection that are called *ethical virtues*.

5. Conclusion

The unity in diversity view of the relation between the human soul and the virtues, so it seems, can help to solve some of the pressing problems concerning both Aristotle's moral psychology and neo-Aristotelian virtue ethics. Let me finally briefly summarize the advantages it provides.

As to the debate on Aristotle's moral psychology, the view, first of all, allows us to see to what extent the soul is the principle of virtue. For exploring the parts of the human soul helps to explain the nature of virtue, the difference between the ethical and the intellectual virtues, and even the different sorts of ethical and intellectual virtues alike; furthermore, it helps to understand why we human beings need the virtues at all if we are to live a good human life. Secondly, the unity view justifies Aristotle's final conclusion in *Nicomachean Ethics*, book X, hence it reveals the unity of the *Nicomachean Ethics*, which is sometimes challenged. Given that it is the intellect that is peculiar to human beings, and given that the intellect is twofold, comprising both practical and speculative thinking, with speculative thinking as the act of the *nous* as such, it cannot come as surprise that the most excellent way of life for us humans is the life of *theoria*, i.e. contemplation. Contemplating about things that cannot be otherwise is, as Aristotle claims, the most supreme intellectual activity for human beings; at the same time, it is the most pleasurable. Living in accordance with the ethical virtues is the second best, since here the intellect is operative as well but in a less supreme way, for it deals with contingencies.

As to neo-Aristotelian virtue ethics, the unity in diversity view does full justice to Anscombe's claim about the necessity of a philosophy of psychology. For it helps to understand, e.g. what type of characteristic a virtue is and how a virtue relates to the actions in, which they are instanced. Of course, there is a lot more to say about how exactly Aristotelian psychology can contribute to modern virtue ethics. But if we do not avoid to study the human soul both on metaphysical and empirical grounds, and if we refrain from substituting philosophical psychology for either social theory or philosophy of language, we will certainly be able to overcome the difficulties some of the neo-Aristotelian accounts of virtue ethics struggle with. With regard to MacIntyre and Foot, here are at least some hints. Concerning Alasdair MacIntyre's account in *After Virtue*, the unity in diversity view allows us to say that the practice of torture can by no means be virtuous since it represents both a lack of prudence, insofar as it is based on the idea of choosing bad means, i.e. inflicting pain on another person, and a lack of character, insofar as it involves the willingness to use such means. Concerning Philippa Foot, the unity view can make perfect sense of someone's refusal to reproduce for the sake of chastity. For it shows that a life devoted to contemplate God is not deficient in any sense but can be a good life.

Dr. Kathi Beier, Hoger Instituut voor Wijsbegeerte, KU Leuven,
kathi_beier[at]web.de

References

Anscombe, G.E.M. "Modern Moral Philosophy," in Goger Crisp, and Michael Slote (eds.). *Virtue Ethics*. Oxford: Oxford University Press, 1997. 26-44.

Aristotle. *Categories*. Transl. by J.L. Ackrill. In Jonathan Barnes (ed.). *The Complete Works of Aristotle*. Vol. 1. Princeton, New Jersey: Princeton University Press, 1984. 3-24.

Aristotle. *De Anima*. Transl. by J.A. Smith. In Jonathan Barnes (ed.). *The Complete Works of Aristotle*. Vol. 1. Princeton, New Jersey: Princeton University Press, 1984. 641-692.

Aristotle. *Nicomachean Ethics*. Translated with Introduction, Notes, and Glossary by Terence Irwin. 2nd Edition. Indianapolis/Cambridge: Hacket Publishing Company, Inc. 1999.

Aristotle. *Politics*. Transl. by B. Jowett. In Jonathan Barnes (ed.). *The Complete Works of Aristotle*. Vol. 2. Princeton, New Jersey: Princeton University Press, 1984. 1986-2129.

Besser-Jones, Lorraine. "The Situationist Critique," in Lorraine Besser-Jones, and Michael Slote (eds.). *The Routledge Companion to Virtue Ethics.* New York: Routledge, 2015. 375-384.

De Young, Rebecca Konyndyke, Colleen McClusky, and Christina Van Dyke. *Aquinas's Ethics: Metaphysical foundations, moral theory, and theological context.* Notre Dame, Ind.: University of Notre Dame Press, 2009.

Flannery, Kevin L. *The Aristotelian Logical Structure of Thomas Aquinas's Moral Theory.* Washington, D.C.: The Catholic University of America Press, 2001.

Doris, John. *Lack of Character: Personality and Moral Behavior.* Cambridge: Cambridge University Press, 2002.

Foot, Philippa. *Natural Goodness.* Oxford: Clarendon Press, 2001.

Goméz-Lobo, Alfonso. "The Ergon-Inference," in John P. Anton, and Anthony Preus (eds.). *Essays in Ancient Greek Philosophy IV: Aristotle's Ethics.* Albany: State University of New York Press, 1991. 42-57.

Harman, Gilbert. "The Nonexistence of Character Traits." *Proceedings of the Aristotelian Society* 100 (1), 2000. 223-226.

Kamtekar, Rachana. "Situationism and Virtue Ethics on the Content of Our Character." *Ethics* 114 (3), 2004. 458-491.

Lutz, Christopher Stephen. *Reading Alasdair MacIntyre's* After Virtue. London: Continuum, 2012.

MacIntyre, Alasdair. *Dependent Rational Animals: Why Human Beings Need the Virtues.* London: Duckworth, 1999.

MacIntyre, Alasdair. *After Virtue: A Study in Moral Theory.* 3rd Edition. Notre Dame, Indiana: University of Notre Dame Press, 2007.

McDowell, John. "Some Issues in Aristotle's Moral Psychology," in *Mind, Value, and Reality.* Cambridge, Mass.: Harvard University Press, 2002. 23-49.

Snow, Nancy. *Virtue as Social Intelligence: An Empirically Grounded Theory.* New York: Routledge, 2010.

Snow, Nancy. "Notes Toward an Empirical Psychology of Virtue: Exploring the Personality Scaffolding of Virtue," in Julia Peters (ed.). *Aristotelian Ethics in Contemporary Perspective.* New York/Abingdon: Routledge, 2013. 130-144.

Thomas Aquinas. *Summa theologiae.* Transl. by Fathers of the English Dominican Province. Benziger Bros. Edition, 1947. (http://www.dhspriory.org/thomas/summa/index.html)

Thompson, Michael. "The Representation of Life," in Rosalind Hursthouse, Gavin Lawrence, and Warren Quinn (eds.). *Virtues and Reasons: Philippa Foot and Moral Theory.* Oxford: Clarendon Press, 1995. 247-296.

Stump, Eleonore. "The Non-Aristotelian Character of Aquinas's Ethics. Aquinas on the Passions." *Faith and Philosophy* 28.1, 2011. 29-43.

Stump, Eleonore. "True Virtue and the Role of Love in the Ethics of Aquinas," in Harm Goris, Lambert Hendriks, and Henk Schoot (eds.). *Faith, Hope, and Love: Thomas Aquinas on Living by the Theological Virtues.* Leuven: Peeters, 2015. 7-24.

Te Velde, Rudi. "The Hybrid Character of the Infused Moral Virtue according to Thomas Aquinas," in Harm Goris, Lambert Hendriks, and Henk Schoot (eds.). *Faith, Hope, and Love: Thomas Aquinas on Living by the Theological Virtues.* Leuven: Peeters, 2015. 25-43.

Whiting, Jennifer. "Aristotle's Function Argument: A Defense." *Ancient Philosophy* 8 (1), 1988. 33-48.

Whiting, Jennifer. "Hylomorphic Virtue: Cosmology, Embryology, and Moral Development in Aristotle." Unpublished Manuscript (to appear in Jennifer Whiting, *Body and Soul*, Oxford: Oxford University Press 2018).

Wilkes, Kathleen V. "The God Man and the Good for Man in Aristotle's Ethics," in Oksenberg Rorty, Amélie (ed.). *Essays on Aristotle's Ethics.* Berkeley: University of California Press, 1980. 341-357.

SUSANNE MOSER (Vienna)

Tugend als Wert: Christoph Halbig und Max Scheler im Vergleich

Abstract

Virtue as Value: A Comparison between Christoph Halbig and Max Scheler

The aim of the following contribution is to compare the virtue conceptions of Christoph Halbig and Max Scheler in order to scrutinize their common positions and differences and thus to answer two questions: Firstly, is it true that Scheler's approach is based on the basic assumptions of the recursive theory of virtues, as Halbig asserts this? Secondly, can the virtues be defined as attitudes (Thomas Hurka, Christopher Halbig), or should they be conceived as qualities of the person (Max Scheler)? In addition, the author examines the connection of virtues and emotions more closely and shows that virtues can be regarded as a kind of transformers from the negative to the positive, because they fix the right way of dealing with negative emotions and because they switch over the negative basic mood into a positive and joyful one. The reflection of these questions is embedded in a constant reference to Aristotle's understanding of virtues.

Keywords: Christoph Halbig, Max Scheler, Thomas Hurka, recursive argument, virtue, value

In den letzten Jahren ist es zu einer starken Wiederbesinnung auf die Tugend gekommen – und dies nicht nur in der fachphilosophischen Diskussion, sondern auch in moralpsychologischen, handlungstheoretischen und wirtschaftlichen Bereichen. In zunehmend komplexer werdenden Situationen wird es immer wichtiger, über Eigenschaften zu verfügen, die dazu verhelfen können angemessen und richtig zu handeln. Diese Tauglichkeit und Kraft, verlässlich gut zu reagieren, liegt dem Begriff der Tugend ursprünglich zugrunde. Erst später wurde er auf den Bereich des Sittlichen reduziert, was dazu führte, dass er immer mehr in den Hintergrund geriet und belächelt, wenn nicht sogar verachtet wurde. Max Scheler macht dies deutlich, wenn er bei der Tugend von einer "alten Jungfer" spricht, – eine Analogie, die nicht ganz ihrer Realität entbehrt, wurde doch der Begriff der Tugend im viktorianischen Zeitalter einzig und allein auf die Keuschheit reduziert.

> Und doch war diese alte, keifende, zahnlose Jungfer zu anderen Zeiten, zum Beispiel in der Blüte des Mittelalters und bei den Hellenen und Römern vor der Kaiserzeit, ein höchst anmutiges, anlockendes und charmevolles Wesen. (Scheler 1919, 13)

Oft denke man bei dem Wort "Tugend" an eine peinliche Kraftanstrengung und vergesse ganz, dass es sich ursprünglich um ein "glückliches Könnens- und Machtbewußtsein" gehandelt habe. Auch dort wo sie in den heutigen öffentlichen Debatten als ein wichtiger ethischer Begriff verstanden wird, ist die Tugend nicht unumstritten. Von denen Einen als wesentlicher Glücksfaktor gepriesen (Seligmann 2002), warnen die Anderen vor der Gefahr eines Tugendterrors (Sarazin 2014). Es erhebt sich also die Frage, worin denn der Wert der Tugend überhaupt besteht und wo die Grenzen einer Tugendethik liegen.

Zunächst von der Absicht getragen, die Defizite der kantischen und utilitaristischen Ethiken zu korrigieren,[1] geht es in den gegenwärtigen philosophischen Debatten um die Klärung des Begriffes der Tugend selbst. Neben denjenigen Ansätzen, welche – unter Rückgriff auf Aristoteles – die Bedeutung der Tugenden für ein gutes und glückliches menschliches Leben betonen (Foot 2001, Hursthouse 2004), liegt der Schwerpunkt nunmehr in den Analysen einzelner Aspekte, seien dies nun Charaktereigenschaften (Slote 1996, 2001; Annas 2004 und 2005), der Nutzen der Tugenden (Zagzebski 1996), oder ihre Aneignung (Vogler 2013, Annas 2004, Müller 2008). Auch stellt sich die Frage, ob das Verständnis des Wesens der Tugend, so wie Aristoteles es vorlegt, aufgrund der darin enthaltenen essentialistischen und metaphysischen Voraussetzungen heute noch nutzbar gemacht werden kann. (Beier 2016, 127)

Ein weiterer Aspekt des Tugendbegriffs besteht in seinem Verständnis als Wert. In seinem kürzlich erschienenen Buch *Der Begriff der Tugend und die Grenzen der Tugendethik* geht Christoph Halbig davon aus, dass erst über eine Axiologie der Tugend die volle Bedeutung der Tugend für die Ethik verstanden werden könne. Es müsse geklärt werden, "was die Tugenden sind und worin genau ihr Wert besteht." (Halbig 2013, 17) Halbig verortet sich in der Nähe Max Schelers, denn "unzweifelhaft steht im Mittelpunkt von Schelers Argumentation das Bemühen um die Rehabilitierung der Tugend als eines zentralen intrinsischen Wertes." (ebd., 66) Das Verständnis der Tugend als Wert entspricht einer bereits länger andauernden Entwicklung immer mehr Bereiche unter den Begriff des Wertes zu subsumieren. Hannah Arendt verweist auf "die aus der neuesten Philosophie so bekannte Transformierung der Güter und Tugenden der traditionellen Philosophie in Werte." (Arendt 2013, 319) Wenn früher von Tugenden oder Pflichten gesprochen wurde, so spricht man heute von Werten.

---

[1] Die erste Generation der neuen Tugendethiker wie z.B. Elisabeth Anscombe, Peter Geach, Iris Murdoch, Philippa Foot, Michael Stocker, Rosalind Hursthouse und Alasdair MacIntyre möchte die Schwierigkeiten des Kantianismus und des Konsequentialismus überwinden. Die Tugendethik sei nicht auf eine "Gesetzeskonzeption von Ethik" angewiesen, der es an einer wirklich gesetzgebenden Instanz mangele (Anscombe 1958). Sie zwinge keine schizophrene Haltung zwischen Handlungsgründen und Handlungsmotiven auf (Stocker 1976) und produziere keine unüberwindliche Kluft zwischen der Natur des Menschen, den moralischen Geboten und den Verboten. (MacIntyre 1984)

Und umgekehrt, wenn heute ein Werteverlust beklagt wird, dann bringt man damit sein Bedauern zum Ausdruck, dass es zu einem Verlust bestimmter Tugenden wie Ehrlichkeit, Mitleid oder Mut gekommen ist.

Ziel meines Beitrages ist es, einen Vergleich zwischen den Tugendauffassungen von Christoph Halbig und Max Scheler zu unternehmen, um das Gemeinsame und die Differenzen sichtbar zu machen und damit zwei Fragen zu beantworten: Erstens, stimmt es, dass Schelers Ansatz wirklich mit den Grundannahmen der rekursiven Theorie der Tugenden übereinstimmt, so wie Halbig dies behauptet? Zweitens, kann man die Tugenden wirklich als Einstellungen definieren, so wie dies Halbig in Anlehnung an Thomas Hurka macht, oder sollte man eher auf diejenigen Ansätze zurückgreifen, welche die Tugenden als Qualitäten der Person verstehen? Darüber hinaus möchte ich den Zusammenhang von Tugenden und Emotionen näher untersuchen und aufzeigen, dass Tugenden als eine Art Transformatoren vom Negativen hin zum Positiven angesehen werden können und zwar zum einen, weil sie den richtigen Umgang mit negativen Emotionen nachhaltig festlegen und zum anderen weil sie deren negative Grundgestimmtheit in eine positive und freudige umpolen. Dabei werden meine Überlegungen eingebettet sein in eine immer wieder aufs Neue vorgenommen Bezugnahme auf Aristoteles und sein Verständnis der Tugend.

1. Das rekursive Argument

Bei der Erarbeitung einer Axiologie der Tugenden orientiert sich Christoph Halbig an Thomas Hurkas *Virtue, Vice and Value*, welches er als das beste Buch über Tugend seit Aristoteles ansieht. (Halbig 2013, 17) Darin entwickelt Hurka seine rekursive Theorie der Tugenden und betont, dass bisher den Tugenden entweder nur ein instrumenteller Wert in Hinsicht auf die Erzielung des Guten oder Richtigen zugestanden worden sei, wodurch sie unterbewertet wurden. Oder, wie dies bei der Tugendethik der Fall sei, habe man sie zum alleinigen Wert erhoben, wodurch sie überbewertet worden seien und wichtige Aspekte des Utilitarismus und der Pflichtenethik übergangen wurden. (Hurka 2001, 3) Hurka leugnet den instrumentellen Wert der Tugenden nicht, aber er gibt ihnen darüber hinaus einen intrinsischen Wert. Ausgehend von einem Zitat von Aristoteles erläutert er den eigenen Argumentationsgang:

> Zu jeder Tätigkeit gibt es eine ihr eigentümliche Lust. Die der guten Tätigkeit eigentümliche Lust nun ist gut, die der schlechten gegenüber schlecht. (Hurka 2001, 23, zitiert nach Aristoteles 2011, 1175b24-30)

Obwohl die Lust ursprünglich keinen Wert an sich darstelle, bekomme sie in Verbindung mit einer guten Tätigkeit einen intrinsischen Wert.²

> Aristotle here affirms the core idea of the recursive characterization: that the value of an attitude, in this case pleasure, depends on the value of its object. (Hurka 2001, 24)

Das rekursive Argument bestehe in der Bezugnahme auf das Gute (*goodness*), woraus sich der intrinsische Wert der Tugend ergebe: "The account takes virtue to consist in a noncausal, and more specifically an intentional, relation to goodness and evil and holds that as this relation, virtue is a further intrinsic good."³ (ebd., 13)

Für Hurka stellt die Tugend nicht den einzigen intrinsischen Wert dar, vielmehr schreibt er auch den Objekten, auf welche die Tugenden Bezug nehmen, einen intrinsischen Wert zu. Für ihn sind "pleasure, knowledge and achievement" (ebd., 12) Güter, die in sich wertvoll sind. Lust sei ein utilitaristisches Gut (*welfarist good*), während Wissen und Leistung perfektionistische Güter seien (*perfectionist goods*). Hurkas rekursive Theorie der Tugenden ist Teil seiner Auseinandersetzung mit umfassenderen Fragen nach dem guten Leben, nach dem Wesen des Menschen und dessen möglicher Vervollkommnung. Bereits in seinem Buch *Perfectionism* plädiert er im Gegensatz zum "*pure perfectionism*", der keinen intrinsischen Wert in der Freude, nicht einmal in der Freude am Guten sehe und auch den Tugenden keinen intrinsischen Wert zuschreibe,⁴ für einen "*Aristotelian perfectionism*", für den das menschliche Gute in der Verwirklichung und Vervollkommnung der menschlichen Natur bestehe: "The human good consists in the development of human nature." (Hurka 1993, 190) Eine Morallehre, die keinerlei Bezüge zu denjenigen Eigenschaften (*properties*) herstelle, die

---

² Hurka verweist darauf, dass Aristoteles an manchen Stellen annehme, dass es Aktivitäten gäbe, die nicht mit Freude verbunden seien, nämlich beim Tun von etwas ganz Niedrigem (Aristoteles 1985, 1174 a 4-9), an anderen Stellen betone er jedoch, dass Freude eine notwendige Begleiterscheinung guter Taten sei.

³ Hurka zitiert auch Franz Brentano, der den rekursiven Gedanken von Aristoteles insofern weiterentwickelt habe, als er die Liebe zum Guten selbst als etwas intrinsisch Wertvolles angenommen habe: "The correctness and higher character of these feelings ... is itself to be counted something that is good. And love of the bad is something that is itself bad." (ebd., 25)

⁴ Hurka weist darauf hin, dass wir bei Kant ein perfektionistische Ideal vorfinden, das in einen Imperativ münde. (Hurka 1993, 17) Kant spricht von der Pflicht des Menschen zur eigenen Vollkommenheit: 1. Es ist ihm Pflicht: "sich aus der Rohigkeit seiner Natur, aus der Tierheit, immer mehr zur Menschheit (...) empor zu arbeiten um der Menschheit, die in ihm wohnt, würdig zu sein." 2) Die Kultur seines Willens bis zur reinsten Tugendgesinnung, da nämlich das Gesetz zugleich die Triebfeder seiner pflichtmäßigen Handlungen wird, zu erheben und ihm aus Pflicht zu gehorchen. (Kant 1993, 516, A14,15)

für die menschliche Natur konstitutiv seien, habe keinerlei moralisches Gewicht.[5] (ebd., 191) In diesem Sinn entwickelt Hurka folgende Definition der Tugend:

> The moral virtues are those attitudes to goods and evils that are intrinsically good, and the moral vices are those attitudes to goods and evils that are intrinsically evil. (Hurka 2001, 20)

Seiner rekursiven Theorie entsprechend, versteht Hurka die Tugenden als eine intrinsisch wertvolle Bezugnahme auf Güter (*goods*) die ihrerseits intrinsisch wertvoll sind. Wie das Verhältnis von Güter (*goods*) und "dem Guten" (*goodness*) zu verstehen ist, bleibt hier allerdings offen.

Christoph Halbig knüpft in seinem 2013 erschienenen Buch *Der Begriff der Tugend und die Grenzen der Tugendethik* an Hurkas Definition der Tugenden an. Der polyvalente Charakter des englischen Wortes "*attitude*", den Hurka verwendet, das sowohl Verhalten, als auch Haltung und Einstellung bedeutet, wird von Halbig mit "Einstellung"[6] übersetzt. Dadurch erhält Halbigs Definition der Tugenden als "intrinsisch wertvolle Einstellungen zu anderen intrinsischen Werten" eine ganz bestimmte Färbung. (Halbig 2013, 18) Denn der Begriff Einstellung verweist zunächst einmal auf eine Sichtweise auf bestimmte Dinge. So werden in der Europäischen Wertestudie die Menschen alle zehn Jahre zu ihren Einstellungen zu Familie, Arbeit, Religion, Politik und Gesellschaft befragt. (Polak 2011, 9) Handelt es sich bei diesen Einstellungen um Tugenden? Sicherlich nicht, auch wenn hier die Einstellung der Europäer zu bestimmten Werten erhoben wird. Halbig ist sich dieser Problematik bewusst, indem er darauf hinweist, dass es sich bei statistischen Erhebungen lediglich um theoretische Einstellungen handle, die außerhalb des Bereiches der Tugend liegen. (Halbig 2013, 55) Bei der statistischen Erfassung gehe es darum, "die Wahrheit über gesellschaftliche Verhältnisse herauszufinden; dem mitfühlenden Menschen geht es darum, im Lichte des Guten eine an-

---

[5] Hurka betont, dass der aristotelische Perfektionismus, so wie er ihn entwickeln möchte, nicht nur auf individuelles Verhalten beschränkt sei, sondern auch das politische Handeln umfasse. Die beste Politik sei diejenige, welche die Vervollkommnung aller Menschen fördere. (Hurka 1993, 147). Karl Marx habe die Vision einer Gesellschaft gehabt, in der jeder Mensch sich an der Entfaltung und Vervollkommnung seines je eigenen individuellen Wesens erfreuen könne, indem er seine körperlichen und mentalen Fähigkeiten in einem Umfeld realisiere. (ebd., 147) Dabei sei er von dem Gedanken ausgegangen, dass dies nur unter der gleichzeitigen Entfaltung aller anderen Mitglieder der Gesellschaft möglich sei. "This idea of Marx's – that each can develop best when all develop – is his greatest contribution to perfectionism." (ebd., 177)

[6] Halbig weist darauf hin, dass Tugenden nicht unmittelbar verhaltenswirksam sein müssen, sondern auf eine bloße Einstellung beschränkt bleiben können. Sie können sich auch in Wünschen oder Erinnerungen manifestieren. Die Tugend des Mitgefühls könne sich darin äußern, dass man Mitgefühl für die Opfer des großen Erdbebens von Lissabon im achtzehnten Jahrhundert verspüre, ohne daran etwas ändern zu können, oder den Wunsch hege "nach einer schmerzlosen Therapie für einen akut Erkrankten, die außerhalb des medizinisch Möglichen liegt." (Halbig 2013, 56)

gemessene Einstellung zu diesem Leid zu finden." (ebd., 56) Halbig betont also, dass es sich bei den Tugenden nicht um irgendwelche Einstellungen handelt, sondern nur um solche, die es uns ermöglichen angemessen auf bestimmte Situationen zu reagieren.

1.1. Angemessenheit

Bei der rekursiven Theorie der Tugenden geht es um eine zweistellige Relation zwischen den Einstellungen und ihren Objekten. Beide möchte Halbig getrennt untersuchen, um eine Antwort darauf geben zu können, ob eine angemessene Einstellung vorliegt. "Sowohl (i) die Ontologie der intrinsischen Werte, die die *Objekte* der Einstellungen bilden, wie (ii) die Ontologie dieser *Einstellungen* selbst bedürfen indes noch einer Klärung." (ebd., 51) Hierbei fällt auf, dass Halbig auf der Objektseite sowohl von Objekten als auch von Werten spricht, wobei er – wie wir noch sehen werden – die Begrifflichkeit dann auch noch auf Güter und Sachverhalte ausdehnt.

Halbig nähert sich der Thematik der Angemessenheit der Tugenden unter anderem über ihr Gegenteil an, nämlich die Laster. Hier, so Halbig, erfahren die Werte nicht die ihnen angemessene Reaktion, weil entweder überhaupt der Wert fehle, wie im Falle der Gleichgültigkeit oder der Rücksichtslosigkeit, oder weil die Reaktion dem Wertcharakter ihrer Objekte zuwiderlaufe, wie im Falle der Böswilligkeit. Ein Schadenfroher freue sich über ein Übel, ein Sadist oder Grausamer über das Leiden des Anderen, ein Zyniker verabscheue das Gute, das er in seiner Umwelt vorfinde, mache es lächerlich und versuche es als subtile Form des Schlechten zu entlarven. (ebd., 193)

Mit Joseph Raz nimmt Halbig drei Stadien einer angemessenen Reaktion auf Werte an (Raz 2001, 161, zitiert nach Halbig 2013, 196): Das erste Stadium bestehe in der Anerkennung, dass ein Wert vorliegt, das zweite in der Anerkennung, dass der Wert als solcher verdiene, erhalten zu werden und das dritte darin, sich auf den Wert einzulassen und ihn im eigenen Leben zur Entfaltung zu bringen. Bedeutet das nun, dass wir einen unmusikalischen Menschen oder Jemanden, der kein Verständnis für Rembrandt hat, als lasterhaft bezeichnen? Halbig gibt hier mit Robert M. Adams zu bedenken, "dass nicht *jeder* Mangel an Interesse am Guten ein Laster ist." (Adams 2006, 45, zitiert nach Halbig 2013, 194) Niemand werde getadelt, weil er sich nicht auf jeden Wert einlasse. Nur die Formen von Gleichgültigkeit verdienen es als lasterhaft bezeichnet zu werden, wenn sie fundamentale Werte betreffen. Es dürfe aber erwartet werden, dass man seine ästhetische Sensibilität in einer angemessenen Breite kultiviere und damit auf ästhetische Werte in angemessener Weise antworte und dass man auch denjenigen Wertbereichen, auf die man sich nicht näher einlasse, den nötigen Respekt entgegenbringe, sich also wehren werde, wenn ein Kunstwerk zerstört werde. Wer diesen normativen Ansprüchen nicht entspreche, könne als lasterhaft charakterisiert werden. "Ihm ist in Bezug auf die Werte des Schönen, Erhabenen etc. ein Laster vorzuhalten, das als ästhetische Stumpfheit bezeichnet werden könnte." (Halbig 2013, 197) Bereits Aristoteles habe die Stumpfheit als das der Zügellosigkeit entgegengesetzte Laster angesehen, das darin bestehe, weniger Freude zu empfinden, als angemessen sei.

Die Beispiele, die Halbig uns gibt, weisen auf die Notwendigkeit einer emotionalen Ansprechbarkeit hin. Der Tugendhafte muss über die entsprechende Sensibilität verfügen, bestimmte Werte überhaupt zu erfassen. Wie dies genau vor sich gehen soll, darüber lässt er uns allerdings im Dunkeln. Auch deutet er an, dass eine Forderung oder ein Ruf von den von uns erfassten Werten an uns ergehe, woraus sich die Notwendigkeit einer bestimmten Reaktion oder Antwort ergebe. In der Angemessenheit dieser Reaktion bzw. Antwort liege der Grund dafür, dass der Tugendhafte Bewunderung und Lob bekomme. Die Ausübung seiner Tugenden verdiene dann insofern Wertschätzung, als sie "die angemessene Antwort auf einen realen Wert" darstelle, (ebd., 46) der nun seinerseits den "Maßstab für die Korrektheit dieser Reaktion" abgebe. (ebd., 44)

Halbigs Untersuchungen über die Tugend sind stark von dem Gedanken getragen, Kriterien für die Bestimmung des moralischen Wertes einer Handlung zu entwickeln. "Die Frage, ob eine richtige Handlung tatsächlich moralischen Wert besitzt oder nicht, ist unabdingbar für unsere moralische Praxis und erfordert den Rekurs auf die Tugenden." (ebd., 365) In der Angemessenheit findet Halbig das Kriterium für die Beurteilung von Handlungen. Es geht ihm bei der Auseinandersetzung mit den Tugenden also weniger um Fragen des guten oder glücklichen Lebens, sondern darum, ob ein Verhalten lobenswert ist oder nicht. Das wird auch daran erkennbar, dass er den Tugenden zwar einen gewissen Beitrag zu einem guten Leben zugesteht, die Opfer jedoch, die dem Tugendhaften abverlangt werden könnten jedoch so groß sein, dass "ihm ein glückliches Leben unmöglich" werde. (ebd., 358)

Eine Einstellung wird für Halbig also zu einer tugendhaften aufgrund der Tatsache, "dass sie einem Wert als ihrem intentionalen Objekt angemessen ist und insofern auch selbst als intrinsisch wertvoll gelten darf." (ebd., 59) Um welche *Art* von Objekten handelt es sich dabei, fragt er weiter? (ebd., 53) Kommen hier nur Sachverhalte in Frage oder auch Personen? Um die Frage zu beantworten, führt er zuerst einige Beispiele an: "Der Sachverhalt, dass jemand bewusst eine Unwahrheit äußert, bildet ohne Zweifel ein geeignetes Objekt der entsprechenden Einstellungen (Ärger darüber, Bereitschaft, die Lüge aufzudecken, etc.) eines ehrlichen Menschen." (ebd., 54) Für Halbig ist es also angemessen, auf einen Sachverhalt der Lüge mit Ärger zu reagieren. Wer Mitleid empfinde, richte sich nach der Person und nicht nach dem Sachverhalt, weshalb es sinnvoll sei einen methodischen Pluralismus mit Blick auf die Bestimmung der Arten von Objekten an zu nehmen, auf welche sich die tugendhaften

Einstellungen beziehen können. (ebd., 54) Der Beantwortung der Frage, um welche Objekte es sich nun genauer handelt weicht Halbig allerdings aus, indem er darauf hinweist, dass er auf eine nähere Bestimmung des *Inhalts* der Liste von Basisgütern verzichten müsse, denn "sie gehört in die allgemeine Werttheorie und setzt die Klärung einer ganzen Reihe von Problemen voraus, die weit über die Theorie der Tugenden hinausweisen." (ebd., 54) Halbig wechselt immer wieder die Begrifflichkeit, indem er zunächst von Werten zu Objekten und dann zu Gütern überwechselt. Auch verzichtet er auf eine Auseinandersetzung mit dem Wertbegriff, obwohl es ja eine seiner Zielsetzungen ist, eine eigene Axiologie der Tugend zu entwickeln. (ebd., 17)

Sehen wir uns die Beispiele von Halbig näher an. Im Fall der Lüge haben wir ein bestimmtes Objekt, nämlich den Sachverhalt, dass jemand die Unwahrheit sagt. Halbig nimmt an, dass der Ehrliche darauf mit Ärger reagieren müsse. Aber ist das wirklich so? Könnte ich nicht auch mit Gelassenheit darauf reagieren, wenn ich sehe, dass mich jemand anlügt. Wenn man von der Tugend der Ehrlichkeit spricht, dann nimmt man alltagssprachlich an, dass jemand ehrlich ist. Dies umfasst neben der Wahrheitsliebe auch den Verzicht darauf, aus den Fehlern Anderer einen Vorteil zu ziehen. So würde ein ehrlicher Mensch darauf hinweisen, dass man ihm zu viel Geld zurückgegeben hat. Wenn ich mich darüber ärgere, dass sich Jemand die Gunst meines Chefs erwirbt, indem er etwas vortäuscht, dann ärgere ich mich selbst als ehrlicher Mensch nicht über die Unwahrheit, sondern darüber, dass jemand meine Pläne durchkreuzen will und damit den Wert meiner Selbstbestimmung verletzt. Die Relation zwischen Tugend und Wert ist also nicht so eindeutig, wie Halbig uns das vorgeben will. Die Tugend der Ehrlichkeit steht nicht nur in Bezug zum Wert der Wahrheit, sondern auch zum Wert des Wohlwollens Anderen gegenüber oder dem Wert der Selbstbestimmung. Umgekehrt gilt, dass ein und derselbe Wert verschiedene Einstellungen nach sich ziehen kann. So kann ich auf Unwahrheit mit Ärger oder mit Gelassenheit reagieren, was zeigt, dass einmal eine tugendhafte Reaktion in Form der Gelassenheit und einmal eine emotionale Reaktion in Form des Ärgers möglich ist.

Anges Heller betont, dass schon Aristoteles darauf hingewiesen habe, dass jede Tugend und jedes Laster auf einen Affekt bezogen ist. (Heller 1972, 47) Die Beziehung der Tugenden zu den Werten sei jedoch noch komplizierter als Aristoteles dies dargestellt habe. "Ganz allgemein gilt in der Tat, dass jede Tugend auf Affekte bezogen ist. Doch ist das eine Binsenweisheit, denn in unseren Beziehungen zu gewissen Werten, in ihrer Realisierung, in unserer Reaktion auf sie, sind die heterogensten Affekte am Werk – wie auch in jeder Art menschlichen Handelns und Denkens." (ebd., 47) Heller weist also darauf hin, dass wir auf bestimmte Werte reagieren und dass diese Reaktionen mit Affekten in Verbindung stehen, auf welche nun ihrerseits die Tugenden bezogen sind. Wenn Halbig von der angemessenen

Einstellung des Ärgers auf den Sachverhalt der Lüge spricht, dann beschreibt er eine emotionale Reaktion auf einen Unwert bzw. eine Wertverletzung. Auch beim Mitleid als angemessene Reaktion auf Leid handelt es sich um eine Emotion. Worin besteht nun das Spezifische der Tugend?

1.2. Emotionen

Halbig erwähnt zwar, dass der Begriff Mitleid nahelege, dass es sich bei dieser Tugend um eine Emotion handle, geht jedoch dem Zusammenhang von Tugenden, Emotionen und Werten nicht weiter nach (Halbig 2013, 32). Wenn – wie die zeitgenössische Gefühlsforschung[7] annimmt – Emotionen als Antwortreaktionen auf Werte bzw. Wertverletzung verstanden werden, dann liegt eine sehr ähnliche Sichtweise vor, wie diejenige, die uns Halbig vorstellt, wenn er Tugenden als angemessene Antworten auf Werte oder Unwerte versteht. Es wäre also lohnend den Zusammenhang von Emotionen und Tugenden näher in Betracht zu ziehen, denn bei den Emotionen ergeben sich ganz ähnliche Fragestellungen wie bei den Tugenden. Ein wichtiger diesbezüglicher Beitrag könnte aus der positiven Psychologie kommen, der es um die Erforschung positiver Emotionen, um positive Charaktereigenschaften, zu denen vor allem die Tugenden gezählt werden, sowie um die Erforschung positiver Institutionen geht, "alles also, was menschliche Tugenden stärkt, die dann ihrerseits positive Emotionen fördern." (Seligman 2003, 15) Seligman beklagt, dass bisher der Fokus immer auf die negativen Emotionen gelegt worden sei. Die Fokussierung auf das Negative könnte meiner Ansicht nach daran liegen, dass den Emotionen stammesgeschichtlich eine Warnfunktion obliegt, weshalb es auch nicht verwunderlich ist, dass von sieben Basisemotionen sechs negativ sind.[8] Den Tugenden kommt dann so etwas wie eine Transformationsfunktion zum Guten im Sinne des Positiven zu, zum Einen weil sie den richtigen Umgang mit Emotionen nachhaltig festlegen und zum Anderen weil sie die negative Grundgestimmtheit in eine positive

---

[7] In der zeitgenössischen Gefühlsforschung wird schon seit Längerem der enge Zusammenhang zwischen Gefühlen und Werten thematisiert und betont, dass den Emotionen eine wichtige Rolle bei der Erfassung von Werten zukommt. (Moser 2013) So spricht Ronald der Sousa in seinem Buch *Die Rationalität des Gefühls* davon, dass Emotionen insofern rational seien, als sie angemessene Reaktionen auf Werte darstellen. In meinem Vergleich zwischen De Sousa und Max Scheler zeige ich auf, dass Scheler Emotionen als Antwortreaktionen auf im Wertfühlen gegebenen Werte versteht, während De Sousa die Emotionen als direkt auf Werte gerichtet annimmt. Neuerdings schließt sich auch Kevin Mulligan der Sichtweise von Scheler an. (Moser 2015, 234)

[8] Der Pionier der Emotionsforschung, Paul Ekman, konnte in großangelegten Forschungsexperimenten in den 1960er Jahren, darunter auch in nichtwestlichen Kulturen, nachweisen, dass es ein universales kulturübergreifendes emotionales Ausdrucksverhalten bei Basisemotionen wie Trauer, Zorn, Überraschung, Angst, Ekel, Verachtung und Freude gibt. (Ekman 2003)

und freudige umpolen. Extrem ausgedrückt: dem Tapferen kann aufgrund seiner Tugendhaftigkeit das Ertragen des Leidvollen sogar Freude bereiten.

Auch Halbig geht der Frage nach, ob es tatsächlich so ist, dass man nur dann von einer Tugend sprechen könne, wenn ihre Ausübungen mit einer positiven affektiven Einstellung, nämlich der Freude, verbunden ist. (Halbig 2013, 90) Aristoteles gehe sogar so weit anzunehmen, dass man nur dann von Tugend sprechen könne, wenn der Tugendhafte Freude empfinde. "Denn wer sich der körperlichen Lüste enthält und sich eben daran freut, der ist besonnen, wer es aber ungern tut, ist zügellos; und wer Furchtbares aushält und sich daran freut oder doch keinen Schmerz empfindet, der ist tapfer, wer es dagegen mit Schmerzen tut, ist feige." (Aristoteles 1104b5-9, zitiert nach Halbig 2013, 88)
Aristoteles nimmt einen fundamentalen Zusammenhang zwischen Tugenden und Emotionen an. Er betont, dass wir es bei der ethischen Tugend vielfach überhaupt "mit den Affekten zu tun (haben), so dass sie in mancher Hinsicht mit den guten Affekten verwandt scheint." (Aristoteles 1985, 1178a15) Aristoteles unterscheidet drei verschiedene psychische Phänomene: Emotionen (*pathos*), Veranlagungen (*dynamis*) im Sinne all dessen, was uns für Emotionen empfänglich macht und die jeweilige Haltung (*hexis*) die es ermöglicht, auf die Emotionen angemessen zu reagieren. (ebd., 1105b20) Der Tugendhafte meide das Übermaß und den Mangel und suche das Mittlere, nicht der Sache nach, sondern in Bezug auf uns selbst. (Aristoteles 2011, 1106b6) So stelle Mut bei der Emotion der Furcht die Mitte (*mesotes*) dar zwischen der Tollkühnheit, welche die Gefahr zu gering und der Feigheit, die sie zu hoch einschätze. Bei der Emotion des Geizes sei die Mitte die Freigebigkeit, die jedoch nicht mit Verschwendung verwechselt werden dürfe. Die ethische Tugend besteht für Aristoteles also darin, angemessen mit den vorhandenen Emotionen umzugehen. Voraussetzung dafür ist, dass überhaupt Emotionen vorhanden sind, also Furcht in der Gefahr und Zorn bei Missachtung. Furchtlosigkeit würde zu Tollkühnheit führen und das Fehlen des Zorngefühls auf Schwäche hinweisen. Die Emotion zeigt uns etwas Wichtiges an, sie schlägt Alarm. Jemand der keine Furcht kennt, würde tollkühn reagieren und nicht lange überleben.

Die emotionale Betreffbarkeit spielt bei Aristoteles also eine große Rolle. Wir sind dafür verantwortlich, unser emotionales Leben dahingehend zu entwickeln, dass wir die entsprechende Sensibilität und Ansprechbarkeit ausbilden, um angemessen reagieren zu können. Darauf weist Aristoteles hin, wenn er sagt:

> Es ist nicht der 'Logos, wie die anderen meinen, Anfang und Führer der Tugend, sondern mehr die Affektivität'. (Aristoteles 1979, II, 7, 1206b17-19, zitiert nach Riedenauer 2000, 235[9])

Aristoteles weist in der *Magnia Moralia* darauf hin, dass die Impulse immer vom affektiven Strebevermögen kommen müssen, weshalb es auch so wichtig sei, dass sich dieses in der "richtigen Verfassung" befinde. Das rationale Element, also die Vernunft, bzw. der Logos, sei dann diejenige Instanz, welche die Zustimmung gebe, wodurch es zur Realisierung, etwa des (Sittlich-)Schönen komme. Würden die Impulse hingegen nur von der Vernunft ausgehen, dann könnte es sein, dass sich die Emotionen, bzw. die irrationalen Elemente widersetzen. "Und das ist der Grund, warum das irrationale Element – vorausgesetzt, dass es in der richtigen Verfassung ist – eher der Anfang zur Tugend hin zu sein scheint als das rationale." (Aristoteles 1979, II, 1206b25-27)

Aristoteles nimmt also nicht, wie Kant, einen Kampf zwischen Vernunft und Gefühl an[10], sondern bettet die Emotionalität in das menschliche Streben ein, das insgesamt am Guten ausgerichtet ist.[11] Aristoteles betont also, dass es nicht nur darum geht, seine zumeist negativen Emotionen im Sinne einer Emotionsregulation[12] im Griff zu haben, sondern darum, sie zu transformieren, sodass man sie dann hat, "wann man soll und worüber und gegen wen und weswegen und wie man soll, das ist die Mitte und das Beste, und das ist die Leistung der Tugend." (Aristoteles 1985, 1106b21-22)

1.3. Die Orientierung am Guten

Im Laufe seiner Auseinandersetzungen mit dem Begriff der Tugend spezifiziert Halbig seine Position, indem er darauf hinweist, dass zur Tugend mehr dazugehört als eine an-

---

[9] Riedenauer übersetzt hier Aristoteles anders als Franz Dirlmeier, dessen Übersetzung folgendermaßen lautet: "es ist nicht das rationale Element, wie die anderen meinen, Anfang und Führer der Tugend, sondern vielmehr das irrationale."(Aristoteles 1979, 1206b17-19) In unserem Kontext erscheinen mir die Begriffe Logos und Affektivität aussagekräftiger.

[10] Für Kant stellen die Antriebe der Natur, also die Gemütskräfte des Menschen keine positiven Ressourcen oder Orientierungshilfen dar, sondern "widerstrebende Kräfte, die also zu bekämpfen und durch die Vernunft, nicht erst künftig, sondern gleich jetzt zu besiegen" sind. (Kant 1993, 509) Kant versteht das Vermögen diesen natürlichen Kräften in uns Widerstand entgegenzubringen als Tugend.

[11] Riedenauer weist darauf hin, dass die Affektivität als eine Form des Strebens ein wesentliches Fundament des aristotelischen Ethikmodells bildet. "Sie verbindet Naturphilosophie, Anthropologie, Psychologie, Ethik und Metaphysik." (Riedenauer 2005, 169) In diesem Sinne spricht er bei Aristoteles von einer Ethikbegründung im Streben. (Riedenauer 2000)

[12] Die Emotionsregulation beschäftigt sich mit den Möglichkeiten des Umgangs von zumeist negativen Emotionen. Eine Fokussierung auf die Reaktionskomponente erfolgte in 1990er Jahren insbesondere im Bereich der Entwicklungspsychologie.

gemessene Einstellung zu bestimmten Objekten, vielmehr gehe es darum, "im Lichte des Guten eine angemessene Einstellung" zu finden. (Halbig 2013, 56) Der Tugendhafte befinde sich in einem kontinuierlichen Prozess der eigenen Reifung in der Orientierung am Guten. (ebd., 362) Dieser Bezug zum Guten werde zunächst über den Bezug zu Gütern hergestellt. Durch Erziehung und vorbildliches Verhalten würden wir lernen den jeweiligen Gütern einen angemessenen Wert zuzumessen.

> Die angemessene Wertschätzung von basalen Gütern verdankt sich zunächst nicht einer Reflexion auf diese Güter selber, sondern der Erfahrung von vorbildlichen und tugendhaften Weisen des Umgangs mit ihnen. (ebd., 365)

Die moralische Entwicklung von Kindern gehe nicht von der Einübung abstrakter Pflichten aus, sondern von gelebten Vorbildern, an denen sie sich orientieren können.
Hier liegt Halbig ganz nahe bei Aristoteles für den das Vorbild des guten Menschen eine zentrale Rolle bei der Erfassung des Guten spielt. Denn "diejenigen Dinge sind schätzenswert, die für den Guten (*spoudaios*) so sind." (Aristoteles 2011, 1176b25) Nur derjenige könne das Gute erkennen und realisieren, der eine tugendhafte Haltung entwickelt habe. Dieser sei nicht nur glücklicher als andere, sondern stelle auch ein Vorbild dar, an dem man sich orientieren könne. Denn das was er anstrebe, sei wertvoll und gut. Die "Gutheit[13] des Charakters" lasse uns die richtigen Ziele setzen, die Klugheit verhelfe uns dann dazu, diese zu realisieren. (ebd., 1145a5) In diesem Sinne spricht Aristoteles davon, dass die Tugend ein Habitus des Wählens sei, der die nach uns bemessene Mitte halte und durch die Vernunft bestimmt werde, "und zwar so, wie ein kluger Mann (*phronimos*) ihn zu bestimmen pflegt." (Aristoteles 1985, 1107a) Allerdings weist er darauf hin, dass nur der gute Mensch klug sein könne, denn es sei "offenkundig unmöglich, klug zu sein, wenn man nicht gut ist." (Aristoteles 2011, 1144a35) Aristoteles ist nicht blind dafür, dass es große Unterschiede zwischen den Menschen gibt: Was der Eine liebe, das verabscheue der Andere. Was dem einen Freude mache, bereite dem anderen Unlust. Dem Fiebernden und dem Gesunden erscheine nicht dasselbe als süß und dem Schwachen und Kräftigen nicht dasselbe als warm. Dies sei jedoch nicht verwunderlich, da Menschen "auf viele Weisen verdorben und geschädigt sein können." (ebd., 1176a20)

Für Aristoteles ist also das Gute dasjenige, das vom vorbildlichen, guten Menschen – und damit auf richtige Art und Weise – geliebt wird. Auch Brentano folgt diesem Gedanken, wenn er sagt:

---

[13] Ursula Wolf übersetzt das griechische Wort für Tugend, *arete*, mit Gutheit um auf die attributive Verwendung deutlich zu machen: wie "Klugheit" zu "klug", so stehe "Gutheit" zu "gut". "Gutsein" wäre zu passivisch und würde die attributive Verwendung nicht anzeigen. (Aristoteles 2011, 348)

> Wir nennen etwas gut, wenn die darauf bezügliche Liebe richtig ist. Das mit richtiger Liebe zu Liebende, das Liebenswerte, ist das Gute im weitesten Sinne des Wortes.[14]
> (Brentano 1889, 17)

Halbig zitiert in dieser Hinsicht Christine Swanton:

> Gut sind zum Beispiel Lust und Freundschaft, wenn wir mit ihnen *richtig* umgehen.
> (Swanton 2003, 36, zitiert nach Halbig 2013, 51)

Swanson geht davon aus, dass die Tugenden eine konstitutive Rolle für diejenigen Entitäten spielen, denen wir einen intrinsischen Wert zuschreiben. Swanson lehnt die *Thesis of Non-Aratic Value* ab, welche die entscheidende Prämisse einer rekursiven Theorie der Tugenden darstellt:

> Tugenden und Laster lassen sich abgeleitet verstehen als Muster von Reaktionen auf oder als nützlich für die Förderung (bzw. jeweils Minimierung) von Basisgütern und -übeln oder intrinsischen Werten und Unwerten, die sich ihrerseits nichtaretarisch verstehen lassen. (Swanson 2003, 34, zitiert nach Halbig 2013, 51)

Swanson verwirft also die Annahme eines notwendigen Rekurses der Tugenden auf andere, ihrerseits unabhängige intrinsische Werte, und besteht darauf, dass sowohl das Gute, als auch die angemessene Einstellung zum Guten nicht unabhängig von der Tugend bestimmt werden kann. Die Lust eines Sadisten, die infolge der rekursiven Theorie als intrinsischer Wert betrachtet werden müsste, verdiene Abscheu aufgrund ihres negativen intrinsischen

---

[14] In seinem 1889 gehaltenen Vortrag *Vom Ursprung sittlicher Erkenntnis* geht Brentano von der Frage aus: "Was nennen wir überhaupt ‚gut'? Und wie gewinnen wir die Erkenntnis, dass etwas gut und besser ist als ein anderes?" (Brentano 1889, 13) Er unterscheidet drei Klassen von psychischen Phänomenen: Vorstellungen, Urteile und Gemütsbewegungen. Gemeinsam ist allen drei, dass sie intentional auf etwas gerichtet sind. Beim Urteilen kommt jedoch zu dem Vorstellen, das in allen drei Klassen vorausgesetzt wird, noch eine zweite intentionale Beziehung zum vorgestellten Gegenstand hinzu, die des Anerkennens oder Verwerfens, während sich diese zweite intentionale Beziehung bei den Gemütsbewegungen in Form eines Liebens oder Hassens vollzieht. (ebd., 15-16) Hierunter fällt für Brentano all das, was Aristoteles unter dem Begriff *orexis* zusammengefasst hat, also das gesamte Strebevermögen mit seinen damit verbundenen Gefühlen. Während man bei den Vorstellungen nicht von richtig oder falsch sprechen könne, gäbe es beim Urteilen analog zur Logik die zwei entgegengesetzten Beziehungsweisen des Anerkennens und des Verwerfens, wobei eine die richtige und die andere falsch sei. "Hier sind wir nun an der Stelle, wo die gesuchten Begriffe des Guten und Schlechten, ebenso wie die des Wahren und Falschen ihren Ursprung nehmen. Wir nennen etwas wahr, wenn die darauf bezügliche Anerkennung richtig ist. Wir nennen etwas gut, wenn die darauf bezügliche Liebe richtig ist. Das mit richtiger Liebe zu Liebende, das Liebenswerte, ist das Gute im weitesten Sinne des Wortes." (ebd., 17) Brentano nimmt, analog zum Evidenzurteil das durch seine "Klarheit" eine "höhere Urteilsweise" darstellt, auch bei den Gemütsbewegungen im Unterschied zu den niederen instinktiven Trieben eine höhere als richtig charakterisierte Liebe an. "Wie die Richtigkeit und Evidenz des Urteils, so zählt darum auch die Richtigkeit und der höhere Charakter der Gemütsthätigkeit selbst zum Guten, während die Liebe zum Schlechten selbst schlecht ist." (ebd., 21)

Wertes, der – im Widerspruch zur rekursiven Sichtweise – durch die Lasterhaftigkeit des Sadisten, mitkonstituiert sei.

Halbig hingegen beharrt darauf, dass Tugenden Bezugnahmen auf Basisgüter oder intrinsische Werte sind, die uns unabhängig von der Erfassung durch einen Tugendhaften gegeben sind. Er hält an der These fest, "dass Tugenden Einstellungen zu intrinsischen Werten bilden, die sich unabhängig von aretaischen Gesichtspunkten individuieren lassen." (Halbig 2013, 53) Wie stellt sich Halbig nun die Erfassung dieser unabhängigen Werte vor? Halbig verweist uns diesbezüglich auf Ideale und Standards, welche die Dimension der Bewertung eröffnen könnten. (ebd., 262) Ohne darauf jedoch näher einzugehen, schließt er sein Buch mit der Metapher des Fernrohres und des Magnetismus. "Idealen im Sinn von Iris Murdochs Metapher des *Magnetismus des Guten*" (Murdoch 1992, zitiert nach Halbig 2013, 365) komme eine inspirierende Kraft ebenso zu wie der Metapher des Fernrohres, die von Copp/Sobel formuliert worden sei.

> Wir betrachten (…) Tugenden nicht als einen Scheinwerfer, der eine Welt durchdringt, die sonst überhaupt keine moralischen Eigenschaften hätte; wir betrachten sie als ein Fernrohr und eine Energiequelle, die aufspürt und strebt und aus diesen Gründen bewundernswert ist. (Copp/Sobel 2004, 552, zitiert nach Halbig 2013, 361)

Halbig ist Wertrealist indem er annimmt an, dass es tatsächlich Werte gibt, die wir nicht erfinden, sondern vorfinden und dass uns das Fernrohr der Tugend dabei behilflich ist. Dabei entsteht der Eindruck, dass uns Werte schwer zugänglich und nur über das Hilfsmittel der Tugend zugänglich seien. Halbig schreibt den Tugenden also eine Werterfassungs- und Wertschließungsfunktion zu. Wie dies genau vor sich geht, darüber lässt er uns allerdings im Dunkeln. Was seine Absichten betrifft, ist er hingegen etwas klarer: Er möchte den Bereich der Pflichten auf den Bereich des Wertes hin überschreiten. Es geht ihm darum, Bewertungskriterien für moralisches Handeln zu finden, die durch den Pflichtbegriff bisher nicht erfassbar sind. (Halbig 2013, 362) Diese glaubt er in der Tugend gefunden zu haben, anhand welcher eine Unterlassung kritisiert werden kann, "auch wenn sie niemals Recht verletzt und keine Pflicht unerfüllt bleibt." (ebd., 363) Er erläutert dies an folgendem Beispiel: Wer sich entschieden habe, generell für eine bestimmte Hilfsorganisation zu spenden, der könne die unvollkommene Pflicht der Wohltätigkeit erfüllen. Wenn er die Not des Nachbarn nicht erkenne, könne ihm dies zwar nicht als Pflichtverletzung angerechnet werden. Er verdiene jedoch Kritik, weil er hinter das Ideal der Wohltätigkeit zurückgefallen sei. (ebd., 362)

An dieser Stelle möchte ich einen Verweis auf die phänomenologische Werttheorie von Hans Jonas und sein *Prinzip Verantwortung* machen. Jonas lehnt die Gesetzes- oder Vertragsethik ab und betont, dass man nicht von Pflichten, sondern von dem "immanenten Anspruch eines an-sich-Guten auf seine Wirklichkeit" ausgehen müsse. (Jonas 2003, 153)

Denn der "Wert" oder das "Gute" sei das Einzige, das ein Sollen begründen könne. (ebd., 100) Jonas sieht die Spezifik des menschlichen Daseins in der Fähigkeit zur Verantwortungsübernahme, d.h. in der Fähigkeit dem Appell des Seins gegenüber offen und empfänglich zu sein. (Moser 2016, 52) Mit Halbig gesprochen: sein Fernrohr ist das Verantwortungsgefühl. Im Gegensatz zu Jonas bietet Halbig uns jedoch keine metaphysische Wertlehre an, aus welcher die Ansprüche abgeleitet werden könnten.

1.4. Handeln aus Gründen

Halbig geht davon aus, dass ein Zusammenhang zwischen Gründen und Werten besteht.[15] Er nimmt an, dass die Gründe für unsere Handlungen in unseren Werten fundiert sind: die "Handlungsgründe sowohl des Großartigen wie des Freigiebigen sind beide fundiert in dem Wert des Wohls anderer." (Halbig 2013, 170) Die rekursive Theorie erlaube es, die Gründe "in den evaluativen Tatsachen zu fundieren, die die Quelle dieser Gründe bilden." (ebd., 170) Das Kriterium der Tugendhaftigkeit bestehe darin, sich von Gründen leiten zu lassen, die in Werten fundiert seien. Der ehrliche Mensch zeichne sich dadurch aus, dass er sich am Wert der Wahrheit orientiere. Seine praktischen Einstellungen werden sich nach Gründen der Art richten: 'das ist einfach falsch', 'traurig, dass er sein Einverständnis mit der Entscheidung des Chefs vorgetäuscht hat', 'die Wahrheit muss ans Licht', oder 'er sollte seine Kinder ermutigen, ihre Meinung offen auszusprechen' richten." (ebd., 151)

Sehen wir uns nun die bezüglich der Tugend der Ehrlichkeit angegebenen Gründe an. Zunächst einmal: "das ist falsch". Hier kann es sich um eine Feststellung oder um einen Ausruf der Verwunderung handeln. Der Forderung, die Wahrheit ans Licht zu bringen, verweist schon eher auf einen möglichen Handlungsgrund, nämlich die Wahrheit aufzudecken zu wollen. Der Ausdruck des Bedauerns, "traurig, dass er sein Einverständnis mit der Entscheidung des Chefs vorgetäuscht hat", verweist auf die Emotion der Trauer, die als eine Reaktion auf einen Verlust, in diesem Falle, des Vertrauens in einen Kollegen verstanden werden kann. Die Aufforderung "er sollte seine Kinder ermutigen, ihre Meinung offen auszusprechen" ist ein Appell zur Werterziehung, in diesem Falle, zu Mut und Offenheit. Halbig stellt uns also mögliche Antwortreaktionen vor, die jemand in verschiedenen Fällen einnehmen kann. Aber kann man von diesen Menschen sagen, dass sie tugendhaft handeln?

---

[15] Halbigs Auseinandersetzung mit den Tugenden stellt eine Fortsetzung seiner Untersuchungen dar, die er 2007 in seinem Buch *Praktische Gründe und die Realität der Moral* veröffentlichte. Dort sei er zu der Erkenntnis gekommen, dass "praktische Gründe ganz allgemein in Werten fundiert sind." (Halbig 2013, 170)

Die Beispiele, die Halbig uns gibt, sind Feststellungen über Etwas oder Jemanden, Aufforderungen und Appelle an Andere etwas zu tun oder überhaupt Beurteilungen Anderer. In allen Fällen liegt eine Fremdbeurteilung vor. Der Grund für die Einstellung zu bestimmten Sachverhalten oder Verhaltensweisen ist hier zwar tatsächlich fundiert in einem Wert, von einem tugendhaften Verhalten würde man normalerweise jedoch nicht sprechen. Von einem tugendhaften Menschen würde man erwarten, dass er sich selber tugendhaft verhält, also nicht lügt, nichts vortäuscht, niemanden übervorteilt. Halbig gibt uns stattdessen Gründe, anhand derer wir bestimmte Situationen und ein bestimmtes Verhalten Anderer beurteilen können.

Außerdem unterschätzt Halbig den Zusammenhang zwischen Emotionen und Werten, wenn er annimmt, dass sich aus den Werten "für den Tugendhaften praktische Gründe, nämlich etwa einen bestehenden Wert durch aktives Handeln zu erhalten, zu fördern, sich über das Bestehen diese Wertes zu freuen, sein Fortbestehen zu wünschen etc." ergeben. (Halbig 2013, 151) Es entsteht der Eindruck, wie wenn wir rein rational Situationen im Lichte von Werten betrachten würden, woraus sich dann Gründe ableiten ließen, die uns zu einem tugendhaften Handeln anleiten. Dieser Eindruck wird noch dadurch verstärkt, dass Halbig den *begrifflichen* Zusammenhang der ethischen Tugenden mit den Verstandestugenden betont.

> Ein ehrlicher Mensch muss zugleich sicherstellen, dass die Überzeugungen, denen er Ausdruck verleiht, tatsächlich auch gerechtfertigt sind. Zudem sollte er in der Lage sein, die eigenen Überzeugungen auf Nachfrage hin zu vertreten und gegen Einwände zu verteidigen. (ebd., 81)

Gerade das ist bei Werten jedoch nicht immer der Fall. Oft sind uns unsere Werte gar nicht bewusst, sie liegen sozusagen wie ein Eisberg unter der Bewusstseinsschwelle und werden erst bei Wertverletzungen sichtbar, bei denen wir dann zumeist emotional reagieren. Und selbst wenn wir uns unserer Werte bewusst sind, gelingt es uns oft nicht, sie zu begründen oder näher zu erklären. Auf die Frage, warum Wahrhaftigkeit gut und Lüge böse sei, antwortete ein Teilnehmer an einer großangelegten Befragung.

> Ich weiß es nicht. Es ist einfach so. Das ist eben ein Grundsatz. Ich möchte mich nicht damit herumquälen, ihn anzuzweifeln. Das ist ein Teil von mir. Ich weiß nicht, woher es kommt, aber es ist sehr wichtig. (Bellah 1987, 27)

1.5. Charaktereigenschaften

Im Laufe seiner weiteren Untersuchungen kommt Halbig zu dem Ergebnis, dass Tugend mehr ist als nur eine Einstellung: Sie sei eine Eigenschaft, die man sich erst aneignen müsse. Es erweise sich "der Erwerb der Tugend durch einen allmählichen Prozess der Habitualisierung, also der Bildung eines entsprechenden Charaktermerkmals, als *begrifflich* notwendig", wenn es sich wirklich um eine Tugend handeln soll. (Halbig 2013, 101) Tugenden erwerbe man durch Einübung tugendhaften Handelns, für das man verantwortlich sei. Nur aufgrund dieser Verantwortlichkeit sei es möglich, jemanden für seine Tugenden zu bewundern.

> Und nur weil die ethischen Tugenden erworben sind, kann sich für sie die Frage nach der Verantwortung überhaupt stellen. (ebd., 149)

Halbig betont, dass wir alltagssprachlich sowohl Handlungen als auch Personen als mutig oder als ehrlich bezeichnen. Er demonstriert dies am Beispiel eines Soldaten, der für seine Feigheit bekannt ist und dennoch äußerst mutig handelt, indem er eine Handgranate in letzter Sekunde wegschleudert und damit das Leben seines Kameraden rettet. Hier liege eine Handlung *out of charakter* vor, die vielleicht sogar den Handelnden selbst später zu verwundern vermag. Wie war es nur möglich, dass ich so mutig reagiert habe?[16] Bin ich jetzt ein mutiger Menschen oder nicht? Hurka nehme an, dass tugendhaftes Verhalten sehr wohl an einzelnen aktuellen Handlungen festgemacht werden könne und hege Zweifel daran ob stabile Charaktermerkmale empirisch überhaupt nachweisbar seien.[17] Halbig wendet sich hier explizit gegen Hurkas Sichtweise, dass der Rekurs auf die Charaktermerkmale des Handelnden, also auf die Person, für die rekursive Theorie überflüssig sei. (ebd., 59) Das Vorliegen einer festen Haltung spiele eine konstitutive Rolle für die Tugendhaftigkeit der aktualen Handlung.

Halbig selbst verortet sich in der Nähe von Max Scheler, der die "Tugenden ausdrücklich im Sinn des ontologischen Primats als Personenwerte" aufgefasst habe. (ebd., 62) Scheler fasse Tugenden als "Beschaffenheiten der Person" auf und nicht als etwas, das für bestimmte Handlungen und Werke, noch gar für die Nutznießung anderer, notwendig sei, sondern als einen "freien Schmuck ihres Trägers." (ebd., 66) Bei Scheler zeige sich, dass der Tugend ein intrinsischer Wert zukomme, d.h. ein Wert, der unabhängig davon ist, wozu sie gut ist. Er bedauert, dass Scheler nie eine Tugendlehre ausgearbeitet habe, wobei man sich des Eindrucks nicht erwehren kann, dass Halbig am liebsten an Schelers Position anknüpfen würde, um seinen eigenen Ansatz besser untermauern zu können. Explizit vertritt Halbig die

---

[16] An dieser Stelle möchte ich auf Jean-Paul Sartre verweisen, der in *Die Transzendenz des Ego* davon spricht, dass das "Ego immer von dem, was es hervorbringt überschritten wird, obwohl es, unter einem anderen Gesichtspunkt, das ist, was es hervorbringt. Von daher jenes klassische Erstaunen: 'ICH, ich habe das tun können!" (Sartre 1994, 73)

[17] Verschiedene Experimente, wie das "Ehrlichkeitsexperiment", das "Samariterexperiment", das "Geldstückexperiment" und das "Milgramexperiment" geben zu der Vermutung Anlass, dass Personen nicht nur durch Charaktermerkmale geleitet werden, sondern durch situative Faktoren wie Zeitdruck, gute Stimmung oder Autorität. (Halbig 2013, 114) Siehe dazu auch: Doris, John M. (2002*) Lack of Charakter: Personality and Moral Behaviour.*

These, dass Scheler "die Grundannahmen der rekursiven Theorie teilt. Unzweifelhaft steht im Mittelpunkt von Schelers Argumentation das Bemühen um die Rehabilitierung der Tugend als eines zentralen intrinsischen Wertes." (ebd., 66) Scheler verstehe Tugenden als Personenwerte, wobei hier das "Können" der Person sowie ihr Bewusstsein für dieses Können im Vordergrund stehe. (ebd., 62) Mit Scheler spricht Halbig dem feigen Soldaten ein solches Können ab. (ebd., 61) Der Soldat habe zwar richtig gehandelt, aber nicht tugendhaft, weil er sich nicht bewusst gewesen sei, dass er die Fähigkeit dazu habe, sein Leben für jemanden Anderen aufs Spiel zu setzen. Seine Handlung könne man vielleicht zum Ausgangspunkt eines Prozesses nehmen, der schließlich zum Erwerb der Tugend des Mutes führe, nicht jedoch zum Anlass dafür, den Soldaten aufgrund dieser einen Handlung schon als mutig zu bezeichnen.

Am Beispiel des Soldaten zeigt sich, dass es Halbig nicht so sehr um die moralische Beurteilung von Handlungen, sondern um diejenige von Personen geht. Das Spezifische der Tugend in Hinsicht auf die Ethik bestehe in ihrem Verhältnis zur Personalität. Daraus ergebe sich die grundlegende "Bestimmung der Tugenden als Vollkommenheiten einer Person." (ebd., 359) Um Tugenden als "personale Vollkommenheiten" verstehen zu können (ebd., 361), müsste Halbig uns jedoch Kriterien angeben, anhand derer wir die Stufen der Vollkommenheit erkennen können. Er müsste seinen Ansatz in einen größeren werttheoretischen Zusammenhang stellen und – wie Hurka dies tut – die Fragen nach dem Wesen des Menschen und dessen möglicher Vervollkommnung abklären. Wenn dies nicht der Fall ist, entsteht die Gefahr einer generellen Moralisierung und eines damit verbundenen Tugendterrors.

Im Folgenden werde ich mich Scheler zuwenden, dessen Auseinandersetzung mit der Tugend in eine umfassende Werttheorie eingebettet ist, um dann in einem weiteren Schritt aufzeigen, inwieweit die rekursive Theorie von Halbig mit Schelers Ansatz kompatibel ist, so wie Halbig dies behauptet.

2. Max Scheler Tugenden als Personenwerte

2.1. Objekte Wertrangordnung

Scheler entwickelt eine objektive Wertrangordnung in der er generell zwischen Sach- und Personenwerten unterscheidet. Das Heilige bildet die oberste Wertqualität in der Rangordnung der Werte und ist laut Scheler maßgeblich dafür verantwortlich, dass sich im Laufe der Geschichte konkrete Gottesvorstellungen herausgebildet haben, die allerdings – wie Scheler zugibt – sehr oft anthropomorphe Züge tragen. Die Personenwerte, zu denen er die Tugenden zählt, siedelt Scheler auf dieser obersten Wertrangebene an, die er dem Heiligen zuordnet, das jedoch nicht mit konkreten religiösen Institutionen verwechselt werden dürfe.

(Scheler 1921, 107) Auf den ersten Blick mag die Verankerung der Person im Heiligen in unserer säkular eingestellten Welt Befremden auslösen. Betrachtet man jedoch den Begriff der Menschenwürde genauer, so wird ersichtlich, dass hier tatsächlich eine Sakralisierung der Person vorliegt, wie Hans Joas in seinem Buch *Die Sakralität der Person. Eine neue Genealogie der Menschenrechte* aufzeigt. (Joas 2011). Für Scheler ist der Mensch derjenigen, der sich selbst, sein Leben und alles Leben transzendiert (Scheler 1921, 298) hin auf das Göttliche: "er ist der Gottsucher". (ebd., 301) Im Menschen und seiner Geschichte öffne sich eine Spalte, durch die eine neue personale Ordnung, nämlich die des Heiligen sichtbar werde. (ebd., 298) Von Tugenden spricht Scheler erst auf der Wertebene des Heiligen, auf welcher die Person angesiedelt ist. Daher ist es auch nicht verwunderlich, dass er bei der Tugend von einem freien "Geschenk der Gnade" spricht. (Scheler 1919, 15)

Für Scheler steht der "Personwert höher (…) als aller Sach-Organisations-Gemeinschaftswert jeder Zeitströmung." (Scheler 1921, XII) Der Wert der Person dürfe nicht von der Beziehung auf eine Gemeinschaft oder auf eine Güterwelt abhängig gemacht werden. Der Gedanke, dass alle Werte den Personenwerten unterzuordnen sind, ist für Scheler so zentral, dass er sein Buch *Der Formalismus in der Ethik und die materiale Wertethik* mit dem Untertitel versieht: "Neuer Versuch der Grundlegung eines ethischen Personalismus".

Auf den unteren Ebenen der Wertrangordnung siedelt Scheler die Sachwerte an. Die unterste Wertrangebene bildet die Ebene des Angenehmen und Nützlichen, gefolgt von der Ebene der Vitalwerte wie Gesundheit und Wohlbefinden, die für alle Sinnenwesen gelten. Auf der dritten Wertebene befinden sich die geistigen Werte wie Schönheit, Wahrheit und Recht, die sich in Kulturgütern wie Kunst, Wissenschaft, Gesetzen, Rechtsordnung und Staat manifestieren. (Scheler 1921, 104) Träger von Sachwerten sind für Scheler die Güter: "Erst in den Gütern werden Werte 'wirklich'". (ebd., 16) Und es sei auch tatsächlich so, dass uns in der natürlichen Einstellung zunächst einmal Güter gegeben sind, an denen wir bestimmte Eigenschaften wahrnehmen (ebd., 55). Güter – als Träger von Werten – dürfen jedoch nicht mit Werten gleichgesetzt werden. Für Scheler ist jede Bildung einer Güterwelt – wie immer sie auch erfolgt – durch eine Rangordnung der Werte bereits geleitet, wie z. B. die Bildung der Kunst einer bestimmten Epoche. Die Wertrangordnung "steckt ihr einen *Spielraum des Möglichen* ab, außerhalb dessen eine Bildung von Gütern nicht erfolgen kann. Sie ist insofern der betreffenden Güterwelt gegenüber *a priori*." (ebd., 18)

Scheler gibt uns Hinweise darauf, woran man die Rangordnung eines Wertes erkennen könne, indem er folgende Kriterien angibt: Dauerhaftigkeit, Teilnahmemöglichkeit möglichst Vieler, Fundierungscharakter, Befriedigung und Nähe zum Absoluten. (ebd., 88). Anders gesagt: Ein Gut ist umso wertvoller, je dauerhafter es ist, je mehr Menschen daran teilhaben können, ohne es aufzubrauchen, je mehr dieses Gut alle anderen Güter befördert und ermöglicht, je mehr Befriedigung es gibt und je näher zum Absoluten es ist.

2.2. Gefühle und Werte

Im Gegensatz zu Halbig setzt sich Scheler ausführlich mit dem Zusammenhang von Gefühlen und Werten auseinander. Das Vorhandensein von Gefühle ist für Scheler das "'Zeichen' für das *Sein* und das *Nichtsein* von Werten". (Scheler 1921, 369) Das emotionale Leben des Menschen ist jedoch je nach Wertrangebene verschieden: Gefühlsempfindungen finden wir auf der Wertebene des Angenehmen, Lebensgefühle auf der Wertebene des Vitalen und Emotionen als Antwortreaktionen auf die im Wertfühlen gegebenen Werte auf der geistigen Ebene, d.h. wir freuen uns über etwas, sind über etwas traurig, sind von etwas berührt oder über etwas begeistert. Auf dieser Ebene spricht Scheler vom intentionalen "Fühlen von Werten, wie angenehm, schön, gut; *hier* erst gewinnt das Fühlen neben seiner intentionalen Natur auch noch eine kognitive Funktion, die es in den beiden ersten Fällen nicht besitzt." (ebd., 264) Die Werte, die sich im intentionalen Fühlen erschließen, fordern regelrecht eine gefühlsmäßige Antwort. Wenn wir uns über etwas freuen, über etwas ärgern oder über etwas traurig sind, zeigt dieses "über" an, dass die Gegenstände hier nicht einfach nur wahrgenommen werden, sondern vor mir stehen "bereits mit im Fühlen gegebenen Wertprädikaten behaftet. Die in den betreffenden Wertverhalten liegenden Wertqualitäten fordern von sich aus gewisse emotionale "Antwortreaktionen". (ebd., 265) Wenn die Forderung der Werte nicht erfüllt werde, dann leiden wir daran, so z.B. sind wir traurig, wenn wir uns über ein Ereignis nicht so freuen können, wie es sein gefühlter Wert verdient, oder nicht so trauern können, wie es der Todesfall eines geliebten Menschen fordert.

Scheler spricht hier das Thema der Angemessenheit von Emotionen ans. Sowohl ein "zu viel" als auch ein "zu wenig" kann fehl am Platz sein. Damit verweist er auf eine Problematik, die bei Aristoteles zentral für die Tugend ist, nämlich die richtige Mitte zu finden. Für Scheler ist die angemessene Reaktion abhängig von den jeweiligen Sinnzusammenhängen, die zu verstehen er in den Bereich des empirischen Forschens verlegt, d.h. in den Bereich der Psychologie, der es um die Erfassung der "*Verständnisgesetze* fremden Seelenlebens" gehe. (ebd., 265) Im Unterschied zum Aristotelischen Tugendverständnis, welches alle emotionalen Ebenen und somit das gesamte Strebevermögen umfasst, spricht Scheler hier nicht von Tugenden, sondern von psychologischen Zusammenhängen, die er in den Bereich der empirischen Forschung verweist.

Von Tugenden spricht Scheler erst auf der höchsten Wertebene des Heiligen, auf welcher die Person angesiedelt ist. Dieser Ebene ordnet er bestimmte Gefühlsqualitäten zu, nämlich die Persönlichkeitsgefühle der Verzweiflung und der Glückseligkeit. Diese sind nicht mehr vor irgendwelchen Handlungen abhängig, sondern betreffen die gesamte Persönlichkeit.

> Wie in der Verzweiflung ein emotionales 'Nein!' im Kerne unserer Personenexistenz und unserer Welt steckt – ohne dass die 'Person' dabei auch nur Reflexionsobjekt ist – so in der Seligkeit – der tiefsten Schicht des Glücksgefühls – ein emotionales 'Ja!' (ebd., 356)

Dieses Gefühl werde nicht mehr "über" etwas ausgelöst, wir können nur selig oder verzweifelt "sein". Seligkeit und Verzweiflung erfüllen vom Kern der Person her unsere ganze Existenz. Scheler spricht davon, dass diese Gefühle "aus dem Quellpunkt der geistigen Akte selbst – gleichsam – hervorzuströmen und alles jeweilig in diesen Akten Gegebene der Innen- und Außenwelt mit ihrem Lichte und ihrem Dunkel zu übergießen" scheinen. (ebd., 356) Scheler nimmt also an, dass die Verfasstheit der Person dafür ausschlaggebend ist, wie wir die Welt insgesamt erleben. Es liegt die Vermutung nahe, dass Scheler das Persönlichkeitsgefühl der Seligkeit dem Tugendhaften zuspricht. Wenn er bei der Tugend von der "inneren Fülle" spricht, die "nach immer weiterer Ausdehnung" drängt (Scheler 1919, 16), dann passt dies zur Metapher des Lichts, welche vom Glückseligen ausgeht. Diese Ausstrahlung, so Scheler, verdanke sich jedoch der Mensch nicht selbst, sie dürfe nicht "gleich einer Naturanlage als angeboren angesehen werden" (ebd., 16), sondern stelle ein "freies Geschenk der Gnade" dar, für das man aufnahmebereit sein müsse. Die Transformation der Person, die in der Tugend stattfindet, wird von Scheler als "das äußerste Gegenteil aller Gewohnheit" angesehen. (ebd., 14) Wolfhart Henckmann spricht in diesem Sinne von einem trans-ethischen Verständnis von Tugend:

> Tugend in diesem trans-ethischen Sinne aufgefasst, geht jeder Pflicht voran. (Henckmann 1998, 128)

Nur was im Bereich des Tunkönnens einer Person liege, könne zur Pflicht gemacht werden.

2.3. Materiale Wertethik

Scheler ist von der Absicht getragen, im Gegensatz zu Kants apriorischer, formaler Ethik eine apriorische, materiale Wertethik zu entwickeln. Scheler teilt mit Kant die Sichtweise, dass allein der Person eine über allen Preis erhabene Würde zukommt. Kant entwürdige jedoch die Person, weil er sie "unter die Herrschaft eines unpersönlichen *Nomos* stellt, dem gehorchend sich erst ihr Personwerden vollziehen soll." (Scheler 1921, 384) Kant verstehe die Person an erster Stelle als Vernunftperson:

Person ist hier das X irgendeiner Vernunftbetätigung; die sittliche Person also das X der dem Sittengesetz gemäßen Willensbetätigung. (ebd., 385)

Im Unterschied zu Kant entwickelt Scheler eine Ethik, die nicht nur an einer formalen Verallgemeinerung, sondern an etwas Materialem, nämlich den Werten orientiert ist. Im Gegensatz zu Kant, der "Gut" und "Böse" nur an den Akten des Willens festmacht[18] und davon ausgeht, dass nichts für gut gelten könne, als der gute Wille, versteht Scheler "Gut" und "Böse" als materiale Werte, deren Träger die Person ist.

> So daß wir vom Standpunkt der Träger aus geradezu definieren können: *'Gut' und 'Böse' sind Personenwerte.* (ebd., 23)

Für Scheler können sittlich gut und böse nur individuelle Personen sowie ihre Willensakte und Handlungen sein. (ebd., 83)

Die Möglichkeit einer apriorischen materialen Wertethik ist für Scheler durch den Zusammenhang von "Gut" und "Böse" mit den übrigen Werten gegeben. Aufgrund der Rangordnung der übrigen Werte sei es nämlich möglich, zu bestimmen, welche Art von Wertrealisierung "gut" oder "böse" sei.

> Für jede materiale Wertsphäre, über welche die Erkenntnis eines Wesens verfügt, gibt es eine ganz bestimmte *materiale* Ethik, in der die sachentsprechenden Vorzugsgesetze zwischen den materialen Werten aufzuweisen sind. (ebd., 21)

Scheler gibt drei apriorische Axiome der materialen Ethik an: Erstens, die Existenz eines positiven Wertes ist selbst ein positiver Wert; [19] zweitens, Gut ist der Wert in der Sphäre des Wollens, der an der Realisierung eines positiven Wertes oder eines höheren (höchsten) Wertes haftet; [20] und drittens, das Kriterium für Gut und Böse besteht in der Übereinstimmung des in der Realisierung intendierten Wertes mit dem Vorzugswerte, resp. im Widerstreite mit dem Nachsetzungswerte. Alles Gut und Böse ist für Scheler notwendig an die Realisierung von Akten gebunden, die ihrerseits wiederum auf Vorzugsakte zurückzuführen sind. Die uns unmittelbar durch unser Vorzugsakte gegebenen Werte stehen zueinander in einem apriorischen Zusammenhang, der uns vor allem Handeln, also apriorisch, gegeben ist.

---

[18] In einem Punkt habe Kant allerdings recht. Wer seinem Nächsten nicht wohltun will, sodass es ihm auf die Realisierung diese Wohles ankommt, sondern nur die Gelegenheit ergreift, in diesem Akte selbst gut zu sein, oder Gutes zu tun, der ist nicht wahrhaft gut, sondern ist in Wahrheit eine Spielart des Pharisäers, der vor sich selbst nur gut erscheinen will. (Scheler 1921, 22)

[19] Die Nichtexistenz eines positiven Wertes ist selber eine negativer Wert. Die Existenz eines negativen Wertes ist selbst ein negativer Wert. Die Nichtexistenz eines negativen Wertes ist selbst ein positiver Wert.

[20] Böse ist der Wert in der Sphäre des Wollens, der an der Realisierung eines negativen oder eines niedrigeren Wertes haftet.

> Der eigentliche Sitz alles Wertapriori (und auch des sittlichen) ist die im *Fühlen, Vorziehen*, in letzter Linie im Lieben und Hassen sich aufbauende *Werterkenntnis* resp. *Werterschauung*, sowie die der Zusammenhänge der Werte, ihres 'Höher' und 'Niedrigerseins', d.h. die *sittliche Erkenntnis*. (ebd., 64)

Scheler betont, dass ein nur auf Wahrnehmen und Denken beschränkter Geist absolut "wertblind" wäre, wie sehr er auch einer inneren, psychischen Wahrnehmung fähig wäre. Nur im fühlenden, lebendigen Verkehr mit der Welt, im Lieben und im Hassen, seien uns die Werte zugänglich.

Für Scheler beruht auf dieser Werterkenntnis und ihrem apriorischen Gehalt das ganze sittliche Wollen:

> Auf dieser Werterkenntnis (…) ist aber das sittliche *Wollen* (…) so fundiert, dass jegliches Wollen (ja jegliches Streben überhaupt) primär auf die Realisierung eines (…) Wertes gerichtet ist. (ebd., 65)

Die Stärke der Gegebenheit des jeweiligen Wertes könne variieren bis hin zur absoluten Evidenz. Hier bekomme das Wollen eine Notwendigkeit, die bei Sokrates dazu geführt habe, anzunehmen, dass die Erkenntnis des Guten automatisch zu einem guten Handeln führe. Das Falsche an der sokratischen Formulierung, sei jedoch ihr Rationalismus, d.h. die Annahme, dass schon die bloße Kenntnis sittlicher Normen – das urteilsmäßig Wissen, was gut sei, ohne Erfüllung im gefühlten Wert selbst – handlungsleitend sei.

Für Kant wiederum sei die Orientierung am Guten deshalb unmöglich, weil all das, was uns in der Erfahrung gegeben sei, immer schon die materialen empirischen, sinnlich bedingten Absichten seien. "Darum gibt es für Kant immer nur das negative Kriterium des sittlich Guten, daß ein gutes Wollen *wider* alle in Frage kommenden 'Neigungen' erfolge." (ebd., 67) Scheler hingegen nimmt an, dass der Sitz des ethischen Apriori in der Sphäre der sittlichen Erkenntnis, nicht aber in derjenigen des Wollens liegt. Er nimmt an, dass es "eine sittliche *Erkenntnis* gibt, die vom sittlichen *Wollen* grundverschieden ist, und die das Wollen des Guten fundiert." (ebd., 78)

Ob jemand sittlich richtig handelt oder nicht hängt nach Scheler von seinen Werten ab, die seinem Streben zugrunde liegen. Die sittlichen Unterschiede zwischen den Menschen liegen für Scheler nicht in den Zwecken, die sie sich setzen und wählen, sondern in ihren Werten, die "den *möglichen Spielraum* für ihre Zwecksetzungen abgeben". (ebd., 37) Für die höherstehende sittliche Natur eines Menschen sei es charakteristisch, dass bereits sein unwillkürliches Streben und Begehren entsprechend einer Vorzugsordnung verlaufe, die der objektiven Rangordnung der Werte entspreche. Die Vorzugsordnung werde hier "zur *inneren Regel des Automatismus* des Strebens selbst und schon der Art und Weise, wie die Strebungen an die zentrale Willenssphäre gelangen." (ebd., 38) Aus dem Besagten wird ersichtlich, dass Scheler den Grundwert des sittlich Guten und des Tugendhaften in der Realisierung des jeweils höheren und wenn möglich des höchsten Wertes sieht. (Schleißheimer 2003, 127)

2.4. Das Sollen

Für Scheler kann man von Tugend nur dann sprechen, wenn ein Sollen vorliegt, sonst "gäbe es keine Tugend, sondern allein 'Tüchtigkeit'". (Scheler 1921, 209) Tugend sei nicht die Tüchtigkeit zu irgendetwas, "sondern zum Wollen und Tun eines als ideal gesollt Gegebenen." (ebd., 245) Hier liegt ein wesentlicher Unterschied zum antiken Tugendverständnis vor, das *arete* im Sinne der "Gutheit" als allgemeine Kategorie der Qualität von Etwas versteht, d.h. "Wie-es-beschaffen-ist", die auch auf handwerkliche und künstlerische Tätigkeiten und ebenso auf Tiere, Werkzeuge und Organe anwendbar ist. (Aristoteles 2011, 1096a25). Aristoteles spricht davon, dass die Qualität der Gutheit (*arete*) etwas oder jemanden in eine gute Verfassung versetze und die Ausübung seiner Funktion (*ergon*) gut mache. (Aristoteles 2011, 1106a15) So mache die Gutheit des Rennpferdes es zu einem guten Rennpferd. Das höchste menschliche Gut als "Tätigkeit (*energeia*) der Seele im Sinn der Gutheit" (Aristoteles 2011, 1098 a16) stellt für Aristoteles das Leben nach der Vernunft dar.

Auch Scheler spricht bezüglich der Tugend von Qualitäten, aber nur in Hinsicht auf die Person. Konkret versteht Scheler unter Tugenden die "Beschaffenheiten der Person" einem Sollen zu entsprechen (Scheler 2007, 83). Die Tugend als "eine *Qualität der Person* selbst" (Scheler 1919, 15), die je nach der Güte der Person variieren kann, beinhalte die Fähigkeit, dem jeweiligen Sollen zu entsprechen. Für Scheler ist alles Sollen in Werten fundiert (Scheler 2007, 79) Scheler unterscheidet zwischen dem idealen Sollen[21] und demjenigen Sollen, das eine Forderung oder einen Befehl enthält. "Wo immer von 'Pflicht' oder von ‚Norm' die Rede ist, da ist nicht das 'ideale' Sollen, sondern bereits diese seine Spezifizierung zu irgendeiner Art des *Imperativischen* gemeint." (ebd., 206) Das könne nun das innere Kommando des Sich-verpflichtet-wissens sein, oder von außen kommende Akte wie "Befehl", "Rat" und "Empfehlung".

Scheler entwickelt seinen Tugendbegriff in Abgrenzung zur formalen Ethik Kants, wobei er davon ausgeht, dass für Kant die Tugend nur ein "*Niederschlag* der einzelnen pflichtgemäßen Akte" ist. (ebd., 24) Man könne jedoch nicht von Pflicht sprechen, wenn man nicht das Können dafür habe, denn dieses Können gehe aller Idee der Pflicht voraus, als eine Bedingung ihrer Möglichkeit. (ebd., 24) In diesem Sinne fehle bei Kant eine eigene Tugendlehre. Was nicht in der Spannweite des "Könnens" eines Wesens liege, das könne zwar als

---

[21] Das Verhältnis zwischen idealem Sollen und Werten ist für Scheler grundsätzlich durch die zwei Axiome geregelt: alles positiv Wertvolle soll sein, und alles negativ Wertvolle soll nicht sein.

Forderung des idealen Sollens noch an es ergehen; es könne aber niemals "Imperativ" für es sein und seine Pflicht heißen. Die Tugend sei fundierend für den sittlichen Wert aller sittlichen Handlungen. Die Tugendlehre gehe somit der Pflichtenlehre voran. (ebd., 24) Scheler lehnt Kants Sichtweise ab, dass man von Tugenden nur sprechen könne, wenn sie mit Opfern und Mühen verbunden seien. Er sieht darin eine ganz bestimmte Art der auf Ressentiment beruhenden Werttäuschung, etwas darum wertvoller zu halten, weil es mehr Kraft, Mühe und Arbeit zu seiner Realisierung in Anspruch nehme. (ebd., 234) Die sittlich höherstehende Persönlichkeit sei jedenfalls diejenige "der die Realisierung dieser Inhalte am wenigsten Mühe macht und kostet; wer am wenigsten Widerstände gegen das Gute hat, der ist der Beste." (ebd., 236)

Für Scheler ist die Tugend als ein lebendiges "Machtbewusstsein zum Guten ganz persönlich und individuell." (Scheler 1919, 16) Das kantische Sittengesetz und die Pflicht seien hingegen nur unpersönliche Surrogate für mangelnde Tugenden: "Pflichten sind übertragbar, Tugenden sind es nicht." (Scheler 1919, 17)

Schelers Begriff der Tugend kann in diesem Sinne als personalistisch verstanden werden. (Hähnel 2015, 78)

Um die Person zu erfassen, so Scheler, müsse man versuchen mit "verstehender Liebe (…) aus dem Gemenge von empirischen Einzelteilen heraus (…) die Linien ihres Wertwesens herauszuschauen und herauszuarbeiten." (ebd., 508) Auf diesem individuellen Wertwerden, nämlich der Person, gründet für Scheler jegliches Sollen, das "als ein ‚Ruf' an diese Person und sie allein ergeht, gleichgültig, ob derselbe "Ruf auch an andere ergeht oder nicht." (ebd., 510) Dies bedeute jedoch nicht, dass die allgemeingültigen Werte vernachlässigt werden müssen, denn "erst die *Zusammenschau und die Durchdringung der allgemeingültigen* sittlichen Werte mit den *individualgültigen*" ergebe die "*volle Evidenz für das Gute-an-sich*. (ebd., 513) In der Tugend verschmelze der allgemeine und der individuelle Wertanspruch: Die Tugend sei ein "glückseliges *Könnens-* und *Machtbewusstsein* zum Wollen und Tun eines in sich selbst und gleichzeitig für *unsere* Individualität, allein Rechten und Guten" zu verstehen. (Scheler 1919, 14) Jeder falsche Individualismus ist für Scheler dadurch ausgeschlossen, dass eine ursprüngliche Mitverantwortlichkeit jeder Person für das Ganze besteht (Solidaritätsprinzip). Scheler legt somit die ganze Sorge für die Gemeinschaft "in das lebendige *Zentrum der individuellen Person.*" (Scheler 1916, XII)

2.5. Tugend als Freude am Können

Scheler weist darauf hin, dass schon Aristoteles das Sollen auf ein Können zurückgeführt hat. Er habe angenommen, dass das Gute dasjenige für ein Wesen sei, für das dieses

Wesen ein eigentümliches und nur ihm zugehöriges "Vermögen" besitze, im Falle des Menschen die Vernunftbetätigung. (Scheler 2007, 241) Dies ermögliche es, dass der Mensch, das realisieren könne, was er solle, nämlich ein Leben nach der Vernunft zu leben. Auch Luther drücke diese Ansicht aus, allerdings in theologischer Sprache, wenn er davon ausgehe, dass der Mensch erst dann gut handle, wenn er durch die Gnade Gottes auch das Können zum Guten besitze. (ebd., 243) Darüber hinaus zeige sich, dass wir das "eigentümliche Bewusstsein der 'Verpflichtung' zu etwas haben, wenn wir uns eines Könnens, einer Macht bewußt werden." (ebd., 241) In jeder sittlich positivwertigen Handlung steigert sich für Scheler die Tugend der Person, "d.h. die erlebte Macht für das gesollt Gute." (ebd., 559) Scheler betont, dass diese erlebte Macht in früheren Zeiten mehr galt, als dasjenige, 'wozu' sie Macht war. (Scheler 1919, 16) Insofern kann man bei Schelers Tugendbegriff von einem intrinsischen Wert sprechen (Hähnel 2015, 78). Denn er steht für sich allein, "nicht da 'für' vorbestimmte Handlungen und Werke, noch gar für die Nutznießung anderer, sondern ein freier Schmuck ihres Träges, etwa wie die Feder auf dem Hut." (Scheler 1919, 15)

Scheler versteht die Tugend als eine Selbstermächtigung zum Guten. Ganz im Sinne Nietzsche geht es ihm um ein Macht- und Kraftbewusstsein, das sich gegen alles richtet, was den Menschen "klein" machen und abwerten will. Wie Nietzsche richtet er sich gegen das Ressentiment, das davon lebt, das Starke und Schöne abzuwerten. Es ist daher auch kein Zufall, dass Scheler in seiner Aufsatzsammlung *Vom Umsturz der Werte*, den Aufsatz *Zur Rehabilitierung der Tugend* demjenigen von *Das Ressentiment im Aufbau der Moralen* voransetzt. Im Gegensatz zu Nietzsche, welcher die Ursache für das Ressentiment im Christentum sieht, wertet Scheler das Christentum auf, weil es durch die Gnade der Liebe den Menschen kräftige und stärke und nicht – so wie Nietzsche angenommen habe – schwäche und klein mache. Es ist daher auch kein Zufall, dass sich Scheler in *Zur Rehabilitierung der Tugend* ausführlich mit zwei Tugenden auseinandersetzt, welche dem Christentum nahestehen, nämlich der Demut und der Ehrfurcht. Während der Stolze – hier denkt er vor allem an den Stoiker – den eigenen moralischen Wert als höchsten ansehe, losgelöst von allen Gütern und Werten, eröffne die Demut dem Demütigen "das Geistesauge für alle Werte der Welt" (Scheler 1916, 25) Während der Stolze sich nichts schenken lasse, werde dem Demütigen "alles geschenkt." (ebd., 25) Scheler nimmt an, dass "das Wertbewusstsein" durch den Stolz verengt wird, bis es nur mehr "auf den bloßen Punkt des Ich" im Sinne der "Unabhängigkeit" reduziert ist. (ebd., 21) Hingegen sei die Demut "ein Modus der Liebe, die sonnenmächtig allein das starre Eis zerbricht, das der schmerzensreiche Stolz um das immer leerere Ich gürtet." (ebd., 24) Seine Beschreibung der Tugend der Ehrfurcht zeigt noch klarer woraufScheler hinauswill: es geht ihm um die Öffnung für das Werthafte der Welt. In der Ehrfurcht sieht er eine "*Haltung, in der man noch etwas hinzuwahrnimmt, das der Ehrfurchtlose nicht sieht und für das er blind ist: das Geheimnis der Dinge und die Werttiefe ihrer Existenz.*" (ebd., 33)

Scheler bringt die Tugend mit der Verantwortung in Verbindung, indem er betont, dass in früheren Zeiten die "innere Fülle" der Tugend nach immer weiterer Ausdehnung der Verantwortung gedrängt habe, sodass derjenige, der sie im Übermaß besaß, sich für alles, was überhaupt in der Welt geschah, leise mitverantwortlich fühlte. Als spezifischer Mangel an Tugend habe gegolten, die Verantwortlichkeit möglichst abzustoßen und nur auf einen möglichst kleinen Kreis des "nicht befohlenen" zu begrenzen. (Scheler 1919, 16) Abgesehen davon, dass Scheler hier eine Idealisierung der Vergangenheit vornimmt, spricht er eine Thematik an, die in der Ethikdebatte seit Hans Jonas von großer Bedeutung ist, nämlich der Zusammenhang von Macht, Können und Verantwortung. Die Macht des Menschen wird für Jonas zur Wurzel des Sollens der Verantwortung. (Jonas 2003, 231) Wie Scheler auch, hebt er die große Bedeutung der Ehrfurcht hervor, denn sie könne uns "vor den Irrwegen unserer Macht" schützen. (Raynova 2016, 22)

> Die Ehrfurcht allein, indem sie uns ein 'Heiliges', das heißt unter keinen Umständen zu Verletzendes enthüllt (und das ist auch ohne positive Religion dem Auge erscheinbar) wird uns auch davor schützen, um der Zukunft willen die Gegenwart zu schänden, jene um den Preis dieser kaufen zu wollen. (Jonas 1979, 393)

Jonas macht seinen Verantwortungsbegriff am Können fest. Anders gesagt, verantwortlich bin ich für alles, was im Wirkungsbereich meines Könnens und meiner Macht liegt und auf diese angewiesen ist oder von ihr bedroht wird, (Moser 2016, 57) wobei die Ehrfurcht mir dabei hilft, die Werthaftigkeit des zu Schützenden zu erfassen.

Die Eigenart des Könnens zeigt sich für Scheler an der besonderen Art von Freude und Befriedigung, die wir am bloßen Können einer Sache haben. (Scheler 2007, 239) Scheler nimmt an, dass jedes positive Wertwachstum mit einer Luststeigerung verbunden ist, wobei sich Werthöhe und Gefühlstiefe entsprechen würden. (ebd., 370)

> Jeder *Vorzug eines höheren Wertes* vor dem niedrigeren Wert ist von einer Steigerung der Tiefe des positiven Gefühls begleitet. (ebd., 370)

Zudem falle uns das Vorziehen des höheren Wertes immer leichter, je öfter dies vorkomme.

2.6. Glückseligkeit

Scheler stellt sich voll in die Tradition derer, die eine notwendige Verbindung zwischen Glückseligkeit und Tugend herstellen: "Dass irgendwelcher Zusammenhang von Glückseligkeit und sittlich positivem Wert der Person, zwischen gutem Verhalten und den es begleitenden positiven Gefühlen bestehe (…) darüber sind alle, die über diese Frage ernsthaft nachgedachten, einer Meinung." (Scheler 2007, 368) Scheler bezieht sich an dieser Stelle nicht explizit auf Aristoteles, obwohl dieser am Eindrücklichsten die Verbindung zwischen Glückseligkeit und Tugend aufgezeigt hat, ja mehr noch, Aristoteles setzt überhaupt die Glückseligkeit mit der tugendhaften Tätigkeit der Seele gleich. (Aristoteles 1985, 1099b26) Je nachdem wie tugendhaft eine Lebensform ist, desto höher oder niedriger ist die Glückseligkeit, die damit verbunden ist. Die höchste Form der Glückseligkeit ist mit der höchsten menschlichen Lebensform, nämlich der vernünftigen, verbunden.

> Ist nun die Vernunft im Vergleich mit dem Menschen etwas Göttliches, so muß auch das Leben nach der Vernunft im Vergleich mit dem menschlichen Leben göttlich sein. (Aristoteles 1985, 1177 b27)

Man solle der Mahnung der Menschen kein Gehör schenken, unser Streben nur auf das Menschliche zu beschränken, sondern alles dazu tun, dem Besten was in uns sei nachzuleben. Denn: "dieses Göttliche in uns ist unser wahres Selbst, wenn anders es unser vornehmster und bester Teil ist. Mithin wäre es ungereimt, wenn einer nicht sein eigenes Leben wollte, sondern das eines anderen." (1985, 1178a2) Erst auf dieser Ebene könne der Mensch die vollendete Glückseligkeit erfahren. (Aristoteles 1985, 1177b25)

Für Scheler stellt die Glückseligkeit die Wurzel und Quelle allen guten Wollens und Handelns dar. Das Glück sei "keineswegs der 'Lohn der Tugend', sowenig als die Tugend Mittel zur Glückseligkeit ist. Wohl aber ist es die Wurzel und die Quelle der Tugend, eine Quelle, die aber selbst schon nur eine Folge der inneren Wesensgüte der Person ist." (Scheler 2007, 373) Schon Spinoza habe diesen Zusammenhang gesehen, nämlich "dass die Glückseligkeit nicht ein Lohn der Tugend, sondern die Tugend selbst" sei.[22] (ebd., 242) Auch Scheler setzt also die Glückseligkeit mit der Tugend gleich. Allerdings koppelt er die Tugend nicht an die jeweilige Tätigkeit bzw. Lebensform, wie Aristoteles dies macht, sondern legt sie in die Person selbst, deren Tugendhaftigkeit er als ein Geschenk der Gnade versteht. In *Das Ressentiment im Aufbau der Moralen* spricht Scheler von einer "Bewegungsumkehr der Liebe" im Christentum. (Scheler 2004, 38) Während die Liebe in der Antike als ein Streben vom Niedrigeren zum Höheren, vom Unvollkommeneren zum Vollkommeneren verstanden worden sei, werde die Liebe im Christentum zu einem Geschenk Gottes und "damit zu einer Quelle der Kraft und Liebesfähigkeit für den Menschen." (Moser 2014, 25)

---

[22] "Lehrsatz 42. Die Glückseligkeit ist nicht der Lohn der Tugend, sonders selbst Tugend; und wir erfreuen uns ihrer nicht deshalb, weil wir die Gelüste hemmen, sondern umgekehrt, weil wir uns ihrer erfreuen, deswegen können wir die Gelüste hemmen." (Spinoza 1994, 295)

Der Begriff der Tugend kann meines Erachtens bei Scheler nur aus dieser Bewegungsumkehr der Liebe heraus verstanden werden. Scheler setzt die Tugend mit einer Kraftquelle gleich, die sich aus dieser Liebe nährt und uns nicht nur in ein freudiges Könnens- und Machtbewusstsein versetzt, sondern uns zugleich auch die Werthaftigkeit der Welt erschließt. Er sieht in der Tugend nicht das Bollwerk gegenüber negativen Emotionen, sondern die kraftvolle Erschließung und Ermöglichung all dessen, was in unserer Persönlichkeit an Schätzen angelegt ist. So gesehen ist es kein Wunder, dass Scheler Spinoza erwähnt, der davon ausgeht, dass – je mehr sich die Seele der göttlichen Liebe oder der Glückseligkeit erfreue – sie umso größere Macht habe über ihre Affekte und dass sie dann umso weniger leide unter ihren schlechten Affekten.

> Mithin hat die Seele infolge davon, dass sie sich dieser göttlichen Liebe oder der Glückseligkeit erfreut, die Gewalt, die Gelüste zu hemmen. (Spinoza 1994, 296)

Scheler folgert daraus, dass man ein Leben der Freude und nicht der Verbote leben sollte. Statt "du sollst nicht", wäre es besser, darauf hinzuweisen: "du kannst dies und jenes". Einem Alkoholiker könne man nicht das Trinken dadurch abgewöhnen, dass man es ihm verbiete, sondern nur dadurch, dass "wir neue Interessen und schlafende Kräfte in ihm entwickeln, ihn auf positive Lebensziele hinweisen, in deren Verfolgung sein Laster gleichsam verschwindet und sozusagen zugedeckt wird." (Scheler 2007, 242)

3. Vergleich und Schlussfolgerungen

Sowohl Halbig als auch Scheler fassen die Tugend als einen intrinsischen Wert auf, d.h. als einen Wert, der um seiner selbst willen geschätzt wird und nicht, weil er für etwas Anderes nützlich ist. Für Scheler sind die Tugenden Personenwerte, die den höchsten Platz in seiner vierstufigen Wertrangordnung einnehmen. Halbig versteht die Tugenden hingegen als angemessene Einstellungen zu anderen intrinsischen Werten. Die Beantwortung der Frage, um welche Werte es sich dabei handelt und ob es so etwas wie eine Wertrangordnung gibt, überlässt er der allgemeinen Werttheorie. Auch wenn Halbig behauptet, dass Schelers Ansatz mit seiner rekursiven Theorie der Tugenden übereinstimmt, haben wir es bei Scheler und Halbig mit zwei komplett verschiedenen Zugängen zu tun. Schelers Überlegungen zur Tugend sind in eine umfassende Werttheorie eingebettet, während Halbig nicht einmal ansatzweise versucht, den Begriff des Wertes zu klären. Sichtbar wird dies insbesondere beim Problem der Werterfassung. Sowohl Halbig als auch Scheler sind Wertrealisten, d.h. sie gehen davon aus, dass die Werte nicht vom Subjekt konstituiert oder erfunden werden, sondern erfasst und gefunden werden. Während Scheler eine subtile

Werterfassungstheorie entwickelt, in der er annimmt, dass wir über ein Wertfühlen verfügen, das uns die Werte erschließt, bleibt diese Thematik bei Halbig völlig im Dunklen. An manchen Stellen gibt Halbig Anlass zur Vermutung, dass die Werterfassung über die Tugenden verlaufen könnte, indem er die Metapher des Fernrohres verwendet, mit dessen Hilfe wir die Werte aufspüren. Bei den Tugenden handelt es sich jedoch keineswegs um bloße Hilfsmittel zur Werterfassung, sondern um eine besondere Verfasstheit der Person, welche das gesamte Strebevermögen umfasst. Während Scheler eine ausdifferenzierte Theorie des emotionalen Lebens entwickelt, in welcher der Zusammenhang von Gefühlen und Werten sichtbar wird, blendet Halbig die Rolle der Emotionen bei der Werterfassung vollständig aus. In seinen Beispielen kommen des Öfteren emotionale Antwortreaktionen auf Wertverletzungen zur Sprache, der Zusammenhang von Tugenden, Emotionen und Werten bleibt jedoch völlig ungeklärt.

Halbig vertritt explizit die These, dass Scheler die Grundannahmen der rekursiven Theorie der Tugenden teilt, welche Tugenden als intrinsisch wertvolle Einstellungen zu anderen intrinsischen Werten versteht. Bereits die Wahl der Begrifflichkeit zeigt an, dass Halbig auf etwas ganz Anderes hinauswill als Scheler. Während bei Scheler die Tugend ein kraftvolles Können im Sinne der Realisierung der je persönlich gegebenen Wertmöglichkeiten darstellt, geht es Halbig darum Bewertungskriterien für die Einstellungen der Menschen zu bestimmten Werten zu entwickeln. In den Tugenden glaubt er den Maßstab dafür gefunden zu haben, ein Verhalten über das Pflichtgemäße hinaus als moralisch wertvoll beurteilen zu können. Da ihm jedoch die Kriterien einer objektiven Wertrangordnung fehlen, ist die Gefahr gegeben, dass dies zu einem Moralisieren, bis hin zu einem Tugendterror führt. Mit der Einstellung durch die Welt zu gehen, das Verhalten der Anderen kritisieren zu wollen, ohne klare Wertvorstellungen zu haben, kann zu einer diffusen moralischen Überforderung führen.

Für Scheler sind die Tugenden Qualitäten der Person, während in Halbigs Verständnis der Tugend als Einstellung der Bezug zur Person gar nicht vorkommt. Dadurch wird es für ihn auch schwierig, den Zusammenhang zwischen Person und Tugend zu erklären und verständlich zu machen, worin denn die Vervollkommnung der Person bestehen könnte, auf die er zum Schluss Bezug nimmt. Das Verständnis der Tugend als Einstellung und die Metapher des Fernrohrs und des Magnetismus des Guten legen nahe, dass Halbig die Tugend als Fähigkeit versteht, sich auf ein Ideal auszurichten, nicht jedoch als eine besondere Verfasstheit der Person selbst. Hier liegt meiner Meinung nach der größte Unterschied zwischen Halbig einerseits und Scheler sowie Aristoteles andererseits. Die beiden letzteren verstehen die Tugenden als eine Art Transformatoren, welche den gesamten Menschen erfassen und nachhaltig verändern. Bei Scheler liegt das Wesentliche der Tugend in der

Persönlichkeitsentwicklung, in der Verwirklichung der ganz individuellen Bestimmung des Menschen. Die Tugend macht es möglich, dass das "volle Licht aller nur möglichen Werte in uns hereinfluten" kann. (Scheler 1916, 24) Während Halbig die Tugenden als Fernrohr für weit von uns entfernte Ideale oder Werte versteht, sind sie bei Scheler Ausdruck der inneren Fülle der Person, an der er die Werterfassung festmacht. Auch Aristoteles setzt die Tugend und die Gutheit der Person gleich. Alles was ich tue geht von dieser Gutheit aus und wird von ihr bestimmt. Die Tugend ist also in der Person selbst verankert und nicht erst in einem Ideal. Allerdings setzt Aristoteles die Tugenden auf allen Ebenen des Strebevermögens an, während Scheler sie nur in der Person verortet. Während Aristoteles "von unten" herkommend die Tugenden als den richtigen Umgang mit Emotionen versteht, zielt Scheler "von oben" darauf ab, die gesamte Persönlichkeit zu verändern. Beide betonen die große Bedeutung der Emotionalität. Aristoteles sieht im irrationalen Seelenanteil den Führer der Tugenden und betont deshalb die Wichtigkeit der richtigen emotionalen Verfasstheit. Scheler hingegen nimmt mit dem Wertfühlen eine eigene, der Vernunft ebenbürtige, dieser jedoch vorgelagerten Instanz an, durch welche die Werte erfasst werden. Die auf der Ebene der Person angesetzten Tugenden bringt er jedoch mit der Liebe in Verbindung, die als ein Gnadengeschenk den Tugendhaften von innen her ermächtigen, das Gute zu vollbringen. Beide Ansätze sind bei Scheler in eine umfassende Metaphysik eingebettet, in der ein innerer Zusammenhang zwischen dem Göttlichen, der Glückseligkeit und der Tugend hergestellt wird. Halbig hingegen geht von einer rationalen Handlungstheorie aus, in der die Werte die Quelle von Handlungsgründen darstellen.

Ganz wesentlich ist für Aristoteles die Freude, die mit der Ausübung der Tugend verbunden ist und die sich, je nach der Art der Tätigkeit bis zur Glückseligkeit steigern kann. Auch für Scheler ist die Tugend mit einem freudigen Gefühl verbunden, nämlich einem glückseligen Könnens- und Machtbewusstsein, das sich in der Realisierung des in uns angelegten individuellen Sollens manifestiert. Sowohl für Aristoteles als auch für Scheler geht es letztendlich darum, die höchst mögliche menschliche Lebensform zu erreichen, die bei beiden auch mit der höchsten Form der Glückseligkeit in Verbindung steht. Bei Scheler ist diese Lebensform ganz persönlich und individuell und kann von Mensch zu Mensch stark variieren. Sein Interesse liegt nicht so sehr bei einer gut funktionierenden Polis, vielmehr wünscht er sich eine Gesellschaftsform, in der das für jeden Einzelnen Gute mit dem der Gesellschaft und mit dem Ansich-Guten zusammen bestehen kann und sich wechselseitig fördert.

Während bei Aristoteles die Tugend durch Gewöhnung und Erziehung erlangt wird, spielt bei Scheler die Gnade eine Rolle, durch welche der Person die Kraft und das Können für die Realisierung der höheren und höchsten Werte ermöglicht wird. Halbig schließt sich

Aristoteles insofern an, als auch er den Erwerb der Tugenden durch Erziehung und Vorbildwirkung annimmt, den Zusammenhang von Tugend und Glück jedoch als problematisch ansieht. Die Freude, die mit der Ausübung der Tugend verbunden ist, sieht er durch die Opfer, die sie abverlangt, gefährdet. Damit folgt er der seit Nietzsche verbreiteten Ansicht, dass Tugenden eher den Anderen nützlich sind, als ihrem Träger. Neueste Erkenntnisse der positiven Psychologie könnten jedoch Aristoteles und Scheler – ganz unabhängig von ihrer metaphysischen Verortung – recht geben, indem sie zeigen, dass Tugenden positive Emotionen fördern, die uns nicht nur zu einem glücklichen und langen Leben verhelfen, sondern auch ein Schutzschild in schwierigen Zeiten gegen Schicksalsschläge bilden. In diesem Sinne können Tugenden als eine Art Transformatoren vom Negativen hin zum Positiven verstanden werden, aber auch als eine Selbstermächtigung dazu, in Freude das jeweils individuell Auferlegte zu bewältigen.

Dr. Susanne Moser, Institut für Axiologische Forschungen, Wien / Universität Wien / Karl Franzens-Universität Graz, susanne.moser[at]univie.ac.at

Literaturhinweise

Adams, Robert Merrihew. *A Theory of Virtue. Excellence in Being for the Good*. Oxford: Clarendon 2006.

Annas, Julia. "Being Virtuous and Doing the Right Thing", *Proceedings of the American Philosophical Association* Vol. 78, No. 2, (2004): 61-75.

Annas, Julia. "Comments on John Doris' *Lack of Character*", *Philosophy and Phenomenological Research* 71, 2005, 636-642.

Anscombe, G.E.M. "Modern Moral Philosophy", in Geach, Mary, and Luke Gormally (eds.). *Human Life, Action and Ethics. Essays by G.E.M. Anscombe*. Exeter: Imprint Academic, 1958, 169-194.

Arendt, Hannah. *Elemente und Ursprünge totaler Herrschaft*. München: Piper, 2013.

Aristoteles. *Magnia Moralia*. Übersetzt von Franz Dirlmeier. Darmstadt: Wissenschaftliche Buchgesellschaft, 1970.

Aristoteles. *Nikomachische Ethik*. Übersetzt von Eugen Rolfes. Hamburg: Felix Meiner, 1985.

Aristoteles. *Nikomachische Ethik*. Übersetzt und herausgegeben von Ursula Wolf. Hamburg: Rowohlt, 2011.

Beier, Kathi. "Tugenden als Qualitäten der Seele", in Beier, Kathi und Thamar Rossi Leidi (Hrsg.). *Substanz denken. Aristoteles und seine Bedeutung für die moderne Metaphysik und Naturwissenschaft*, Würzburg: Königshausen und Neumann, 2016, 127-146.

Bellah, Robert, Richard Madsen, and William Sullivan. *Gewohnheiten des Herzens. Individualismus und Gemeinsinn in der amerikanischen Gesellschaft*. Köln: Bund-Verlag, 1987.

Brentano, Franz. *Vom Ursprung sittlicher Erkenntnis*. Leipzig: Duncker & Humblot, 1889.

Copp, David und David Sobel. "Morality and Virtue. An Assessment of Some Recent Work in Virtue Ethics", in *Ethics* Vol. 114, No. 3 (2004): 514-554.

Doris, John M. *Lack of Charakter: Personality and Moral Behaviour*. New York: Cambridge University Press, 2002.

Ekman, Paul. *Gefühle lesen*. Heidelberg: Spectrum Verlag, 2010.

Foot, Philippa. *Natural Goodness*. Oxford: Clarendon, 2001.

Geach, Peter. *The Virtues*. Cambridge: Cambridge University Press, 1977.

Hähnel, Martin. *Das Ethos der Ethik. Zur Anthropologie der Tugend*. Wiesbaden: Springer, 2015.

Halbig, Christoph. *Praktische Gründe und die Realität der Moral*. Frankfurt am Main: Vittorio Klostermann, 2007.

Halbig, Christoph. *Der Begriff der Tugend und die Grenzen der Tugendethik*. Berlin: Suhrkamp, 2013.

Heller, Agnes. *Hypothese über eine marxistische Theorie der Werte*. Frankfurt am Main: Suhrkamp, 1972.

Hurka, Thomas. *Perfectionism*. New York: Oxford University Press, 1993.

Henckmann, Wolfhart. *Max Scheler*. München: Beck, 1998.

Hurka, Thomas. *Virtue, Vice and Value*. New York: Oxford University Press, 2001.

Hursthouse, Rosalind. "On the Grounding of the Virtues in Human Nature", in Szaif, Jan und Matthias Lutz-Bachmann (Hresg.). *Was ist das für den Menschen Gute? / What Is Good for a Human Being?* Berlin, New York: Walter de Gruyter, 2004, 263-275.

Joas, Hans. *Die Sakralität der Person - Eine neue Genealogie der Menschenrechte*. Frankfurt am Main: Suhrkamp, 2011.

Kant, Immanuel. *Die Metaphysik der Sitten*. Frankfurt am Main: Suhrkamp, 1993.

MacIntyre, Alasdair. *Der Verlust der Tugend. Zur moralischen Krise der Gegenwart*. Frankfurt am Main: Suhrkamp, 1984.

Moser, Susanne. "Philosophie der Gefühle zwischen Feeling-Theorien, Kognitionstheorien und Axiologie", *Labyrinth*, Vol.16, Nr.1 (2014): 77-91.

Moser, Susanne. "Vom Wert der Liebe", *Labyrinth*, Vol.16, Nr.2 (2014): 20-47.

Moser, Susanne. "Werte und Gefühle: Max Scheler und Ronald der Sousa im Vergleich", in Brigitte Buchhammer (Hrsg.). *Neuere Aspekte in der Philosophie: aktuelle Projekte von Philosophinnen am Forschungsstandort Österreich*. Wien: Axia Academic Publishers 2015, 213-246.

Moser, Susanne. "Verantwortung im Spannungsfeld zwischen Machtentfaltung und Verletzlichkeit: Die Umkehr des Verantwortungsverständnisses bei Hans Jonas", *Labyrinth*, Vol.18, Nr.1 (2016): 58-78.

Murdoch, Iris. *Metaphysics as a Guide to Morals*. London: Penguin Books, 1994.

Polak, Regina (Hrsg.). *Zukunft. Werte. Europa. Die Europäische Wertestudie 1990-2010: Österreich im Vergleich.* Wien: Böhlau 2011.

Raynova, Yvanka B. "Phänomenologie als Antwort und Verantwortung. Von Husserl bis Derrida", *Labyrinth*, Vol. 18, Nr.1 (2016): 5-30.

Raz, Joseph. *Value, Respect, and Attachment*. Cambrigde: University Press, 2001.

Riedenauer, Markus. *Orexis und Eupraxia. Ethikbegründung im Streben bei Aristoteles*. Würzburg: Königshausen & Neumann, 2000.

Riedenauer, Markus. "Menschliches Streben bei Aristoteles. Von affektiver Betreffbarkeit zu vernünftigem Handeln", in Murillo, José Sánchez de und Martin Thurner (Hrsg.). *Aufgang. Jahrbuch für Denken, Dichten, Musik*, Band 2. Stuttgart: Kohlhammer, 2005.

Sarazin, Thilo. *Der neue Tugendterror. Über die Grenzen der Meinungsfreiheit in Deutschland*. München: Deutsche Verlags-Anstalt, 2014.

Sartre, Jean-Paul. *Die Transzendenz des Ego. Philosophische Essays 1931-1939*. Reinbeck bei Hamburg: Rowohlt, 1994.

Seligmann, Martin. *Der Glücksfaktor. Warum Optimisten länger leben*. Köln: Bastei Lübbe AG, 2003.

Scheler, Max. "Zur Rehabilitierung der Tugend", in ders. *Vom Umsturz der Werte*. Leipzig: Der neue Geist Verlag, 1919, 12-42.

Scheler, Max. *Der Formalismus in der Ethik und die materiale Wertethik*. Halle: Max Niemeyer, 1921.

Scheler, Max. *Das Ressentiment im Aufbau der Moralen*. Frankfurt am Main: Vittorio Klostermann, 2004.

Schleißheimer, Bernhard. *Ethik heute. Die Frage nach dem guten Leben*. Würzburg: Königshausen & Neumann, 2003.

Slote, Michael. "Agent-based Virtue Ethics", in *Midwest Studies in Philosophy* Vol 20, No. 1 (1996): 83-101.

Slote, Michael. *Morals from Motives*. Oxford: Oxford University Press, 2001.

Stocker, Michael. "Die Schizophrenie moderner ethischer Theorien", in Rippe, Klaus Peter und Peter Schaber (Hrsg.). *Tugendethik*, Stuttgart: Reclam, 1976, 19-41.

Swanson, Christine. *Virtue Ethics. A Pluralistic View*. Oxford: Oxford University Press 2003.
Vogler, Candace. "Natural Virtue and Proper Upbringing", in Julia Peters (ed.). *Aristotelian Ethics in Contemporary Perspective*. New York, London: Routledge, 2013, 145-157.
Zagzebski, Linda Trinkaus. *Virtues of the Mind*. Cambridge: Cambridge University Press, 1996.

YVANKA B. RAYNOVA (Sofia/Vienna)
Paul Ricœurs Suche nach einer Neubegründung der Menschenrechte und der Würde durch die Fähigkeiten und die Anwendung der *phronèsis*

Abstract

Paul Ricoeur's Search for a New Foundation of Human Rights and Dignity by Means of the Capabilities and his Application of phronesis

The aim of the following article is to reconstruct Paul Ricoeur's concepts of human rights and human dignity by exploring some little-known texts, and to exemplify how these concepts are connected to a specific philosophical conception of human being, which is grounded in a Dialectics between transcendence and incarnation, freedom and dependence, identity and difference, capability and fallibility (fragility). In doing so, I will argue that Ricœur interprets human dignity, which he has never explicitly defined, through the prism of human capabilities, especially of the capability of being responsible. This interpretation allows him to take a differentiated position in the current bioethical debates on the rights of "potential persons" (Embrio) and to illustrate how the Aristotelian phronèsis can be used in (bio)ethical cases where decisions are difficult to take.

Keywords: Paul Ricœur, human rights, dignity, capabilities, responsibility, ethics, phronesis

---

In vielen einschlägigen Artikeln zur Würde des Menschen, wie z. B. in der französischen Ausgabe der Wikipedia[1] und der *Encyclopédie de l'Agora*[2] sowie in einigen Fachpublikationen (siehe Seifert 2003, 65), wird oft folgende "Definition der Menschenwürde" Paul Ricœur zugeschrieben: "Quelque chose est dû à l'être humain du fait qu'il est humain" ("Es steht dem Menschen etwas zu, durch die Tatsache, dass er ein menschliches Wesen ist"). Das Zitat stimmt zwar, aber die Autorinnen und Autoren der genannten Beiträge haben Ricœurs Artikel "Pour l'être humain du seul fait qu'il est humain" (Ricœur 1988, 233-237), aus der es entnommen wurde, so wie es aussieht nie gelesen; nicht nur, weil die Literaturangaben mangelhaft sind – es fehlt bei manchen der Aufsatztitel, auch die Seitenangaben sind ungenau –, sondern weil Ricœur in diesem Text überhaupt nicht über *Würde*, sondern über *Menschenrechte* spricht. Das Wort "Würde" (*dignité*) kommt gar nicht vor. Ich werde die ungekürzte Textpassage, aus der diese scheinbare "Definition" der Würde des Menschen herausgerissen wurde, später anführen. Hier möchte ich nur hervorheben, dass ohne den gesamten Ricœur'schen Artikel unter die Lupe zu nehmen, um sich den Kontext sowie Ricœurs Thesen genauer anzuschauen, aus dieser Textpassage allein kaum klar wird, worum es Ricœur ei-

---

[1] Siehe "Dignité", *Wikipedia* (https://fr.wikipedia.org/wiki/Dignit%C3%A9)
[2] Siehe "Dignité", *Encyclopédie de l'Agora* (http://agora.qc.ca/dossiers/Dignite)

gentlich geht. Kein Wunder also, wenn es zu abfälligen Kommentaren gekommen ist, wie z. B. bei Marc Halévy:

> Tut mir leid Herr Ricœur, aber nichts steht dem Menschen zu allein durch die Tatsache, dass er ein menschliches Wesen ist. Oder man müsste dann unter dem Adjektiv "menschlich" etwas ganz Anderes verstehen als das bloße Faktum, der Gattung homo sapiens demens anzugehören. Wenn das aber der Fall wäre, dann würden sehr wenige von den menschlichen Tieren eine Würde besitzen (...) Die Würde des Menschen besteht in seinen Werken und nicht in ihm selbst.[3]

Abgesehen davon, dass das Thema "homo sapiens demens" ein weitaus komplexeres ist,[4] als dass man es mit einem Satz abtun könnte, ist der ganze Kommentar problematisch. Erstens: Da es Ricœur hier nicht um Würde geht, ist die alte Debatte, ob die Würde dem Menschen inhärent sei, oder ob sie durch gewisse Leistungen verdient werden müsse, irrelevant. Für Ricœur geht es allein um die Frage, ob und weshalb die Menschenrechte als Rechtsforderungen dem Menschen als solchen zustehen und wie Menschenrechte überhaupt begründet werden können. Zweitens: Halévy unterstellt hier etwas, das mit dem Artikel nichts zu tun hat, nämlich, dass Ricœur die Würde sakralisiert und dem Menschen, der – so Halévy – nur ein "homo sapiens demens" sei, einen absoluten Wert im Kant'schen Sinne zuschreibe. So etwas steht aber weder im Text selbst, noch anderswo bei Ricœur. Wer sein Früh- und Spätwerk kennt, weiß sehr wohl, dass er den Menschen nicht nur als ein "fähiges", sondern auch als ein "fehlbares" und manchmal "unfähiges" Wesen thematisiert hat.

Das Ziel des folgenden Beitrags ist es, ausgehend von diesem wenig bekannten Text – "Pour l'être humain du seul fait qu'il est humain" – zu zeigen, inwiefern die Menschenrechte bei Ricœur mit einem bestimmten philosophischen Menschenbild verbunden sind, das auf der Dialektik zwischen Transzendenz und Inkarnation, Freiheit und Abhängigkeit, Identität und Differenz, Fähigkeit und Fehlbarkeit/Fragilität gründet. Dabei werde ich die These vertreten, dass Ricœur die Menschenwürde, die er nie explizit definiert hat, durch das Prisma der

---

[3] Die deutsche Übersetzung ist von mir, Y.R. Der Text im Original lautet: "Désolé, monsieur Ricœur, rien n'est dû à l'homme du seul fait qu'il est humain. Ou alors, il faudrait mettre dans l'adjectif "humain" tout autre chose que le seul fait d'appartenir au genre homo sapiens demens. Et si tel devait être le cas, bien peu d'animaux humains se pareraient d'une quelconque dignité (...) La dignité de l'homme est dans ses œuvres, et non en lui" (Marc Halévy. "Dignité humaine", online: http://www.noetique.eu/articles/anthropologie/dignite-humaine). Halévy, der bei Ilja Prigojine dissertiert hat und mit dem Namen des Nobelpreisträgers überall im Netz kokettiert, bezeichnet sich als Physiker und Philosoph, Spezialist für Freimaurerphilosophie und Esoterik, Zukunftsexperte, Krisenmanager usw. Ich kann seine wissenschaftlichen und philosophischen Kompetenzen nicht beurteilen, aber es steht für mich fest, dass er weder Ricœurs Text gelesen hat, noch sich in seiner Philosophie auskennt. Auch seine weiteren Kommentare zum Würdebegriff bei Kant, Plato und Augustinus, die in dieselbe Richtung gehen, zeugen von oberflächlichen Kenntnissen und Lektüren aus "zweiter Hand".

[4] Um im französischsprachigen Kontext zu bleiben, möchte ich hier auf die sehr differenzierten Analysen von Edgar Morin verweisen, für den "homo sapiens demens" ein instabiler und antagonistischer Begriff ist, mit dem man nicht nur den Menschen als ein Wesen bezeichnet, das sich zwischen Weisheit und Verrücktheit befindet, sondern auch die Möglichkeit eines Übergangs der Weisheit in Verrücktheit und umgekehrt (siehe Edgar Morin 2013).

menschlichen Fähigkeiten betrachtet und folglich aus der Fähigkeit Verantwortung zu übernehmen her interpretiert. Des Weiteren wird gezeigt wie diese Interpretation es ihm ermöglicht eine differenzierte Position in Bezug auf die gegenwärtigen bioethischen Debatten über die Rechte "potentieller Personen" (Embrio) einzunehmen und wie die Aristotelische *phronèsis* bei schwierigen (bio)ethischen Entscheidungen Anwendung finden kann.

1. Menschsein und Menschenrechte

Wenn man den Titel des Ricœur'schen Textes, "Pour l'être humain du seul fait qu'il est humain", außerhalb seines konkreten Kontextes betrachtet, könnte man annehmen, dass es sich hier um einen philosophisch-anthropologischen Beitrag handelt, nicht zuletzt auch weil die Philosophie Paul Ricœurs von vielen als eine Variante der philosophischen Anthropologie aufgefasst wird.[5] Der Text wurde jedoch aus einem bestimmten Anlass verfasst, der im ersten Augenblick wenig mit philosophischer Anthropologie zu tun hat. Er ist Teil eines Sammelbandes, der dem 50. Jubiläum der *Allgemeinen Deklaration der Menschenrechte* von 1948 gewidmet ist und einen Vergleich mit der *Déclaration des droits de l'homme* von 1789 anstrebt. In seiner Einleitung zu diesem Band betont der Herausgeber Jean-François de Raymond die doppeldeutige Rezeption der Menschenrechte, die bei den einen Ehrfurcht, bei den anderen jedoch Verdacht erregen. Im Zeitalter der Globalisierung habe die Idee der Menschenrechte einen breiten Konsens bei Regierungen und internationalen Organisationen gefunden, woraus der Verdacht geschöpft werde, es handle sich um eine neue Ideologie. Dies, so Raymond, sei jedoch nicht der Fall, ganz im Gegenteil, die Menschenrechte seien vielmehr eine ständige Ideologiekritik im Namen eines kritischen Humanismus:

> In Wirklichkeit überschreitet die Idee der Menschenrechte die politischen und kulturellen Spaltungen. Sie entgeht der parteiischen Aneignung und entblößt ironisch die Ideologien. Sie stellt die dringende Frage: "homme de quel(s) droit(s)?" - "Mensch mit welchen Rechten und aus welchem Recht?" – und erfordert die Antwort eines kritischen Humanismus. Die Idee der Menschenrechte verwandelt die Krise des Denkens in ein Denken der Krise.[6]

Durch den Ausdruck: "homme de quel(s) droit(s)?" werden mindestens zwei Fragen aufgeworfen: Inwiefern hat der Mensch Anrecht auf irgendwelche Rechte? Welche Rechte stehen dem Menschen als Menschen zu?

Ricœurs Artikel stellt meines Erachtens einen Versuch dar, diese Fragen historisch und philosophisch aufzugreifen, um das zugrunde liegende Spannungsverhältnis, das mit

---

[5] Diese Ansicht wird seit Langem von Jean Greisch vertreten und auch von vielen anderen übernommen (siehe Greisch 2009, 2, 8, 41 ff).

[6] Die deutsche Übersetzung ist von mir, Y.R. Der Text im Original lautet: "En réalité, l'idée des droits de l'homme traverse les clivages politiques et culturels. Elle échappe à l'annexion partisane et dénude ironiquement les idéologies. Elle pose l'irréductible question: "homme de quel(s) droit(s)?" et exige la réponse d'un humanisme critique. L'idée des droits de l'homme transforme la crise de la pensée en pensée de la crise (Raymond, 1988, 5).

der Ambiguität des menschlichen Seins zusammenhängt, aufzuzeigen. Er geht dabei in mehreren Schritten vor.

Der erste Schritt stellt eine rein semantische Textanalyse der *Allgemeinen Deklaration der Menschenrechte* von 1948 sowie der zwei UNO-Zivilpakte von 1966 dar – dem *Internationalen Pakt über wirtschaftliche, soziale und kulturelle Rechte* und *dem Internationalen Pakt über bürgerliche und politische Rechte*. Ricœur bezeichnet diese Dokumente als "Triumph des Individuums", da sie den Individuen, aber auch Gruppen von Individuen grundlegende "subjektive Rechte" einräumen. Somit wären einerseits den Regierungen und Institutionen Handlungsgrenzen gesetzt, und andererseits werde die Initiative der Rechtssubjekte gefördert. Das Neue an diesen Dokumenten bestehe darin, dass die Menschenrechte zum ersten Mal in Form eines völkerrechtlichen Abkommens verfasst worden seien. Dadurch habe die internationale Rechtspraxis ihren Schutz über das Staatliche hinaus auf Individuen und Gruppen ausgeweitet. Auch die sozialen Rechte, wie z. B. das Arbeitsrecht, seien als individuelle Rechte definiert worden. Nach Ricœur stellen diese Dokumente einen wesentlichen Fortschritt gegenüber den bisherigen Menschenrechtsdeklarationen dar. Zugleich würden sie jedoch zwei große Lücken aufweisen. Erstens: Manche Formulierungen würden mehrdeutige Begriffe beinhalten und könnten dadurch auf verschiedene, sogar entgegengesetzte Weise ausgelegt werden:

> (...) der Text selbst gibt keine Anleitung zur Interpretation der Begriffe, zum Beispiel, wenn gesagt wird, dass gewisse Beschränkungen erlaubt seien mit dem Ziel "die berechtigten Forderungen der Moral, der öffentlichen Ordnung und des Gemeinwohls im Allgemeinen in der demokratischen Gesellschaft zu erfüllen"; doch alle diese Begriffe, wie wir wissen, haben mehrere Bedeutungen...[7]

Zweitens: Obwohl die einzelnen Staaten Berichte über die Umsetzung der Menschenrechte vorlegen müssen und die Rechtssubjekte Klagen einreichen können, habe das internationale Recht keine Einrichtungen, um den Respekt vor diesen Rechten zu erzwingen und strafrechtlich gegen Verstöße vorzugehen. Hier sei vermerkt, dass dieser Text im Jahr 1988 geschrieben wurde und die damalige Situation beschreibt, die sich seither, insbesondere mit der Europäischen Union, wesentlich verändert hat.

In einem zweiten Schritt schlägt Ricœur eine philosophische Interpretation vor. Diese besteht in zwei Stufen. Zunächst soll der ursprüngliche philosophische Kontext, aus dem die Menschenrechte ihren Sinn beziehen, identifiziert werden. Danach soll ergründet werden, ob es auch andere, womöglich adäquatere Kontexte gibt, die auf philosophischen Quellen und Kulturen beruhen, welche sich wesentlich von der ursprünglichen Philosophie und Kultur, die die Menschenrechte hervorgebracht hat, unterscheiden. Denn jeder Text, so Ricœur, könne sich dem ursprünglichen Kontext entziehen und sich in andere Kontexte einschreiben, durch die er wiederum eine neue Orientierung und eine neue philosophische Basis bekomme.

---

[7] Die deutsche Übersetzung ist von mir, Y.R. Der Text im französischen Original lautet: "...le texte même ne fournit pas de guide pour interpréter les termes, par exemple lorsqu'il est dit que les limitations sont permises dans le but "de satisfaire aux justes exigences de la morale, de l'ordre public et du bien-être général dans une société démocratique" : tous ces termes employés ici, on le sait, ont plus d'un sens..." (Ricœur 1988, 234).

Ricœur beginnt mit dem Hinweis, dass die philosophischen und konzeptuellen Quellen der *Allgemeinen Deklaration der Menschenrechte* von 1948 sowie der Präambeln der Zivilpakte von 1966 ihren Ursprung in dem bahnbrechenden Denken der europäischen Philosophie des 17. und des 18. Jahrhunderts haben, angefangen mit Hugo Grotius und John Locke, mit den Enzyklopädisten, Montesquieu und Jean-Jacque Rousseau, bis hin zu Immanuel Kant und dem Utilitarismus. Nach diesen Denktraditionen, so Ricœur, besitzt das Individuum das Vermögen Entscheidungen zu treffen als eine ihm eigene Fähigkeit, die ihm weder gewährt noch abgesprochen werden darf. In diesem Sinne gehe die Souveränität des Individuums der Souveränität des Staates voran. Für Ricœur ist jedoch die Idee der "unveräußerlichen" Menschenrechte mit vielen Problemen behaftet. Wenn das subjektive Recht etwas ist, das dem Individuum inhärent ist, dann kann dieses sich auch entscheiden, darauf zu verzichten. Es müsste also der Freiheit auf Verzicht eine Grenze gesetzt werden, damit die Rechte als unveräußerlich gelten können.

Ricœur betont daher in einem zweiten Schritt die Notwendigkeit der Neubegründung der Menschenrechte auf einer breiteren philosophischen Grundlage, da die Menschenrechte seit 1789 zunehmend einen moralischen Hintergrund bekommen haben und auch sozialpolitisch weiterentwickelt wurden. In der Periode zwischen 1948 und 1966 sei nicht nur der Katalog der Menschenrechte erweitert worden – zu den Bürgerrechten wurden eine Menge sozialer und kultureller Rechte hinzugefügt, – sondern auch die Art und Weise ihrer Anwendung. Während die Menschenrechtserklärung von 1948 die Nichteinmischung der Staatsmacht verlangte, d. h. die negative Verpflichtung des Staates betonte, wiesen die Zivilpakte von 1966 auf die positiven Verpflichtungen des Staates hin, da die Verwirklichung der Menschenrechte nur durch bestimmte gesellschaftliche Maßnahmen als möglich aufgefasst wurde. Das hatte zur Folge, dass die freie individuelle Initiative immer mehr durch gesellschaftliche Vorgaben, welche die verschiedenen Staaten nach eigenem Ermessen definierten, abhängig gemacht und von diesen allmählich abgelöst wurde. Diese Neuorientierung, so Ricœur, habe zu einer Veränderung des Referenten geführt – als Subjekt sei nunmehr das Volk mit seiner kulturellen Prägung in Kraft gesetzt worden, anstatt des einzelnen Menschen." (Ricœur 1988, 236) So habe in den Zivilpakten von 1966 das Gemeinwesen den Platz der universellen Menschenrechte eingenommen ("L'universalité cède la place de la généralité"), wodurch die Antithese zwischen Individuum und Gemeinschaft virulent geworden sei.

Doch der eigentliche Grund, warum die Suche nach einer besseren Begründung der Menschenrechte gerechtfertigt ist, besteht nach Ricœur in etwas viel Grundlegenderem; sie ist von der Erkenntnis getragen, dass es eine Forderung gibt, die viel älter ist als alle philosophischen Formulierungen:

> Zu jeder Zeit und in jeder Kultur gab es einen Schrei, ein Sprichwort, ein Lied, ein Märchen, eine Weisheitsüberlieferung, welche die Botschaft von dem Bedürfnis der Menschenrechte übermittelt haben. Auch wenn der Begriff der Menschenrechte kein universeller ist, war die Forderung immer dieselbe, nämlich: "es steht dem Menschen etwas

zu, durch die Tatsache, dass er ein menschliches Wesen ist". Nur deshalb können die Menschenrechte durch ein positives Recht dekretiert, anerkannt und verkündet werden.[8]

Dies ist die ungekürzte Textpassage, aus der die Ricœur zugeschriebene Definition der Menschenwürde herausgenommen wurde. Daraus wird ersichtlich, dass es Ricœur hier nicht um die Würde geht, sondern vielmehr darum, dass die Menschenrechte dem Menschen immer schon aufgrund seines Seins zustehen und keine bloße Erfindung eines fortgeschrittenen Rechtssystems sind. Diese Erkenntnis habe Einzug auch in die europäische Philosophie gefunden, was man an den philosophischen Konzepten von Person, Subjekt und Freiheit, die in den Deklarationen verwendet wurden, ablesen kann. Deren Mehrdeutigkeit habe jedoch zu mannigfaltigen Interpretationen geführt. Zugleich zeige dies die wichtige Rolle der Philosophie: Man bedürfe der philosophischen Auslegung, weil die Diskussion auf rein rechtlichem Niveau nicht ausreiche, um die "zwei ethischen Dimensionen" der menschlichen "Natur" zu erfassen, nämlich die Dimensionen der Nichtbedingtheit und der Bedingtheit, der Transzendenz und der Inkarnation. Jeder Menschenrechtskatalog sei, so schließt Ricœur, nur ein Kompromiss zwischen diesen beiden Dimensionen, doch, man solle nicht erwarten, dass die Erweiterung des Katalogs diesen latenten Konflikt schlichten werde. Vielmehr sollten wir uns vor der Gefahr schützen, die grundlegenden Forderungen in einer unendlichen Multiplizierung der Menschenrechte untergehen zu lassen (ebd., 237).

Im Folgenden möchte ich den Grundgedanken des Artikels "Pour l'être humain du seul fait qu'il est humain" aufgreifen, um ihn danach durch andere Ricœur-Texte zu entschlüsseln.

Wie ich zu Beginn hervorgehoben habe, ist Ricœurs Artikel einer rechtlichen und nicht primär einer philosophisch-anthropologischen Thematik gewidmet. Es ist jedoch kein Zufall, dass die Menschenrechtsproblematik letztendlich in die philosophische Anthropologie mündet, welche nach seiner Argumentation die Grundlage für die Rechtsansprüche des Menschen bildet, denn für Ricœur sind die Menschenrechte immer auf ein bestimmtes Menschenbild zurückzuführen. Das kommt im Text meines Erachtens klar heraus. Was aber unklar bleibt, ist die Frage nach dem Menschenbild selbst sowie nach den Schlussfolgerungen, die er daraus zu ziehen scheint. Anders ausgedrückt, es bleibt folgende Frage offen: Was ist es, was den Menschen als Menschen ausmacht und ihm als solchen das Recht auf Rechtsansprüche gibt? Ricœur antwortet darauf ganz allgemein, es sei die Erkenntnis der zwei "ethischen Dimensionen" des Menschen – der *Transzendenz*, d. h. der Nichtbedingtheit als Freiheit der Entscheidung und der Wahl, und der *Inkarnation* als bedingter Faktizität –, deren Spannungsverhältnis sich in der Philosophie wie auch im Rechtsdenken niedergeschlagen habe. Genau genommen sind das aber keine ethischen, sondern anthropologische oder ontologische Dimensionen, wobei es nicht ersichtlich wird, inwiefern sie das menschliche Wesen zu ethischen oder rechtlichen Ansprüchen berechtigen. Um diese Unklarheiten zu klären,

---

[8] Die deutsche Übersetzung ist von mir, Y.R. Der Text im Original lautet: "À toute époque et dans toute culture, une plainte, un cri, un proverbe, une chanson, un conte, un traité de sagesse ont dit le message : si le concept de droits de l'homme n'est pas universel, il n'y en a pas moins, chez tous les hommes, dans toutes les cultures, le besoin, l'attente, le sens de ces droits. L'exigence a toujours été que "quelque chose est dû à l'être humain du fait qu'il est humain". C'est pourquoi les droits de l'homme ne peuvent être décrétés par aucun droit positif, ils ne peuvent être reconnus et proclamés." (Ricœur 1988, 236)

werde ich mich anderen Ricœur-Texten zuwenden, welche die Verbindung zwischen philosophischer Anthropologie, Ethik und Recht einerseits, und Menschenwürde, Rechte und Verantwortung andererseits, deutlicher artikulieren.

2. Menschenwürde und Verantwortung

Der Artikel "Pour l'être humain du seul fait qu'il est humain" (1988) endet mit der Warnung vor einer unendlichen Ausdehnung der Menschenrechte. Zehn Jahre später, in einem Vortrag unter dem Titel "Responsabilité: limitée ou illimitée?" (Ricœur 1998), den er auf einer Konferenz über "Das Verbrechen gegen die Menschlichkeit: Maßstab der Verantwortung?" gehalten hat, warnt Ricœur wiederum vor einer unendlichen Ausdehnung der Verantwortung und einer inflationären Verwendung des Verantwortungsbegriffes.

An der Konferenz, die von der Pariser Diözese und der Pariser Anwaltschaft organisiert wurde, nahmen Juristen, Geistliche und Wissenschaftler teil. Das Interessante an den Beiträgen, die später in einem Sammelband veröffentlicht wurden, ist meines Erachtens die Betonung der Verbindung zwischen Menschenwürde und Verantwortung. So hob der Rektor des Katholischen Instituts in Paris, Patrick Valdrini, hervor, dass die Kirche die Menschenwürde mit der Ausübung von Verantwortung verbinde (Valdrini 1998, 31). Auch der Anwalt Théo Klein erklärte anhand der biblischen Geschichte von Kain und Abel, dass die Würde in der Verantwortung der Menschen für einander bestünde (Klein 1998, 120). Ricœur bietet seinerseits eine philosophische Auslegung der Verantwortung an, die man in drei Fragen resümieren könnte: Was bedeutet Verantwortung? Wofür sind wir verantwortlich? Bis wohin reicht unsere Verantwortung?

Er beginnt mit der Erläuterung, dass das Konzept der Verantwortung auf einem älteren basiere, nämlich dem der Zurechnungsfähigkeit, dieses jedoch wesentlich bereichere. Die Zurechnungsfähigkeit sei die menschliche Fähigkeit etwas zu tun, sodass diese Handlung dem Agierenden dann zugerechnet werden könne. Ricœur geht hier also von seiner Auffassung des fähigen Menschen aus, der autonom denken und handeln kann, und vergleicht sodann die Zurechnung mit einem Konto, welches Kredit und Debit besitzt. Das Konzept der Zurechnungsfähigkeit könne primär ganz neutral aufgefasst werden, im Sinne von einer Zuschreibung, z. B. wenn man sagt, das Bild X sei das Werk von diesem oder jenem Maler. Aber es könne auch eine moralische und rechtliche Färbung bekommen, wenn die Handlung als gut oder verwerflich, als ein Delikt oder gar als eine Straftat qualifiziert werde. Im moralischen sowie im rechtlichen Sinn sei die Zurechnung oft mit einer Schuldzuschreibung gleichgesetzt worden, wobei der Täter für die jeweilige Handlung zur Verantwortung gezogen werden könne. Der Täter, dem eine gewisse Handlung zugerechnet werde, müsse sich in diesem Fall vor jemandem für etwas verantworten. Was bedeutet das aber konkreter?

Ricœur geht hier zunächst etymologisch vor, indem er auf das Wort "Antwort" in dem Begriff "Verantwortung" hinweist und den Akzent auf dessen doppelte Anwendungsweise setzt. Man solle, erläutert er, das "Antworten-auf" (*répondre à*) vom "Ver-antworten-für" (*répondre de*) unterscheiden. Anders gesagt, die Antwort *auf* einen Appell, eine Bitte, einen Hilferuf usw. unterscheide sich wesentlich von der Antwort als einem Ver-antwortlich-sein-*für* etwas oder jemanden. Während sich die Zurechnung auf eine schon begangene Handlung beziehe, sei das Ver-antwortlich-sein-*für* (*répondre de*) zukunftsweisend, da es ein Projekt impliziere, für das ich Verantwortung trage. Es verweise auf andere Subjekte, für die ich verantwortlich bin oder vor denen ich mich zu verantworten habe. So z. B. sind die Eltern für das Wohl ihrer Kinder verantwortlich oder das Staatsoberhaupt ist *für* die Angelegenheiten des Staates *vor* dem Parlament verantwortlich (Ricœur 1998, 24-25). Doch wodurch kommt uns dieser Auftrag zu, auf den wir antworten und für den wir uns vor Anderen verantworten müssen?

Ricœur wendet sich hier an das berühmte Werk von Hans Jonas *Das Prinzip Verantwortung: Versuch einer Ethik für die technologische Zivilisation* (1979), nach dessen Verständnis wir als Individuen oder Kollektive für das Zerbrechliche und Verderbliche verantwortlich sind. Weil alle Lebewesen fragil, verletzlich und verderblich seien und die Zerstörungskräfte in unserer Zeit ständig wachsen, habe Jonas den Imperativ aufgestellt: "Handle so, dass die Effekte deiner Handlungen mit einem würdigen Leben auf Erden kompatibel sind" (ebd., 25). Daher stellt sich für Ricœur die Frage, bis wohin wir für die Anderen und für unsere Umwelt verantwortlich sind: Handelt es sich dabei um eine begrenzte oder unbegrenzte, um eine gänzliche oder partielle bzw. geteilte Verantwortung? Ricœurs Antwort geht in zwei Richtungen, in die der Moral und in die des Strafrechts, um ein Paradox aufzuzeigen, das die Begrenztheit des menschlichen Seins und dadurch auch die Grenzen der Verantwortung veranschaulichen soll.

Auf der Ebene der Moral stellt die Verantwortung für Ricœur ein Paradox dar, weil sie zwei widersprüchliche Dinge versöhnen soll. Einerseits schreiben wir jemandem aufgrund seiner Freiheit Verantwortung zu, wenn wir ihn als den Urheber gewisser Handlungen ansehen; andererseits ist die Verantwortung aber auch etwas, das erst in einem Erziehungs- und Bildungsprozess angeregt wird, damit es beim Zögling zu einer moralischen Entfaltung seines Verantwortungsbewusstseins kommt. Anders gesagt, die Verantwortungsfähigkeit wird vorausgesetzt, ist aber dennoch etwas, das erst herausgebildet werden muss. Ricœur erläutert dies anhand der menschlichen Zerbrechlichkeit:

> Es ist die Zerbrechlichkeit, welche die Verantwortung zur Voraussetzung und zugleich zur Aufgabe macht. Wir sind für ein zerbrechliches Sein verantwortlich, aber die Zerbrechlichkeit ist die eines verantwortlichen Seins. In diesem Paradox bewegt sich das Denken, nämlich zwischen einer potentiell grenzlosen Verantwortung und ihrer Grenzen.[9]

Um dies besser zu veranschaulichen, gibt er zwei Beispiele, die in zwei entgegengesetzte Richtungen gehen, jedoch zum selben Resultat führen. Das eine geht in Richtung Minderung der Verantwortung, ohne diese zu annullieren, wenn man es mit Tätern zu tun hat, die unfähig sind, das Delikt zu verstehen. Das andere Beispiel fordert hingegen dazu auf, den Anderen für seine Straftat als verantwortlich anzuerkennen und ihn dementsprechend zu behandeln. Dieses Bespiel, das Ricœur gibt, ist für unser Anliegen von grundlegender Bedeutung, weil er die Verantwortung hier in einen direkten Zusammenhang zur Würde des Menschen bringt:

---

[9] Die deutsche Übersetzung ist von mir, Y.R. Der Text im französischen Original lautet: "C'est la fragilité qui fait que la responsabilité est à la fois une présupposition et une tâche. Nous sommes responsables d'un être fragile, mais la fragilité est celle d'un être responsable. C'est dans les formes de ce paradoxe que s'opère la pensée, la graduation et donc la limitation de la responsabilité potentiellement illimitée" (ebd., 27-28).

Wenn man einem Angeklagten, der verurteilt wurde, gänzlich die Verantwortung für seine Tat entzieht, wird man nie seine Teilnahme und Mitwirkung an einer Rehabilitierung oder Resozialisierung erlangen. Wenn das Ziel der Strafe darin besteht, dem Verurteilten die getilgte Schuld zu vergelten und seine Bürgerrechte zurück zu geben, dann muss er ständig würdig behandelt werden, das heißt als verantwortlich.[10]

Ricœur gibt diese Beispiele, um das Paradox der menschlichen Fähigkeiten – wenn ich mich so ausdrücken darf – aufzuzeigen. Der Mensch ist nämlich sowohl fähig als auch fehlbar und in manchen Fällen sogar unfähig, weil er eben unvollkommen und fragil ist. Ähnlich wie Heidegger, der die Endlichkeit des Menschen artikuliert, hebt Ricœur die Zerbrechlichkeit und die Begrenztheit des fähigen Menschen hervor als Bestandteil der "Disproportion oder der antinomischen Struktur des menschlichen Seins" (Ricœur 2013, 22)[11]. Darüber hinaus gebe es auch Menschen, die noch nicht reif oder behindert sind und für die gesorgt werden müsse.

Der Erzieher, der Lehrer, der Richter ist mit amputierten, verletzten Modalitäten der Ausübung der Verantwortung konfrontiert. Dies ist meines Erachtens eine Einladung dazu, neue Formen des Strafrechts zu suchen, z. B. bei der Pflegschaft, verstanden als Gesamtheit der Maßnahmen um Menschen, die für sich selbst nicht sorgen können, aber für sich sorgen müssen, sie gegen sich selbst zu schützen. Es ist wichtig daran zu glauben, dass diese Menschen verantwortungsfähig, zurechnungsfähig sind, sonst wäre die Erziehung wie eine Art Dressur von wilden Tieren.[12]

Wenn also die Würde des Menschen mit der menschlichen Fähigkeit zur Verantwortung zusammenfällt, sodass auch "verantwortungslose", strafbare Handlungen und Verfehlungen letztendlich nichts daran ändern, dass der Mensch trotzdem Mensch, also ein "fähiges Wesen" ist und bleibt, dann scheint Ricœur ein Befürworter der inhärenten Würde des Menschen zu sein. Und tatsächlich, es gibt einige Textpassagen in seinen Werken, die dafürsprechen und auf die ich hinweisen möchte. Es stellt sich hier jedoch die Frage, ob der Mensch seine Würde verspielen kann, z. B. durch verschiedene Gräueltaten. Ricœur gibt hier keine eindeutige Antwort, vielmehr mahnt er zur Vorsicht, wie man rechtlich und moralisch urteilt und

---

[10] Die deutsche Übersetzung ist von mir, Y.R. Der Text im französischen Original lautet: "Si vous privez entièrement un inculpé, devenu un condamné, de la responsabilité de son acte, vous n'obtiendrez jamais sa participation, sa collaboration à quelque entreprise de réhabilitation ou de resocialisation que ce soit. Si la finalité de la peine est de rendre au condamné, sa peine purgée, la plénitude de ses droits civiques, il faut qu'il ait été constamment traité dignement, c'est-à-dire comme responsable." (ebd., 28).

[11] Es sei hier erwähnt, dass die menschliche Disproportion das Hauptthema des ersten Bandes seiner Phänomenologie der Schuld darstellt (siehe Ricœur 1971, 18ff).

[12] Die deutsche Übersetzung ist von mir, Y.R. Der Text im französischen Original lautet: "L'éducateur, l'enseignant, le juge, sont en face de modalités amputées, blessées, de l'exercice de la responsabilité. Modalités qui invitent, selon moi, à rechercher des formes nouvelles d'exercice du droit pénal, sous la forme, par exemple, de la tutelle, si l'on entend par là l'ensemble des mesures susceptibles de protéger contre eux-mêmes des êtres incapables de se prendre en charge mais destines à se prendre en charge. Il importe de croire que de tels êtres sont capables de responsabilité, d'imputabilité. Sinon, l'éducation deviendrait un dressage de bêtes sauvages" (Ricœur 1988, 28).

Andere verurteilt. Er verweist auch auf die Hoffnung als theologischer Tugend, die darauf setzt, "dass das *imago Dei* nie gänzlich zerstört werden könne, egal wie verfallen ein Mensch auch sein mag" (ebd., 28). Dies ist leider nur eine Randbemerkung, die nicht weiter ausgeführt wird und aus der nicht herauszulesen ist, ob Ricœur zur Zeit des Vortrags immer noch an die Unzerstörbarkeit der Würde im Sinne eines *imago Dei* glaubte, so wie er es Jahre zuvor getan hatte (Ricœur 1974, 124-147), oder ob er die Hoffnung als "theologische Tugend" nur deswegen erwähnt hat, weil sein Vortrag in einem klerikalen Rahmen gehalten wurde. Sein Beitrag endet jedenfalls mit dem eindeutigen Schluss, dass hyperbolisierte Auffassungen wie die, dass man für alles vor allen verantwortlich sei, inakzeptabel seien, da das menschliche Sein viel zu fragil sei, um für das ganze Übel der Welt verantwortlich gemacht zu werden (Ricœur 1998, 30).

Ricœur betont also einerseits, dass die Essenz der Würde in der Fähigkeit Verantwortung zu übernehmen besteht, andererseits hebt er aber die menschliche Zerbrechlichkeit hervor, um die Fehlbarkeit und die Begrenztheit der Verantwortung zu artikulieren. Wenn aber nicht nur der Mensch, sondern auch seine natürliche Umgebung bzw. alle Lebewesen zerbrechlich sind und er deswegen auch für sie gewisse Verantwortung zu tragen hat, wie Ricœur Jonas folgend argumentiert, dann stellt sich die Frage: Wie hängen Würde und Recht auf Leben zusammen? Heißt es nun, dass alle Lebewesen ein Recht auf Leben haben, das geschützt werden muss, jedoch nur der Mensch Würdebesitzer ist und demzufolge nur er ein würdiges Leben auf Erden verdiene? Oder nochmals anders gefragt, gibt es eine Würde der Kreatur oder ist die Würde nur ein Prärogativ des Menschen bzw. der Person? Ricœur gibt in diesem Beitrag keine Antwort darauf. Deshalb werde ich versuchen, anhand diverser Stellen in seinem Früh- und Spätwerk eine mögliche Antwort darauf zu finden.

In seinem Frühwerk hat Ricœur das Thema der Würde in einer Kant'schen und zugleich in einer christlichen Perspektive gestellt. In *Le volontaire et l'involontaire* (1949) wird die Würde aus einem ethischen und zugleich rechtlichen Anspruch der Gleichwertigkeit der Menschen heraus interpretiert:

> Die Forderung nach Gerechtigkeit, die geschichtlich in verschiedensten Formen Ausdruck gefunden hat, besteht in der radikalen Behauptung, dass der Andere mir gegenüber einen Wert hat, dass seine Bedürfnisse genauso viel zählen wie die meinigen, dass seine Meinungen aus dem Zentrum einer Perspektive und Bewertung entspringen, die dieselbe Würde besitzt wie mein eigenes Ich. Der Andere ist ein Du: das ist die Behauptung, die unterschwellig die Maxime der Gerechtigkeit leitet, sowohl in ihrem antiken Ausdruck – *neminem laedere, suum cuique tribueré* –, als auch in ihrer kantischen Form – behandle die Person immer als Ziel und niemals als Mittel. Im Prinzip besteht die Forderung nach Gerechtigkeit in einer Dezentrierung der Perspektive durch welcher die Perspektive des Anderen (seine Bedürfnisse und Forderungen) meine eigene Perspektive ins Gleichgewicht bringt.[13]

---

[13] Die deutsche Übersetzung ist von mir, Y.R. Der Text im französischen Original lautet: "L'exigence de justice, qui s'incarne historiquement dans des formes essentiellement variables, a sa racine dans l'affirmation radicale que l'autre vaut en face de moi, que ses besoins valent comme les miens, que ses opinions procèdent d'un centre de perspective et d'évaluation qui a la même dignité que moi. L'autre est

Diese Gleichwertigkeit zwischen mir und dem Anderen wird in *Histoire et vérité* (1955/dt. 1974) durch die besondere Stellung des Menschen erklärt. Der Mensch stellt das Ebenbild Gottes als "Zeugung eines persönlichen und gemeinschaftlichen Wesens" (Ricœur 1974, 126) dar, wobei ein jeder dieses Bild in sich trägt. Das *imago Dei* wird als "die sehr persönliche und sehr einsame Fähigkeit des Menschen, zu denken und Entscheidungen zu treffen" (ebd., 125) definiert. Obwohl Ricœur hier das Wort Würde nicht verwendet, kann man erahnen, dass die Gottesebenbildlichkeit des Menschen zugleich die Basis seiner Würde darstellt, weil die Fähigkeiten des Denkens und Entscheidens die Bedingung der Verantwortung als Zurechnungsfähigkeit bilden. Da der Mensch als frei erschaffen wurde[14] und sich immer frei zu entscheiden habe, sei er auch zum Ungehorsam und zum Bösen fähig (ebd., 146), was zur Beschädigung des Ebenbildes Gottes führen könne. Ricœur konkretisiert dies anhand von Kants Auffassung der Leidenschaften der Habsucht, der Herrschsucht und der Ehrsucht, um zu zeigen wie "die Schöpfung *durch* das Böse und mittels der Gnade" (ebd.) fortgeführt werde. Das Epos des Menschen verlaufe, so Ricœur, durch die Geschichte der Entfremdung des Ebenbildes Gottes als einer Umkehrung des Menschlichen im Unmenschlichen, gesteuert durch die Leidenschaften, um dann zu einer Erlösung zu gelangen. Diese bestünde im Sieg über die Habsucht, Herrschsucht und Ehrsucht durch den Überfluss an Gnade und Liebe sowie durch die imaginative Kraft, die zur Konversion und Veränderung unserer Existenz führe: "Jede *echte* Bekehrung ist in erster Linie eine Umwälzung unserer Leitbilder; wenn der Mensch seine Imagination verändert, dann verändert er seine Existenz" (ebd., 145). Doch Ricœur setzt in diesem Aufsatz nicht allein auf den Menschen und seine Fähigkeiten (Denken, Wählen, Entscheiden, Sprechen, Imaginieren usw.), sondern primär auf die Großzügigkeit und die Gnade Gottes, auf die wir vertrauen und der wir uns anvertrauen sollten:

> Vielleicht ist es erforderlich, die gefahrvolle Schulung des Menschen im Guten und im Bösen mit Gottes Großmut zu verbinden und sich seiner Nachsicht anzuvertrauen. – Ich will dort aufhören wo ich begonnen habe; da ich dieses Gespräch auf die Interpretation der Kirchenväter vom Bilde Gottes aufzubauen gewagt habe, will ich ein letztes Mal auf die Kirchenväter zurückkommen (…) 'Indem also Gott sich großmütig zeigte', schreibt Irenäus, 'lernte der Mensch das Gute des Gehorsams und das Böse des Ungehorsams, damit das Auge seines Geistes beides kennen lernte, für die Wahl des Besseren sich einsichtig entscheide und niemals träge oder nachlässig in den Geboten Gottes werde …' Auch für Tertullian ist der Mensch in freier Zustimmung zum Bilde Gottes geworden: 'Das Bild und das Gleichnis Gottes müssen also frei in Willen und Entscheidung gesetzt werden, weil gerade hierin das Bild und das Gleichnis Gottes sich bestimmt'. (ebd., 146-147)

---

un toi: telle est l'affirmation qui anime souterrainement la maxime de la justice, aussi bien sous sa forme antique: *neminem laedere, suum cuique tribueré*, que sous sa forme kantienne : traiter la personne comme une fin et non comme un moyen. L'exigence de justice consiste donc, dans son principe, en un décentrement de perspective par lequel la perspective d'autrui – le besoin, la revendication d'autrui – équilibre ma perspective" (Ricœur 1949, 120).

[14] Erinnern wir uns hier an der Artikel 1 der *Allgemeinen Erklärung der Menschenrechte*: "Alle Menschen sind frei und gleich an Würde und Rechten geboren. Sie sind mit Vernunft und Gewissen begabt und sollen einander im Geiste der Brüderlichkeit begegnen." (*Allgemeine Erklärung der Menschenrechte*, online: http://www.un.org/depts/german/menschenrechte/aemr.pdf)

3. Die Würde "potentieller Menschen" und die Anwendung der *phronèsis*

In Ricœurs Spätwerk *Soi-même comme un autre* (1990) fällt jedoch diese christliche Perspektive weg. Und so wird "das Auge des Geistes", das "die Wahl des Besseren" ermöglicht, durch das Kant'sche Klugheitsurteil und das aristotelische Konzept der *phronèsis* als "praktischer Weisheit", d. h. als Abwägung der Vor- und Nachteile bei der Wahl gewisser Lebensentwürfe und Handlungen in der Praxis, ersetzt (Ricœur 1996, 216). Die Würdeproblematik wird hier in einen viel komplexeren Zusammenhang gestellt, nämlich in den Kontext der aktuellen Debatten über "die Achtung der Person beim 'werdenden Leben.'" (ebd., 327). Ricœur weist auf das Konfliktpotenzial des zweiten kantischen Imperativs hin: Die Menschheit in der eigenen Person und der des Anderen als Zweck an sich selbst und nicht bloß als Mittel zu behandeln. Obwohl es eine schmale Grenzlinie zwischen der universalistischen Seite des Imperativs, welche die Idee der Menschheit repräsentiere, und der pluralistischen Idee der einzelnen Personen gebe, sei dies Kant zufolge kein Gegensatz, "insofern der Begriff der Menschheit die Würde bezeichnet, aufgrund derer Personen achtenswert sind, und zwar – wenn man so sagen darf – ihrer Pluralität zum Trotz. Die Möglichkeit eines Konfliktes ergibt sich jedoch dann, wenn sich die Andersheit der Personen (…) unter bestimmten besonderen Umständen als nicht mehr mit der Idee der Menschheit tragenden Universalität der Regeln koordinierbar erweist; die Achtung neigt dann dazu, sich in Achtung des Gesetzes und Achtung der Personen aufzuspalten." (ebd., 318) In solchen Fällen würde die praktische Weisheit darin bestehen, bestimmte Verhaltensformen zu erfinden, "die der von der Fürsorge verlangten Ausnahme weitestgehend entsprechen und zugleich die Regel so wenig wie möglich zu verletzen." (ebd., 325) Mit "erfinden" meint Ricœur hier, dass es bezüglich komplexer Situationen, in denen Entscheidungen getroffen werden müssen, keine fertigen Antworten gibt, sondern dass alle Pros und Kontras kontextuell zu prüfen und abzuwägen sind, inklusive möglicher Konsequenzen, auch wenn sie nicht immer vorhersehbar sind. Ricœur gibt verschiedene Beispiele, um die diesbezüglichen Schwierigkeiten zu veranschaulichen. Ich werde hier nur eines in Betracht ziehen, welches direkt das Problem der Würde anspricht.

Die Idee der Würde bei Kant basiere, erläutert Ricœur, auf einem Gegensatz – dem Gegensatz zwischen Person und Ding. Die Person als "vernünftige Natur" *existiere* als Zweck an sich, ihr allein komme Wert und Würde zu, im Kontrast zum Ding, das keine Würde habe, das als Zweck behandelt und dementsprechend gehandhabt und verändert werden dürfe. Nun aber stellen die neuesten Erkenntnisse über Embryo und Fötus den dichotomischen Charakter dieser ethisch-ontologischen Erwägungen infrage, denn der Embryo und der Fötus sind weder Dinge noch Personen. Ricœur zitiert diesbezüglich die Philosophin und Psychiaterin Anne Fagot, die sagt:

> Es besteht ein Konflikt zwischen dem Prinzip der Achtung, die man dem menschlichen Wesen schuldet, und der Instrumentalisierung dieses Wesens im embryonalen und fötalen Status – es sei denn, ein menschliches Embryo wäre keine menschliche *Person* (ebd., 327).

Um diesen Konflikt zu erfassen und zu bestimmen, wie die praktische Weisheit zu verstehen sei, konfrontiert uns Ricœur mit zwei entgegengesetzten Thesen. Die eine bringt das biologische Kriterium ins Spiel und argumentiert, dass das genetische Erbgut, welches die biologische Individualität bestimmt, schon seit der Zeugung konstituiert ist. Daraus wird, in der moderatesten Form, die ethische Folgerung gezogen, dass der Embryo ein Recht auf Leben hat und im Zweifelsfall eine Tötung nicht vorgenommen werden darf. Dieses Argument beruhe, so Ricœur, auf einem Substantialismus, der dem Zwischenbereich zwischen Ding und Person nicht gerecht wird und eine Ontologie der Entwicklung unmöglich macht. Aber auch die entgegengesetzte These, die auf der kantischen Ethik aufbaue, trage in sich dasselbe Problem:

> Wenn man die Idee der Würde allein mit vollentwickelten Vermögen wie etwa der Autonomie des Willens verknüpft, dann sind nur erwachsene, gebildete und 'aufgeklärte' Individuen Personen. Strenggenommen "kann die Gemeinschaft der Personen entscheiden, die Wesen, die sich noch unterhalb des 'minimalen' Autonomievermögens befinden, zu schützen (wie man die Natur schützt), nicht aber, sie zu achten (wie man die Autonomie der Personen achtet)" (A. Fagot). Man sieht also nicht wie sich eine rein moralische These der Achtung in dieser Debatte Gehör verschaffen könnte, es sei denn, auch sie wäre von einer minimalen Ontologie der Entwicklung begleitet. Diese würde der Idee des Vermögens, wie sie einer Logik des 'Alles oder Nichts' entspricht, die Idee der Fähigkeit hinzufügen, die Aktualisierungsgrade erlaubt. (ebd., 328)

Ricœur sieht sehr wohl das Problem, das entsteht, wenn man die Würde allein an den Personenbegriff koppelt: Alle nicht zurechnungsfähigen Menschen, Debile, seelisch Gestörte, Alzheimer-Kranke, aber auch Kinder, Unmündige und "Unaufgeklärte" würden herausfallen. Im Falle des Embryos und des Fötus verkompliziert sich das Problem jedoch nochmals. Deswegen sieht Ricœur – Anne Fagots Argumentation folgend – den Ausweg in einer progressiven Ontologie, die das Konzept der "potentiellen menschlichen Person" enthält. Dieser Ansatz wurde bereits von verschiedenen Expertenkommissionen, inklusive dem französischen konsultativen Ethikkomitee, aufgenommen. Beim Begriff der "potentiellen menschlichen Person" wird davon ausgegangen, "dass das embryonale Wesen ein in der Entwicklung befindliches Wesen ist und daß unsere moralischen Verpflichtungen gegenüber einer lebenden Zelle, dann gegenüber einem fünf Monate alten Fötus, dann gegenüber einem fünf Jahre alten Kind, nicht dieselben sein können." (ebd., 329)

Ricœur begrüßt dieses Konzept einerseits, weil es ermöglicht, den Bereich zwischen Ding und Person jenseits der Extreme der substantialistischen Ontologie und des engen Personalismus zu erfassen, und andererseits, weil es mit seiner Dialektik von *mêmeté* (die Selbigkeits-Identität als fortbestehende Eigenschaften, die den Menschen als ein und denselben charakterisieren) und *ipséité* (das Selbst als persönliche, sich wandelnde Identität) im Einklang zu sein scheint. Wir sollten auch in Betracht ziehen, dass zwischen Würde der Person und Würde des Menschen ein wesentlicher Unterschied besteht, auch wenn Ricœur selbst diesen Unterschied nicht explizit thematisiert. Denn wie wir schon im Artikel "Pour l'être humain du seul fait qu'il est humain" gesehen haben, geht es ihm in der Menschenrechtsproblematik um das Menschliche und nicht um die Person – alle Menschen, egal ob gesund oder krank, klug oder unmündig, haben die gleichen Rechte. Beim Embryo handelt es sich aber um ein Zwischenwesen, das noch kein Mensch ist, weshalb sich die Frage stellt: Welche Rechte hat der Embryo als "potentieller Mensch"? Ricœurs Antwort spricht mehrere sehr wichtige Dinge an, die man sich genauer anschauen sollte.

> Auch wenn die Wissenschaft allein befähigt ist, die Schwellen der Entwicklung zu beschreiben, so geht doch die Bewertung der jeweiligen Rechte und Pflichten aus einer wahren moralischen Erfindung hervor, die nach einer den biologischen Stufen vergleichbaren Progression qualitativ verschiedene Rechte abstufen wird: das Recht nicht zu leiden, das Recht auf Schutz (...) und das Recht auf Achtung, sobald sich so etwas wie eine wenn auch asymmetrische Austauschbeziehung präverbaler Zeichen zwischen dem Fötus und seine Mutter abzeichnet. Diese Wechselbeziehung zwischen der Beschreibung der Schwellen und der Bewertung der Rechte und Pflichten, im Zwischenbereich von 'Person' und 'Ding', berechtigt dazu, die Bioethik dem Bereich des Klugheitsurteils zuzurechnen. (ebd.)

In dieser Passage weist Ricœur darauf hin, dass die Bewertungen im bioethischen Bereich einer "wahren moralischen Erfindung" bedürfen, d. h., dass es hier keine apriorischen oder vorgegebenen Normen gibt, sondern dass man parallel zum biologischen Wissen über die Stufen der Entwicklung eine Abstufung von Rechten und Pflichten erarbeiten sollte, die nur durch einen Dialog zwischen den Wissenschaften und der Philosophie zustande kommen kann. Denn mit der Entwicklung der Wissenschaften und der neuen Technologien ist es zu einer Verkomplizierung der rechtlichen und ethischen bzw. axiologisch-normativen Fragestellungen gekommen. Exaktes Wissen, Werttheorie und Praxis bedürfen also einander und müssten demnach Hand in Hand gehen, um kontextbezogene Antworten auf die Herausforderungen zu (er)finden. Anders gesagt, eine universalistische Ethik reicht genauso wenig aus wie biologistische Rechtfertigungen. Dasselbe hat später Jürgen Habermas sehr gut in einer Replik zu Dieter E. Zimmermann klargelegt:

> Eine rationale Erörterung von Fragen der Bioethik verlangt gewiß eine hinreichende Kenntnis der einschlägigen naturwissenschaftlichen Diskussionen und Tatsachen. Aber normative Fragen lassen sich ohne Bezugnahme auf normative Gesichtspunkte nicht vernünftig behandeln (...) Die Biologie kann uns moralische Überlegungen nicht abnehmen. Und die Bioethik sollte uns nicht auf biologistische Abwege bringen. Andererseits sind normative Gesichtspunkte umstritten und die moralische Eingliederung neuer Phänomene erst recht. Das gilt auch für den Versuch, den möglichen Konsequenzen des Klonens von menschlichen Organismen mit Kantischen Begriffen beizukommen. (Habermas 1998)

Ricœurs Auslegung legt nahe, dass es einen Unterschied zwischen Würde und Achtung gibt. Würde ist für ihn ein engerer Begriff, der sich nur auf Menschen und Personen bezieht, Achtung hingegen ein breiterer, der sowohl auf Zwischenwesen, die man als "potentielle Personen oder "potentielle Menschen" auffassen kann, als auch auf alle Lebewesen angewendet werden kann. Dies ermöglicht eine differenziertere Auffassung von Würde und Verantwortung, die sich der Fallen des Reduktionismus und Essentialismus entzieht.

Indem Ricœur die Bioethik dem Klugheitsurteil zuweist, stellt sich nunmehr die Frage, wie die *phronèsis* im bioethischen Kontext konkret aussehen könnte. Ricœur verweist hier an erster Stelle auf die Mäßigung bzw. auf die "rechte Mitte" – die aristotelische *mesotès* – die uns die praktische Weisheit lehrt. In Anbetracht unserer Verantwortung gegenüber zukünftigen Generationen, sollte man die Wagnisse, zu denen die technischen Errungenschaften ermutigen, mit Besonnenheit abwägen. Dies wäre z. B. der Fall bei der Manipulation überzähliger Embryos, aber auch im Falle von Schwangerschaftsabbrüchen. Hier bedürfe es "eines sehr weit entwickelten moralischen Taktgefühls." (Ricœur 1996, 330) Ricœur weist jedoch darauf hin, dass die "rechte Mitte" etwas anderes sei als nur ein fauler Kompromiss:

> Im allgemeinen bestehen die schwerwiegendsten moralischen Entscheidungen darin, eine Grenze zwischen dem Erlaubten und dem Verbotenen in solchen Zonen zu ziehen, die selbst 'in der Mitte' liegen und die sich daher den allzu vertrauten Dichotomien widersetzen. (ebd., 330-331)

Um die Willkür des moralischen Situationsurteils zu verringern, sei es klug den Rat der Kompetentesten einzuholen und somit vom Pluralitätscharakter der Debatte zu profitieren. Dabei sollte man sich vergewissern, ob sich die entgegengesetzten Positionen auf das gleiche Prinzip der Achtung berufen und sich nur durch den Umfang des Anwendungsbereiches unterscheiden, insbesondere in der Grauzone zwischen Ding und vollentwickelter moralischer Person. Nicht zuletzt sollte die Achtung der Person Hand in Hand gehen mit der bemühenden Fürsorge um den Schutz der Person, einschließlich dem Schutz "potentieller Personen". Diese Fürsorge sei nicht als eine "naive" zu verstehen, sondern als eine "kritische" Fürsorge, die durch die doppelte Prüfung der moralischen Bedingungen der Achtung und der erzeugten Konflikte hindurchgegangen sei (ebd., 331).

Diese Leitsätze aus dem Bereich der praktischen Weisheit, die Ricœur hier ganz allgemein formuliert, sollten jedoch nicht als universelle Prinzipien verstanden werden. Denn die praktische Weisheit als Endzweck der Ricœur'schen Ethik ist immer kontextbezogen und zielt darauf ab, "die *phronèsis* im Sinne des Aristoteles über die *Moralität* im Sinne Kants mit der *Sittlichkeit* im Sinne Hegels zu versöhnen." (ebd., 351) Die *phronèsis*, die eine Balance zwischen Formalismus und Kontextualismus herstellt, ist somit die kritische Instanz, die ein moralisches Situationsurteil ermöglicht und die auf dem Gebiet der zwischenmenschlichen Beziehungen die Form einer "kritischen Fürsorge" annimmt.

Prof. Dr. Yvanka B. Raynova, Institute for the Study of Societies and Knowledge – Bulgarian Academy of Sciences, Sofia / Institut für Axiologische Forschungen, Wien,
raynova[at]iaf.ac.at

Literaturangaben

Greisch, Jean. *Fehlbarkeit und Fähigkeit. Die philosophische Anthropologie Paul Ricœurs.* Berlin: Lit Verlag, 2009.

Habermas, Jürgen. "Nicht die Natur verbietet das Klonen. Wir müssen selbst entscheiden", in *Die Zeit*, 19 Februar 1998, online: http://www.zeit.de/ 1998/09/klonen.txt.19980219.xml

Klein, Théo. "Le pardon et la dignité", in (Coll.), *Le crime contre l'humanité : mesure de la responsabilité ?* Paris : CERP, 1998, 119-127.

Morin, Edgar. *Comment repenser l'humain?* online: http://e-south.blog.lemonde.fr/2013/06/03/comment-repenser-lhumain-une-reflexion-dedgar-morin/.

Raymond, Jean-François de. "Les droits de l'homme : Une anti-idéologie", in ders. (éd.). *Les enjeux des droits de l'homme*. Paris: Librairie Larousse, 1988.

Ricœur, Paul. "Das Bild Gottes und das Epos des Menschen", in ders. *Geschichte und Wahrheit*. München: List Verlag, 1974, 124-147.

Ricœur, Paul. "L'antinomie de la réalité humaine et le problème de l'anthropologie philosophique", in ders. *Anthropologie philosophique. Ecrits et conférences 3*. Paris: Seuil, 2013, 21-49.

Ricœur, Paul. "Pour l'être humain du seul fait qu'il est humain", in Jean-François de Raymond (éd.). *Les enjeux des droits de l'homme*. Paris: Librairie Larousse, 1988, 233-237.

Ricœur, Paul. "Responsabilité : limitée ou illimitée ?" in (Coll.). *Le crime contre l'humanité : mesure de la responsabilité ?* Paris : CERP, 1998, 24-25.

Ricœur, Paul. *Das Selbst als ein Anderer*. München: Wilhelm Fink Verlag, 1996.

Ricœur, Paul. *Die Fehlbarkeit des Menschen. Phänomenologie der Schuld I*. Freiburg, München: Alber 1971.

Ricœur, Paul. *Le volontaire et l'involontaire*. Paris: Aubier, 1949.

s.a. . "Dignité", *Encyclopédie de l'Agora*, online: http://agora.qc.ca/dossiers/Dignite

s.a. .."Dignité", *Wikipedia*, online: https://fr.wikipedia.org/wiki/Dignit%C3%A9

s.a. *Allgemeine Erklärung der Menschenrechte*, online: http://www.un.org/depts/german/ menschenrechte/aemr.pdf

Seifert, Josef. "Dimensionen und Quellen der Menschenwürde", in Walter Schweidler (Hrsg.). *Menschenleben – Menschenwürde: interdisziplinäres Symposium zur Bioethik*. Münster: Lit Verlag, 2003, 51-92.

Valdrini, Patrick. "Eglise, peines et responsabilité", in (Coll.). *Le crime contre l'humanité : mesure de la responsabilité ?* Paris : CERP, 1998, 31-40.

SABEEN AHMED (Nashville, TN)

The Genesis of Secular Politics in Medieval Philosophy:
The King of Averroes and the Emperor of Dante

Abstract

In contemporary political discourse, the "clash of civilizations" rhetoric often undergirds philosophical analyses of "democracy" both at home and abroad. This is nowhere better articulated than in Jacques Derrida's Rogues, *in which he describes Islam as the only religious or theocratic culture that would "inspire and declare any resistance to democracy" (Derrida 2005, 29). Curiously, Derrida attributes the failings of democracy in Islam to the lack of reference to Aristotle's* Politics *in the writings of the medieval Muslim philosophers. This paper aims to analyze this gross misconception of Islamic philosophy and illuminate the thoroughgoing influence the Muslim philosophers had on their Christian successors, those who are so often credited as foundations of Western political philosophy. In so doing, I compare the ideal states presented by Averroes and Dante – in which Aristotelian influence is intimately interlaced – and offer an analysis thereof as heralds of what we might call the secularization of the political, inspiring those democratic values that Derrida believes to be absent in the rich philosophy of the Middle Ages.*

Keywords: Averroes, Dante, Aristotle, medieval philosophy, political philosophy, secularism, democracy, religion

---

> *Poi ch'innalzai un poco piu' le ciglia,*
> *vidi 'l maestro di color che sanno*
> *seder tra filosofica famiglia*
> *Euclide geometra e Tolomeo,*
> *Ipocrate, Avicenna e Galieno*
> *Averois, che 'l gran comento feo.*
> Dante Alighieri[1]

Questions concerning democracy, secularism, and religion – intimately intertwined while concomitantly in tension with one another – have pressed upon the minds of such con-

---

[1] *When I had lifted up my brows a little /The Master I beheld of those / who know,/ Sit with his philosophic family./ Euclid, geometrician, and Ptolemy,/ Galen, Hippocrates, and Avicenna,/ Averroes, who the great Comment made.* (Alighieri 2012, 18-19)

temporary political thinkers as John Rawls, Jürgen Habermas, and Noam Chomsky, with roots in the canonical writings of John Stuart Mill, John Locke, and the Founding Fathers of the United States of America. They are questions that lie at the heart of our understanding of politics both within and without, particularly sharp against the backdrop of the "clash of civilizations" rhetoric materializing in today's fear of terrorism and, more to the point, of Islam. So stark and simplistic is the binary drawn between "us" Westerners and "them" Muslims that the only comprehensible manner of conceptualizing it, without the effort of critical reflection, is by labeling them – those seen as coming from a political world dominated by a religion of hate – anti-democratic. Indeed, Jacques Derrida himself, otherwise so carefully nuanced in his philosophical analyses, describes Islam as the only religious or theocratic culture that would "inspire and declare any resistance to democracy" (Derrida 2005, 29).

Despite its shockingly rudimentary presentation, Derrida's conceptualization is not, on the surface, terribly unfounded. He is, after all, writing in an age in which fear of the "Other" is especially visceral, whether in the East or the West. What is more curious is Derrida's attribution of these "failings" of democracy to the Muslim philosophers of the Middle Ages, and particularly to the absence of Aristotle's *Politics* in their writings. This negligence, he says, had a

> symptomatic, if not determining, significance, just like the privilege granted by this Muslim theologico-political philosophy to the Platonic them of the philosopher king or absolute monarch, a privilege that goes hand in hand with the severe judgment brought against democracy. (Derrida 2005, 32)

This meager image presented by Derrida can only be the result of contemporary discourses on Islamic politics, or the "politicization" of Islam, that fuels blinding fear thereof. Indeed, Derrida himself concedes that he is following the opinions of "certain historians and interpreters of Islam today" (Derrida 2005, 32), suggesting a lack of critical evaluation that is, unfortunately, an apt representation of much of today's scholarship on politics in the Muslim world. Nonetheless, the emphasis placed on Islamic philosophy warrants critical attention. For Derrida, the political writings of the Muslim philosophers primarily have recourse to Aristotle's *Nicomachean Ethics* and Plato's *Republic*, reducing the intricacies of Islamic philosophy to disappointing oversimplification.[2] Rather than take into consideration the sociopolitical context of the age – or indeed, acknowledge the explicit endorsement of monarchical rule in the subsequent writings of medieval Christian philosophers – Derrida instead general-

---

[2] Derrida fails to mention, as well, that the appeal to Plato's *Republic rather* than Aristotle's *Politics* was due to the simple fact that the *Politics* were physically unavailable to the Muslim philosophers of the Middle Ages.

izes the writings of the Muslim philosophers as the foundation of the democratic failings of Islamic states today.

In the following paper, I analyze this gross misconception of Islamic philosophy and illuminate the thoroughgoing influence the Muslim philosophers had on their Christian successors.[3] Much of Islamic philosophy's connection to Christian philosophy is tied to (Peripatetic) Islamic philosophy (*falsafa*)'s attempt to reconcile reason and revelation, "remaining faithful to both Aristotle . . . and to one's religion" (Stone 2007, 137). Ibn Rushd (Averroes, Latinized) was especially critical in the survival of Aristotelian philosophy – evinced by his masterful Commentaries on Aristotle's works – and Aristotelian influence is clearly evident in his own philosophy. Indeed, so influential were Averroes' writings on the Greek philosophers that his branch of radical Aristotelianism – called Averroism by his followers – was a point of substantial controversy during the infamous Parisian Condemnations of 1277. Even following their denunciation, Aristotelianism and Averroism thrived in Venice and Padua where, in fact, "Averroes [seemed] to have been taken more seriously than [Thomas] Aquinas" (Stone 2007, 137).[4]

Given his lasting impression upon the intellectual work of his successors, I take Averroes as my central figure of analysis, as both an illuminating point of contact between Islamic and Greek philosophy, and as a central component of the intellectual exchange between medieval Muslim and Christian philosophers. Of his works, I examine his political texts – particularly the *Decisive Treatise* and several of his Commentaries – in the context of his Peripatetic background in order to illustrate the nuanced relationship between reason and revelation – secularism and religion – in the state. In order to further elucidate Averroes' impact on subsequent Christian writings, I turn to Dante Alighieri's *Monarchy* as a text both exalting and critical of Averroism. As a thinker whose life overlapped with the Parisian condemnations and whose intellectual upbringing is decorated with Aristotelian influence, Dante provides an especially unique foil to the Muslim scholar. Indeed, so profound was Averroes' impact on Dante that Averroes – "che 'l gran comento feo" (Alighieri 2012, 19) – was given "special attention for his intellectual achievement" (Schildgen 2007, 115), exemplified by his

---

[3] This is not to say that their works did not impact those of the medieval Jewish philosophers; Moses Maimonides, in fact, credits Averroes' Commentaries on Aristotle as hugely influential in his own philosophical development. The scope of this paper, however, does not admit space for this particular discussion, whose richness truly warrants an analysis of its own.

[4] This is especially apparent in the writings of such Italian philosophers as Pietro Pomponazzi, Alessandro Achillini, and Marsilius of Padua. Indeed, the influence of Aristotle and Averroes on Aquinas himself was so significant that he refers to them explicitly throughout the *Summa Theologiæ*.

privileged standing alongside such illustrious thinkers as Socrates and Aristotle in the *Divine Comedy*.

Using Aristotle – the "Father of Political Science" – as the foundation of their respective theories alongside critical exegesis of their respective Scriptures, both Averroes and Dante introduce conceptualizations of the state that are, I posit, heralds of what we might call the secularization of the political. The shadow of Aristotle is cast throughout this analysis, with his notion of *Eudaimonia* interlaced throughout Averroes' and Dante's constructions of the state and as the guiding force of their political theories. Neither philosopher advances the state as a *democracy*, to be certain – and on this note there is some truth in Derrida's claim – but the values each philosopher promotes are closely aligned contemporary theories of liberal democracy and liberalism more broadly. Ultimately, I contest Derrida's generalization of Islamic writing as a profound disservice to the complex reality of Islamic medieval philosophy and propose that, even if not democracy, the Muslim philosophers and their Christian successors were essential to the development of a secularist thought we still find integral to Western political philosophy today.

1. Averroes and the Unity of Truth

In order to properly assess the significance of his writings, it would do us well to situate Averroes within his historical moment and the atmosphere of intellectual hostility in which he was a central figure. In so doing, the terrain and motivation of his philosophical analyses may not only offer a more nuanced understanding of his ideal state, but prefigure the fate of Islamic philosophy both within the Muslim world and in the worlds of its Christian and Jewish neighbors. Averroes (1126-1198), a polymath of the medieval period, was notable amongst his contemporaries for integrating the teachings of the Greek philosophers with an understanding of Islam that, due to its rationalist approach, did not maintain popularity among Muslim scholars in the centuries following his death. Indeed, even within his own life Averroes witnessed considerable backlash against his methodology and Islamic *falsafah* – Peripatetic, rational philosophy – writ large. More than his Commentaries, Averroes is remembered principally for his defense of Aristotelianism against charges of heterodoxy raised by the *mūtakallimūn* – practitioners of scholastic theology – and, especially, Ash'ari theologian Abū Hāmid al-Ghazālī.[5]

---

[5] See Averroes' response to Ghazālī's *The Incoherence of the Philosopher* (*Tahāfut al-Falāsifa*) in his, suitably titled, *The Incoherence of the Incoherence* (*Tahāfut al-Tahāfut*) [see Al-Ghazālī 2000]. Nevertheless, the impact of al-Ghazālī's treatise, as is well known, initiated the irreversible shift of Islamic

Despite the protestations of his opponents, Averroes was deeply committed to articulating the theoretical consistencies between scripture and philosophy, both through close Qur'anic exegesis and by means of a comprehensive philosophical rehabilitation of Aristotle. As noted by Catarina Belo, "Averroes was renowned in the Latin Middle Ages as the Aristotle commentator par excellence, and he consciously endeavored to restore Aristotle's original thought and purge it from distortions accreted to it by his predecessors in the Islamic tradition" (Belo 2009, 417).[6] As such, Averroes was firmly in the philosophical theater of his contemporaries – Muslim and Jewish alike – in his commitment to the reconciliation of Aristotelianism with scripture, and remembered in particular with regard to his sophisticated argument for the unity of truth:

> Since this Law is true and calls to the reflection leading to cognizance of the truth, we, the Muslim community, know firmly that demonstrative reflection does not lead to differing with what is set down in the Law. *For truth does not contradict truth*; rather, it agrees with it and bears witness to it. (Averroes 2002a, 8-9, my emphasis S.A.)[7]

Not only does this declaration reinforce the compatibility of Aristotelianism and the Qur'an, but it also served as the foundation for Averroes' criticism of the *Mutakallimūn*. Because he held that Qur'anic truths and philosophical truths were one and the same, Averroes was of the opinion that few were properly capable of embarking on the philosophical endeavor to truth and should, instead, accept those articulated in scripture as given. Indeed, Averroes' *Decisive Treatise* enumerates three classes of interpretation corresponding with three classes of readers of the Qur'an: the philosophers, the dialectical theologians (*Mutakallimūn*), and the multitude, each of whom learned by means of philosophical demonstration, dialectical theology, and rhetoric, respectively.

---

and philosophical scholarship away from the Peripatetic school and, in due course, *falsafah* declined under increasing politico-legal support of Sufi and kalām traditions.

[6] Averroes was nevertheless deeply indebted to al-Farabi and Ibn Sina, both of whom wrote extensively on the nature of the Active Intellect and set the groundwork for Averroes' own analyses on the subject (see Davidson 1972).

[7] Nonetheless, there was great controversy surrounding the "unity of truth" doctrine – particularly in Christian Europe – which, among other factors, prompted the banning of Averroist texts in the Condemnations. Under certain readings, Averroes was understood to have suggested the existence of two separate and distinct domains of truth: one "religious" and one "philosophical." Averroes, however, explicitly denounces this reading in the *Decisive Treatise*, as noted above. For an extensive analysis of the "double truth" controversy (see Heller-Roazen 2006).

Averroes justified his reconciliation of these interpretive methods with an exegetical analysis of Qur'anic verse 3:7, which is itself cited at various lengths throughout the *Decisive Treatise*. The Qur'anic verse itself reads:

> He it is Who has sent down the Book upon thee; therein are signs determined; they are the Mother of the Book, and others symbolic. As for those whose hearts are given to swerving, they follow that of it which is symbolic, seeking temptation and seeking its interpretation. And none know its interpretation save God and those firmly rooted in knowledge. They say: "We believe in it; all is from our Lord." And none remember, save those who possess intellect. (Nasr 2015, 129-132, 3:7)[8]

For Averroes, no one save Allah and those adept in demonstration – those who "possess intellect" – were the proper (and sole) knowers of the true interpretation of religious text.[9]

---

[8] In most translations of the verse, the penultimate sentence focuses exclusively on Allah as the knower of the true meaning behind the "ambiguous" verses, suggesting that there exists no human mind capable of comprehending the divine truths. To this day it stands as a point of contention, particularly because the original Arabic transcription of the Qur'an lacked punctuation altogether, making it difficult for the reader to gauge the precise delineations between the "interpreters" discussed in the verses. For example, Majid Fakhry's translation of the verse states that "As to those in whose hearts there is vacillation, they follow what is ambiguous in it, seeking sedition and intending to interpret it. However, no one except Allah knows its interpretation. Those well-grounded in knowledge say: 'We believe in it; all is from our Lord'; yet none remembers save those possessed of understanding!" (Fakhry 2000, 54, 3:7). Contrarily, Islamic scholar Farid Esack notes that, "if one ignores the full stop and proceeds, then one arrives at an entirely different meaning: 'None save God *and* those whose hearts are rooted in knowledge know their actual meaning'" (Esack 2005, 58). Given Averroes' commitment to the compatibility of reason and revelation, we may safely assume that it is Esack's reading – and Nasr's translation as used above – that he and his contemporaries would have invoked during the medieval era. Nasr, too, notes that, "taken as a whole, the genre of Quranic exegesis includes the dimension of interpretation known to the medieval Western world as the literal, moral, allegorical, and anagogical" (Nasr 2015, 131, 3:7). Indeed, Averroes himself devotes considerable attention to analyzing those "well-grounded in science" – as distinct from the dialectical theologians and the "rhetorical people, who are the overwhelming multitude" (Averroes 2002a, 26) – as the ordained interpreters of ambiguity in the Qur'an.

[9] Although outside the scope of this analysis, Averroes' understanding can be further strengthened by the reading of his "First Intellect" as articulated in Richard C. Taylor's translation of the *Long Commentary on the* De Anima in which the First Intellect is, effectively, God. However, because the First Intellect is also pure intelligence by definition, it necessarily follows that the First Intellect embodies "knowledge" of the intelligibles; God, in other words, is pure intelligence. Averroes' understanding of immortality as union with the Active Intellect – that which is the progenitor of intelligibles to the rational agent – thus illustrates precisely how man is capable of attaining knowledge of God's divine

Those lacking the intellectual capacities to engage syllogistically with scripture, on the contrary, were to accept the parables as transcribed, lest they would fall into doubt and stray from the truth: "If the beliefs based on the literal sense of the divine Law are taken away from the non-philosophers who do not understand the allegorical sense, because they required intellectual abilities for understanding it, then these non-philosophers will fall into nihilism" (Fraenkel 2008, 120). Accordingly, Averroes cautioned against the promulgation of philosophical truths to the multitude, a position which drove his charge against the *Mūtakallimūn*, who, "by declaring... corrupt beliefs to the multitude... [had] become the reason for the multitude's and their own perdition in this world and in the hereafter" (Averroes 2002a, 27).[10] Fundamentally, the heart of Averroes' argument reified a unity of truth understood through divergent mediums: one by means of philosophy; the other by means of the Qu'ran.

Averroes' integration of philosophical principles with revelation is most evident in his unparalleled Commentaries on Aristotle's works.[11] Indeed, it is by appeal to Aristotelian doctrines that Averroes reconciles the paradox of immortality as illustrated in the Qur'an with the Peripatetic denial of individual immortality, not only for affirmation of their compatibility, but also as a key theorization undergirding his entire political philosophy.[12] Averroes' clearest analysis of immortality appears in his Commentaries on Aristotle's *On the Soul* read through the lens of his Islamic perspective. Aristotle's own theory on the intellect is, infamously, a source of frustration due to the brief and ambiguous explanations given in not only *On the Soul*, but also the *Posterior Analytics* and *On the Generation of Animals*, to say nothing of the countless efforts made by his successors to parse out his distinction between the passive ("potential") and active ("agent") intellects. For our purposes, however, a general summation will suffice.

In *On the Soul*, Aristotle postulates that the duality of passivity and activity is to be found in all things, manifested as the "protean potentiality of their matter and the active and

---

truths. See footnotes 14-16 for further elucidation on the Active Intellect and the controversy surrounding Averroes' position on the First Intellect.

[10] We might notice here the similarities between Averroes' denunciation of the *mutakallimūn* and Socrates' denunciation of the sophists in Plato's *Republic*.

[11] These Commentaries are subsequently taken up as the authoritative interpretations of Aristotelian philosophy by such Christian thinkers as Thomas Aquinas and Pietro Pomponazzi. Aquinas in fact challenges Averroes' Doctrine of Immortality and offers his own interpretation thereof in *On the Unity of the Intellect Against Averroists*. For a detailed reading on the controversy surrounding Averroes' Doctrine of Immortality, see Mohammed 1985.

[12] Immortality itself is further crucial to the Muslim philosophers' justification of the ideal state, as it serves as the motivating impetus for living in accordance with virtue in the Islamic tradition.

productive art or agency that allows them to realize their potentials" (Goodman 2003, 132).[13] In the case of objects of knowledge – which for Aristotle are always true – the passive intellect of the rational being is that which "can become all things" (Aristotle 1981, 51) but without content, until the agent intellect actualizes its potentiality by illuminating the intelligibles thereto: "the [potential] intellect only receives the intelligibles which exist in it when the [potential] intellect is perfected by the agent intellect and illuminated by it" (Averroes 2009, 333). The active intellect, then, is essentially what makes the intelligibles (objects of knowledge) comprehensible to the intellecting subject by actualizing the intellectual potentiality therein.

Averroes builds upon this theme throughout his philosophical tenure, such that his Aristotelian approach would harmonize with the metaphorical illustration of immortality described in the Qur'an, poetically painted in evocative images of either Heaven or Hell.[14]

---

[13] See also Aristotle's *Posterior Analytics* II.19 (Aristotle 1991, 138-139).

[14] Averroes grappled with Aristotle's conceptions of the passive and active intellects throughout his philosophical career, reading and critiquing the theories of his Muslim predecessors – particularly those of Ibn Sina and Ibn Bajja – and ultimately reconciling Aristotle's notion of the soul with Alexander of Aphrodisias' interpretation of *On the Soul*. The idea of the Active Intellect was one that resonated deeply with the Muslim thinkers, "because it arose in philosophical argument, offered to answer a question, and responded to the need to connect knowing with God" (Goodman 2003, 150). According to Herbert Davidson, "no less than seven of Averroes' compositions treat the subject of human intellect formally – while others do so incidentally" (Davidson 1992, 262). Averroes' precise positions on the First Intellect and the Active Intellect change shape even throughout his own three Commentaries on *On the Soul*. Indeed, as established in footnote 9, *The Long Commentary* suggests an equivalence between the First Intellect and God. It must be noted, however, that Averroes' mature position on the matter remains a matter of controversy; in particular, Alfred Ivry offers the most significant counterpoint to Davidson's analysis, as his translation of the *Middle Commentary* posits the First Intellect as pure Intellect, rather than as analogous with God. Much of the disagreement between Davidson and Ivry is due to the fact that Averroes is known to have gone back to his Commentaries at different stages of his philosophical tenure and changed his position therewithin. There is no guarantee, in other words, that the *Long Commentary* contains Averroes' final position on the ambiguity of the First Intellect. Indeed, Ivry is of the position that "one text served as the source for the other (…) I have given my reasons for believing the *Long* is the source of the *Middle*" (Ivry 1997, 155). The ongoing debate about Averroes' ultimate position on the matter has significant implications on our reading of Averroes' doctrine of immortality today; however, it is unequivocal that the Commentary available to Averroes' Christian successors – and the one believed to be definitively used by Aquinas, Dante, and Marsilius of Padua – was *The Long Commentary*. Thus understood, Dante's understanding of God is very much in line with a reading of the First Intellect as Allah, and for the purposes of this paper, it is enough for us to accept Averroes' position as articulated in *The Long Commentary*. My accepting the Davidson reading, however, does not imply that I subsequently accept *The Long Commentary* as Averroes' ultimate position on the First

Averroes, following Alexander of Aphrodisias' interpretation of the Aristotelian intellect, theorizes the intellect as a "disposition" within the soul – human intelligence – encompassing two functions,

> one of which is the producing of intelligibles and the other is the receiving of them. By virtue of producing intelligibles, it is called agent, while, by virtue of receiving them, it is called passive, though in itself it is one thing. (Averroes 2002b, 112)

Contra Aristotle, however, Averroes' conceptualization of the external Active Intellect is deeply imbricated in a complex cosmology in which it – the "last of the primary intelligences" – is "the cause of human thought" (Davidson 1992, 225).[15] Human intelligence, in its purest form, is one with the Active Intellect, and the Active Intellect is, hence, the perfection of the human intellect. Indeed, we may understand the Active Intellect as "both external and our own, divine and within us," and, accordingly, "Averroes elevates what is intellectual in us, locating human rationality not beside but within the Active Intellect" (Goodman 2003, 151, cf. 159).[16] More simply, it is the nature of the passive intellect to receive the intelligible forms, and it is accordingly toward the Active Intellect that man strives for unity through performance of his function as a rational being. This philosophical ascent traces the journey of man's mortal life toward immortality and, indeed, because the Active Intellect is incorporeal and immortal, so too does man become when his intellect attains perfection.[17] To be sure,

---

Intellect; I do not here take a stance one way or another. For a brief outline of Davidson's position (see Davidson 1972, particularly 220-222). For a more nuanced reading of Ivry's position, see Ivry 1995. For an excellent overview of the Ivry-Davidson debate (see Taylor 2012, particularly 269-273).

[15] My capitalization of Active Intellect is a reflection of Averroes' rendering of the Active Intellect as the Tenth Intelligence, or the final of the celestial spheres, that gives form to the sublunary realm. For a more comprehensive articulation of Averroist cosmology, see Averroes' *On Aristotle's Metaphysics* and *Parva Naturalia*. Davidson offers a meticulous analysis of these and other Commentaries in *Alfarabi, Avicenna, and Averroes, on Intellect* (1972).

[16] Averroes' understanding of "human intellect" is the intellect *in potencia* alongside an active intellect – derivative of the Tenth Intelligence – that exists in each of us, able to receive the objects of knowledge from the celestial Active Intellect. This is a conceptualization that is doubtlessly inspired by Alexander of Aphrodisias, who "saw the Active Intellect at work in our processes of thought, anchoring the capabilities that differentiate rationality from mindlessness. To make sense of this work of the Active Intellect, he spoke of a *nous thyrathen*, a mind within us that is externally derived" (Goodman 2003, 151). By Aristotle's own articulation, this mind – the active intellect within the rational subject – is untouchable by death: "when separated [from the body], it is *as such* just that [i.e. intellect], and only this [part of the soul] is immortal and eternal" (Aristotle 1981, 51).

[17] The relationship between intellectual perfection and (moral) virtuosity merits brief elucidation, as it often generates perplexity among scholars even today. In Averroes' Commentaries (and those of many of his predecessors), the primacy of intellectual proficiency appears to subdue the ethical dimension of

this rendering of immortality is a radical departure from the vision of individual immortality poeticized in the Qur'an, which Averroes himself denied. Rather, immortality is attained through union of the human intellect with the celestial Active Intellect; in essence, it is the return of the immortal intellect to its progenitor, and it is to this progenitor that all human intellects endeavor.

So understood, Averroes' theory of immortality is delicately woven into the tapestry of his political philosophy, which draws yet again from Aristotle by virtue of the *Nicomachean Ethics* as well as from al-Farabi's thesis on the perfect state. Indeed, al-Farabi is widely considered the herald of political philosophy in Islam (and graced with the title of "Second Teacher" by his successors, the "First" being, of course, Aristotle) due in large part to his *Philosophy of Plato and Aristotle*, within which he conceptualizes the ideal state as an integration of the Platonic structure of the *Republic* with the Aristotelian notion of *Eudaimonia*.[18] Aristotle's understanding of *Eudaimonia* as the "chief good" or the end to which all men aim, alongside his further qualification of man's end as "activity of the soul and actions in accordance with virtue" (Aristotle 2000, 12), were especially conducive to integration with the principles outlined in the Qur'an – those of living the virtuous life, or that which would reward man with "earthly happiness in this life and supreme happiness in the life beyond" (Alfarabi 2001, 13). Averroes, writing in the footsteps of al-Farabi, doubtlessly held this theologico-political reconceptualization of the state in mind – concomitant with his own understanding of the "life beyond" – while crafting his Commentaries on Plato and Aristotle.[19] As such, though the structural architecture of Averroes' ideal state appears Platonic, the spirit thereof is thoroughly Aristotelian.

---

virtuosity that serves as the cornerstone of religious scripture. The most cogent interpretation – and the one I take as conforming to the spirit of the texts – is the existence of a moral dimension to the intellectual virtues themselves, particularly if following Socrates' assertion that 'to know the good is to do the good' (see *Gorgias* 460b, *Meno* 87c, and *Apology* 37a [Plato 1997] for variations on this theme). Indeed, if it is through philosophizing that one may attain immortality, then there certainly must exist an element of virtuosity in the act of philosophizing itself; man's intellect as desiderative of knowledge imbues the very notion of intellectual curiosity a moral dimension. Coupled with Averroes' adoption of the Aristotelian notion of man, we may extend these virtues into the realm of sociality, ensuring that the true philosopher, the embodiment of the soul in accordance with virtue, is always, accordingly, virtuous in his rapport with his fellow men. As such, although the non-philosopher lacks the theoretical virtues of the philosopher, her capacity to live in accordance with the moral virtues of faith elevates her to the status of the philosopher in practice. I thank Dr. Lenn E. Goodman for his helpful insight on this matter.

[18] This is most clearly articulated in al-Farabi's *The Attainment of Happiness*.
[19] For an excellent overview of al-Farabi's influence on Averroes in this regard, see Fraenkel 2008.

Just as Aristotle's man is a social and political being, so too did Averroes hold that the state is the necessary theater in which man is able to attain his end: "to acquire his virtue a man has need of other people. Hence he is political by nature" (Averroes 1974, 5). In Platonic fashion, it is the Ruler in particular who is tasked with implementing and maintaining the state that is capable of doing so; she is the figure – the political leader with knowledge "of the spheres of the body and of the soul alike" (Aristotle 2000, 20) – in possession of the theoretical understanding of man's end and the practical understanding of its realization. She is, more simply, the philosopher, or harbors at the very least "a philosophic nature, for in choosing the things with a view to knowledge and wisdom [s]he is by nature virtuous" (Averroes 1974, 16). More salient, however, is that she is aware of the variations in interpretive capacities of her people and has the judgment to guide them by whatever manner of education best suits them:

> [t]his government can only come into being if it is possible – and perchance happens – that the king is a philosopher . . . the philosopher, according to the primary intention, is the one who has attained the theoretical sciences [by virtue of] the four conditions that have been enumerated in the books on demonstration [i.e. theoretical, deliberative, moral, and practical virtues]. One of those conditions is that [s]he have the ability to discover them [sc., the theoretical sciences] and to teach them. (Averroes 1974, 71)

The medium by which the ruler guides the masses are of two kinds: demonstrative arguments or imitation. Understanding that promulgation of philosophical arguments would confound the non-philosophical masses into nihilism, the ruler accordingly must "establish the opinions in their souls through rhetorical and poetical arguments" (Averroes 1974, 10). It is religion, thus, that opens their eyes and minds, utilizing vivid metaphor and winsome language to unfurl their imaginative faculties to the inimitable divine truths so vibrantly proffered. The Qur'an, in other words, is the rhetoric of philosophy – an imitation to be sure, but one for whom the masses, "believing what they endeavor to believe of [what pertains to] knowledge of the first principle and of their final cause, as far as it is in their nature to believe, is useful with regard to the other moral virtues and practical arts" (Averroes 1974, 10-11).[20] Through its imagery of the afterlife, especially, the Qur'an provides the impetus needed to persuade the masses to live virtuously both in soul and in practice, ensuring their immortality:

---

[20] Al-Farabi himself proposes that "[religion] imitates the classes of supreme happiness – that is, the ends of the acts of the human virtues – by their likenesses among the goods that are believed to be the ends. It imitates the classes of true happiness by means of the ones that are believed to be happiness" (Alfarabi 2001, 45).

once the moral virtues and practical arts are established in their souls in this first way they can also be led toward performing the actions of these arts and virtues through the two kinds of arguments together, namely persuasive and affective arguments, which will move them toward the [good] qualities. (Averroes 1974, 11)

The office of Averroes' ruler is synonymous with that of the "king," "Lawgiver," and "Imam," all whose connotations are decidedly secular. (Although the term "Imam" as understood in common parlance often represents a religious leader, Averroes endorses the literal, originary definition thereof: "*imam* in Arabic means one who is followed in his actions. He who is followed in these actions by which he is a philosopher, is an Imam in the absolute sense" [Averroes 1974, 72].) Prophethood, it should be noted, is never cited as a necessary condition for rulership; when mentioned, it is a remark made in passing solely to clarify that "it would be with respect to what is *preferable*, not out of necessity" (Averroes 1974, 72, my emphasis). The prophet-ruled state Averroes has in mind is unquestionably the *umma* (community of Muslims) under the leadership of the Prophet Muhammad, which, for the Muslim thinkers, exemplified the most perfect constitution of the state. Since the time of the Prophet had passed well before Averroes' writing, we may safely infer that he is not prescribing the implementation of a "religious" state at all; following his Doctrine of Unity, the *sharī'a* and the truths of philosophy are, after all, one and the same. Though religion is considered by the Muslim philosophers to be an imitation of philosophy – less rigorous in its demonstrative argumentation and analogization of the first premises (referring to the nature of God and immortality) by means of imagery that would be most accessible to the unphilosophical – it provides the same justification for the life of virtue as does the philosophical attainment of intellectual perfection. It is not by Averroes, in fact, but by al-Farabi that this notion is most elegantly articulated:

> [i]f [the knowledge of the beings] are known by imagining them through similitudes that imitate them, and assent to what is imagined of them is caused by persuasive methods, then the ancients call what comprise these cognitions religion… For both [religion and philosophy] supply knowledge about the first principle and cause of the beings, and both give an account of the ultimate end for the sake of which man is made – that is, supreme happiness. (Alfarabi 2001, 44)

Though the forms of understanding are distinct, the essences therein remain identical: the philosopher knows that it is through the cultivation of a virtuous soul that man attains immortality, and it is through virtuosity in deed that his soul is made virtuous.

It would be reductive (and indeed, specious) to interpret Averroes' state as a theocracy; it much more clearly conforms, rather, to the Platonic meritocracy of the *Republic*, with the virtuous and most intellectually proficient as those tasked with rulership. In reality, Averroes staunchly *opposes* any conservative declaration prohibiting philosophical reasoning and engagement with the Greek philosophers; for him, doing so is a violation of the Book itself: "totally forbidding demonstrative books bars from what the Law calls to, because it is a wrong to the best sort of people and the best sort of existing things" (Averroes 2002a, 22). Although religion does occupy a significant role therein, it certainly does not play as integral a role in the structural actualization of the Muslim state as Derrida presumes. Indeed, despite its rejection of democracy – a rejection that is prevalent in the writings of Plato and Aristotle themselves – Averroes' state fully embodies the ideals of virtue, reasoning, peace, and political harmony that are taken up by Western, "secularist" and democratic political philosophers in his wake. To overlook this is not only historically irresponsible, but also an unfortunate injustice that perpetuates the dogmatic belief in the intellectual superiority of the West over the East that has, for centuries, contaminated our ability to cultivate peace between one another.

2. Dante and the two Suns

Following the reconquest of Sicily and the Iberian Peninsula in the twelfth century, Arabic texts (as well as Arabic translations of ancient Greek works) were assimilated into the Latin translation movement of the twelfth century and made available to Christian scholars in Europe. The dissemination of Aristotelian and Averroist writings quickly kindled a hotbed of controversy and debate among religious authorities – particularly for their rejection of individual immortality and potential to inspire heretical scholarship that might undermine the authority of the Papacy – which ultimately ignited the infamous Condemnations of 1270-1277.[21] More precisely, "the rationalizing approach to the knowledge of divine things" was

---

[21] The Oxford and Parisian Condemnations – administered by the Bishop of Paris, Étienne Tempier, and the Archbishop of Canterbury, Robert Kilwardby – proscribed the teaching of Aristotelian and Averroist doctrines, principally for the perceived "double truth" theory they advanced. The Condemnation of 1277 enumerated 219 banned propositions, motivated primarily by the difficulty of subordinating Averroism and Aristotelianism under the more Neoplatonic Augustinianism of the schools of theology (or, more simply, the difficulty of subordinating Averroism and Aristotelianism under the theology of the Catholic faith). As articulated in the *Condemnation*:

> some students of the arts in Paris are exceeding the boundaries of their own faculty and are presuming to treat and discuss, as if they were debatable in schools, certain obvious and loathsome errors (...) For they say that these things are true according to philosophy but not according to the Catholic faith, as if there were two contrary truths and as if the truth of Sacred Scripture were contradicted by the truth in the sayings of the accursed pagans. (Kilma et al., 2007, 180)

the match that fueled "fierce confrontations within Christianity and Islam . . . as the inherent danger of heresy or apostasy emerged" (Schildgen 2007, 128).

Concomitant to the Condemnations was a period of theologico-political turmoil in Florence, of which Dante Alighieri (1265-1321) was a firsthand observer. Heir to a family fully immersed in the grim sociopolitical climate eclipsing Florence, Dante was witness to the tumultuous religious and political developments dividing the Florentine *Guelphs* – of which he was a part – and the *Ghibellines*, or, those supporting the Papacy and those supporting the Holy Roman Emperor, respectively. In the aftermath of the later schism within the *Guelphs*, Dante aligned with the Whites amidst his disaffection with the growing encroachment of Pope Boniface VIII in the political affairs of the Holy Roman Emperor.[22] Indeed, his repudiation thereof is visible throughout the *Divine Comedy*:

> Repeatedly in the great poem and in several of his letters, Dante excoriated the Florentines for the violence, factionalism, and instability of their politics, for their excessive pursuit and consumption of wealth, and, worst of all, for their criminal resistance to what he considered the divinely ordained authority of the Roman emperor. (Najemy 2007, 236)

Dante's blistering criticisms of the Florentines is very much a product of his disillusion with Papal corruption, the civil factions engendered by the unending politico-religious turmoil, and especially, his own exile following the Black-led *coup d'état* in November of 1301. Accordingly, Dante's philosophy reflects a clear demarcation between political and religious institutions, seen not only in his *Monarchy*, but also in his magnum opus, the *Divine Comedy* which, in many ways, is a culmination of the author's philosophical background[23]:

Excellent analyses of the Condemnations and the "double truth" controversy are given by Walter Principe (Principe 1985) and Ali Ghorbani Sini (Sini 2013).

[22] For an exhaustive overview of Dante's Florence (see Nejemy 2007).

[23] We should also recognize the distinction in mediums of transmission between the *Divine Comedy* – poetic and metaphorical – against the syllogistic methodology of the *Monarchy*, the first read in the Italian vernacular while the second is written in Latin. In much the same way as Averroes' endorsement of rhetoric as the educational tool for the masses, Dante, too, has a very specific audience in mind for the *Comedy*. (The purposive nature of his linguistic commitments suggest as much.) While the means of communication used by the general public was the vulgar tongue (Italian), only the religious and political elites were versed in Latin. Indeed, the allegorical spirit of the *Comedy* shines light upon the allegiance of poetry and theology "as a means to express the inexpressible," and in thoroughly Averroist fashion, the poem "suggests that theological truth can only be mediated through poetic language" (Schildgen 2007, 117). Dante's faith in the beauty of language as revelatory is further strengthened by his ennobling the Augustan poet Virgil as the guide of the protagonist Dante in the *Inferno*: thou [Vir-

> *Men, therefore, need restraint by law, and need*
> *a monarch over them who sees at least*
> *the towers of The True City. Laws, indeed,*
>
> *there are, but who puts the nations to their proof?*
> *No one. The shepherd who now leads mankind*
> *can chew the cud, but lacks the cloven hoof*
> *[...]*
> *The bad state of the modern world is due –*
> *as you may see, then – to bad leadership;*
> *and not to natural corruption in you.*
>
> *Rome used to shine in two suns when her rod*
> *made the world good, and each showered her its way:*
> *one to the ordered world, and one to God.*
>
> *Now one declining sun puts out the other* (Alighieri 2003, 422; 423)

The verses above plainly evince man's need of law and an authority to enforce it; however, like Averroes' philosopher-ruler, Dante's monarch, too, "sees . . . the towers of The True City," or life beyond death attained through virtue and good deeds on earth. The monarch is not fully divorced from religion, but neither is she the "shepherd who . . . lacks the cloven hoof" who leads mankind in Dante's present (unmistakably a reference to Pope Boniface VIII). Dante furthers his critique of Papal authority by crediting "bad leadership" as the cause of the modern world's spiritual and religious failings. Instead, Dante elevates the status of the Roman Empire – the most harmonious age in man's history, as he writes in the *Monarchy* – as the time in which the "two suns" shined. The two suns – representing the temporal and spiritual realms – reveal the "ways" to the temporal world and the heavenly world, illuminating man's path to virtue on earth to ensure blessings of immortality once reunited with God. Just Aristotle's marks of honor and perfection embrace the two spheres of body and soul, Dante's vision of the Roman Empire is one in which the two suns illuminate the graces of earth and heaven.

God is, of course, the Biblical God; unlike Averroes' appeal to a cosmology of Intelligences, Dante's understanding of man's supreme end of immortality – individual rather than universal – is equivalent to his arrival at the Heavenly Kingdom. That this is inconsistent with Averroist and Aristotelian conceptions of man's end – the life of virtue realized through

---

gil] art my master, and my author thou,/ thou art alone the one from whom I took / the beautiful style that has done honour to me (Alighieri 2012, 5).

contemplation and subsequent intellectual immortality – was certainly apparent to Dante. Indeed, Dante rejected the Aristotelian object of contemplation of a Supreme Being as different in kind from the Biblical God, no less than Averroes' denial of individual immortality.[24] Nevertheless, Dante manages to bridge the seeming impasse between the philosophical life and the religious afterlife through his division of the two realms and, subsequently, the two "ends" toward which man strives: "while the earthly end is centered on philosophy and the perfection of man's natural virtues, the heavenly end absorbs philosophy into the specifically Christian virtues of faith, hope and charity" (Weinrib 2005, 86). In keeping with his Catholic faith, Dante further holds that "the enjoyment of God's beatitude cannot be reached through philosophy alone" (Weinrib 2005, 86). Although the Aristotelian and Averroist philosophies are in many ways incompatible with Dante's orthodox devotion to Christianity, the virtues of Aristotelian ethics, for him, are very much in accord with the Biblical precedent of the moral life in the service of a "higher" being, *id est*, God.

Dante's *Monarchy* more precisely articulates the delineation of reason and revelation in the context of man's social and political life. Indeed, so explicit does he make the distinction between politics and religion that he appears to cache an argument for the separation of church and state: "the *De Monarchia* contains groundbreaking thought on the theory of the secular state, such that Dante may rightly be called a significant figure in the development in Western political theory" (Derek 1991, 328). The architecture of *Monarchy* is beautifully constructed, with each section seamlessly shepherding the next, stylistically philosophical in a manner reminiscent of Aristotle's own writings. *Monarchy* is divided into three books, almost dialectical in nature, elucidating his philosophically inspired understanding of political theory as a means of criticizing the encroachment of papal influence in the affairs of secular (political) power.[25] By focusing primarily on the status of the temporal world, Dante holds fast to the philosophical understanding of man's end as "temporal felicity of the human race . . . [defined] as the full exercise of the intellectual and moral virtues" (Davis 2007, 266)[26], and it is within this schema that the status of the monarch is fully developed.

---

[24] Contra Aristotle and Averroes, Dante's *Convivio* reveals "Avicenna, al-Ghazālī, Plato, and Pythagoras [as] his authorities on the nature of the soul" (Schildgen 2007, 114). See Schildgen 2007 for a lovely elucidation of the Islamic influence underpinning Dante's integration of philosophy with Christianity.
[25] The imagery of the two suns – which, in *Monarchy*, Dante calls the "two great lights" – materializes most unambiguously as the "Roman Pope and the Roman Prince" (Dante 1996a, 64).
[26] Dante more fully explores the nature of the intellectual soul in Canto XXV of the *Purgatorio* (Alighieri 2003, 502-503), which is itself influenced in no small part by Aristotle's *On the Generation of Animals* (see Boitani 2007).

In the spirit of his Greek and Muslim predecessors, and as indicated above, Dante establishes man's (earthly) end, or "highest potentiality," as "his intellectual potentiality or faculty" whose realization cannot be undertaken if not collectively, as "the human race, through whom the whole of this potentiality can be actualized" (Dante 1996a, 7).[27] The function of mankind as a whole, then, is "constantly to actualize the full intellectual potential of humanity, primarily through thought and secondarily through action (as a function and extension of thought)" (Dante 1996a, 8). Dante focuses primarily on the need for action, and, accordingly, the state emerges as the natural and necessary context in which man is to attain his end in practice. Dante's understanding of man's end as extensive to all of mankind motivates his promotion of a unitary state with a single ruler to direct mankind thereto.

Greco-Islamic background notwithstanding, Dante likens the structure of the state to divine organization, as "mankind most closely resembles God when it is most a unity, since the true measure of unity is in Him alone" (Dante 1996a, 13). And because the afterlife is the Kingdom of Heaven, it is only fitting that this unitary state takes the shape of a monarchy; God, after all, is spiritual "king of all earth" (Psalm 47:7), the King in whose service each man, through his obedience to the monarch, ultimately lives and breathes. Accordingly, Dante advocates for a *single, world* monarchy, a universal political community or federation of states subject to a single sovereign monarch tasked with maintaining order therein. It is a sentiment echoed in *De Vulgari Eloquentia*, in which Dante declares that, for him, "the whole world is a homeland" (Dante 1996b, 13). The monarch of this global empire accordingly governs "those matters which are common to all men and of relevance to all . . . by a common law" (Dante 1996a, 25), by extension promoting a version of secular cosmopolitanism – tasked with upholding justice, as "the world is ordered in the best possible way when justice is at its strongest in it (Dante 1996a, 15) – that is itself deferential to the will of God.[28] Because the art of governance consists both in understanding man's end and creating and enforcing laws that will guide her subjects thereto, Dante's monarch is, unequivocally, and much like Averroes' ruler, also the philosopher.

---

[27] This vision of the intellect is drawn explicitly from Averroes, who, per Dante, "is in agreement with this opinion in his commentary on the *De anima*" (Dante 1996a, 7).

[28] Bracketing its religious motivation, Dante's appeal to a (universal) monarchy rather than a republic is likely also to have been borne from his rejection of "not only Florence and its politics, but the whole idea of the city as the proper and natural form of political association" (Najemy 2007, 238). Indeed, Dante's elevation of the monarchy as the form of government most faithful to God is entirely consistent with his belief in "the necessity of the empire as the sole reasonable warranty against the sinister spirals of violence" and factionalization "splintering" his Florence (Mazzotta 2007, 10).

The secular elements of Dante's theory are further reinforced by his obeisance to the pagan Emperor Augustus as the ideal representative of the virtuous monarch. Rather than appeal to such a Christian emperor as Constantine – who, in fact, Dante believed to be especially corrupt rather than emblematic[29] – Dante affirms the pre-Christian Roman Empire as the one "founded on *right*," not only by the "light of human reason but also by the radiance of *divine authority*" (Dante 1996a, 31, my emphasis). It was the Augustan Empire that was most emblematic of the spiritually and politically pure monarch of Dante's imaginings; through the construction of laws aimed at the common good of mankind, it exemplified those virtues held in the highest, divine regard:

> Thus it is clear that whoever has the good of the community as his goal has the achievement of right as his goal. Therefore if the Romans had the good of the community as their goal, it will be true to say that the achievement of right was their goal. That the Roman people in conquering the world did have the good of which we have spoken as their goal is shown by their deeds, for, having repressed all greed (which is always harmful to the community) and cherishing universal peace and freedom, that holy, dutiful and glorious people can be seen to have disregarded personal advantage in order to promote the public interest for the benefit of mankind. (Dante 1996a, 40)

It is these values – peace, freedom, generosity, and, especially, justice – that Dante believes are integral to both the state and the monarch for inspiring the moral flourishing of mankind, rather than its domination: "his ideology of empire posits the universal dominion of the monarch, who is concerned with administering justice rather than with conquering new territories" (Ascoli 2007, 56). Indeed, these are the values that Christ himself advocates, and for this reason Christ, on Dante's account, "acknowledged the validity of . . . the edict of Augustus" (Dante 1996a, 59).

Despite her supreme political authority – justified most vividly in Book III wherein Dante rebukes clerical arguments allowing "papal usurpations of imperial power" (Davis 2007, 267) – Dante is nonetheless careful not to bestow upon the monarch *religious* authority in any capacity. To be sure, Dante never denounces the role of the Papacy as an institution; he in fact concurrently holds that the authority of the temporal monarchy owes its power to the heavenly sphere, insofar as the temporal realm "receive[s] from [the spiritual realm] the capacity to operate more efficaciously through the light of grace which in heaven and on earth the blessing of the supreme Pontiff infuses into it" (Dante 1996a, 72). The Papacy reigns supreme in all matters of religion, offering spiritual guidance *alongside* the political guidance of the monarch. Inasmuch as there exist two lights, two suns, two kingdoms, and

---

[29] See Book II of *Monarchy*.

two ends, mankind is in need of both the Emperor and the Pope; the first to lead it to its earthly end and the second to lead it to its spiritual end.

Much like Averroes and the philosophers before him, Dante highlights the singular importance of the Monarch's intellectual capacities in conjunction with the Pope's religious authority: while "the emperor relies on philosophical teachings to lead men to their human goal of temporal happiness, the pope relies on theological teachings to lead men to the divine goal of salvation" (Davis 2007, 257). Dante illustrates how, just as the tragic poets of his age were masters of their craft once they had "true affinity with [the illustrious vernacular]" of Italy, so too is it "the case with other customs and symbols of authority" (Dante 1996b, 47), appealing to the practical and theoretical virtues expected of both Monarch and Pope.

3. A Return to the Medieval, Today

Both Averroes and Dante were well attuned to the controversial natures of their theories and expected that, given the religio-political contexts of the societies in which they were writing, they would draw controversy. Indeed, not only did they anticipate retaliation, but in many ways worked to facilitate it. One of the keenest points of contact between the two philosophers lies in Dante's biting charge against the *Decretalists* – those who engaged in exegetical analyses of papal decretals in the context of church discipline – and others who argued that the Papcy had legitimate authority to intervene in the affairs of the state. On Dante's account, the *Decretalists* interpreted the "two great lights" as signifying "a greater light and a lesser light – so that one might rule the day and the other rule the night; these they took in an *allegorical sense to mean the two powers*, i.e. the spiritual and the temporal" (Dante 1996a, 69). Most striking about Dante's denunciation is the similarities it shares with Averroes' charge against the *Mutakallimūn* who, according to Averroes, deliberately interpreted the Law in such a way as to delegitimize the role of reason in affairs of religion and politics. Further, both Averroes and Dante felt that the *Mutakallimūn* and *Decretalists* aimed to undermine the authority of philosophy through endorsing a hierarchal chain of authority: the subordination of earthly power under heavenly power, which would, thereby, position religious and theological offices above that of the ruler. Any adherence to the tenets of rational philosophy was subsequently met with charges of heresy from religious authorities who, by Averroes' and Dante's estimations, endeavored to consolidate material as well as spiritual authority rather than uphold the virtuous truths and practices of God's Books.

Averroes and Dante were fierce proponents of man's intellectual capacities, and from this conviction advocated societies reflective of precisely those virtues that capable men, by means of their rational faculties, could comprehend and actualize. Although distinct in their methodologies in significant ways, it would be inequitable to deny the secular elements – particularly Aristotelian – undergirding their approaches to political philosophy, not by disputing religion, but rather by using scripture to demonstrate the spiritual and practical compatibilities of reason and revelation. By appeal to their Greek predecessors, each philosopher espoused the flourishing of mankind and held faithfully to the authority of a virtuous ruler – the exemplar of practical and theoretical reasoning both – to guide mankind thereto. The common denominator in both of their political works is the indispensable role of *philosophy itself* within the state:

> The emperor… presides over the moral world. It is his duty to put the ethical teachings of philosophers, especially Aristotle, into effect . . . Each needs the other, for the imperial authority without the philosophical is dangerous, and the philosophical without the imperial is weak. (Davis 2007, 259)

It is this loyalty to philosophy – a philosophy inspired principally by the writings of Aristotle – that lends secular elements to both Averroes' and Dante's conceptualizations of the state, of the role of reason in understanding and organizing the affairs of man while never losing sight of the preeminence of the divine.

Textual particularities aside, both philosophers offer invaluable insight into the religio-political climates of their time, and to reduce either's work to mere generalizations is to overlook the stunning pluralism and nuanced complexities embedded in the beginnings of Western secularism. Derrida himself would have done well to heed their profoundly historico-philosophically informed analyses of religious and political affairs. Indeed, in light of the devolution of Western, "secularist" democracy to some of the most frightening forms of populism and fanaticism thus far witnessed, it is perhaps unbridled democracy, that deserves scrutiny under the lens of philosophical criticism. By rethinking our methodology and sensitivity to historico-political context in a manner similar to that offered in this analysis, we may embark on a new understanding of the role of the secular today. And the reintegration of medieval philosophical thought – the intellectual acuity of which is presciently relevant – would provide a welcome voice in the ever-ongoing dialogue of politics and religion.

Sabeen Ahmed, PhD Cand., Dept. of Philosophy, Vanderbilt University,
sabeen.ahmed[at]vanderbilt.edu

References

Alfarabi. *Philosophy of Plato and Aristotle*. Trans. Muhsin Mahdi. Ithaca: Cornell University Press, 2001.

Al-Ghazālī. *The Incoherence of the Philosophers*. Trans. Michael E. Marmura. Provo: Brigham Young University Press, 2000.

Alighieri, Dante. *Monarchy*. Ed. Prue Shaw. Cambridge: Cambridge University Press, 1996a.

Alighieri, Dante. *De Vulgari Eloquentia*. Trans. Steven Botterill. Cambridge: Cambridge Univeristy Press, 1996b.

Alighieri, Dante. *The Divine Comedy: The Inferno, The Purgatorio, and The Paradiso*. Trans. John Ciardi. New York: New American Library, 2003.

Alighieri, Dante. *The Divine Comedy/La Divina Commedia*. Trans. Henry Wadsworth Longfellow. Oxford: Benediction Classics, 2012.

Aristotle. *On The Soul*. Trans. Hippocrates G. Apostle. Grinnell: The Peripatetic Press, 1981.

Aristotle. *Politics*. Trans. Hippocrates G. Apostle and Lloyd P. Gerson. Grinnell: The Peripatetic Press, 1986.

Aristotle. *Selected Works*. Trans. Hippocrates G. Apostle and Lloyd P. Gerson. Grinnell: The Peripatetic Press, 1991.

Aristotle. *Nicomachean Ethics*. Trans. Roger Crisp. Cambridge: Cambridge University Press, 2000.

Ascoli, Albert Russell. "From *auctor* to author: Dante before the *Commedia*." In *The Cambridge Companion to Dante*. 46-66. Ed. Rachel Jacoff. Cambridge: Cambridge University Press, 2007.

Averroes. *Averroes on Plato's* Republic. Trans. Ralph Lerner. London: Cornell University Press, 1974.

Averroes. *Decisive Treatise and Epistle Dedicatory*. Trans. Charles E. Butterworth. Provo: Brigham Young University, 2002a.

Averroes. *Middle Commentary on Aristotle's* De anima. Trans. Alfred L. Ivry. Provo: Brigham Young University Press, 2002b.

Averroes. *Long Commentary on the* De Anima *of Aristotle*. Trans. Richard C. Taylor. New Haven: Yale University Press, 2009.

Averroes. *Averroes on Aristotle's Metaphysics*. Trans. Rüdiger Arnzen. Berlin: De Gruyter, 2010.

Averroes. *Averroes' Tahafut Al-Tahafut (The Incoherence of the Incoherence) Volumes I and II*. Trans. Simon Van Den Bergh. Cambridge: E. J. W. Gibb Memorial Trust, 2012.

Belo, Catarina. "Essence and Existence in Avicenna and Averroes." *Al-Qantara* XXX 2 (2009): 403-426.

Boitani, Piero. "The poetry and poetics of the creation." In *The Cambridge Companion to Dante*. 218-235. Ed. Rachel Jacoff. Cambridge: Cambridge University Press, 2007.

Davidson, Herbert A. "Alfarabi and Avicenna on the Active Intellect." *Viator* 3 (1972): 109-178.

Davidson, Herbert A. *Alfarabi, Avicenna, and Averroes, on Intellect: Their Cosmologies, Theories of the Active Intellect, and Theories of Human Intellect*. New York: Oxford University Press, 1992.

Davis, Charles Till. "Dante and the empire." In *The Cambridge Companion to Dante*. 257-269. Ed. Rachel Jacoff. Cambridge: Cambridge University Press, 2007.

Davis, Derek. "Seeds of the Secular State: Dante's Political Philosophy as Seen in the *De Monarchia*." *Journal of Church and State* 33:2 (1991): 327-346.

Derrida, Jacques. *Rogues: Two Essays on Reason*. Trans. Pascale-Anne Brault and Michael Naas. Stanford: Stanford University Press, 2005.

Esack, Farid. *The Qur'an: A User's Guide*. Oxford: Oneworld, 2005.

Fakhry, Majid. *An Interpretation of the Qur'an*. London: Garnet Publishing Limited, 2000.

Fraenkel, Carlos. "Philosophy and Exegesis in al-Farabi, Averroes, and Maimonides." *Laval thèologique et philosophique* 64:1 (2008): 105-125

Goodman, Lenn. *Islamic Humanism*. Oxford: Oxford University Press, 2003.

Heller-Roazen, Daniel. "Philosophy before the Law: Averroë's *Decisive Treatise*." *Critical Inquiry* 32:3 (2006): 412-442.

Hendrix, John S. "Philosophy of Intellect in the Long Commentary on the De Anima of Averroes." *School of Architecture, Art, and Historic Preservation Faculty Publicatios.* Paper 26 (2012).

Ivry, Alfred L. "Averroes' Middle and Long Commentaries on the *De Anima*." *Arabic Sciences and Philosophy* 5 (1995): 153-155.

Ivry, Alfred L. "Response [to Davidson]." *Arabic Sciences and Philosophy* 7:1 (1997): 153-155.

Kilma, Gyula/ Allhof, Fritz/Vaidya, Anand Jayprakash (eds.). "Selections from the Condemnation of 1277," in idem, *Medieval Philosophy: Essential Readings with Commentary*, Oxford: Blackwell Publishing Ltd, 2007, 180-189.

Leaman, Oliver. *Averroes and His Philosophy*. New York: Routledge, 1997.

Mazzotta, Giuseppe. "Life of Dante." In *The Cambridge Companion to Dante*. Ed. Rachel Jacoff. Cambridge: Cambridge University Press, 2007.

Mohammed, Ovey N. *Averroës' Doctrine of Immortality: A Matter of Controversy*. Waterloo: Wilfrid Laurier University Press, 1985.

Najemi, John M. "Dante and Florence." In *The Cambridge Companion to Dante*. 236-256. Ed. Rachel Jacoff. Cambridge: Cambridge University Press, 2007.

Nasr, Seyyed Hossein. *Islamic Philosophy: From its Origin to the Present*. New York: State University of New York Press, 2006.

Nasr, Seyyed Hossein, Ed. *The Study Quran: A New Translation and Commentary*. New York: HarperCollins Publishers, 2015.

Plato. *Complete Works*. Trans. John M. Cooper. Indianapolis: Hackett Publishing Co., 1997.

Principe, Walter H. "Bishops, Theologians, and Philosophers in Conflict at the Universities of Paris and Oxford: The Condemnations of 1270 and 1277." *Proceedings of the Fortieth Annual Convention of the Catholic Theological Society of America.* 5-8 June 1985: 114-126.

Schildgen, Brenda Deen. "Philosophers, Theologians, and the Islamic Legacy in Dante: 'Inferno' 4 versus 'Paradiso' 4." *Dante Studies, with the Annual Report of the Dante Society* 125 (2007): 113-132.

Sini, Ali Ghorbani. "The Clerical Double Truth Theory in Thirteenth Century." *Interdisciplinary Journal of Contemporary Research in Business* 5:5 (2013): 64-70.

Stone, Gregory B. "Dante and the 'Falasifa': Religion as Imagination." *Dante Studies, with the Annual Report of the Dante Society* 125 (2007): 133-156.

Taylor, Richard C. "Separate Material Intellect in Averroes' Mature Philosophy." In *Words, Texts and Concepts Cruising the Mediterranean Sea.* 289-309. Eds. Gerhard Endress, Rüdiger Arnzen, and J. Thielmann. Dudley: Peeters Publishers, 2004.

Taylor, Richard C. "Textual and Philosophical Issues in Averroes' *Long Commentary* on the *De Anima* of Aristotle." In *The Letter Before the Spirit: The Importance of Text Editions for the Study of the Reception of Aristotle.* 267-288. Ed. Aafke M.I. van Oppenraay. Leiden: Brill, 2012.

Tornay, Stephen Chak. "Averroes' Doctrine of the Mind." *The Philosophical Review*, 52:3 (1943): 270-288.

Weinrib, Jacob E. "Dante's Philosophical Hierarchy." *Aporia* 15:1 (2005): 85-100.

www.ingramcontent.com/pod-product-compliance
Lightning Source LLC
Chambersburg PA
CBHW080804300426
44114CB00020B/2820